Nationalism, Marxism, and Modern Central Europe

Nationalism, Marxism, and Modern Central Europe

A Biography of Kazimierz Kelles-Krauz, 1872–1905

TIMOTHY SNYDER

OXFORD
UNIVERSITY PRESS

OXFORD
UNIVERSITY PRESS

Oxford University Press is a department of the University of Oxford. It furthers the University's objective of excellence in research, scholarship, and education by publishing worldwide. Oxford is a registered trade mark of Oxford University Press in the UK and certain other countries.

Published in the United States of America by Oxford University Press
198 Madison Avenue, New York, NY 10016, United States of America.

First published by the Ukrainian Research Institute, Harvard University, 1997,
and distributed by Harvard University Press

Library of Congress Cataloging-in-Publication Data
Names: Snyder, Timothy, author.
Title: Nationalism, Marxism, and modern Central Europe: a biography of
Kazimierz Kelles-Krauz, 1872–1905 / Timothy Snyder.
Description: New York, NY : Oxford University Press, 2018. |
"First published by the Ukrainian Research Institute, Harvard University, 1997
and distributed by Harvard University Press." |
Includes bibliographical references and index.
Identifiers: LCCN 2017025071 (print) | LCCN 2017025894 (ebook) |
ISBN 9780190846091 (Updf) | ISBN 9780190846107 (Epub) |
ISBN 9780190846084 (pbk. : alk. paper) |
ISBN 9780190846077 (hardcover : alk. paper)
Subjects: LCSH: Kelles-Krauz, Kazimierz, 1872–1905. | Socialists—Poland—Biography. |
Sociologists—Poland—Biography. | Nationalism and socialism—Poland.
Classification: LCC HX315.7.A8 (ebook) | LCC HX315.7.A8 K47 2017 (print) |
DDC 335.092 [B]—dc23
LC record available at https://lccn.loc.gov/2017025071

1 3 5 7 9 8 6 4 2

Paperback Printed by WebCom, Inc., Canada
Hardback Printed by Bridgeport National Bindery, Inc., United States of America

To my parents

Contents

List of Illustrations and Maps

Preface to the First Edition

A GREAT FIGURE in the intellectual and political histories of Central Europe has been neglected. This work is a narrative and chronological biography of Kazimierz Kelles-Krauz (1872–1905), the leading theorist of the main current of Polish socialism, the Polish Socialist Party (PPS), and a creative and farsighted social thinker. Though scarcely remembered in Poland and altogether unknown elsewhere, Kelles-Krauz was one of the most important Polish political activists of the late nineteenth and early twentieth centuries. He was a figure of exceptional political imagination, who anticipated and devoted great attention to the problems that would arise in a restored Poland and a modernizing Central Europe. He urged recognition of the national status of the non-Polish inhabitants of the former Polish-Lithuanian Commonwealth, proposed that Poles support the national aspirations of their eastern neighbors, and was outstanding in his advocacy of Polish-Jewish reconciliation. Though a Marxist, he believed that socialism could only be built within the democratic nation-state, and his subtle understanding of political sociology set him apart from his socialist peers. As a scholar, Kelles-Krauz was an early and trenchant challenger to his day's dominant positivist methodology, and was probably the first to provide a convincing sociological explanation of the arrival of modern nationalism. His pioneering work in this area anticipated major positions of prominent scholars of our own day.

The first chapter of this work, which treats the years 1872–1894, investigates Kelles-Krauz's intellectual and political formation. Kelles-Krauz was of noble origins, although his father had lost the family estates for taking part in the rising of 1863. Kelles-Krauz respected the patriotic and ethical values he learned at home, but by the age of eighteen he was already a convinced socialist. He was educated during the Russification of schools, and took part in secret self-education circles with his fellow students. They were impressed by the changes that industrialization had brought to Polish lands in Russia, and drawn to Western science and Western political ideas as a means to create a modern, unified Poland. Although they rejected the Warsaw positivists' program of legal work in favor of the socialist call to action, they retained the positivists' basic notion that science could guide politics.

Expelled from school for taking part in a student plot to steal an exam question, Kelles-Krauz emigrated to Paris in 1891 in order to study at the Sorbonne. He immediately entered into the peculiar world of the colony of Polish students and socialists, which was characterized by the tension between the political freedoms of France and the real risks brought by the Franco-Russian alliance. Soon after Polish socialists met in Paris to form a united Polish Socialist Party in November 1892, a spy for the Russian secret police began to report on Kelles-Krauz. Kelles-Krauz did not immediately join the new party, taking part instead in a group of Polish social democrats whose Marxism was more in line with his own. The exposure to the politics of conspiracy in emigration was the next lesson in Kelles-Krauz's political education.

The second chapter (1894–1896) concerns Kelles-Krauz's first years in the PPS. When faced in 1894 with the choice between the PPS, whose program included Polish national independence, and Rosa Luxemburg's rival party, Social-Democracy of the Kingdom of Poland (SDKP), whose program did not, Kelles-Krauz joined the former. He emerged as the leader of the Paris Section of the foreign organization of the PPS, and began a doomed campaign to change the program of that foreign organization. His first pamphlet as a member of the PPS was directed toward this end, and its criticism of other European socialist parties and unauthorized publication earned Kelles-Krauz an early rebuke from party leaders. It also marked the debut of his career as a Marxist offering Marxist arguments for Polish independence. In 1895, Kelles-Krauz was named the editor of a new party organ, *Le Bulletin Officiel du Parti Socialiste Polonais*. Kelles-Krauz's articles in the journal served to draw the attention of west European socialists to politics within the Russian Empire and to the PPS program.

At the end of 1895, Kelles-Krauz persuaded PPS leaders to propose a resolution to the 1896 congress of the Second International stating that Polish independence was in the interest of the international working class. The efforts of Kelles-Krauz and other PPS leaders to gain support for this resolution revealed the attitudes of the major parties and figures of the Second International toward the Polish question and the national question in general. Here Rosa Luxemburg played a special role, for her arguments against the PPS resolution ensured that it could not be treated merely as a gesture to the PPS. In the end, Kelles-Krauz's resolution failed, and a vague resolution endorsing the right of all nationalities to pursue autonomy was passed instead. This outcome fortified the conviction of PPS leaders that international socialism would be of little help to their cause, and taught Kelles-Krauz that few Marxists would understand the desirability of new nation-states. The experience of 1896 strengthened his commitment to the PPS, and established him as one of its leading figures.

The third chapter, which covers the years 1897–1901, discusses the changes in Kelles-Krauz's political positions which followed the failure of this resolution. He continued to believe that a correctly elaborated Marxist justification for Polish national independence would help the PPS's cause, and directed some effort to this end. His continuing work in the *Bulletin* was designed to persuade French socialists to oppose the Franco-Russian alliance. Kelles-Krauz came to believe that internationalism, properly understood, implied that socialists should take an interest in questions of international affairs, and that the working classes of each nation should try to exert some influence on the foreign policies of their particular states in the interest of European progress. These efforts found little resonance within the Second International, whose leaders preferred to oppose categories of behavior such as "imperialism" and "colonialism" rather than form a common policy on particular issues such as tsarist imperialism, the seizure of Alsace-Lorraine, or the emerging nations of the Balkans.

By this time, Kelles-Krauz had made his name among French sociologists. He had been a member of the Institut International de Sociologie since 1894, and participated in its congresses until he left Paris in 1901. The first papers he presented to this body elaborated his theory of "revolutionary retrospection," according to which revolutionaries seek their ideals in the past. Opposing the widely-held view of "evolutionary" progress, Kelles-Krauz argued that a gap between material conditions and human needs leads not to rational adaptation, but to longings for a better society which take their form from ideas drawn from tradition. To this claim he later joined effective methodological arguments against the use of biological analogies within sociology. In 1900, Kelles-Krauz was invited to present his understanding of Marxist sociology to a congress of the Institute. His presentation of a phenomenalist social psychology was so different from what his fellow sociologists expected that they ignored his paper in favor of attacking the more conventional interpretations of Marxism favored by German social democrats.

Kelles-Krauz would write on the place of art in capitalist society and on the history of sociology after his move to Vienna in 1901. In the main,

however, the final chapter (1901–1905) concerns Kelles-Krauz's political and scholarly work on the national question. His attempts to support
Polish socialism in Germany left him all the more cynical about socialist
internationalism. His observation of the national question in Austria led
him to believe that the emergence of the modern nation was the key event
of the nineteenth century. His work on the Jewish question led him to
a sophisticated analysis of the origins of modern nationalism, which he
then used to justify the program of the PPS. He also spoke up in a personal capacity to urge his party and the Polish public to regard Jewish
national sentiments as being of the same character as their own.

Kelles-Krauz thought that the national question should be of natural
concern to socialists, and took the opposition of the majority of German
socialists to the Polish program of national independence as a sign of the
decadence of German Marxism. He treated the revisionism debate as an
occasion to criticize all of its major participants: Kautsky, Luxemburg, and
Bernstein. He set out his own understanding of the relation between theory and practice, in which sociology serves revolutionaries as an "applied
science." A Marxist himself, he took care to frame his political strategies in
terms of progress from one stage to the next, and defended the view that
national liberation and the formation of nation-states were preconditions
to social justice. Believing that national aspirations were a natural result of
economic modernization, he defended the right of each nation to a state.
He defended this view consistently, unhesitatingly applying it to realms
of former Polish dominance such as Lithuania, Ukraine, and Belarus. He
recognized that the age of the nation-state must also be the age of the
national minority, and advanced policy proposals designed to protect the
rights of minorities in a future Poland.

During the revolution of 1905, Kelles-Krauz served as link between
the right and left wings of the PPS. He died of tuberculosis at the revolution's height. The conclusion seeks to establish Kelles-Krauz's place
within Polish political history and the history of social thought by way of
comparisons to four of his contemporaries (all best known for achievements after 1905): Józef Piłsudski, Rosa Luxemburg, Max Weber, and
György Lukács. It emphasizes that his contribution to social thought on
the national question is deserving not only of a place in the histories of
socialism and sociology, but of recognition and reference by scholars of
our own times.

This political and intellectual biography is the first significant effort
in that direction. I have attempted to show Kelles-Krauz's as one voice
in intellectual debates and political struggles which are interesting in

their own right, and to present Kelles-Krauz's views in such a way as to add to our knowledge of these events. At the same time, chronology and narrative allow us to understand how Kelles-Krauz's views yielded to change over time and in response to changing circumstances. Also, insofar as this biography is useful because Kelles-Krauz was a characteristic figure, context is necessary to grasp when, how, and why this is so. By the same token, context must be reconstructed in order to perceive just when, how, and why Kelles-Krauz was exceptional within his several milieux.

There is a limit to this method, however. Every biographer faces two distinct and conflicting demands. On the one hand, he must be true to the times, concerns, and idioms of his subject. On the other, he must present his subject in a language accessible to his readers, and must make some allowance for what his readers will find to be of interest. In my view, there is no synthesis which can resolve these conflicting demands, only better and worse attempts to take both into account. While keeping my own voice low, I have tried in two ways to avoid the pitfalls of extreme contextualism. First of all, though I present ideas within their contexts, I have also at the margin selected which ideas I consider to be interesting: either for their own sake, or because they illuminate other figures or motivate stories worth telling. For example, I have written the better part of a chapter on Kelles-Krauz's resolution for the 1896 London congress, but I have dispensed with Kelles-Krauz's views on the agricultural question in a footnote. Second, I have departed completely from narrative in the conclusion, where I will offer my own views as to why Kelles-Krauz's life and ideas should be of interest.

This method creates numerous questions of proportion, and I have been fortunate to benefit from much good advice. More generally, any such effort engenders many debts, which for me are a pleasure to acknowledge. This project has shown me an ideal of academic cooperation which I dare not expect to continue. I wish above all to thank Mr. Timothy Garton Ash of St. Antony's College, Oxford, and Professor Jerzy Jedlicki of the Institute of History of the Polish Academy of Sciences, who jointly supervised my doctoral thesis. Mr. Garton Ash was what every Oxford supervisor should be, and Professor Jedlicki demonstrated exceptional care. By force of example, both have taught me invaluable lessons about the craft of history, and about the relation of academic history to politics and life. I consider it an honor to have worked under their guidance.

Two professors at Brown University, Mary Gluck and Ambassador Thomas W. Simons, Jr., taught me to love the endeavor of history. I thank xvi *Preface to the First Edition*

my first Oxford supervisor, Professor Charles Feinstein of All Souls College, for a rewarding introduction to graduate studies. My college advisor Dr. Martin Conway was my most important tie to Balliol College, and the main reason I shall remember it fondly. Professor Leszek Kołakowski of All Souls College gave time and expertise at both the beginning and the end of this work. Mme Céline Gervais of the University of Paris kindly offered the benefit of her knowledge and research, and read the entire thesis. Professor Robert Blobaum of West Virginia University volunteered to read each chapter upon its completion, and sent me valuable comments. Professor Andrzej Walicki of the University of Notre Dame read the thesis (twice!) and allowed me ample opportunity to profit from his extraordinary erudition. Mr. Stuart Rachels also read the thesis from beginning to end with great care. Professor Jerzy Szacki of the University of Warsaw, Dr. John Klier of University College, London, Mr. Jeffrey Dolven, Mr. Daniel Markovits, Mr. Kevin Stack, and Ms. Heike Remy were good enough to read sections of the thesis. Ms. Remy helped me with German sources, while Dr. Waldemar Czajkowski helped me with Russian. The aid of Dr. Milada Vachudová allowed me to negotiate the archives of the Russian secret police. Dr. Dariusz Drewniak of the Institute of History of the Polish Academy of Sciences sent me original research. I have learned much from conversations with Professor Norman Davies of the University of London, Dr. Harry Shukman of St. Antony's College, Professor Chimen Abramsky, Dr. Jan Kancewicz, and Professor Feliks Tych. The final form of this book owes much to the hard work of my editor, Robert De Lossa. I would also like to thank Tom and Peggy Simons, Andrzej and Agnieszka Waśkiewicz, and Krystyna Hartmanowa for their help during my various stays in Poland. I must also note that my parents, Dr. E. E. Snyder and Christine Hadley Snyder, took time from their visit to Paris to review the introduction and conclusion. This book is the culmination of an education that they have supported in innumerable ways for two decades, and it is thus dedicated to them.

That final year of research and writing in Paris was supported by a dissertation fellowship from the American Council of Learned Societies. I am grateful to Balliol College for a grant which allowed me to visit the Hoover Institution, and to the Institute of Sociology of Warsaw University for repeatedly playing the role of academic host in Poland. My three years in Oxford were funded by a British Marshall Scholarship, and I think it proper to note here that I am very grateful for the opportunities the Marshall program has brought me.

Preface to the Second Edition

THIS BOOK IS my doctoral dissertation, originally published in 1997 by the Harvard Ukrainian Research Institute and distributed by Harvard University Press. That edition has long been unavailable. This new one includes an index, which the first edition lacked. Aside from a few minor corrections, the text has not been altered.

There are, I think, good reasons for this. If I undertook today to write a biography of Kazimierz Kelles-Krauz, it would be a different book. Perhaps I would be more attentive to the Russian and German sources, rather than so highly focused on the Polish and French, languages which in the early 1990s I took such pleasure in learning. I believe I understand more now than I did then about some of the themes of this book, such as Habsburg nationality policy or Jewish politics in partitioned Poland. On the other hand, I can no longer see these issues from the specific perspective developed as I researched Kelles-Krauz and his milieu. I no longer agree with some of the judgments formulated here, but there is no strong reason to prefer my position today over my conclusions of two decades ago. Indeed, there are propositions in this book, perhaps even correct or useful ones, which I am sure I would not be able to formulate now. Such reflections, of course, are completely theoretical; it is only thanks to earlier work that I passed on to later languages, themes, and conclusions.

My biographies of Henryk Józewski (*Sketches from a Secret War*, 2005) and of Wilhelm von Habsburg (*The Red Prince*, 2008), studies of men two decades or so younger than Kelles-Krauz, consider dilemmas of post-imperial statehood that he had predicted. My second book, on the origins of modern nationalism (*The Reconstruction of Nations*, 2002), owes something to Kelles-Krauz's insight that national movements traduce the past in patterned ways that arise from social change as well as political goals. My histories of political atrocity in twentieth-century Europe (*Bloodlands*, 2010; *Black Earth*, 2015) drew from the territorial perspective of that second book, but also from thinking about the relationship between nationalism and socialism, which was Kelles-Krauz's main subject. Even my published conversation with Tony Judt (*Thinking the Twentieth Century*, 2012) has some relation to the dissertation, since he offered me a fellowship after my doctoral work on a Polish Marxist had guaranteed me durable unemployment, and that is how our friendship began. In Kelles-Krauz himself I had a model of the scholar who engages in the politics of urgent moments. In that way we might see a relationship between this book and my political manifesto (*On Tyranny*, 2017)

   After all of this intervening time and work, I read this book today as the work of a man half my age, with different preoccupations, and perhaps some intrinsic ability to identify with its youthful subject. The second chapter, for example, was written by one student in his twenties living in Paris about another student in his twenties living in Paris, a happy coincidence in which I am loathe now to interfere. I can't recall in every respect what it was like to be the person who picked up a bound copy of his dissertation from a French printer who had insisted on the cover's proper color and then ran for the Métro to get to the Gare du Nord to catch a channel train to London in order to submit his work in Oxford and then returned to Paris the same day to have a late dinner with his parents. I do however remember that person well enough to be confident that he would have objected to later alterations to his work. Getting to the end of a book, whether as author, reader, or editor, is the work of a particular moment. So this biography remains in substance as it was, improved in form by the kind attention of Susan Ferber of Oxford University Press.

Krasnogruda, 29 July 2017

1. Kazimierz Kelles-Krauz in school uniform, Radom, 1890.

2. Kazimierz Kelles-Krauz (seated, middle), with friends Władysław Bukowiński (left) and Zygmunt Rostkowski (right), Radom, 1891.

3. Maria Goldsteynówna, future wife of Kazimierz Kelles-Krauz, Radom, 1890.

4. Polish student group "Spójnia" in Paris. In the third row, from the left: Kazimierz Kelles-Krauz, Maria Kelles-Krauzowa, and (fourth from the left) Bolesław Motz.

5. Kazimierz Kelles-Krauz at his desk, Paris.

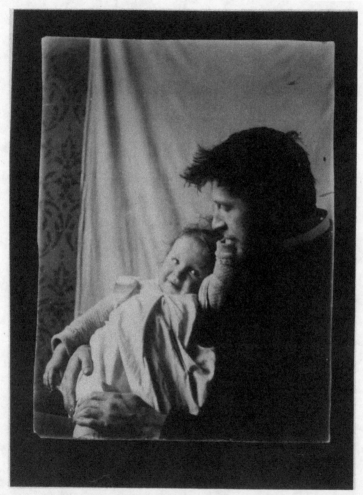

6. Kazimierz Kelles-Krauz with daughter Janina, Paris, 1900.

7. Kazimierz Kelles-Krauz, Cracow, 1904.

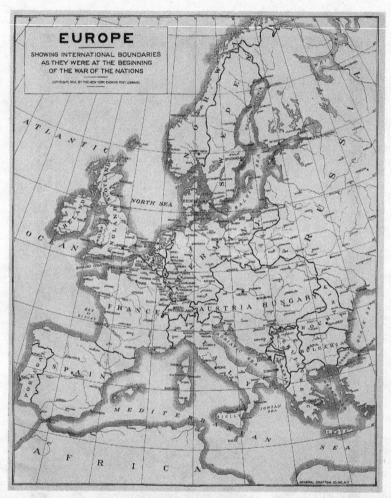

MAP I. "Europe: Showing International Boundaries as They Were at the Beginning of the War of the Nations." General Drafting Co., Inc. for the *New York Evening Post*, 1914.

Reproduced courtesy of the Harvard Map Collection, Pusey Library, Harvard University.

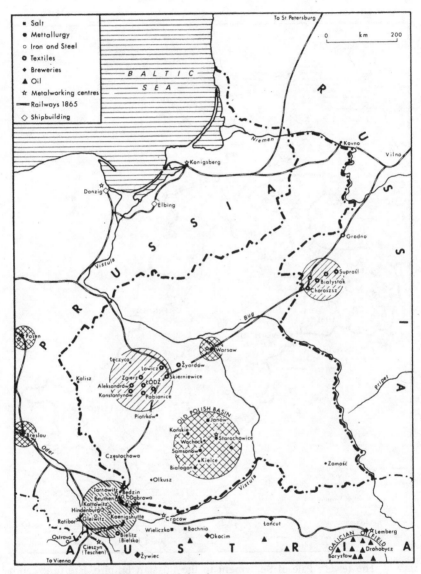

MAP 2. Industrialization in Polish lands, c. 1900.

Reproduced courtesy of Norman Davies. From his *God's Playground: A History of Poland*, vol. 1, p. 166. Oxford, 1982.

MAP 3. The Jewish Pale of Settlement in the Russian Empire, late nineteenth century.

Reproduced courtesy of Norman Davies. From his *God's Playground: A History of Poland*, vol. 1, p. 243. Oxford, 1982.

List of Abbreviations

Bund   Allgemeyner Idisher Arbeyterbund in Lita, Poylen un
            Rusland [Central Union of Jewish Workers in Lithuania,
            Poland, and Russia]
Institute   Institut International de Sociologie [International Institute
            of Sociology]
KZPPS   Komitet Zagraniczny Polskiej Partii Socjalistycznej [Foreign
            Committee of the Polish Socialist Party]
PPS   Polska Partia Socjalistyczna [Polish Socialist Party]
PPSD   Polska Partia Socjalno-demokratyczna [Polish Social-
            Democratic Party, affiliated with Austrian social democracy]
PPSzp   Polska Partia Socjalistyczna zaboru pruskiego [Polish
            Socialist Party of the Prussian Partition]
RSDRP   Russkaia Sotsial-demokraticheskaia Rabochaia Partiia
            [Russian Social-Democratic Workers' Party]
SDKP   Socjaldemokracja Królestwa Polskiego [Social-Democracy of
            the Kingdom of Poland]
SDKPiL   Socjaldemokracja Królestwa Polskiego i Litwy [Social-
            Democracy of the Kingdom of Poland and Lithuania]
SPD   Sozialdemokratische Partei Deutschlands [Social-Democratic
            Party of Germany]
Union   Union of Polish Socialists Abroad
ZZSP   Związek Zagraniczny Socjalistów Polskich [Union of Polish
            Socialists Abroad]

*Nationalism, Marxism,
and Modern Central Europe*

Introduction

WHY WRITE A BIOGRAPHY? Why devote years of energy and thought, or indeed any time at all, to a single figure, rather than to some broader subject? Assuming that such an endeavor is justified in principle, why one figure and not another? Why write the life of a Polish political intellectual, and why this Polish political intellectual rather than another? I will offer four answers to these questions, and attempt to explain how my methods meet their demands.

A biography may be interesting because its subject is in some sense *typical* of his nation, class, generation, or period. Kazimierz Kelles-Krauz faced the two overlapping intellectual problems of the emerging Polish intelligentsia of the Russian partition during the last quarter of the nineteenth century: first, the desire for national reconstruction and social reformation in conditions of repression and after the failure of the rising of 1863; and second, the discontinuity between the new ideas of science and their related political ideologies, and the continuing force of national tradition. Kelles-Krauz's life experiences were also typical of this new group: his descent from déclassé nobility; his ambivalent relationship to a father who had fought in the Polish rising against Russian rule in 1863; his participation in secret self-education circles as a schoolboy; his emigration to Paris for a university degree. As he aged, his life as a party activist and writer was typical of Polish political intellectuals in more general ways: he lived under the pressures of conspiracy, the constraints of writing for a living, and the insecurities of immigration. As we shall see, Kelles-Krauz's thought reflected a tripartite view of history characteristic of the Polish intelligentsia. Hence, the narrative of his life casts some light on the origins of this intelligentsia, the political class which would bring modern political ideologies to Russian Poland, lead Poland's first mass parties, and build the Second Polish Republic.

Most conventionally, a biography may be justified because its subject was *influential*. He is treated as a factor in history: his life must be understood in order to grasp certain chains of causation. This is probably the weakest justification for a biography of Kelles-Krauz. It is true that he provided a necessary link between the right and left wings of the Polish Socialist Party (PPS), and that his death contributed to the party's eventual split into its Marxist and patriotic fractions. His advocacy of the democratic nation-state as the best means of satisfying both national and class aspirations had no influence on either of these fractions, nor on any other Polish political formation. His work in sociology left some slight traces in France, Belgium, and especially Poland. His tradition of Marxist patriotism had little influence in the decades immediately following his death, but would be contested by the Polish left after the Second World War. His Marxist philosophy would inspire the Polish philosopher Stanisław Brzozowski. His views on Jewish nationality exerted some influence on the debate of Polish progressives on the Jewish question, and his death ended the career of one of the most articulate Polish advocates of Polish-Jewish reconciliation.

Kelles-Krauz is most interesting precisely because so many of his political and intellectual positions were *exceptional*; because he was, one might argue, "ahead of his time." At a time when Marxists were generally indifferent to the national question, he justified the nation-state and sought to explain the arrival of modern nationalism. While Marxists saw international relations in terms of general categories such as "peace" and "imperialism," he suggested that socialist parties take concrete positions on the foreign policies of their respective states. At a time when most Marxists were determinists, Kelles-Krauz proposed a subtle explanation of historical change which allowed generous room for autonomous traditions and human freedom. While most of his contemporaries followed Engels in treating Marxism as a "dialectic of nature," Kelles-Krauz insisted that Marxism consisted in research methods which applied to society only. While Second International socialists treated Marxism as a theory concerning the economy, Kelles-Krauz preferred to discuss the alienation of modern man within capitalist society. At a time when the young discipline of sociology was teething on the positivist version of Marxism offered by the Second International's leading thinkers, Kelles-Krauz proposed treating Marxism as a means to transcend sociology's own inclination to ape the natural sciences. To some extent, these positions can be traced to

Polish academic and political traditions. Yet more than any other Polish sociologist, Kelles-Krauz confronted the assumptions of the day's West European sociology with audacity and intelligence. More than any other Polish political activist, he worked to find a coherent resolution to the rival problems of national liberation and social revolution. More than any other Polish patriot, Kelles-Krauz accepted that the Polish case was one of many equally laudable struggles for national liberation, and sought to understand nationalism in scholarly terms. While Polish socialists who regarded national independence as an integral part of the Polish socialist program were usually not Marxists (and vice versa), Kelles-Krauz was both patriot and Marxist.

It is one thing to take unusual positions which have little influence on one's peers; it is quite another when these positions have scholarly value and anticipate later concerns and conclusions. As a Marxist thinker, Kelles-Krauz operated within the categories which are associated with Lukács and Western Marxism. As a sociologist, he correctly predicted the end of his day's naive positivism and organicism, and set out a method which in some respects anticipated Weber's. His most important work, as both socialist and sociologist, concerned nationalism, and here he anticipated the key elements of the debate which has grown up around the work of Benedict Anderson, Eric Hobsbawm, and especially Ernest Gellner in the last decade.

Fourth and finally, a biography may be *illuminating*: following the course of a single life may animate milieux and provide vantage points on questions of larger interest. As we trace Kelles-Krauz's attempts to bring the European left around to his understanding of national issues (concretely, his efforts to pass a resolution at the London congress of the Second International in favor of Polish independence, to persuade French socialists to oppose the Franco-Russian alliance, to win an autonomous role for Polish socialism in Germany, to teach Austrian socialists that their empire was doomed to collapse, and to justify to the Polish left the national rights of Jews) we find ourselves learning a great deal not only about the national thinking but about the nationalism of the Second International's parties and leading figures. Nationalism has traditionally confounded the left, and Kelles-Krauz's attempts to bring national issues to the attention of socialists during the golden age of the Second International help us to find the roots of this problem.

Kelles-Krauz's path illuminates other problems as well. His attitude toward the revisionism debate within German social democracy is not significant because he was able to influence its course, but because the arguments he directed against its three major protagonists (Karl Kautsky, Eduard Bernstein, and Rosa Luxemburg) provide us with a means of perceiving dynamics within German social democracy that were invisible from inside the party. This holds for his own party as well: because Kelles-Krauz was the most capable theorist of the Polish Socialist Party, his presence and work forced what was a very pragmatic party leadership to reveal its theoretical assumptions and make explicit its strategies. In general, a thorough description of Kelles-Krauz's role in the party must add to our knowledge of the PPS, the most successful conspiratorial organization in Russian Poland, and the party which provided much of the political elite of independent interwar Poland. Finally, Kelles-Krauz's attempts to create a Marxist sociology help us to understand the relationships between these two academic countercultures.

In the same way, the biography offers new views of familiar figures. In general, the perspective offered by Kelles-Krauz's concerns reveals unappreciated sides of the notables of the *fin-de-siècle* left. This is especially true of the two great figures of the Polish left of the era, Rosa Luxemburg and Józef Piłsudski. If one knew nothing about Kelles-Krauz, one would not know that Rosa Luxemburg had an energetic and intelligent opponent on the national question, who offered Marxist arguments which she never answered. One would not know that Luxemburg was so troubled by this interlocutor that she stooped to a campaign of personal attacks which culminated in a public revelation of his pseudonyms and details of his personal life. Likewise, Kelles-Krauz's relationship with Józef Piłsudski presents the latter rather differently than might be expected. Kelles-Krauz, on the left of the PPS, respected Piłsudski's practical skills and charisma. Piłsudski was agnostic rather than hostile to Kelles-Krauz's Marxism, and considered chess and discussion with a Marxist theorist relaxing, rather than taxing. The record of Kelles-Krauz's political life illuminates the alternatives available to both Piłsudski and Luxemburg, just as a description of his struggles to find a middle ground helps reveal the attractions of these extremes.

I

From Radom to Paris, 1872–1894

KAZIMIERZ RADOSŁAW ELEHARD KELLES-KRAUZ was born on 22 March 1872 in Szczebrzeszyń, in the Russian partition of Poland. The name says much about the history of the family. The first known progenitor is a certain Baron von Krause from Bavaria, a Knight of the Sword who took part in the conquest of Livonia (present-day Estonia and Latvia) in the early part of the thirteenth century. This Baron von Krause settled near Dorpat (now Tartu, Estonia), and built a castle on lands which were known as Kelles; his descendants were known by this second surname.

In the mid-sixteenth century, the Livonian state was crumbling under the weight of internal strife and aggression from the east. Dorpat fell to Tsar Ivan IV in 1558; Livonian nobles swore homage to Polish King Zygmunt August in 1561. The Polish-Lithuanian Commonwealth conquered these lands from Russia in 1582, and royal reviews of 1583 and 1585 confirmed that one Elehard Krause was entitled to the title of baron. (At some point, it became customary for the eldest son of each generation of the Krause line to bear the name Elehard.) Elehard's son or grandson Eginhard fought with distinction against the Swedes in 1600–1607. This loyalty may well have preserved the family's holdings, as Polish and Lithuanian nobles were allowed to seize property from Livonian nobles who did not support the Polish-Lithuanian cause.[1]

The Polish "wojewód derpski" was short lived. The Swedes took Dorpat in 1625, and were granted the city and its surrounding lands by treaty ten years later. Wars over Livonia continued, and Russia took Dorpat again in 1704. At some point in the seventeenth or eighteenth century the Krauses abandoned their ancestral estates and moved south to present-day Lithuania. Russian rule overtook them there, when the Polish-Lithuanian Commonwealth was partitioned for the third time in 1795. In the early nineteenth century we find Baron Jan and Baroness Franciszka (née Rurykowicz-Olechnowicz) von Kelles-Krauz residing in Lithuanian estates called Mićkuny and Medykany. These lands were the birthright of their son Michał Wilhelm Elehard von Kelles-Krauz, born in 1842. Michał Kelles-Krauz fought for Poland in the 1863 rising under Edmund Różycki in Volhynia, and when he returned to Lithuania these properties had been seized by the Russian government.[2]

Unlike hundreds of his comrades in arms, Michał was not executed; unlike thousands of his fellow Lithuanian gentry, he was not exiled to Siberia. He may have escaped with a relatively light punishment by grace of his choice to fight so far from home. His surname and background probably helped, as there were many Baltic Germans in the Russian bureaucracy, and Michał had important friends in both Warsaw and Vilnius. Upon leaving Lithuania, he was able to find a series of posts in excise offices, first in Szczebrzeszyń, then in Końskie, and finally in Radom. He was married to Matylda (née Daniewska), a niece of Piotr Wysocki, who had led the military conspiracy that preceded the 1830 rising. The couple settled in Radom no later than 1882, for in that year their eldest child (of six), Kazimierz, was enrolled in Radom's school.

Matylda died in 1883, leaving Michał to rear their sons and daughters.[3] Michał maintained a modest home in Radom on his bureaucrat's pension, and even sent his sons to school. With occasional help from his father-in-law, the retired mathematics teacher Jakub Daniewski, he raised his children in an atmosphere of learning and patriotism.[4] In the seven years between his wife's death and his eldest son's exit from the household at the age of eighteen, he and Kazimierz seem to have been on exceptionally good terms. At that age in 1890, Kazimierz wrote of his father that; "Each of us has in the other a true and sincere friend. Of course, we differ, my strivings sometimes conflict with his goals and principles, but never has that honest and understanding man shown anything but toleration to his children."[5] The difference between the "strivings" of young Kazimierz, at eighteen already a convinced socialist,[6] and the "principles" of his father, a patriotic noble defeated on the battlefields of 1863, deserves a moment of reflection.

Generations

Among educated Poles over the course of the nineteenth century, the early-modern definition of the nation as its gentry was being replaced by the modern understanding of the nation as the sum of all its members.[7] This change coincided with the emergence of a sizable intelligentsia, in the sense of a "group of educated people cut off from both the masses and the traditional sources of power, and tending to seek ways to lead the former against the latter."[8] The notion of such an intelligentsia predated the rising of 1863; two Poles, Bronisław Trentowski in Paris and Karol Libelt in Poznań, had used the term as early as 1844, both in the context of the "government of souls"; and in 1862 Ludwik Gumplowicz had called the intelligentsia (as opposed to the gentry) the "alpha and omega of the nation."[9] Yet it was after 1863 that economic, political, and cultural changes within Russian Poland put an end to the political predominance of the Polish gentry, and brought this intelligentsia to the fore as the unrivaled national political class. In what did these changes consist?

The dispensation of the lands of the former Polish-Lithuanian Commonwealth among Russia, Austria, and Prussia (or the German Empire from 1871) was unchanged after 1863. These powers had agreed to three partitions (though Austria abstained from the second) of the Polish-Lithuanian Commonwealth, the last of which, in 1795, had removed Poland from the map. At the Congress of Vienna in 1814 they had decided on a modified division of these territories, which (with minor changes) lasted until the First World War. Prussia held formerly Polish lands stretching from the Baltic sea to Silesia, and Austria was lord of Galicia. The majority of the former Polish-Lithuanian territories fell to Russia, which divided its gains into two categories. Lands east of a line marked roughly (from north to south) by the Baltic Sea, the Niemen River, Kaunas, Hrodna, Białystok, Berestia, and Volodymyr, were simply absorbed into the Empire. From his remaining Polish territories Alexander I formed in 1814 a "Kingdom of Poland," known as the "Congress Kingdom," with its own ministries and a measure of autonomy. This autonomy was severely limited after the Polish rising of 1830–1831; but the Congress Kingdom, now ruled by a Russian general as the emperor's viceroy, continued to exist. Although it included only about one-seventh of the territory and one-fifth of the population of the pre-partition Polish-Lithuanian Commonwealth, the Congress Kingdom was the closest approximation of a Polish state to be found.

The distinction between the Congress Kingdom and the rest of the Russian Empire was erased after the rising of 1863.[10] In 1865 the Congress Kingdom's governing bodies were dissolved, to be replaced by local administrative, treasury, postal, and school authorities designed on the Russian model and subordinate to imperial ministries in Petersburg.

Governors-General of Warsaw (as the tsar's agent was called from 1874) could send persons suspected of political crimes to military courts, and even exile suspects to Siberia without any trial at all. These lands were under martial law almost without cease from 1864 to 1914, and were usually excluded from Alexander II's modest reforms. The press was preventatively censored, and discussions of political questions were forbidden. The term "Congress Kingdom" fell out of Russian usage, and was replaced by the "Privislianskii Krai," or "country by the Vistula."[11]

The Roman Catholic Church also lost its relatively privileged position. Hundreds of its priests were exiled or imprisoned after 1863, and at least 37 were executed. By 1870, not a single bishop who had held office in 1863 remained in his seat. The majority of monasteries and nunneries were suppressed, and the appointment of priests was made subject to confirmation by the state. Pastoral letters were censored, and trips abroad were forbidden. Bishops of dioceses within the former Congress Kingdom were forbidden contact with the Vatican, except through the mediation of a Roman Catholic College in Petersburg.[12] In the last decades of the nineteenth century, the Church failed to meet elementary religious needs of Polish Catholics, especially in the burgeoning cities. In politics, it moved "from a policy of moderate opposition and cautious confrontation characteristic of the late 1850s and early 1860s to one based on fear and calculated loyalty."[13]

After Alexander III succeeded the assassinated Alexander II in 1881, Russian repression was increasingly directed against Polish culture. Alexander III pursued a policy of Russification throughout the entire Empire, not sparing even the peoples who had proven loyal subjects.[14] He appointed Governor-General I. V. Gurko (1883–1894), who removed the Polish language from all levels of administration and the courts.[15] Poles were almost completely purged from upper and middle levels of bureaucracies, and Russians were drawn in by bonuses to take their places. Whereas before 1863 Poles could work in any but the top governmental positions, by the 1880s we tend to find them in railroads, post offices and excise offices.[16]

Another fundamental change within the lands of the former Congress Kingdom after 1863 was an industrial revolution, which in Piotr Wandycz's view was complete by about 1890.[17] Its first cause is to be sought in the countryside. The tsar's emancipation decrees of 1864 had increased the net amount of land held by peasants, but class divisions among them widened, and the number of landless peasants quadrupled. The influx of cheap grain from America and cheap wool from Australia in the 1880s led to an agricultural crisis which accelerated this process.[18] This new pool of labor sought employment in urban industries, where another basic transformation was underway.

After Alexander II decided in 1878 to expand the imperial rail system, orders for wagons and rails flooded the Congress Kingdom's metallurgical industry. From 1878 to 1886 coal production increased from 400,000 to two million tons, and production of iron and steel from 18,000 to 128,000 tons. Rail lines constituted an important investment in the infrastructure of the lands of the Congress Kingdom. By 1865 Warsaw and Łódź were connected by rail to Petersburg, by 1867 to Moscow and Kyiv. Between 1864 and 1884 rail cargo increased twenty-fold. In 1864, the Congress Kingdom had 635 kilometers of tracks; by 1890 this figure had reached 2,084. Rail links to eastern markets were crucial, as the Congress Kingdom sent the vast majority of its finished products to Russia. In the 1870s and 1880s industry within the Congress Kingdom held a privileged place within the Russian economy: it was protected from outside competition by increasing tariffs, and was assured of orders from the rest of the Empire. Its iron and steel products, and a flourishing textiles industry based in Łódź, were supported by Russian demand. These industries benefited from the advantages of backwardness by importing modern machinery from western Europe.[19]

The results were imposing. The value of total industrial production within the Congress Kingdom increased six-fold between 1864 and 1885, and the number of industrial workers nearly doubled in the same period from 80,000 to 150,000. These changes were localized: almost all of these industrial workers were to be found in Warsaw, Łódź, Żyrardów, or the Dąbrowa basin. This industrial revolution, arriving so quickly to an essentially agrarian land, brought with it the kind of urban misery that Engels had described two generations earlier. The average working day in large factories was between twelve and fourteen hours, and sixteen-hour days and work on Sundays and holidays was not exceptional. Workers lived in overcrowded apartments, several families often sharing a single room. Half of all of Warsaw's workers died before reaching the age of fifty.[20]

Radom, where the Kelles-Krauz family finally settled, played its own modest part in these transformations. The Dęblin-Dąbrowa railway linked the city with the rest of the imperial economy in 1885. The rail line helped Radom to begin an economic boom, which was to help triple the city's population—from 12,000 in 1885 to 36,000 in 1905—in the space of twenty years. Though not a major industrial center, Radom was one of the relatively few cities in the Empire to see some effects of industrialization in the 1880s.[21]

The characteristic figure of Radom's industrialization was the worker-peasant, who kept strong ties with the country while earning wages in the city.[22] He often worked as a tanner, for tanning had been the major industry in Radom since the middle ages. Radom's first modern tannery was built by a German who moved from Poznań in order to avoid Russian tariffs. When Kelles-Krauz was a student, there were three large tanneries operating, and a fourth was under construction. In 1888, Radom was the second largest center of tannery, after Warsaw, in Russian Poland.[23] Moreover, Radom was also within reach of Warsaw and Łódź, and students in Radom's schools were well aware of the strikes and industrial turmoil in these neighboring cities.

The end of the Congress Kingdom's autonomy and arrival of the industrial revolution meant that Kazimierz Kelles-Krauz's generation was born into a new political and economic order. For them, the modernization of the Congress Kingdom's economy was the normal state of affairs, whereas for their parents it was a disorienting change. Students of Kazimierz's age were touched by the repression which had followed the 1863 rising; but unlike their parents, they had never known anything else. For these students, a fixed and sharp boundary between the home, where Polish was spoken and Poland was treasured, and public life, where Russian was spoken and Poland was considered not to exist, was a given fact. Russian schools made up the greater part of their public life, for Polish schools had been another casualty of 1863. Between 1866 and 1869 Russian was introduced as the language of instruction—only religion was taught in Polish.[24]

Especially after Alexander III's accession in 1881, the school system became a political tool, designed to create loyal subjects who were professionally competent, but unable to think independently. Polish students were taught to fear Russian power, yet love Russian culture.[25] Alexander Apukhtin, curator of the Warsaw Educational District (1879–1897), accepted the task of Russification with enthusiasm. He was supported by Governor-General I. V. Gurko, who expected from Polish students "a better knowledge of the Russian language and of its grammatical rules than from Russians themselves."[26] Students were beaten for speaking Polish within the schoolyard, and even for committing errors in Russian characteristic of Poles.[27]

Russification of schools was only the first of many difficulties Kelles-Krauz's generation had to face. The few schools whose diplomas allowed students to apply to university were overfull.[28] Students were expected to master vast amounts of material by rote memorization, working at home. The amount of homework was so large that almost every younger student who could afford to do so hired a tutor from among the older students. This arrangement helped older students pay their school fees and their rent, but reduced the amount of time they had for their own review.[29]

The bulk of lectures covered the Russian, Greek, and Latin languages (with an emphasis on grammar)—subjects which were calculated to take a great deal of time to master, and to do little to promote independent thinking.[30] The history of the Russian Empire comprised almost the entirety of the history curriculum, and was presented in an extremely chauvinistic fashion. Polish history was not taught as a discrete subject.

The history text most often recalled in memoirs of former students is that of D. I. Ilovaiskii, who among other things praised Catherine the Great for freeing Poland from the Jesuits.[31] Russian literature was taught in conjunction with Russian history, although no works written after 1830 were studied.

Students were not allowed to own books of their own choosing, nor to borrow them from libraries. Russian authorities strove to ensure that students read only what was thought good for them, at home as well as in school. In general, school supervisors did their best to blur the line between school and home, public and private, Empire and Poland. School inspectors spied on students in and out of school. On Sundays and holidays, students were required to perform state or religious ceremonies *en masse*.[32] Extracurricular activities and school libraries were designed to attract students unwittingly to Russian culture.

Some of the consequences of this education policy were predictable enough. Many students dropped out of school, and the ones who graduated typically required ten or eleven years to finish the eight classes.[33] Many future notables of interwar Poland were troubled by memories of their schooling to the end of their lives: Józef Piłsudski, for example, wrote that even after exile in Siberia and time in prison his worst nightmares were of school, where all he had been taught to love and respect was scorned.[34] "What might such a school attain?" asked a graduate of Kelles-Krauz's school in Radom. "Only the exhaustion of the mind, weakening of the nerves, constriction of individuality, and the feverish desire to graduate."[35]

Radom's school was run after 1883 by V. I. Smorodinov. Smorodinov was an old hand in Poland, having taught in Konin, Kalisz, and Piotrków before moving to Radom. From 1873 he had served as school inspector in Radom, and thus had ten years of experience as head of discipline before being appointed school supervisor.[36] Smorodinov was named to this post at a time when cultural Russification was the order of the day, in the early years of Alexander Ill's reign, and was under the orders of Apukhtin in Warsaw. But Smorodinov acted from belief as well as from obligation, taking personal charge of every aspect of Russification, from music to discipline.[37] His students called him "the little Apukhtin."

But as Smorodinov wrote in his memoirs, he was quite aware that the school was failing in its mission.[38] Until 1880, he recalled, there had been no significant disciplinary problems. From that time on, the situation worsened by degrees, and he saw the stamp of "anti-tsarism" and "Polish chauvinism" on some of the students' activities.[39] But even this most devoted of Russia's educational specialists had only the faintest idea of the degree of secret student activity around him. By the late 1880s, his school no longer decided the course of the education of his best students. When Kazimierz and his fellows, in uncomfortable school uniforms, marched across Radom's cobbled square, passed rows of Russian flags, and stepped into the neoclassical school building, they were entering a theater.[40] All day they pretended to be students. After school they learned from and taught each other, in an impressively organized way. Through secret education circles, they learned the subjects they missed at school, practiced the conspiracy that was necessary for all political endeavors before 1918, and built a private, free sphere of life.

"In many ways, Russification was counterproductive, as it insured the rise of underground education, beyond the government's control."[41] In Radom, where the attempt at government control was at its most ambitious, we find the most elaborate attempt at circumvention. But similar circles were to be found in most schools in Russian Poland: Poles studied in twenty four schools, of which at least fifteen had such circles by 1889–1890, Kazimierz Kelles-Krauz's eighth and last year at Radom.[42] They emerged from below, for the most part independently of one another, and at about the same time.[43] (Their appearance coincided with secret illegal courses for girls, including the famous Flying University from 1885).[44] The various circles engaged in similar activities: they read forbidden academic and political material, kept libraries, published handwritten journals, and conspired to keep their activities secret. In these early years, they were not unified politically, only by the common quest for knowledge. Almost without exception, every prominent Polish politician (regardless of orientation) and scholar (regardless of field) of the Second Republic who hailed from Russian Poland had taken part in such a circle in his or her student days.

The appearance of these circles cannot be explained simply as a reaction to Russification, although they were certainly that. Russification of schools, although it worsened after 1881, began in 1866, some twenty years before circles began to form. Part of the explanation for this gap is probably generational. The seventh- and eighth-year students of 1888 (the year that Kelles-Krauz and others formed a first circle in Radom), for example, were born in the late 1860s or early 1870s, and thus had no memory of the 1863 rising or of the calamities of its immediate aftermath. These students (usually children of gentry) imbibed the romantic patriotism of their parents, but could not understand the resignation and passivity which accompanied it. Their parents remained in something like a state of shock for the rest of their lives, hoping to preserve what they had not yet lost: and only the young generation could take up Poland's political predicament with animation and dedication.[45] Students were conspiring before the invader, who oppressed, and before their parents, who feared. With two contradictory sources of external authority, both suspect, students were pushed back onto their own resources.

One of these resources was the natural tendency of boys to form cliques and clubs. Another was the glittering attraction of modern ideas (chiefly the belief that science could resolve social problems) and modern political thought (mainly the ideologies of patriotism and socialism). With neither teachers nor parents (in many cases) to guide their choice of readings and interpretations, the appeal must have been all the more irresistable. Yet, the attractiveness of modern ideas and modern politics was not a simple function of generational alienation and attempts at Russification. The ideas which these students interpreted, vulgarized, and adapted to their own situation had to come from somewhere. Books were crucial to the formation of secret circles, not only because of their content, but because of their simple physical existence. Because students could not read any unassigned works without facing expulsion, every book had to be secret. There were in fact two categories of forbidden writings: books which were not assigned, and writings which had not been approved by the censor. The latter were illegal, and their possession was a crime punishable by imprisonment—all the more reason for conspiracy. Naturally, the riskier a subject, the more tempting it was: only illegal propaganda was more attractive than the undertaught subjects of science and Polish history.

In the years just before the formation of the circles, students in the lands of the former Congress Kingdom had sought the propaganda of Russian revolutionaries. At the turn of the 1870s and 1880s Russia had seemed to offer the most vital revolutionary movement in Europe, and the heroic feats of Russian *narodniki* attracted the attention of Polish students, many of whom enrolled in Russian universities. For a scant and exceptional period, leaders of Polish political groups acknowledged the superiority of their comrades to the east. The leader of the first Polish socialist party, Ludwik Waryński, had studied in Petersburg.[46] Ignacy Hryniewiecki, the assassin of Alexander II, was a Pole. His attitude was typical: so long as the action was in Russia, he would remain in Russia. Ironically, his act helped ensure that independent Polish activity would begin, for the repression that followed the assassination in 1881 broke the Russian revolutionary organizations *Narodnaia Volia* (The People's Will) and *Chornyi Peredel* (Black Repartition).

By the time Polish students began to form circles in the mid-1880s, faith among youth in a revolution coming from the east had all but died (though it was to last another five years or so in émigré outposts like Geneva).[47] Waryński had founded the first Polish socialist party, and had used a famous trial in 1880 to publicize the socialist program.[48] In 1886 Russian Poland had its first socialist martyrs, said to be the first mortal casualties of resistance to Russian rule since 1864.[49] Because this first party, Proletariat, was quickly crushed, its achievements were known only as legend to the student circles. Still, as Kelles-Krauz was to remember later in life, the legend was inspiring.[50] Though Proletariat was anti-patriotic, it showed that resistance was possible by Poles on Polish soil. The simple fact of loss of life provided an example of courage, and the commemoration of martyrdom became an annual occasion for propaganda.

This domestic example dovetailed with literature smuggled in from abroad. During the course of the 1880s, the émigré writings of Bolesław Limanowski (1835–1935), a patriotic socialist and sociologist, and of Zygmunt Miłkowski (1824–1915), the founder of the Polish League in 1887, helped turn young minds back to the possibility of political change that would begin in Poland.[51] Throughout the 1880s, Limanowski stood for non-Marxist, patriotic socialism, while Stanisław Mendelson (1858–1913) and other socialist émigrés opposed any effort to regain national independence.[52] Miłkowski's Polish League marked the political beginning of modern Polish patriotism, and as a self-conscious alternative to socialism ended the socialists' monopoly on political organization. It soon controlled a conspiratorial student group, Zet, and subordinated the populist Warsaw newspaper *Głos* to its views.

Works of science and history joined the writings of Limanowski, Miłkowski and others in students' secret libraries. Although Polish historiography was flourishing in Warsaw and Cracow, the quality of the available Polish history texts was quite low; students seemed to have placed a good deal of stock in the *Historical Songs* of Julian Niemcewicz, published with accompanying music in 1816.[53] The works of the Polish romantic poets Adam Mickiewicz and Juliusz Słowacki were much sought after, but extremely difficult to come by—in uncensored editions at any rate. Of much greater immediate influence were works of science and philosophy translated into Polish and Russian. As the 1880s passed, more and more west European books were becoming available, often in translations by Polish socialists just a few years older than the students themselves.[54] As one former student put it, there was a "cult of science" beside the "cult of Mickiewicz."[55] This cult of science corresponded to a tendency which we now refer to as "positivist": it embraced the new social sciences; it offered the hope that social problems were subject to resolution by scientific method; its saints were Darwin, Comte, Spencer, and Buckle.

Positivism and Its Discontents

"Warsaw positivism" was the final important influence upon the intellectual atmosphere of the secret circles. It was a movement of journalists, and its origins can be dated from the formation of *Przegląd Tygodniowy* in 1867. As a movement rather than school of thought, it defies precise characterization. It was a reaction to the failed uprising of 1863, and an attempt to find some means of national survival under the repression which followed. Warsaw positivists regarded it as their purpose to save the Polish nation (which under conditions of censorship was naturally considered under the rubric of "society") from its historical backwardness and traditional romanticism, and to find the intellectual tools by which the Polish nation might gain sufficient internal strength to one day reclaim its independence.[56]

The intellectual toolbox was imported from western Europe. These journalists borrowed from Auguste Comte the term "positivism" and the belief in the possibility of social science, but their conception of society was similar to Herbert Spencer's. Warsaw positivists accepted Spencer's idea that society was a self-regulating and harmoniously functioning organism.[57] Spencer's belief that economic development was the key to social progress allowed for optimism in the context of the Congress Kingdom's industrialization. Spencer's notion that state intervention could only hamper this progress was even more convenient, since Warsaw positivists could count on no help whatsoever from the Russian state.[58] Departing from Spencer, Warsaw positivism did not imagine that progress would follow of its own accord, and appealed to intellectuals to play particular roles in society in the name of duty and citizenship.[59] They called for "work at the foundations," a voluntary effort by intellectuals to educate peasants and workers and thus raise the level of Polish civilization.[60] By the notion of "organic work" they identified bourgeois virtues with national virtues, and argued that intellectuals who promoted entrepreneurship and collective resourcefulness were best serving their society.[61] In general, the attitude of the Warsaw positivists toward the intellectual was ambiguous: on the one hand, they urged him to drop his romantic pretensions and take a productive part in society; on the other, they treated him as a superhuman being able to fill all the gaps of Polish society, culture, and politics.[62] Adam Smith, meet Adam Mickiewicz.

By the 1880s, it was clear that the program of the Warsaw positivists was insufficient to build the kind of stateless civil society they had in mind. Positivists wished to work within the law, but the existing law was a tool of the invader. They sought to educate the population, but existing education was a tool of Russification. They imagined that capitalism would end Poland's eternal problem of rural poverty and backwardness, but instead poverty was transferred to the cities. (They reacted flexibly by advocating state protection of labor, but the Russian state was not cooperative.) Educated Poles who attempted to find work in the capitalist economy were often disappointed. German firms investing in Poland hired German engineers, and the young capitalist economy did not offer many attractive jobs for qualified technicians. The problem of the oversupply of intellectuals—whose attendant insecurity added a sense of class urgency to the positivist program[63]—remained unresolved. In fact, it worsened in the 1870s and 1880s as former civil servants expelled from government work (where as many as 70 percent of school graduates had found employment in the 1870s) and Poles fleeing even harsher repression in the eastern lands joined the chase after a very limited number of jobs.[64]

From the early 1880s, some of these restless surplus intellectuals were Marxists, who made their names as critics of positivism.[65] Marxists did not believe that social problems could be solved within the existing political order, counting instead on an international revolution of the working classes. However, in conditions of censorship, their offensive took place on more theoretical grounds. Stanisław Krusiński criticized the positivists' understanding of society as an organism, arguing instead that it was divided into hostile classes. Bronisław Białobłocki offered a new perspective on the problem of the oversupply of intellectuals, maintaining that the emergence of a "thinking proletariat" was a welcome development. While the Marxists polemicized with the positivists, the two groups had much in common. Although Marxists rejected the view of society as an organism, they agreed that a science of society was possible. Positivists had argued, as against romantic traditions of Polish exceptionalism, that Poland was simply behind in a general scheme of historical progress; the Marxists accepted this as well. Whereas positivists imagined that education would bring the peasantry into the national community, Marxists saw in the industrial working class the future saviors of humanity, but in both cases, the intellectual mediates between the group in question and its historical destiny.[66] Indeed, both positivists and Marxists were concerned with the problem of the intelligentsia. Positivists sometimes treated the intelligentsia as a potential middle class, and sometimes as a distinct group with a special social calling; Marxists opted clearly for the latter, though the role was reserved for intellectuals holding a particular set of beliefs.[67] In any case, irrespective of what positivists and Marxists said on this question, their behavior revealed both groups to be parts of a highly self-conscious intelligentsia.

Poland's first Marxist intellectuals carried out these debates on the pages of the positivists' own legal and censored journals, the most important of which was Aleksander Świętochowski's *Prawda* (founded in 1881). In this way their ideas reached students, who pooled their money to subscribe to *Prawda, Głos,* and other Warsaw weeklies. By the end of the 1880s, positivism had yielded to socialism among Polish students and urban intellectuals, but its legacy was to be lasting and powerful. For Kelles-Krauz and his peers, positivism was the discredited ideology of an older generation inclined to adjust to the verdict of 1863. But even as these students rejected positivism's anti-politics in favor of socialism's call to action, they accepted many of its intellectual assumptions.

Radom's Republic of Ideas

By the late 1880s there were several circles of Radom students, aware of each other's existence, but nonetheless conspiring one before the other.[68] One of these was formed in the fall of 1888 by a group of friends who met at the house of Franciszek Malczewski. The idea of formalizing these meetings and building a secret library was not Kelles-Krauz's, though he was one of the first members (along with his childhood friends Władysław Bukowiński and Zygmunt Rostkowski).[69] Malczewski, an old bachelor serving as a bureaucrat in Radom, was a willing host. Though not a socialist, he was sympathetic to socialism's aspirations, and passed on his atheism, lay morality, and patriotism to his guests.[70] The group called themselves "Malczewianie" in his honor, though the official name of their circle was "Aryele" (after Ariel, Prospero's spirit in *The Tempest*).[71] Other adults helped as well. The editor of *Gazeta Radomska*, Hugo Wróblewski, printed articles and poems written by the circle's members, including several by Kelles-Krauz.[72] The art teacher Hipolit Pinko also welcomed the Aryele into his home. His three daughters were a part of the group.[73] (Which is not to say his attitude was unambiguous: he was Smorodinov's favorite teacher, and agreed to paint portraits of the tsar and the like.[74]) Men like Malczewski, Wróblewski, and Pinko played an important role. There were few enough of them, so Kazimierz and his friends could continue to nourish their self-image as a special generation, but such men gave indispensable practical help.

Kelles-Krauz's Aryele were opposed by a new set, called *Kombinacja* (Combination). The latter group was apparently more positivist and materialist in orientation, although it is difficult to imagine that the Aryele were in fact not positivists. The Aryele subscribed to the positivists' *Prawda* as well as *Głos*. (*Głos*, founded in 1886, was *Prawda's* main rival for the Warsaw intellectual readership. It called itself "populist" and claimed that the future of Poland depended upon the development of the Polish people and the unity of Polish society. This was a challenge to the old class divisions in the countryside, but also to socialism with its idea of the class struggle. While *Prawda* published socialists such as Ludwik Krzywicki, *Głos* reflected the views of the patriotic Polish League.[75]) *Prawda* had pedagogical aims, and thus allowed students to keep abreast, in a rough and tumble way, of European scholarship. Through *Prawda* they would also have learned of a new academic discipline that was popular among Warsaw positivists and Marxists, sociology.[76] Both the Aryele and the Kombinacja had secret libraries filled with science and Polish history, the subjects they lacked at school.

The difference between the groups was probably one of emphasis. Aryele was the more patriotic of the two, the more aesthetically inclined, and even admitted girls. Its romantic and materialist tendencies existed side by side. As a member of the circle recalls: "When I was led into Malczewski's group, I was astonished to hear the obdurate materialist Kelles-Krauz reciting erotica."[77] When Kelles-Krauz's Aryele met each Sunday, they discussed history, science, and politics, but ended with poetry. Poetry also found its way into the circles' two handwritten journals, *Ul* (*The Hive*) and *Ziarno* (*The Seed*).[78] But in all discussions, regardless of form, the most common theme was resistance. One of Kelles-Krauz's youthful poems bore the title "One Must Struggle."[79]

In 1889–1890, Kelles-Krauz's eighth and final school year in Radom, he was the acknowledged leader of the group.[80] He and the other members of the circle were very close friends, whose ideals and mutual sympathy had been fortified by the comradeship of conspiracy. Although Smorodinov never learned of the existence of the group, he did in May 1890 catch Kelles-Krauz breaking school rules, and expelled him before he could graduate. Once Kelles-Krauz was expelled from school in Radom, he was unable to attend university in Russian Poland, and eventually chose to emigrate to France. This event, so important for the course of Kelles-Krauz's life, is passed over briefly in his letters and in the memoirs of his friends. The crime for which he was punished was not the noblest he committed; only Smorodinov discusses it in any detail.[81]

The examinations of final-year students, held in May and June, were extremely demanding. The most difficult was the Russian essay, which many students failed each year. Exam questions were settled in advance in Petersburg, sent to Apukhtin's office in Warsaw, and from there delivered to school directors. Every student in every school in the former Congress Kingdom thus answered the same questions. Each year, students from many schools would try to get hold of the questions in advance. When they succeeded, they would pass on the questions to other schools.[82] Students in Radom made several such attempts.[83] In the spring of 1890, Kelles-Krauz was caught up in just such a plot, a cooperative effort by students in Radom and Piotrków.

In order to steal the exam question without leaving a trace, it was necessary to break into a school supervisor's office, find the proper envelope, open it and copy the question, return the question to another envelope closed with the seal of the education ministry, and return the envelope to the office. A thief and a forger had to be hired. Students in Radom and Piotrków paid for these services, planning to ask students from each school to help cover costs. The main organizer of the plot, in Piotrków, wanted nothing for himself, save a written answer to the essay question by Radom's top student.[84] After the essay question was purloined during a party in Piotrków, Kelles-Krauz wrote the promised answer. Once he finished, he sent the question and the answer on to other schools, using as his messenger a friend disguised in fake mustache and pince-nez. Though the scheme was beautifully planned, a single leak (in Lublin) was enough to ruin it. The day before the exam in Russian was to be given (12 May) telegrams with a new essay question were sent to all of the schools in the country. On May 21 and 22, the Radom school was closed down for an official investigation. A student revealed Kelles-Krauz's participation, and on 25 May Kelles-Krauz was summoned to talk to the school inspector. On 29 May his house was searched. Soon after, he joined the handful of boys from several schools who were expelled.[85] Smorodinov was so angered by the behavior of his best student that three years later, when Michał's second wife came to register Kazimierz's brother Stanisław, he exploded: "What, another Krauz?" to which Julia Kelles-Krauzowa replied, "And not the last!" pointing proudly to her pregnant belly.[86]

Kelles-Krauz was in a difficult position. Without a diploma, he could not attend university; and without a university degree, he could not fulfill the goals he had set for himself in life. As a youth, he planned to become a lawyer or scholar, and to work as a socialist agitator at the same time. He did intend to spend some time abroad during his studies, but had in mind nothing more than a conventional study tour. He meant to live out his life in Poland.[87] Kelles-Krauz was to spend much of the next year searching for a way to graduate from secondary school, hoping afterwards to continue his studies at the University of Warsaw.

Orońsk

His expulsion did not change his summer plans. As during previous summers, he stayed with his friend Władysław Pruszak in a country estate in Orońsko (now Orońsk), a village fifteen miles to the south of Radom.[88] Pruszak's mother had married the romantic painter Józef Brandt, and the family hired Kelles-Krauz to tutor their two daughters.[89] While Brandt sat by the house painting seventeenth-century Polish knights, Kelles-Krauz set off to propagate socialism among his hired hands and nearby small-holders. This was the only extended agitation he was ever to carry out among Poles in Poland, and it seems that it went quite well.[90]

Kelles-Krauz seems to have spent much of his time with these farm workers and their families. He was able to describe their dances, their gossip, their eating habits, and their religiosity. He learned that they did not use the Polish polite form of address "pan" to refer to Brandt in his absence, and that they wanted schools for their children. He gained their trust by teaching their children to read. He learned that the adults attached something close to a mystical importance to books, and sat for hours while he read history aloud to them. He found that the peasants attempted to draw out a moral from each reading, as though it had been a fable. They were eager to learn, and would ask him endless questions. He read social-ist propaganda to a smaller, trusted group, with much the same result. One of its members told Kelles-Krauz where a cache of arms left over from 1863 was hidden. Kelles-Krauz wrote later that as a "pure internationalist" at the time, he did not counsel a national rising.[91]

As a boy of eighteen in that summer of 1890, he agitated using his own material, a long pamphlet he later entitled "Is there no serfdom now?" As he recalled, his smaller circle received it enthusiastically.[92] Based on good first-hand knowledge of the conditions of his audience, this pamphlet was the best piece of agitation Kelles-Krauz ever wrote, and eventually the most influential.[93] It took the form of a conversation between a knowledgeable and well-traveled socialist worker and a group of farm laborers. Its general argument, which spoke well enough to the condition of small landowners and hired laborers at the time, was that the tsar's land reform of 1864 had not given them economic freedom. It ended with an appeal for farm work-ers to join the socialist party.

Unfortunately for Kelles-Krauz, there was virtually no such thing at the time. Though he assured the peasants that he had been sent by "the party," in fact he was acting quite on his own. In Kelles-Krauz's recollection, the strongest of the tiny Polish socialist parties in the summer of 1890 was the Union of Polish Workers.[94] Though the Union of Polish Workers (whose chief ideologist was the sociologist Ludwik Krzywicki) had rejected terror, advocated by Proletariat, it was still a doctrinaire Marxist party, hoping to win gains for urban workers by economic means. Proletariat (broken in 1884 and refounded in 1888 as the Second Proletariat) now accepted the sociologist Ludwik Kulczycki's view that the next goal of Polish socialists should be a constitution for all of the lands of the Russian Empire, rather than the dictatorship of the proletariat. It had been all but destroyed by arrests the fall previous. Both parties had very few members, and had very little reach outside Warsaw, let alone into the countryside.[95]

The weakness of the Warsaw parties embarrassed Kelles-Krauz on this occasion, but it liberated him as well. Because he was independent, he could preach as he liked to the peasants. He told them, for example, that there had been socialism in the distant past, and thus socialism could come again.[96] He was free to read what he liked, form his own understanding of socialism, and hope that he might lead a Polish party someday. As Kelles-Krauz left Orońsk in September, he still had nine months before him in which he could read and think, provided he could get his hands on books. This was to be a critical time in his intellectual development, as during these months the outlines of his own version of socialism, based upon a distinct view of historical progress, began to take shape. In a few years time his notion of historical cycles was to be central to much of his sociology, and to provide one of the bases for a major challenge to the Second International orthodoxy of Karl Kautsky and German social democracy.

Vilnius

Kelles-Krauz's immediate task, after leaving Orońsk, was to find an appropriate venue for his exams. He also hoped to be exempted from military service, so that he might continue his studies immediately after graduation. With these goals before him, Kelles-Krauz set out for Vilnius in September 1890, where he was to stay with relatives. The Dowiatts were the family of Michał's stepfather, and they (like the Brandts) had daughters for Kazimierz to teach.[97] Feliks Dowiatt, a former officer, had little trouble obtaining dispensation from military service for Kelles-Krauz.[98] Kelles-Krauz had extremely weak eyes, which caused him occasional pain from the time of his childhood, and thus had a genuine medical excuse.[99]

The problem of the exams proved more difficult. Kelles-Krauz tried to secure permission to take his exams in Vilnius, but learned in December that his petition had been denied.[100] He returned home for the holidays and to discuss his next steps with his father. He had another reason to return to Radom. On Christmas Eve he asked for the hand of his girl-friend Maria Goldsteynówna.[101] Her father gave his permission, and she accepted. As Kazimierz was then eighteen and with uncertain prospects, and Maria a year younger, it was understood that the engagement was to be a long one.

Maria was the love of Kazimierz's life. As should become clear, Kelles-Krauz lived an impossibly exhausting life, and it is difficult to imagine that it would have taken anything like the coherent form it did without Maria's support. Until the end of his days, whenever the two were separated, Kazimierz wrote to Maria the first day possible, and the passion and caring that fill his letters are unmistakably sincere (and unusually enduring). She had been a comrade in student conspiracy in Radom, and had been Kazimierz's girlfriend since the 1889–1890 school year. The relation between Kazimierz's love for her, and his devotion to the "Idea" of socialism was manifold and powerful.

His letters to her in 1890, the first year of three for which they were to be apart, give some idea of this. Filled with poetry and citations from socialist texts, his love for her and his devotion to the cause mingle and overlap. From the first, he writes to her, Maria had won him by her socialism. "I would not have stopped loving Miss K., if not for the fact that I loved the Idea more than her, and she did not want to be the servant of the Idea; you will always struggle at my side and I can love you and the Idea simultaneously, each through the other . . . "[102] Love was subordinated to struggle, ("Only one Idea, only one social good do I love more and set higher than you: but I would not consider myself worthy of your love if it were otherwise"[103]), and also a weapon in the struggle ("But I want to have beside me an equal/a soul believing in the future with a face like a rainbow/A woman allied in the hatred of evil/with me . . . "[104]). In principle, she is his equal in the struggle, though at times his rhetoric gives Kazimierz away. "I always long for a wide field of action, for fame, for popularity . . . "[105] "If I—forgive the arrogance—approach in some way the worthiness of a king, then you will not be a queen only because you are my comrade, my wife (for you will be her in all probability), but you yourself will deserve at least some of the light of the halo by which the future will crown the brow of those who work for the oppressed."[106] "I will leave behind me a path worth following, and I will not lack for strength . . . Only, my love, never leave me, stay with me through the difficult times that await me!"[107] He worried that the coming revolution might find them apart: "I fear only one thing: that political and social conditions will tear us apart for good; we are standing on a pan-European volcano, which at any moment will erupt, and we after all will not be standing to one side with folded arms. I at any rate cannot imagine any great turmoil taking place without my participation."[108]

The association of love and struggle also had a more prosaic cause. In Radom, love (like learning) was clandestine. Kazimierz and Maria met in secret places, discussed taboo subjects, read forbidden books. This conspiracy before Russian police power blended into conspiracy before the older generation. Maria received Kazimierz's letters care of a friend, the daughter of Hipolit Pinko.[109] She justly feared that her father would demand to see the letters, as he indeed did when he learned of their existence.[110] To Kazimierz and Maria, his expulsion from school and her father's suspicions seemed to be elements of a social system bound to keep them apart. As the years passed after their engagement, this feeling that only an unjust society could impede the fulfillment of their desire grew stronger, and contributed to Kazimierz's later interest in romantic love and the family as spheres of life affected by industrialization.

Kazimierz and Maria had several weeks together in Radom that winter (1890–1891), but Kazimierz was busy studying and trying to find a way to take his exams. He and his father traveled to Warsaw, where they tried and failed to arrange a meeting with Apukhtin.[111] When Kazimierz returned to Vilnius in late January, he and Maria had to content themselves once again with letters. His correspondence reveals his intellectual preoccupations, and in particular the books which he found useful. These he tended to describe to Maria, in order to persuade her to read them. In these descriptions, two books stand out as especially formative.

Wandering Ideas

The first is a novel entitled *Looking Backward*, written by the American progressive journalist Edward Bellamy in 1887.[112] Serialized in *Głos* in 1890, it was immensely popular among Polish students. It recounts the story of Julian West, an upper-class Bostonian, who awakens from a "mesmeric" trance in the year 2000 to find a socialist paradise. The chief attraction of the book to Kelles-Krauz and other young Polish socialists was that Bellamy's utopia was carefully described and seemed scientific.[113] Bellamy also offered a bit of consolation to those who must suffer under capitalism, which he treated as a necessary stage of human development.[114] Another attractive feature was Bellamy's emphasis on the primeval goodness of human nature, which would return when capitalism was replaced by socialism.[115] In socialism, all obstacles to human desires will vanish, and romantic love will flourish as never before.[116]

Bellamy sketched a model of historical progress which was to appear in the writings of Kelles-Krauz and other Polish socialists and sociologists until the First World War. Human nature is essentially good, but has been corrupted by the advance of capitalism. In turn, even as we struggle under capitalism, we understand its necessity, for it builds the industrial infrastructure of a future paradise. When capitalism's work is done, we must only nationalize private property. Then man's lost nature will be restored to him, and he will live morally on the higher material level that industrialization has made possible. In the meantime, the key to the transition is knowledge.

Ludwik Krzywicki, in trying to explain how socialism becomes popular in backward countries, created the theory of the "wandering idea." According to this theory, ideas which speak to the historical conditions of one nation may be passed on to another, more backward nation, and accelerate the course of its development. Bellamy was inspired to write a novel by what he had learned as a journalist of American monopoly capitalism. But despite its American origins and goals, the book was an inspiration to a generation of young Polish socialists.[117] Kelles-Krauz wrote that the picture presented by Bellamy was so beautiful, and yet so justified on scholarly foundations, that he was all the more inspired to struggle against whatever stood in the way of such a future.[118]

The second book, *Ancient Society,* by the early anthropologist Lewis Henry Morgan, was also written by an American, and published in 1877, a year before *Looking Backward.*[119] Morgan wrote that all human groups are equal in intelligence and abilities, and pass through the same stages of civilization.[120] Changes in the means of production are the source of historical progress, and some civilizations are currently behind others simply because the raw materials they have at hand are less suitable to inventions.[121] Europe and North America are the home of civilization, to be sure, as defined by the "monogamian" marriage and the institution of private property.[122] But Morgan predicted the advent of a still higher society. In a paragraph that fairly leaps off the page after five hundred pages of somber analysis, he wrote:

Since the advent of civilization, the outgrowth of property has been so immense, its forms so diversified, its uses so expanding and its management so intelligent in the interests of its owners, that it has become, on the part of the people, an unmanageable power. The human mind stands bewildered in the presence of its own creation. The time will come, nevertheless, when human intelligence will rise to mastery over property, and define the relations of the state to the property it protects, as well as the obligations and the limits

of the rights of its owners. The interests of society are paramount
to individual interests, and the two must be brought into harmo-
nious relations. A mere property career is not the final destiny of
mankind, if progress is to be the law of the future as it has been in
the past. The time which has passed since civilization began is but a
fragment of man's past existence; and but a fragment of the ages yet
to come. The dissolution of society bids fair to become the termina-
tion of a career of which property is the end and aim; because such a
career contains the elements of self-destruction. Democracy in government, brotherhood in society, equality in rights and privileges,
and universal education, foreshadow the next higher plan of society
to which experience, intelligence, and knowledge are steadily tending. It will be a revival, in a higher form, of the liberty, equality, and
fraternity of the ancient gentes.[123]

That paragraph was exceptionally important for Kelles-Krauz and his generation. In these words, Morgan united the idea of progress with that of
a golden age in the past. Morgan claimed that a golden age of the past
presaged a future socialist utopia, and added that man's "property career"
was a necessary bridge from the former to the latter. Morgan's bulky work
seemed to prove not only the existence of primitive communism, but the
inevitability of its restoration within an industrially advanced society. As
such, it provided one of the main supports for a view of history which we
will find in Kelles-Krauz and in many of his contemporaries. *Origins of the
Family* was for Polish Marxism what the *Anti-Dühring* was for German.[124]
For young socialists such as Kelles-Krauz the endorsement given to
Morgan by Engels completed the effect.[125]

Kielce

While teaching Dowiatt's daughters about primitive communism in the
spring of 1891, Kelles-Krauz learned that his father had secured for him
permission, from Apukhtin, to take his exams. He chose the school in
Kielce, not far from home, and whose director was known to be sympathetic to Poles.[126] Arriving on 21 April, a few weeks before exams, he studied day and night.[127] He still found time, though, to take part in the local
student circle. Students in Kielce had begun to organize in 1889–1890,
and had been helped by an emissary from Radom. By spring 1891 Kielce's
organization was mature; Kelles-Krauz could write for its two organs, and

sample Bellamy, Limanowski, Jeż, Marx, Draper, and the romantic poets in its library.

His reputation preceded him: he was known as the best student in Radom, and as a socialist who had already published articles in *Głos* and *Prawda*.[128] Having digested Bellamy and Morgan, Kelles-Krauz came equipped with his own theory of socialism, which he called revolutionary retrospection. As one of his classmates remembered: "Extraordinarily capable, educated and politically and socially sophisticated beyond his years (he was then 19), with the gift of oratory, tremendous skills in agitation, and very amicable, he inspired us all and exerted on many of us a decided influence in the direction of international socialism."[129] Kelles-Krauz and his new comrades studied for exams enervated by the events of early May 1891. Some thirty thousand workers observed the May 1 holiday in the lands of the former Congress Kingdom.[130] A student, one of many who tried to commemorate the centenary of the Polish constitution on 3 May, committed suicide in his jail cell.[131] Kelles-Krauz passed his final exams on 12 June, and returned home to Radom.[132]

Warsaw

After once again spending the summer in Orońsk,[133] Kelles-Krauz registered in October 1891 at the faculty of law of the Imperial University of Warsaw. The university was much like an imperial school writ large; its primary task was Russification rather than education.[134] The university's one thousand or so students (four-fifths of whom were Poles)[135] were spied upon by their fellows and by their teachers, and required to wear uniforms so their activities could be more easily recorded.[136] Its lectures were in Russian, and though it could boast a few good Russian professors, none of its four faculties—History and Philology, Mathematics and Physics, Law, and Medicine—enjoyed any kind of academic distinction.[137] The result was much the same as in the school circles.[138] Students knew that the university apparatus would give them accreditation, but that they would have to teach themselves.

Yet students at university were older, brighter, had the experience of years in circles in school, and had often consciously chosen to study in Warsaw rather than at better imperial universities further east. Instead of simply learning in secret, they formed larger organizations with political and ethical goals. Most Polish students joined Brotherly Aid, which aimed to set generally accepted standards of ethics, and lent money to especially needy students.[139] Other secret organizations ran student honor courts, organized economic self-help, and kept hidden libraries. Many students tutored young women (who were forbidden entrance to university) or workers.[140] Devoted to a "religion of knowledge" inspired by the new certainties of materialism,[141] students hoped to transform their university into a "Republic of Ideas," whose achievements would radiate outwards.[142] The sharp discontinuity between their formal studies and this eagerness for learning is demonstrated best by the fact that the university's prominent alumni are almost invariably known in fields other than the ones in which they took a degree.[143]

Public political activity at the university was virtually impossible. The Second Proletariat shied from recruiting students for fear of deconspiracy,[144] though when the Union of Polish Workers was decimated by arrests in November 1891, some of those behind bars were students.[145] Such daredevils had patriotic alternatives by now as well. Kelles-Krauz's later comrade in the PPS, Stanisław Wojciechowski, was a member of both the patriotic organization Zet, and of a new socialist party, Unification. (This party, a fragment of Proletariat, was the brainchild of the sociologist Edward Abramowski. Abramowski, who had been a leader of Proletariat, realized that terror was driving potential members into the arms of the Union of Polish Workers. He founded Unification in the hopes of unifying the two parties under his leadership.)[146] Kelles-Krauz was apparently not a member of any of these socialist parties.[147]

Though the line between patriotism and socialism was still somewhat fluid, in the school year before Kelles-Krauz's arrival two fairly distinct tendencies had appeared within the main secret political organization on campus, the Central Student Circle. Wojciechowski distinguished himself in Circle debates as a leader of the "patriots," whereas Kelles-Krauz looked for his place among the "internationalists."[148] These two students well exemplify the two main paths which led Poles to socialism in these years. At this time in his life, Kelles-Krauz was convinced that the international socialist revolution would soon arrive; and that the science which had predicted this revolution would guide socialists of all European states to its realization. Wojciechowski saw in socialism a philosophy of action, a way to break through the passivity of political life in the Congress Kingdom after 1864; and he saw in the emerging Polish working class the best means to win an independent and democratic Polish republic. "Internationalists" such as Kelles-Krauz were likely to be Marxists, "patriots" such as Wojciechowski were likely to draw from the Polish romantic tradition.[149]

Former members of circles at school could join the Central Student Circle, and usually did. But they brought their regional loyalties, and their politics, with them. Students of all political orientations, save conservative, formed their own smaller circles.[150] In autumn 1891, students from Kielce and Radom formed such a smaller circle,[151] called the Circle of the Young, and elected Kelles-Krauz their leader.[152] Smaller groups such as the Circle of the Young were the real units of self-education (although students would also group by discipline, so as not to lose mastery of technical terminology in Polish). Its program consisted of the social sciences, which could not be formally studied: economics, anthropology, sociology, and psychology. The small circles also served as link between the university and the schools, passing down books, propaganda, and technique to student circles back home.[153]

Kelles-Krauz's university career in Warsaw was fated to be short. He was expelled after Smorodinov sent a report about him to the university, and left for Radom on 14 December.[154] He parted with his friends from the Circle of the Young, and left behind Maria, who had begun her studies at the Warsaw conservatory.[155] Two days later he departed for Paris. During his journey, he wrote to her: "What a contemptible system, my darling, which tears lovers away from each other for no reason, and forces one to wander abroad in search of learning, and the other, for lack of funds and facing resistance within her family, to stay with a broken heart, when she might more happily and usefully live elsewhere." He also wrote that her father had given him a cross on a chain as a parting gift, and asked in the presence of both families that he wear it. Kazimierz refused, wishing to teach his younger relatives that they must act according to their principles. In the young man's atheism we may see one source of Dr. Goldsteyn's reservations.[156]

Paris

After tours by relatives and friends of the family of Vienna and Munich, Kelles-Krauz pulled into the Gare du Nord on 27 December 1891.[157] He was met by the young patriotic socialist Jan Lorentowicz (1868–1940), fresh from a court of honor of Poles which had adjudged his connections to Brazilian revolutionaries.[158] Lorentowicz brought Kelles-Krauz home, and they stayed up late talking.

Kelles-Krauz was no doubt curious about the lives of Poles in Paris. There were about six thousand,[159] stereotypically divided between émigrés of 1863 on the right bank, and students and socialists on the left bank.[160] The generation of 1863 had assimilated,[161] and was prosperous enough to support schools, libraries, and nursing homes.[162] As one Pole remembers the division, on the right bank were "aristocrats," on the left, "socialists."[163] (We might just as well read the division as "gentry" and "intelligentsia.") Another recalled this sharp feeling of generation difference: "Socialist youth had little contact with the older emigration. They didn't like us, and we didn't seek inspiration in them. We respected them as documents of an honored past. We lived by seeking for Poland, and for all of humanity, a better future, and believed that our part would be victory, and not the defeat borne by our fathers in 1863 and our grandfathers in 1831."[164]

Younger people, clustered around avenue des Gobelins and boulevards St. Michel, de Port-Royal, Arago, and St. Marcel, formed a peculiar kind of ghetto. Polish students (such as Maria Skłodowska, later known as Marie Curie) had been leaving the country in a steady flow since 1863:[165] in the 1890s, nearly thirty percent of all university students from the Congress Kingdom were studying abroad.[166] New arrivals joined old in the same buildings, and the colony's isolated character was reinforced.[167] Everyone knew everyone else, and everyone knew too much about everyone else, for gossip reigned supreme. The colony compensated for missing family and friends, and provided lovers and spouses.[168] We might say grandly that younger Poles created an ersatz Poland in France; one of them remembers the colony rather as a village in the midst of a big city.[169]

Women, forbidden from attending university in the Russian Empire, came to Paris to study. Their numbers were thus more or less constant. The number of men, however, varied with political tides within Poland. Women generally had more money, and had good lives awaiting them at home. The men were usually poor, often could not safely return home, and of necessity planned political lives for themselves in Paris. For these reasons, and because there were several men for each woman, an engagement was regarded as a coup by men—and a disaster by families of women at home in Poland. Lacking the means, the incentive, and often the French, the men tended to extend their studies over absurdly long periods.[170] Lorentowicz, writing in later life, recalled cases of men who stayed for eight years without learning to speak a single sentence of proper French.[171] Both men and women usually studied medicine or other trades (there were no polytechnics in the former Congress Kingdom), though there were some of each at the Sorbonne.[172]

When Lorentowicz brought Kelles-Krauz to the six-story house on 20, rue de la Glacière, he introduced him to a particularly intense corner of this new world. There was a free room on the sixth floor, and Kelles-Krauz moved in. He joined a group of a dozen young men, most of whom were at least nominally students, and most of whom were socialists of one variety or another. They tended to argue about politics well into the night, sleep late, then argue into the afternoon about who was to buy the food. Duels and courts of honor, ancient traditions of the Polish nobility, were frequent. This testified not so much to Polish obsession with tradition as to a kind of émigré oversensitivity: these young men were not only away from the homeland they thought they were fated to save, they were also poor and not particularly well nourished. One of them spent a day picking up coins from the street, and his friends thought the amount he found astonishingly large. Another claimed he could study without food for a week so long as he lay immobile in bed. A third, having sold an article, was turned upside down for his coins. They ate at Koch's restaurant on the ground floor; Koch gave some of them meals on credit on the understanding that they would pay back the debt from their future earnings as doctors.[173]

Kelles-Krauz wrote to Maria that he pitied his new friends, who could not separate themselves from the dirt of the world, and even seemed to seek it out.[174] He himself was a more orderly soul. He earned his keep by writing for the *Kurier Warszawski,* the most important daily in the former Congress Kingdom.[175] The *Kurier Warszawski* was not only a legal newspaper, but also increasingly conservative: Kelles-Krauz lived by interpreting events in a way he considered false and misleading; he called his reports "literary prostitution."[176] His second major commitment of time was to study: he enrolled at the Sorbonne, planning to study "physical sciences" (geology, chemistry, physics) for two years, "natural sciences" (botany, geography, zoology) for another two, and then begin studies of sociology. During the spring term he duly attended his four hours of daily lectures,[177] but almost at once began to read sociology on his own time.[178] He thus spent most of his time away from home, attending lectures, reading in the Bibliothèque Nationale, and writing articles and letters to Maria from cafés.

He seems not to have been drawn into the politics of his house, a hotbed of patriotic, non-Marxist socialism, in the spirit of the charismatic Stanisław Barański. Barański had been a member of Proletariat while still in school, and had been expelled from the University of Warsaw, where he was already preaching the interdependence of patriotism and socialism.[179] After emigrating to Paris, he founded in 1888 the National Socialist Commune,[180] and from 1889 edited the group's journal, *Pobudka* (*Reveille*). His hope was to join the old patriotic ideals to the common human values brought to the fore by socialism.[181] This was also the ideal of Bolesław Limanowski, now living in Paris,[182] who wrote for almost every issue of *Pobudka*.[183] When Barański died, Lorentowicz took over the editorship. When Kelles-Krauz arrived in Paris, Lorentowicz was the leader of patriotic socialists.[184]

As the residents and frequent guests of Kelles-Krauz's house more or less made up the Commune, he could not help but be confronted by its ideas. For the first time, given his clear leadership in Radom, and his short stay at university, his internationalist Marxism met a stiff challenge. He was not won over, but he began to take the national question into account. His letters to Maria still show an obstinate resistance to national sentiments,[185] but by July 1892 his first known attempts at publishing in the socialist press find him acknowledging the need for national independence in the program of a future Polish socialist party. In an article intended for *Gazeta Robotnicza* in Berlin, Kelles-Krauz argued that socialists must strive for national independence, because the working class needed it. At the same time, they must not encourage workers to yield to nationalism, or themselves fall into the salon socialism of the Commune. This article attracted the attention of Bolesław Antoni Jędrzejowski and Stanisław Mendelson, men who were to lead the PPS. They intended to contact Kelles-Krauz in Paris—characteristically, they were well aware of Kelles-Krauz's identity, despite his pseudonymous writing.[186] As Kelles-Krauz was already making a name for himself in Paris, it was difficult for him to keep his identity a secret from Polish socialists who wanted to know. He was apparently the most respected of the Marxists even in 1892, and had already attracted more students to his orbit than Lorentowicz had to the Commune.[187]

But before Jędrzejowski and Mendelson could send someone to Paris to find him, Kelles-Krauz left to spend the summer in Radom and Orońsk. He arrived on 31 July.[188] Maria's problems may have drawn him home. Just after Kazimierz had left her in Warsaw a stranger had knocked on her door, asking about her identity. A few days later, after Maria had left for the holidays, Russian gendarmes had searched the place for evidence of self-education circle meetings. Maria's housemate, when asked, said falsely that Maria did not intend to return to Warsaw. When Maria did return, she had to find another flat, but was unable to do so. Meanwhile, Dr. Goldsteyn had to travel to Warsaw to plead his daughter's innocence.[189]

Like Kazimierz, Maria thus lost a year of education. It is unclear whether the police knew what they were about in the winter of 1891, but we do know that when Maria returned to conservatory in the fall of 1892 she took an active part in secret circles.[190]

In October 1892, Kazimierz was called back to Radom for his father's wedding. His father Michał and Maria's sister Julia had fallen in love and decided to marry while Kazimierz was in Paris. In view of the morés of the time, the match between a fifty-year-old Polish nobleman and a much younger woman was quite unusual. Kazimierz and Maria were quite supportive, though their own circumstances (and the continued resistance of her father) made such a step impossible for them. Kelles-Krauz spent the end of October in Warsaw, meeting with friends and editors. These two groups overlapped: Władysław Bukowiński, his closest friend from Radom, was now working for *Prawda,* and in all likelihood helped Kelles-Krauz gain access to its pages.[191]

On his way back to Paris he stopped in Berlin on 15 November, and stayed with Ludwik Krzywicki. The two had probably met while Kelles-Krauz was a student, and Krzywicki a party activist, in Warsaw. Krzywicki (1859–1941) was more than a decade older than Kelles-Krauz, and already a well-known party authority and sociologist. So famous, in fact, that he felt obliged to spend a year in Berlin hiding from Russian police. He welcomed Kelles-Krauz, and took him to listen to the proceedings of the yearly congress of the *Sozialdemokratische Partei Deutschlands* (hereafter, "SPD") which had begun the day previous.[192] The SPD had been legal for two years, and had just rewritten its program at Erfurt on a more Marxist basis. The aura of martyrdom which it had acquired while banned by Bismarck (1878–1890) now combined with the prestige of a large, organized and theoretically coherent party. The SPD was becoming the standard model for socialist parties, and its example had not gone unnoticed in Poland.[193] Unbeknownst to Kelles-Krauz, leading Polish socialists had decided to meet to form a united party.[194]

Kelles-Krauz returned to Paris on 17 November 1892, the first day of negotiations on the formation of a united Polish Socialist Party. That night, when he returned home to find his room a pigsty and his friend Ignacy Urbach sitting on his bed writing, he may have learned about the negotiations.[195] If not, he learned about them soon enough, as his friend and rival Lorentowicz took part. When the talks ended on 23 November, Lorentowicz returned home not as the leader of a clique of students in Paris, but as a member of the *Centralizacja,* the émigré group founded to organize and lead the PPS. As Kelles-Krauz listened to Lorentowicz recount the negotiations, he must have felt keenly that he had been left out.

The major novelty of the PPS program was that it postulated an independent Poland as a "minimum program." This was a provision not to be found in the SPD program (although all of its practical planks presumed the existence of a united German state), but was also new to Polish socialist platforms. The past few years, however, had made the connection between national and social goals more or less clear. In 1890 and 1891 Stanisław Mendelson, the most important of the émigré socialists, had arrived at a conclusion reached by younger men some years before: that Polish socialism must have a non-Russian strategy, which must include taking action against the Empire without waiting for a new Russian party to form.[196]

Events of 1 May 1892 confirmed the consensus forming around this view. When the Second International had passed (in 1889) a motion declaring May 1 to be a workers' holiday, the reaction of national parties varied considerably. The Germans, for example, insisted that a May Day general strike would risk the loss of their legal status, and some of them thought that some sort of celebration on the following Sunday would suffice. After a fiery speech by Wilhelm Liebknecht, the party decided to commemorate the holiday on its proper day—by meetings held after working hours.[197] The Poles in the Russian partition treated the holiday quite differently.[198] In 1892, even though May 1 fell on a Sunday, Polish workers in Łódź struck on Monday. By Wednesday, all factories in Łódź were closed, and by Thursday non-industrial workers were striking as well.[199] In all, something like sixty thousand workers stayed home from work or demonstrated. Factory owners were inclined to compromise on wage demands, but they were prevented from doing so by Russian policy. On Friday the regional governor declared a state of emergency, called in the police, and provoked antisemitic acts as a pretext for his action. (Peasants in nearby villages were told that in Łódź Jews were murdering Poles). More than a hundred workers were killed.[200]

The strike showed the possibilities for a Polish movement, but it also demonstrated an inextricable connection between economic and political gains. According to the ideology of existing Polish socialist parties, the strike should have been a success. Economic hardship bred economic demands, which should have brought an economic result. Instead, political factors intervened, in the form of Russian gendarmes and Cossacks on horseback. Waves of arrests had already begun to discredit the possibility of apolitical socialism in the Russian partition:[201] after May 1892

Kelles-Krauz, and older socialists as well, concluded that political means are needed even for economic ends.[202] From there, it was only a small step to the need for Polish independence, for it was difficult to imagine sufficient legal changes taking place within an empire which banned trade unions and used deadly force against demonstrations.[203] Not all Polish socialists took this last step, however. Among those who accepted the need for political action were some who advocated setting for Polish socialists the goal of a constitution for the lands of the Russian Empire, rather than Polish independence. Many Polish socialists also realized that political action was necessary, but cast about without embracing either of these two options.[204]

1 May 1892 brought into focus another aspect of the issue. Polish workers had been put down by imperial Russian police, but they had been striking against German capitalists. Increasing Russian trade barriers at the end of the 1870s had encouraged German firms to move across the border into the Russian Empire. Most factory owners in Łódź were Germans, and a large part of the remainder were Jews.[205] This was typical: the lands of the former Congress Kingdom were by far the most industrialized part of the Russian Empire, but most of its industry was in the hands of Germans and Jews.[206] A historian who took part in the Polish socialist movement concluded that rising national feeling among workers forced the issue of Polish independence on party leaders.[207]

Lorentowicz probably recalled to Kelles-Krauz how Bolesław Limanowski, chosen to chair the negotiations, had been astonished when the Marxist Mendelson proposed adding national independence to the program.[208] For a decade Limanowski and Mendelson had represented the extremes of Polish socialism, but the recognized need for independence now opened up an easy dialogue between them. The proposal carried without much debate. The most difficult question was terror, a troublesome part of the legacy of early Polish socialism.[209] In the end, it was included in the program, but only to be applied in exceptional cases. Cooperation with Russian socialists, who for some time had lacked a party of their own, was mentioned briefly and vaguely. It was decided to form a Union of Polish Socialists Abroad to oversee the foundation and direction of the new party in Russian Poland. The Union was to be led by an executive committee, or *Centralizacja*.[210]

Almost as soon as it had been chosen, the *Centralizacja* encountered Russian repression, meted out by the French police. Russia and France had signed a military pact in 1891, and the French were generally eager to keep their ally happy by helping in such cases.[211] At the request of the Russian embassy, on 7 January 1893 Interior Minister Émile Loubet applied an 1849 law allowing for the expulsion of dangerous foreigners to the new group. The *Centralizacja* moved its operations to London.[212] The Paris flats of its members were searched, and their papers passed to the Russian secret police. The Russian secret police, or Okhrana, had chosen Paris as the site for the headquarters of its European operations in 1883.[213] The Paris Okhrana wasted no time following up its new leads.

The Paris Okhrana had many tools at its disposal. As we have seen, it could usually count on the cooperation of the French police. Also, its three Russian case officers each "controlled" around ten informants within the socialist movement.[214] On 15 January 1893 one of its French agents filed a report on the Polish socialists who remained in Paris after the raid and expulsions.[215] The same agent, after being given names found among the papers seized in the raid, provided a second list of profiles. Among these names was that of Kazimierz Kelles-Krauz. From 23 January 1893 the Okhrana thus knew his full name and title, his date of birth, his address, and of his scholarly inclinations, his friendship with Lorentowicz, and his connections with Polish and Russian socialists and workers.[216] Even though Kelles-Krauz was not at first connected with the new party, the Okhrana already knew of him. Before he was important to Polish socialism, he was known to the Russian police apparatus.

The combination of France's political freedoms, the Franco-Russian alliance, and the peculiar style of life in the Polish colony created numerous problems for Poles who wished to practice politics. They lived in a hothouse environment, where secrets were very hard to keep. Yet many of them lived in the colony precisely because they had secrets about their past, or about their ideas for the future, that were well worth keeping. The PPS, after a few initial glitches, managed to keep its level of conspiracy within Russian Poland extremely high. Poles in Paris, tempted by the freedoms of French life and the omnipresence of Polish friends, had more trouble keeping quiet. Very, very few were actually agents of the Okhrana, but an agent could count on the trust of friends.

Kelles-Krauz was a victim of this very principle. In early 1893, he decided to steer clear of the new PPS, and he and a handful of friends remained loyal to their group of Marxist social democrats. Stanisław and Władysław Grabski, Estera Golde, Cezaryna Wojnarowska, Ignacy Urbach, and Antoni Złotnicki were apparently the other members of the circle.[217] Urbach was Kelles-Krauz's closest friend within the group. Urbach was the son of a rich man, and upon his father's death had inherited a goodly sum. This he squandered traveling with friends across Europe, and ended up a street peddler in Paris. He learned the Paris underground, and taught Kelles-Krauz about a side of the city he might not have learned much about otherwise.[218] Kelles-Krauz followed his example, and while a single man in Paris learned the songs and stories of Parisian workers, thieves and prostitutes.[219] Urbach had written for *Pobudka,* but had been drawn by Kelles-Krauz's influence into the group of social democrats. Ironically, his shift left would lead him to join Rosa Luxemburg's SDKP (Social-Democracy of the Kingdom of Poland), and to drift out of Kelles-Krauz's favor.[220] Kelles-Krauz began to think, correctly, that Urbach talked too much. Eventually he came to consider Urbach an agent, which was probably not true. Urbach did repeat what he knew of Kelles-Krauz to another friend of his, a worker called Bolesław Malankiewicz.[221]

Malankiewicz had been a journeyman brazier and anarcho-socialist, and had seen difficult years. At the age of seventeen, in 1884, he had been chosen by Polish socialists in Cracow to assassinate the Cracow chief of police, who also reported to the Okhrana. Malankiewicz agreed to sacrifice his own life in order to get close enough to deliver the bomb. Then, the plan was changed, and he was directed to throw the bomb through an office window. He dutifully climbed up the wall of the building, only to find that he had been directed to the wrong window. The clerk inside began to yell at him. Malankiewicz lost his concentration, fell, and dropped his bomb, which exploded behind him. He lost one eye, and the other was damaged. He confessed in the hospital, and the Cracow socialists were soon in prison.[222]

After Malankiewicz's release, he drifted among Polish socialist émigré colonies, first to Zurich, then to London and finally to Paris. His spirit was broken by prison, and he had neither a wealthy family at home nor the skills to support himself as a writer. In Zurich he swindled other immigrants out of their money. In London he unsuccessfully counterfeited Russian currency, selling the scheme to other socialists as an antitsarist plot. In 1892, having been turned down by the British police, he sold his services to the Russian Okhrana.[223] Malankiewicz wrote directly to P.I. Rachkovskii, director of its Paris bureau. Like Malankiewicz, Rachkovskii had himself once been a revolutionary.[224] He ran the Paris bureau from 1884 to 1902, and was regarded as very effective.[225] Rachkovskii received more than one hundred reports from Malankiewicz between 1893 and 1896, and on the basis of these reports ordered numerous arrests at the Russian border.[226]

One can see why Kelles-Krauz suspected that Urbach was the agent. When the Okhrana asked Malankiewicz for information or documents, Malankiewicz often simply asked Urbach.[227] In at least one instance, Urbach then asked Kelles-Krauz for information that the Okhrana desired.[228] Malankiewicz was so dependent on Urbach for news that he fretted when he had not talked to him for two days.[229] In 1892 and 1893 Urbach stayed for days at a time with both Kelles-Krauz and Malankiewicz, so he was close both to the man who would become the most important Polish socialist in Paris, and to the Okhrana's best informer on Polish socialism in Paris.[230] Even after Urbach and Kelles-Krauz drifted apart, Urbach knew enough about his activities to keep Malankiewicz's checks coming.

Malankiewicz's was an extreme case, but the Polish colony was filled with strife caused by the difficulties faced by older socialists, freed from prison or exile, trying to adapt to life in Paris. In February 1893, Kelles-Krauz was asked to escort the body of one such man, Ludwik Sawicki, to Berlin. Sawicki had committed suicide in a question of honor. He had joined the original Proletariat in the early 1880s, and had been sentenced to a year in prison followed by five in exile in Siberia. When freed in 1889, he moved to Paris to study medicine. Despite the efforts of Lorentowicz and others, he refused to hear of an independent Poland, and instead joined an association of Russian students. There he met a man that he had known in exile, Wacław Handelsman. Handelsman was now using another name, as he had been convicted by a court of honor of Proletariat in Siberia of betraying comrades to the police. The verdict was known among Polish immigrants, and Sawicki set out to prove Handelsman's guilt. Handelsman demanded a trial.

At the trial, on 9 February 1893, Handelsman admitted that he had been found guilty by the court of honor in Siberia, and tried to defend himself against the substantive charge that he betrayed comrades to the police. Sawicki would not hear of this: in his view, when Handelsman confessed to his identity, the case was closed. The court of honor, made up of Polish socialists such as Bolesław Limanowski, Cezaryna Wojnarowska, and Antoni Złotnicki, decided that it could not pass a verdict without hearing evidence about the substantive issue. Sawicki was shattered. Two days later, Handelsman slapped his face on the street, challenging him to a duel. That day Sawicki killed himself by poison. Kelles-Krauz was immensely saddened. He and Sawicki had known each other well; Kelles-Krauz had served as his second in a duel the previous year. He agreed to escort the body to Berlin. When the Okhrana learned of Sawicki's death, the Russian embassy had the French police seal off his apartment, appealing to its right under treaty conventions to the possessions (such as the personal papers) of its subjects.[231]

In the end, Kelles-Krauz did not travel with Sawicki's remains to Berlin. When he did go to Berlin a few months later, it was on another sad errand: to care for his good friend from Radom Zygmunt Rostkowski, who had been diagnosed with a brain disorder. While there, he learned that his other close friend from Radom, Władysław Bukowiński, had also contracted a neural disorder. Kelles-Krauz could not but feel isolated. As he wrote to Maria, "So both of my closest friends, which, you remember, I said constituted with me a single soul, who were always to go forth with me on the field of knowledge, have fallen behind, undeserving, for reasons independent of themselves; they've been cut off, and I must leave them behind, as I remain as close to them as ever." A few days later, Stefan Kania, a friend of Kelles-Krauz's from Orońsk, shot himself three times and died. In a letter to Kelles-Krauz, he wrote: "I will kill myself at 11:00 today, please forgive me." Kama's brother killed himself in turn.[232] Kelles-Krauz had expected much from the friends of his youth, and this series of tragedies (coming after Sawicki's suicide in February, and the death of Kelles-Krauz's brother Bohdan of tuberculosis in March)[233] was devastating.

These personal tragedies did not keep Kelles-Krauz from politics, even during the scant three days he spent in Berlin. His fellow social democrat Stanisław Grabski was passing through Berlin at the same time, and was arrested by the German police. Grabski had been expelled from Germany, and was therefore travelling under an assumed name and in disguise. He had abandoned his fashionable (among socialists in Paris, that is) beret and red tie in favor of a brown hat and conservative suit, and dyed his mustache and hair red. The German gendarme who arrested Grabski told him that he never would have recognized him by day, but that his movements by night were unmistakable.[234] When Kelles-Krauz learned of the arrest from Stanisław Przybyszewski, he wrote to comrades in Paris. In particular, he wanted to warn Estera Golde, whose letters had been on Grabski's person when he was arrested.[235]

Grabski was arrested around 8 June, held only a few days, and then released.[236] But Kelles-Krauz's suspicions were well-founded: on 22 June a

Paris agent filed a report on Estera Golde with the Okhrana. The report concerned the group of social democrats, and mentioned Kelles-Krauz as one of the Polish revolutionaries with whom Golde had frequent contact.[237] Estera Golde was the second most important woman in Kelles-Krauz's life.[238] Like Kelles-Krauz, she studied science at the Sorbonne in the early 1890s, and like him was committed to Marxism. In Maria's absence, she provided him with a sustaining and inspiring enthusiasm for his ideas.[239] When Golde left to agitate in Poland in late summer, Kelles-Krauz instructed Maria to help her.[240] Golde could not avail herself of Maria's help, as she was arrested and imprisoned not long after crossing the border.

The difficulties of the spring and summer of 1893 left little time for Kelles-Krauz's academic work. Already working full time as a journalist, during the school year Kelles-Krauz was burdened with about eight hours of lectures and homework a day. Science and mathematics were his weak points, not least because his previous coursework in these subjects had been so cursory. The paucity of science and math in school curricula had made these subjects more alluring, but not any easier; and there is a great deal of difference between reading popularizers with friends and studying the natural sciences at a foreign university. He did not take his exams in July 1893, and was granted instead of a diploma a certificate declaring that he had proven himself capable of further studies in physics.[241]

Polska Partia Socjalistyczna

Kelles-Krauz had begun to think that his original plan to take up the social sciences only after four years of grounding in the natural sciences was a mistake. Still, when he set out for home in early September 1893, he had every intention of returning shortly to Paris to continue his studies, though perhaps with a new academic plan, and certainly with Maria. In the nearly three years of his engagement to Maria, he had seen very little of her. His life was now in Paris, and he returned to Poland to bring her back.

Once in Poland, Kelles-Krauz made his usual rounds, meeting with editors and friends in Warsaw, spending a few weeks in Orońsk, and seeing Maria when he could. Just as the time of his departure was nearing, he was arrested without formal accusation, held in prison for eight days, and then released. His passport was held for seven months, until his innocence was satisfactorily proven. The eventual charge was that he was writing for Luxemburg's newspaper, *Sprawa Robotnicza,* which he truthfully denied.[242] The course of the judicial procedure corresponded to what the Okhrana knew of him: he was arrested during his first stay in Poland after being mentioned in informers' reports; at first there was no definite charge, as the Okhrana knew little more about him; then, when Malankiewicz wrote in January 1894 that one of Urbach's friends wrote for *Sprawa Robotnicza*, the police tried this charge; and when it failed to stick, they let him go.[243] The available evidence fits this interpretation: but is also possible that Kelles-Krauz was right to believe that he was arrested in Radom simply to give young socialists there a warning.[244]

Kelles-Krauz spent the academic year in Poland instead of Paris. He missed not only a year of university, but also the chance to play a role in one of the most significant episodes in modern Polish political history. The PPS was established in Poland in the spring of 1893, and by the summer of 1894 its character and leadership were settled. It had split in summer 1893, the dissenting majority forming Luxemburg's SDKP.[245] The first issue of the SDKP organ, *Sprawa Robotnicza*, appeared just before the Zurich congress of the Second International in August 1893. At the congress, the PPS denied the mandates of the SDKP delegation, marking the character of future relations between the parties.[246]

Though the PPS had been reduced to a handful of members by the split, it built itself up in the fall of 1893 through the hard work of Józef Piłsudski, Stanisław Wojciechowski, and Jan Strożecki (the future husband of Estera Golde). In February 1894, in Strożecki's flat in Warsaw, the PPS held its second congress. There the party wrote its statutes, decided to publish a journal called *Robotnik*, and chose its six-member directing committee. Two of the six were also members of the National League, the patriotic organization recently founded by Roman Dmowski. Dmowski had led a coup within the Polish League in April 1893, changing its name, and eventually moving its ideology toward a more virulent nationalism. At the same time, two of the six were distinctly further left than their fellows. As it happened, these two wings were removed by arrests, which left Józef Piłsudski and Stanisław Wojciechowski in effective control of the party.[247] The two of them published *Robotnik* from 12 July 1893, devoting most of its space to the struggle with the tsar, and very little to economic issues. Despite serious opposition within the party, they were able to keep any mention of a Russian constitution out of the party program.[248]

Because Kelles-Krauz had remained outside the PPS while in Paris, he had no chance to help direct the course of the young party's development once in Poland. Likewise, he was also helpless to influence the course of events in Paris from Poland. Under police supervision, he was reduced to writing in code, even about his own situation. For example, in response to an inquiry from Urbach, he wrote in allegorical style about a "patient" who has been able to leave the "hospital," but who must remain in Poland until the "cure" has taken its full course. (He had been freed from prison, but could not leave the country.)[249] Kelles-Krauz was nevertheless drawn into the new party's activities. After spending some months with Maria and her family, he returned to Warsaw around May 1894. There, in between trips to editors (where he collected articles that had been kept out of print by the censor) and friends, Kelles-Krauz visited Jan Strożecki.

In the spring and summer of 1893, Strożecki's one-room flat on Niecała 12, shared with two other boarders, was the virtual headquarters of the PPS. Strożecki rented the flat from a generous couple downstairs, who fed him and his friends, and did their best to keep the rather flamboyant young man from getting himself caught.[250] It was here that Kelles-Krauz learned of the congresses and the achievements of the PPS. He doubtless also learned of the first congress of the rival SDKP, held in March 1893 in Warsaw.[251] Kelles-Krauz thought that the PPS did not sufficiently ground the goal of national independence in the class interests of workers. But given the choice between a party that supported independence, and one that explicitly rejected it, and urged on by Strożecki, Kelles-Krauz chose the PPS. Among the leaders of the early PPS, Strożecki was the only Marxist,[252] and this must have helped him attract Kelles-Krauz.

Strożecki convinced Kelles-Krauz to help start a PPS cell in Radom. Radom workers had been politically active since 1892, and in 1894 eighty of them had celebrated May Day. With help from Radom's student circle, Kelles-Krauz succeeded in transforming the unorganized meetings of workers in Radom (chiefly railroadmen and tanners) into an unorganized section of the PPS.[253] Strożecki visited Radom to inaugurate the new section, and was arrested shortly thereafter. Kelles-Krauz had therefore recruited for a party with which he no longer had any personal ties.

Kelles-Krauz knew that he would have to build his political reputation anew upon his return to Paris. Though some of his friends may have been waiting for his return to make their final decision,[254] his group of social democrats had split in his absence, in about equal numbers joining the PPS, the SDKP, and a socialist front organization of the National League. More, he had decided to start a new academic life, in the new field of sociology. When he at last received permission to leave the country, he married Maria[255] and packed his bags. By the time the Kelles-Krauzes reached France on 10 July 1894, the Okhrana had been warned of their impending arrival.[256]

2

Dependence and Independence, 1894–1896

KELLES-KRAUZ'S RETURN TO Paris in July 1894 marked his passage into personal, academic, and political adulthood. Whereas previously he had been personally, academically, and politically free (if materially poor), hereafter he was to live within a set of clearly defined loyalties (though he remained poor). After his return to Paris, he would live with his wife, and not in a house full of students. He and Maria lived for a time in the group house on rue de la Glacière, but she could not stand the constant flow of guests who left messes and kept her husband from his work.[1] They moved just around the corner to 42, boulevard Arago.[2] Likewise, Kelles-Krauz was no longer only a student, but a sociologist. He presented a paper in October 1894 at the first congress of the Institut International de Sociologie, and was named an associate member of the new body. Finally, in late 1894 he helped to found a Paris Section of the Union of Polish Socialists Abroad, the foreign organization of the PPS.

Upon his return to Paris, Kelles-Krauz was uncertain that the Union was the only possible legitimate foreign representative of the PPS, and only two months of probing convinced him that he had no chance of founding a rival organization.[3] In his absence, the days of leading informal groups of students in Paris had closed, and the days of choosing political parties had begun. But even though Kelles-Krauz had taken time to survey the political terrain in Paris before contacting the Union, its internal dynamics were not apparent to the outsider. The little he did know inclined him away from the organization.[4] Still, he had to make a choice. Especially as he had already worked for the PPS, the Union must have seemed the lesser of evils in comparison with Rosa Luxemburg's SDKP, which opposed Polish independence, and the group of socialists around the journal *Przegląd Socjalistyczny,* which was associated with the National League. As his later actions would reveal, Kelles-Krauz was confident that he could quickly influence the Union from within. But just as he was set-tling into Paris, a further power struggle was shaping the Union and the PPS, the course of which demonstrates quite clearly why he was bound to run into difficulties.

Centralizacja

The conflict was over a substantial programmatic issue. At the top of the PPS program was the goal of an independent, democratic, Polish repub-lic. Yet in 1894, most members of the PPS believed that the party should cooperate with Russian socialists in their struggle to transform the Empire into a constitutional republic. A Russian constitution, they believed, would put the PPS in a better position to struggle for Polish independence. The most prominent expositor of this reasoning was the Warsaw activ-ist Ludwik Kulczycki, who in the summer of 1894 sent an article along these lines to *Przedświt,* the official journal of the Union in London. Its edi-tor, Witold Jodko-Narkiewicz (1864–1924), refused to print the article, but argued against its contents nonetheless in a series of articles published that autumn.

In these articles, entitled "Stages," Jodko argued that the PPS had not clearly enunciated its goal of independence during the first two years of its existence in the hope that the Russian movement might prove an ally. Yet there was still no Russian party worthy of the name, and the PPS should now announce clearly and simply that it strives for national independence. In the final article he made his key argument: that Russian society is so backward that the Russian people, given the opportunity, would vote for the continued occupation of Poland.[5] The Union's *Centralizacja* in London did not control the party at home: Jodko's views, though expressed in the party's theoretical journal, were not binding. As it happened, Jodko's arti-cles were cut out of the issues of *Przedświt* which reached Warsaw by party members, and a letter of censure under the party seal was sent to him.[6]

The incident reveals London's attitude. Jodko and his best friend Bolesław Antoni Jędrzejowski (1867–1914) were the most important party activists in London. They were a few years older than Kelles-Krauz, and had both been members of Proletariat; Jędrzejowski had been imprisoned in the Warsaw Citadel. Jodko had moved toward accepting independence in the party program in 1891 and 1892, and was one of the main orga-nizers of the Paris Congress of 1892. The congress had been held in Jędrzejowski's flat, though he was somewhat slower than Jodko in shed-ding his Proletariat past.[7] (During the discussion of terrorism at the con-gress, one party activist tried to clear the air by saying that no terrorists were present. "Yes there are!" replied another, pointing to Jędrzejowski).[8] But by 1894, both men believed that the party's first goal must be national independence and—with the conviction of the converted—dismissed cooperation with Russians and internationalist Marxism. Jodko's "Stages" were a failed attempt to bring the bulk of the party around to this view.

The "Stages" incident also revealed the means London would employ in struggles within the party. Jodko simply chose not to publish Kulczycki's article, even though it represented a majority opinion within the PPS. Because he and Jędrzejowski edited *Przedświt*, they could decide what would and would not appear. Though the party in the Russian partition was not subordinate to the *Centralizacja*, the Union (which Kelles-Krauz was to join) was. The Union's statute provided for the possibility of sections in cities besides London, but these sections were placed under London's control. Just as party cells within the Russian partition were subordinate to the PPS's directing council between party congresses, so sections of the Union were subordinate to the *Centralizacja* between Union congresses. All relations between sections, or between sections and the PPS, passed through London.[9] Moreover, unlike the party in the Russian partition, such sections had few means of resistance.

The members of these sections were, like the Londoners, émigrés, often with little hope of returning home. They studied or worked; they had lives outside the party. The Londoners, though, lived for the party: they worked full-time on its publications and organization, and usually held no other job.[10] This complete dedication, combined with their experience in Proletariat, lay behind the Londoners' feeling of superiority over the groups of students, scattered across Europe, who made up the rest of the Union.

The Paris Section

On 7 September 1894 Kelles-Krauz wrote to London that, after consulta-tion with Strożecki, he had agreed to found a Paris Section of the Union.[11] Paris had been the major center of Polish émigré socialism in the first years of the 1890s, but the arrests of the Union's leaders in January 1893 had prevented the new organization from establishing itself there. London had been working to remedy the situation: in 1893 they had tried to recruit Kelles-Krauz's group of social democrats. That group had dissolved in Kelles-Krauz's absence, but in the summer of 1894, he found several of its former members, such as Stanisław Grabski, working for *Przegląd Socjalistyczny*. These friends of Kelles-Krauz (and other prominent Polish socialists, such as Bolesław Limanowski and Bolesław Motz) were surely attracted to the prospect of publishing their own journal.[12] Their sponsor was Roman Dmowski's National League, which hoped to wean socialist intellectuals away from internationalism.

In 1894, the National League could still seem a legitimate socialist alternative. Its student organization (which funded *Przegląd*) was led by Zygmunt Balicki, who was also a member of the Union and had been offered a spot on the *Centralizacja*. Balicki's case was not exceptional: as we have seen, leaders of the PPS were simultaneously members of the National League. In 1893 and 1894, the PPS and National League each penetrated the other, and if the PPS flirted with the idea of a merger, the National League had considered an amicable division of labor.[13]

When Kelles-Krauz offered to recruit this group as the nucleus of a new Paris Section of the Union, London accepted "with pleasure."[14] For London, Kelles-Krauz was a new means of drawing Paris socialists away from Balicki and Dmowski. London had been trying to recruit the group all year,[15] and was apparently close to success when Kelles-Krauz appeared on the scene. Kelles-Krauz's offer should also be seen in the light of his attempt to return to a leading role among socialists in Paris. He had been absent for the better part of a year, and had lost his political moorings. Were he able to transform the *Przegląd Socjalistyczny* group into a Paris Section of the PPS, he would have a fresh start. Though he had not known the man whom he was later to call the "head and heart" of the group, Bolesław Motz (1865–1935),[16] he did know several of its members, and must have anticipated that he could compete with Motz on an equal footing for leadership within a new formation. Kelles-Krauz's interests and those of London were thus in harmony.

Kelles-Krauz's efforts may have helped, as the group did join the Union, but they were not decisive. London had someone else working for them in Paris (perhaps Bolesław Limanowski), for London informed Kelles-Krauz that the group had decided to form a section, not the other way around. The group made its decision on 5 October, and on 14 October Wojciechowski wrote Kelles-Krauz from London, informing him of the success, and telling him that "there is nothing more for you to do."[17] In formally requesting Union membership on 17 October, Kelles-Krauz closed on this note: "I trust that a spirit of coterie does not prevail, and that the right of free criticism is sacred in the Union?"[18]

Three days later, the Paris Section of the Union of Polish Socialists Abroad met for the first time. Limanowski read a letter from the *Centralizacja* welcoming ten members of the former *Przegląd Socjalistyczny* and a few outsiders, such as Maria Kelles-Krauzowa, into the Union. Kelles-Krauz was chosen secretary for external affairs, and Motz was elected treasurer. Kelles-Krauz and Motz were to become rivals for leadership within the Paris Section.[19] Motz was several years older than Kelles-Krauz, and as a student in Petersburg had been a member of *Narodnaia Volia*. Suspected of involvement in a plot to assassinate the tsar, he had left for Paris to study medicine.[20] It seems that Motz thought himself better qualified to lead the Paris Section, and over the years begrudged Kelles-Krauz his growing reputation. According to one member of the section, Kelles-Krauz led through speeches and open dialogue, whereas Motz preferred to work for his own goals behind the scenes.[21] Motz's post as treasurer was appropriate, in that over the years (especially after finishing his studies in bacteriology and becoming a physician) he gave the most money to the section. Kelles-Krauz's position, though, allowed him to establish and develop a dialogue with London.

Klasowość

Kelles-Krauz lost no time in launching his bid for leadership within the Paris Section, and for reform within the Union and PPS. During a meeting of the Paris Section on 2 December 1894, he presented his just-completed pamphlet, "The Class Character of Our Program." The Paris Section endorsed the pamphlet, and set about publishing it. Kelles-Krauz did not mention the pamphlet to London until 18 December, and then only to note that it was being printed and sent to all sections of the Union in time for the upcoming first congress of the Union, which was to be held on 25 December.[22] The following day he sent London several copies, and asked for help in the distribution.[23]

"Class Character" is thus one of the few of Kelles-Krauz's early political writings in which his views are expressed fully and freely, for he was writing under neither political nor party censorship. He is speaking for a group which had its doubts about the Union: "The majority of us saw in the Union certain organizational and tactical faults." The remedy he suggests is "the right and obligation of free criticism and free initiative." Extreme centralization, which is demanded by conditions in the Russian Empire, is not necessary abroad. Everywhere it is harmful: "Many, conceiving that party discipline demands absolute agreement with party leaders, or at least with a majority, willingly abandon free and open organization, closing themselves into the prison from which we wish to rescue our socialist movement." Kelles-Krauz believed that the fetish of centralization is partly a result of exaggerated imitation of the SPD of the Bismarckera, and argues that the experience of the French Allemanists has proven that it is possible to combine openness with discipline.[24]

The article proposed that the *Centralizacja* should allow every matter that did not demand absolute secrecy to be handled by the sections, and that new initiatives should also come from below: "the direction of activity should not be forced down from above, by a few of the most active individuals, but should rather flow upward from public opinion . . . " The rule that all contact between the Union and the PPS should be mediated by the *Centralizacja* must then be changed. The leaders of the PPS should reach "an understanding not with a few individuals, but with the entire Union, with all of its adherents abroad; only knowledge of the mood of individual sections could assure them that." The future of the party depends on the widest possible openness, combined with full agreement about the basic program.[25]

Kelles-Krauz is explicit and emphatic in his support of the program of national independence. He recognizes that the ongoing quarrel over the desirability of working to win a Russian constitution divided the PPS, and that Rosa Luxemburg's SDKP stood to gain from the conflict. (The SDKP opposed Polish independence, and at its first congress in March 1894 had included the struggle for a Russian constitution within its program.) He understands that opposition to the inclusion of the goal of a Russian constitution within its program opens the PPS to charges of "social patriotism" from Luxemburg, and even agrees with her that it risks drawing non-socialist "elements" into the party. But he unambiguously declares that: "The program not only does not contradict the principle of socialism, but flows naturally from that principle . . . "[26] He then sets out to defend it from attacks by the SDKP, addressing in turn precisely these two issues: the political goal of a constitution, and the risk of contaminating the class character of the PPS.

He begins his discussion of the programmatic issue by reviewing the SDKP's program.[27] He cites the protocols of the SDKP's first congress, which indicated that the goal of the party was "To gain for our country a government chosen by the whole nation, and gain that government for our workers' cause."[28] Kelles-Krauz then tries to reconcile this statement with the SDKP's programmatic goal of a constitution for the Russian Empire. Perhaps recalling the nationalist stance of Russian liberals during the Polish rising of 1863,[29] Kelles-Krauz argues that a constitution for the lands of the Russian Empire would be no guarantor of Polish freedom. "It seems not at all established that a future Russian constitution, most graciously conferred by Nicholas II, or proclaimed by a bureaucratic-military committee the day after said Nicholas was blown into the sky, would advance quite so far in its liberalism."[30] In speaking thus of a "constitution" for "our nation" or for "our country," Rosa Luxemburg is misleading the workers. She will not say that the constitution is for Poland, because that is not what she wants or expects; but she will not admit that the constitution, nation and country she has in mind are Russian.

He then responds to the SDKP charge that the PPS does not indicate the means by which it will gain national independence. Kelles-Krauz's answer is simple: no one can be sure at what point any party program will be implemented, because moments of opportunity depend upon circumstances beyond any party's ability to predict. In the case of the PPS program, such a favorable constellation of factors is possible: it may result from a war between the partitioning powers, or from an internal collapse of the Russian Empire. The party's task is to prepare workers for that moment, so that they will be able to lead the fight for independence and for the widest possible freedoms in a new Polish constitution. Any breakdown in Russia, Kelles-Krauz cautions, will cause a struggle for constitutions, in the plural, "for on the territory of this empire economic conditions are so widely divergent, that to speak of just one constitution is utopian."[31]

The SDKP's rejection of national independence, Kelles-Krauz concludes, is the result of "the very purest Marxism," of "the kind of Marxism which forced Marx to declare 'I will never be a Marxist.' "[32] This famous remark of Marx's had been directed against the major French Marxist party, led by Jules Guesde—and Kelles-Krauz has just this parallel in mind.[33] Noting the good relations between the Luxemburgists and the Guesdists, he compares their programs. Just as the SDKP proved its shortsightedness and doctrinaire Marxism by opting for a Russian constitution at its last congress, the Guesdists did the same by rejecting the general strike at theirs. In doing so, they accepted a tactic, according to Kelles-Krauz, "simply contrary to scientific socialism."[34] He has in mind a particular argument, used by both Luxemburg and Guesde: that when the working class is strong enough for national independence (Luxemburg), or for a general strike (Guesde), it will then be strong enough to start a revolution, so there is no point in concentrating attention on any goal but the final one.

This way of thinking clearly infuriates Kelles-Krauz, and his anger pushes him still further in his criticism of the Guesde's *Parti Ouvrier Français*, and even of August Bebel's SPD:

> Do you not see something similar [to the SDKP program] in the struggle of western socialist parties? Recall that the official repre- sentatives of Marxism, Bebel from one, Guesde from the other side of the Rhine, are beating down the idea of a general strike, that revo- lutionary, courageous tactic of Nieuwenhuis and Allemane. Word for word the same: in order to carry out a general strike, we must organize the whole working class, which would be a sufficient con- dition for carrying out a socialist revolution: then we would make a revolution, and the general strike would be completely superfluous! Clear and simple, like two plus two is four. But only at first glance.[35]

The general strike is necessary, argues Kelles-Krauz, because the revolu- tion will not come at one blow. "Many have become used to seeing the revolution as an immediate and complete transformation of the social structure": this is "a dream."[36] Instead, the revolution is a long process, demanding a continuous increase in political consciousness among work- ers. The general strike serves as a kind of political practice, which by its very nature will be of, by, and for workers. As workers feel their own political power through the general strike, they become conscious of the possibility for more fundamental political change through class politics. His model was thus the series of strikes in Belgium for general suffrage,[37] rather than the hope of the French trade union leader Fernand Pelloutier that a general strike would, by itself, transform society.[38] Here, as elsewhere, Kelles-Krauz seems to have been inspired by the example of the Dutch socialist Domela Nieuwenhuis at the 1893 Zurich congress of the Second International. Nieuwenhuis had called the Germans "patriots," and saw his resolution in favor of the general strike lose by a huge margin.[39]

According to Kelles-Krauz, in Russian Poland the struggle for national independence must take the place of the general strike. First, the general strike cannot work without national independence. If Polish workers tried a general strike now, the Russian government could find loyal Russians to take their place. But, he points out, even the most reactionary conceivable future government of an independent Poland would never dare to try such a tactic. Second, the effort to gain national independence will prepare workers for the political struggle to follow. Both national independence and the general strike are the kinds of concrete tools that make a revolution possible: "Those who do not understand that the revolutionary crisis will take place in stages and be subject everywhere to local conditions, must always oppose both the general strike and the workers' struggle for an independent Poland, with the help of their vulgar, quasi-'scientific' syllogisms."[40]

Kelles-Krauz then turns to the second point at issue between the PPS and SDKP: tactics. By opposing national independence, Rosa Luxemburg hoped to keep her party purely proletarian. According to her approach, if a party is to pursue class goals, it must not adopt a program which will draw in the petty bourgeoisie. Kelles-Krauz believes that for Luxemburg this tactical issue is the "heart of the matter." Though he mocks her for fearing a "phantom," elsewhere in his pamphlet he reveals that he too believes in such a danger.[41] He thinks that the petty bourgeoisie has already ruined French and German socialism, and warns that such a danger now lies before the PPS. He advises his own party not to imitate the SPD and the Guesdists, and cites Allemane to the effect that bourgeois allies will desert the cause at the critical moment. Just as radicals in France and reformers in Germany will abandon socialism when they are offered spots in the government, so petty bourgeois patriots will betray the PPS when independence is won.[42]

For Kelles-Krauz, the resolution of this tactical problem is to be found in the conscious preservation of the class character of the party. The PPS must make its demands for national independence absolutely clear, which *Robotnik* had thus far failed to do.[43] At the same time, it must remember and teach that Polish independence is for the proletariat, not the other way around. To this end, Kelles-Krauz advocates that non-socialist patriots be expelled from the party and no longer allowed to publish on the pages of *Przedświt*.[44] The issue of double allegiance to the National League and the PPS was at this time a pressing one, and so we may regard this as the last of Kelles-Krauz's recommendations to the forthcoming Union congress.[45]

Klasowość and the PPS

This lengthy pamphlet was addressed to four groups: in descending order of immediacy, to the new Paris Section, to the Union and PPS, to the SDKP, and to French and German socialist parties. (It was never to reach this last group, though there would be a close call.) The new Paris Section seems to have been swept away. As Luxemburg remembered, the Paris Section was full of Allemanists in early 1895.[46] But it was Motz, not Kelles-Krauz, who was delegated to attend the Union congress where the pamphlet was to be discussed.[47] Thus Kelles-Krauz was not present in Zurich in the last days of December, when the Union and the PPS—represented by Józef Piłsudski—debated the pamphlet.[48] This congress was Piłsudski's introduction to the Union, whose members (except for Jodko and Wojciechowski) he met for the first time.[49] It seems likely that Kelles-Krauz's pamphlet gave Piłsudski and the right of the Union a way to close ranks.[50] It is certainly the case that December 1894 marked the beginning of close ties and a pronounced spirit of cooperation between Piłsudski, Wojciechowski, Jodko, and Jędrzejowski.

The Union passed a resolution denying Kelles-Krauz's every charge, and noting the political damage that open criticism on Kelles-Krauz's model could cause the party. The pamphlet contained very strongly-phrased accusations, and was sanctioned by the Paris Section, and thus would have been taken by outsiders at face value rather than as part of a larger discussion. "Class Character" also criticized the leading French and German socialist parties without cause: given that the new PPS was weak and desirous of German support, and that Kelles-Krauz was defending Nieuwenhuis against the SPD and the majority of socialists (Friedrich Engels himself believed that Nieuwenhuis's plan "would ruin all the socialist parties in Europe"[51]), this was perhaps the most serious charge. Further, the pamphlet was published in a non-Union printing house, which risked that it would fall into the hands of non-members. The Union ordered all remaining copies of the pamphlet sealed in the party archive, and reprimanded the Paris Section.[52]

The pamphlet had been published by Adolf Reiff, a Polish printer in Paris. He was widely known and used by Polish socialists: indeed, he played an important role in the development of Polish socialism. Stanisław Wojciechowski, who was to print *Robotnik,* and Aleksander Dębski, who printed *Przedświt,* both apprenticed with Reiff. So members of the Union who spoke of the possibility that materials given to Reiff might pass into non-party circles knew whereof they spoke, and in the event, their fears were justified. For Luxemburg also published with Reiff, and the two of them were on good terms. By March 1895 she had a copy of "Class Character," and she had indeed learned of its existence from Reiff. Despite the pamphlet's pseudonymous byline, she also knew that Kelles-Krauz was the author.[53]

Klasowość and Rosa Luxemburg

In this unintended fashion, Kelles-Krauz's pamphlet reached its third intended audience, the SDKP. "Class Character" began a decade of debate between Kelles-Krauz and Luxemburg on the relationship between socialism and Polish independence, and it is thus worthwhile to pause a moment to compare their positions. Luxemburg was staying in Paris for a few months in late 1894 and early 1895, to publish a few issues of her *Sprawa Robotnicza* and work in libraries.[54] It is possible that she and Kelles-Krauz met personally during this period, for they both were working in the Bibliothèque Nationale, and had common acquaintances. Indeed, they had much in common. Like Kelles-Krauz, Luxemburg had left the Congress Kingdom to study abroad. Also like Kelles-Krauz, she had studied science first, and then switched to the study of society. (She was writing a doctorate about economics within the faculty of law at Zurich.) She was in Zurich what Kelles-Krauz was becoming in Paris: a leader of Polish émigré socialist intellectuals and students.

The SDKP was led by a tightly knit émigré group. Luxemburg, her lover Leon Jogiches, and their friends Adolf Warszawski and Julian Marchlewski were about the same age, lived in Zurich at the same time, and knew each other well even before the party was founded.[55] These intellectuals were quite conscious of the uses of the Second International: *Sprawa Robotnicza*, for example, was founded just in time to grant Luxemburg a mandate for its 1893 Zurich congress. Luxemburg was very bright and formidably industrious, able singlehandedly to write and edit *Sprawa Robotnicza*. The journal was funded by Jogiches, who was heir to a family fortune.[56] Luxemburg was thus in the unique position of writing and editing the organ of a political party. Like Kelles-Krauz, she was a prolific correspondent; but whereas he wrote his love letters to Maria and his political letters to his sponsors in London, Luxemburg wrote about both in letters to Jogiches. This lent her correspondence, and in some measure her life (until she broke with Jogiches in 1907) a certain unusual economy.

Kelles-Krauz's efforts to establish himself in Paris and in the Union were an unexpected boon to Luxemburg and her Zurich friends. "It's a pity [that "Class Character" was forbidden publication]," wrote Luxemburg to Jogiches, "because from every point of view it could have rendered us countless services." She knew that such frank criticism of the SPD could only hurt the PPS's international reputation, and recognized that Kelles-Krauz's attempt to identify "scientific socialism" with syndicalism was doomed to failure. She laughed that the Paris Section understood "Guesdist" to be an insult and was amused that Kelles-Krauz tried to discredit the SDKP by identifying it with Bebel and Guesde, two of the leading figures of the Second International. She concluded that the pamphlet was a sign of the internal disarray of the PPS, and was much encouraged.[57] She soon sent copies of the pamphlet to Jogiches and Marchlewski.[58] As we shall see, a good occasion to exploit the pamphlet against the PPS soon presented itself.

While Luxemburg was in Paris, she wrote and published her first brochure on patriotism and socialism. It is unknown whether Luxemburg had read "Class Character" before finishing "An Independent Poland and the Worker's Cause" in March 1895.[59] In any event, a comparison of their views of patriotism and socialism should set the stage for debates to come. Luxemburg is unambiguous in her opposition to Polish statehood. Henceforth there could be no supposing, even for rhetorical purposes such as Kelles-Krauz's, that the SDKP program meant anything other than "a single constitution for the territories of the Russian Empire" when it spoke of "a constitution." The arguments against Polish independence are legion, if sometimes shallowly defended. Workers, she begins, suffer just as much in western Europe as in Russia, for independent states also have means of repression.[60] A new Polish state would not change the lot of the working class, for independence would not change property relations.[61] All governments equally serve the capitalist class, and it is therefore futile to strive for any goal besides the socialist revolution.[62] In any case, she argues, (resorting to the argument which Kelles-Krauz regarded as so counterproductive) if the workers were strong enough to win national independence, they would also be able to start a socialist revolution.[63]

The premise of these arguments is that political life under capitalism is everywhere the same. Luxemburg hoped to blunt the edge of the *Robotnik* and *Przedświt* line, which emphasized the differences between Poland and lands farther east. Leaders of the Union and the PPS generally held that Russia was qualitatively more backward than Poland, and therefore qualitatively less revolutionary.[64] They opposed the healthy PPS organization to scattered and feeble Russian socialist groups, the industry of Warsaw and Łódź to Russia's endless steppes, and Poland's republican tradition to Russia's heritage of Asiatic despotism. Piłsudski's articles went furthest in treating Poland's fate as a matter for Poles to decide.[65] Though Kelles-Krauz was not on principle opposed to cooperation with Russian socialists (unlike Piłsudski he had no reflexive dislike of all things Russian[66]), he also carefully distinguished between Polish lands and Russian, as his argument about the futility of a Russian constitution in "Class Character" revealed. Leaders of the SDKP, on the other hand, tended to blur differences between the Russian partition of Poland and Russia: to argue that Russia and Poland were at about the same stage of development, or in Rosa Luxemburg's case, that industrialization was forming from Poland and Russia an "organic" whole.

In "Independent Poland," Luxemburg is thus concerned to protect workers from PPS agitation to the effect that Poland's superiority justifies the struggle for independence rather than an imperial constitution. Believing that the socialist revolution will replace existing states with an international socialist republic, she wants socialist parties to be organized by state rather than by nation, and believes that national struggles would sap the Polish proletariat's energy and divide it from its Russian comrades.[67] She presents an abridged version of her organic incorporation argument: Poland's bourgeoisie is interested in preserving trade ties with Russia, and is thus opposed to independence.[68] At the same time, she argues that the PPS has exaggerated the economic gap between Poland and Russia.[69]

One suspects that Luxemburg exaggerated for effect. She knew perfectly well the difference between political life in the Russian Empire and in, say, Switzerland, having fled the former to live freely in the latter. She was also doubtless aware that the reasons she gave (in this pamphlet) against Polish independence did not form a coherent whole. But she was agitating, not theorizing. Luxemburg was convinced that the best way to build an effective socialist party was to keep the petty bourgeois nationalists out, and to that end she was supplying workers with simple, ready arguments to use against patriotic slogans.

A concern for tactics is not what distinguished Luxemburg's approach from Kelles-Krauz's. At this stage in his career, Kelles-Krauz also sought to keep his socialist party proletarian, but had to seek after more subtle means than simply ignoring national issues.[70] For while Luxemburg held that meaningful political and social change would take the form of a sudden international revolution carried out by parties organized against existing (imperial or nation-) states, Kelles-Krauz believed that meaningful political change would take place in stages, that the character of these stages depended upon local conditions, and that most of these stages required the nation-state. His "Class Character" was thus a plan to build a Poland which can become socialist; her "Independent Poland" aimed to prepare Polish workers for an international revolution. For Luxemburg, a Polish state was a dangerous distraction for the working class; for Kelles-Krauz it was a necessity.

1895

In spring 1895 Luxemburg left Paris for Zurich. By June, when her party held its second congress, it was already so weakened by arrests that only five delegates appeared.[71] By the end of 1895 her party had effectively disappeared on Polish soil, its remnants joining the PPS.[72] Luxemburg and other SDKP intellectuals dispersed through Europe, forming close ties with, and often eventually joining, French and German parties. Kelles-Krauz was in a completely different position. Though the PPS was also weakened by arrests during 1895, it showed no signs of disappearing. As we shall see, those very arrests left the PPS with a united leadership. Kelles-Krauz belonged to the party with the brighter future, but Luxemburg still had her own Zurich formation, the possibility of reviving her own organ, and her freedom. Kelles-Krauz's lot during 1895 was to remain in Paris, to consolidate his position within the Paris Section, and to try to find a way to change the Union from within.

The Union was an extremely centralized organization, and for that very reason a very personal one. The *Centralizacja* in London directed the Union, but because Jodko and Jędrzejowski were best friends, it made little difference that for a time Jędrzejowski was in the *Centralizacja* and Jodko was not. Kelles-Krauz had demonstrated that he considered himself an outsider with reforming zeal—especially as Jodko and Jędrzejowski had not yet met him personally, they were bound to distrust him at first. It would be wrong to say that Kelles-Krauz sought any immediate compromise with them in 1895, but during the course of the year he at least became more familiar. He wrote to London almost daily, and at one point during the year resolved to write at least once a day.[73] Kelles-Krauz was astonishingly prolific, and these epistles were often quite long. He often chastised London for not replying soon enough, though one feels that he was setting a terribly high standard. In any event, as Kelles-Krauz wrote about his views at length and without compromise, he slowly became a known quantity.

This is not to say that he and London came to terms on very many issues. Indeed, disagreement was the rule. Kelles-Krauz believed, for example, that the PPS should not treat the SPD as a model, while Jodko and Jędrzejowski were German speakers who regarded Wilhelm Liebknecht and the SPD as the PPS's natural patrons.[74] Kelles-Krauz expected that Russian socialists would soon form a united party, while London thought that this was years away.[75] Kelles-Krauz was especially sensitive to issues of ethics, and worried that London did not have any evidence to back its claim that a leading member of the SDKP was an Okhrana agent.[76]

Kelles-Krauz was also a Marxist. He urged London to keep up good relations with the Allemanists, on the grounds that, identifying Marxism with the general strike, he considered them to be good Marxists.[77] At the same time, living in Paris gave Kelles-Krauz everyday experience of the difficulty of explaining the need for Polish independence to other Marxists. When Kelles-Krauz told Allemane, for example, that the difference between the PPS and the SDKP was that the former supported Polish independence, he received the reply that the PPS were just "patriots."[78] (Unlike his pupil, Allemane apparently saw no connection between the general strike and national independence.) Kelles-Krauz continued to believe that the way around this problem was for the PPS to emphasize the class basis of its demand for national independence.[79] London, however, placed its hopes in a national strategy: rather than prove that national independence followed from Marxism, they hoped to persuade the leaders of the SPD to support the program of Polish national independence. Kelles-Krauz thought that the path to international political support led through Marx; London thought that it led through Berlin.

The most ink was spilled over "Class Character" and the principle of decentralization. The Paris Section met several times in January 1895 to discuss ways of reopening the issues discussed in the pamphlet.[80] Eventually realizing that "Class Character" would not serve as a tool to remake the Union, the Paris Section submitted a number of motions to decentralize authority within the organization, most of which failed.[81] The main effect of this flurry of motions was to stigmatize Kelles-Krauz and the Paris Section before other members of the Union. As Romuald Mielczarski, a member of the Union section in Antwerp, wrote to London in April: "As to the communications from Paris, it's as clear as could be that Comrade Luśnia is a novice in the socialist school, and thinks that activity consists of endless haggling about the program and the like."[82] Jędrzejowski wrote to Kelles-Krauz in the same spirit:

> The Paris Section joined the Union at a time when the statute was already a fait accompli, the section did not take part in the discussion which preceded it . . . Though we are convinced that some of your criticisms are valid, we are also convinced that you yourself have not pointed out adequate solutions. Your plans are just as academic as is, in some measure, the statute itself. So why is it, that having little experience in the Union, and not knowing its previous history, you want to waste your time trying to replace an imperfect statute with something worse?[83]

Kelles-Krauz and his *Przegląd Socjalistyczny* group had entered the Union with the expectation that they could change the Union from within, and in the event could not. As 1895 passed, Kelles-Krauz's enthusiasm for decentralization cooled.[84] This occurred in part, perhaps, because of the futility of further effort, and perhaps also because his own experience was teaching him just how unruly a group of young émigré Polish intellectuals could be.[85]

This year of constant epistolary debate over programmatic and other issues is only explicable in light the profound importance these socialists attached to words. As a very young man and a Marxist, Kelles-Krauz was an extreme example of this, but the phenomenon was general. For Polish socialists, this fascination with words was in part a side effect of conspiracy and emigration. Because the PPS's intellectuals were spread around Europe and rarely able to meet in person, party programs and congress resolutions took on an added importance. They provided the premises for the debates and polemics which are the daily bread of political intellectuals. Programs also served as psychological ballast for these more or less isolated intellectuals, devoted to a cause with an uncertain future. There is a camaraderie of conspiracy, but one of its conditions is a feeling of agreement about ends. It must have been especially important to individuals to believe that their understanding of socialism was represented within the party to which they dedicated so much of their lives. Since at this point the PPS did little more than produce and distribute propaganda, the relationship between the party's publications and its identity was all the clearer.

The PPS and its Publications

While Kelles-Krauz and the Paris Section were haggling with London, power within the party continued to shift toward Piłsudski and Wojciechowski in the Russian partition, and Jędrzejowski and Jodko in London. The Londoners stood by their opposition to including the demand for a Russian constitution within the PPS program, and Piłsudski and Wojciechowski tried to move the party at home in this direction. The hand of Piłsudski is visible in some of the resolutions passed by the PPS's Third Congress on 29 June 1895 in the Ponar forest near Vilnius. (The word "congress" is a grand one: it should be kept in mind that PPS congresses were very small gatherings of individuals within a very small conspiratorial party.) One resolution endorsed the strategy of stirring up nationalism among other subject peoples of the Russian Empire, in the hope of hastening its collapse.

Still, Piłsudski and Wojciechowski did not have the votes to put the issue of a Russian constitution to rest. After being named to the party's directing committee (along with Piłsudski and Kulczycki), Wojciechowski proposed a motion to the effect that articles should not be cut from *Przedświt* by party members. (He had in mind the fate of Jodko's "Stages.") The motion failed, and Wojciechowski resigned from his place on the party's directing committee. What is more, Kulczycki was able to pass a motion in favor of adding the struggle for a Russian constitution to the party program. (The vote was 6–3, with Piłsudski, Wojciechowski, and Piłsudski's man Aleksander Sulkiewicz voting against. Piłsudski had managed to get Sulkiewicz elected to the directing committee in Wojciechowski's place.) Piłsudski and Wojciechowski agreed, as a compromise, to place a programmatic article in *Robotnik*, instead of amending the actual program. In the end, they failed to do even this.[86] Because they controlled *Robotnik*, the constitution issue was dead until the next congress.

Shortly after the congress, arrests of Piłsudski's rivals once again consolidated his position. Kulczycki, the leading advocate of designating a Russian constitution as a goal within the party program, was arrested in September 1895, and Wojciechowski returned to the party's directing committee to take his place.[87] The leadership of the PPS was now united: in opposing the goal of a Russian constitution, in supporting national independence, and in not considering Marxism to be integral to the PPS's goals. All believed that *Robotnik* should receive priority over verbal agitation and concentrate on national rather than class issues. The remnants of the SDKP began to join the PPS shortly thereafter, and Piłsudski and

Wojciechowski had every reason to feel confident of their position.[88] The very wave of arrests that had helped Piłsudski and Wojciechowski consolidate their authority also confirmed to them the correctness of their tactics: conspiracy and *Robotnik*, not the open agitation that had led Strożecki, Kulczycki, and much of the SDKP to prison.[89] Wojciechowski was a member of the *Centralizacja* and had lived in London, and knew Jodko and Jędrzejowski well. Piłsudski had met them at Zurich; when he moved to London for six months in March of 1896 the personal ties among these men grew closer still.[90]

If arrests of political opponents are set aside, the two keys to the success of these patriotic socialists were centralization and control of the press. When Kelles-Krauz began to write for *Przedświt*, he had to learn to live with the lack of editorial control. Kelles-Krauz's first two articles appeared in the May 1895 issue. The first covered demonstrations by Polish workers in Paris on 1 May, and emphasized that workers wanted national independence.[91] This went in without a hitch. The second article discussed French celebrations of May Day, and argued that because French workers had political rights, the holiday lost much of its meaning. The editors intervened in the article to note that this was not the view of the party.[92] Kelles-Krauz's remaining articles for *Przedświt* in 1895 were usually little more than political reporting from a socialist point of view, and this more or less protected them from editorial intervention. His reports in 1895 and 1896 kept Polish socialists aware of such issues as the balance of power in the French parliament,[93] the fall of Bourgeois's radical government,[94] the success of socialist parties in local elections,[95] and Guesdist congresses.[96] He covered the massive strike and lockout of glass workers in Carmaux in July-September 1895, caused by the firing of a worker who had the audacity to be elected to a regional council.[97]

London published Kelles-Krauz's views when it suited them, as in the case of his article "In the question of 'paralellism'." As in "Class Character," Kelles-Krauz here advocates the expulsion of non-socialist patriots from socialist organizations. The PPS had approved this strategy at its third congress in June 1895, but non-socialist patriots remained in the Union. It is against these émigré patriots, Zygmunt Balicki in particular, that Kelles-Krauz turns his arguments. Only workers, he begins, have an "integral" interest in independence. All other classes can be bought off by some form of concession from the tsar, but the workers must have full political freedom in order to struggle for their own interests and eventually transform the capitalist system. The PPS must therefore "monopolize" all of the progressive tasks left to it by the bourgeoisie, in the sense that it must relate them all to the ultimate goal of a socialist republic. Accepting allies who share the immediate goal of an independent Poland can only retard working-class consciousness, and risks that the independent Poland actually attained by this alliance will be founded on a constitution unfavorable to socialist demands.[98] London did not share all of Kelles-Krauz's concerns, but his arguments were useful tools in the new effort to separate the PPS and Union from the National League, and were therefore welcome. Whereas the early 1890s had witnessed attempts to unite socialists and patriots in one party, by this time the effort to separate the PPS from Dmowski's National Democrats was well underway.

The Paris Section and its Successes

Ironically, Kelles-Krauz's editorial difficulties began in earnest when he was chosen to edit and direct a new *Bulletin Officiel du Parti Socialiste Polonais*, the purposes of which were to inform European socialists about the PPS program and to provide copy for European socialist newspapers.[99] The Paris Section nominated Kelles-Krauz for the job in March 1895, and London approved the choice. London could not have considered Kelles-Krauz the ideal candidate, but he had two rare and indispensable qualifications: he was willing to take the job. and could write French prose virtually with the skill of a native. The latter distinguished him from most of the Paris Section—over the four years that he was to edit the *Bulletin*, he would never have more than one assistant, and often made do with none. These qualities insulated his candidature from the criticisms his rival Bolesław Motz sent to London:

> It's very strange to me that after Luśnia's pamphlet you would give him the editorship of the *Bulletin*. He is extraordinarily kind and energetic, but he has no gift for organization whatsoever. He's also ambitious, and won't allow anyone to correct him in even the smallest matters. I'm certain that this combination will guarantee the failure of the enterprise. Better to change your decision sooner than later.[100]

In the event, the enterprise bore a few modest successes. Though mainly used by west European socialists and newspapers, it was also read in the Russian Empire by socialists and, in Piłsudski's words, "a few big fish, ministers and governors-general."[101] Kelles-Krauz was responsible for the contents of each issue, and usually wrote all of the articles. He had to send them to London for review, however, and complained that "rewritings will be the death of me."[102] Some of London's criticisms were truly pedantic, as when certain of Kelles-Krauz's French usages (which he had picked up from socialist journals) were questioned.[103] But because Kelles-Krauz was the only one capable of doing the job, he had some leverage. Early on he warned London that he must either have editorial control, or work simply as a technical assistant, correcting the French of other authors.[104] It never came to that, and on each issue Kelles-Krauz and London found a *modus vivendi*. Kelles-Krauz certainly lost some battles. In 1895, for example, he thought that the SDKP was not to be regarded as a foe, but as an ally with a flawed program.[105] But though he wished to cover its successes in the *Bulletin*,[106] no favorable articles about the party actually appeared. Still, he had a greater degree of editorial control than he would have found in any other party publication, and was able to freely choose the issues he would cover.

For example, Kelles-Krauz knew that the Fifth International Prison Congress was to be held in Paris, beginning 30 June 1895. Prison conditions are an issue of natural interest to any revolutionary, especially to those who were subjects of the tsar. Kelles-Krauz knew a little about the subject from his own experience, and had learned more by working in a joint PPS-SDKP committee which gathered money for political prisoners in the Russian Empire.[107] He devoted the entire second number of the *Bulletin* to a "Lettre Ouverte du Parti Social iste Polonais au Ve Congrès Pénitentiaire Internationale." He began with a brief sketch of political conditions in the Russian partition of Poland, concluding: "You can imagine the situation of political prisoners in such conditions." But he wisely did not leave the matter to the imagination of his west European readers, describing instead the fearful conditions that prevailed in imperial prisons. He proposed that the congress pass resolutions opposing inhumane prison conditions, administrative sentencing, preventive detention, and the Okhrana; as well as one supporting the inviolability of the right to asylum; and one appointing a special commission to monitor the tsar.[108] The European mainstream press picked up the story,[109] and the congress passed a resolution opposing the administrative sentencing of political crimes in the Russian Empire.[110]

Though Kelles-Krauz's name did not appear in the *Bulletin*, even in pseudonymous form, this new responsibility confirmed his status as the leading Polish socialist in Paris. He and Estera Golde, a member of the section since returning to Paris at the end of 1894,[111] distributed the journal, and were therefore known among French socialists. Kelles-Krauz was also popular among the Association of Polish Workers in Paris, and (often alongside Golde) spoke at its meetings.[112] More, socialists from southern Europe (Portugal, Serbia, Romania) sought his counsel.[113] Kelles-Krauz had eclipsed Motz, and by the end of 1895 was the leader of the Paris Section.[114]

This prominence was not necessarily to his advantage, for the Paris Section had to be on guard against the Okhrana. Several of Kelles-Krauz's letters either report the discovery of informers, or ask London for information about those he suspected of being spies. One issue of *Bulletin* printed the photograph of a known Russian *provocateur*, who was at large despite Russian reports of his arrest.[115] These precautions were certainly justified, but they did not prevent the Okhrana from following Kelles-Krauz's activities. Malankiewicz continued to file reports throughout 1895. By April 1895, he was recommending that the police should turn its attention first of all to the Kelles-Krauzes, calling their apartment the center of the revolutionary Polish intelligentsia in Paris.[116] He referred to Polish socialism in Paris as the "clique of the Krauzes,"[117] and as "Krauz, Golde, et comp."[118]

Interestingly, Malankiewicz had been unmasked as an Okhrana agent by Polish workers in Paris as early as 27 July 1894, two weeks after Kelles-Krauz's return to Paris. A Polish worker wrote to the Okhrana's Paris chief Rachkovskii, using the return address "Imperial Russe Agent Provocateur Malankiewicz." In a childlike hand, the worker wrote that "your *agent provocateur* Malankiewicz was exposed yesterday," and suggested that Malankiewicz be paid more to keep him from inventing false information.[119] This led to the absurd situation of Malankiewicz pleading to his own boss that he was never a *provocateur,* just an informer,[120] and to his less amusing request that decisive action be taken against the "intrigues" that had engulfed him.[121] Although Malankiewicz was condemned by the Association of Polish Workers, Polish socialist intellectuals in Paris either never heard of the charge (which is unlikely), or did not believe it. Urbach remained close to Malankiewicz, and Kelles-Krauz did not believe that Malankiewicz was an agent.[122]

Independence

By the end of 1895, Kelles-Krauz's dedication and dialogue had brought him much closer, personally if not politically, to Jodko and Jędrzejowski. Toward the end of the year, Kelles-Krauz and London had found a common project. In October 1895 Kelles-Krauz persuaded Jodko and Jędrzejowski that the PPS should propose a resolution stating that Polish independence was in the interest of the international working class to the forthcoming London congress of the Second International, to be held in July and August 1896. In a letter full of enthusiasm, he wrote: "The whole civilized world would be galvanized by this blow to the tsar from the international proletariat."[123] Kelles-Krauz recognized that such a resolution should only be proposed if its acceptance was certain, and predicted "that it will gain full support."[124] A few days later, a more hesitant Jędrzejowski agreed that the PPS should take "this risky step."[125]

Kelles-Krauz met Jodko and Jędrzejowski personally for the first time at the second congress of the Union in Geneva in late December 1895.[126] At this congress, he was formally named a *"mąż zaufania"* of the Union, (literally, "man of trust," a term hailing from at least the 1863 rising, signifying that he was to be privy to much more Union and PPS business than previously), and elected to the *Centralizacja*.[127] This congress, following the lead of the PPS's third congress of June 1895, resolved that no member of the Union could belong to other political organizations.[128] Kelles-Krauz had remained a proponent of such a move throughout 1895,[129] and so won his first programmatic battle. National League activists, most notably Balicki, had to leave the Union.

The congress devoted a great deal of time to the forthcoming London congress of the Second International. In particular, the Union discussed whether or not they would try to prevent Luxemburg and her allies from taking part. The PPS could consider such a step because congresses of the Second International were formally constituted of national delegations, rather than individuals. Thus Germans approved the mandates of Germans, the French the mandates of Frenchmen, and so on. The goal of approving mandates was to ensure that each delegate represented a properly socialist, which is to say not an anarchist, organization.[130] This procedure was carried out by majority vote, so it was open to abuse. The PPS, which expected to field a large delegation in London, could simply reject the mandates of conationals whom it did not wish to see participate.

There was a precedent: the Zurich congress of August 1893. There, the PPS had voted to reject the mandates of Luxemburg and Julian Marchlewski (both had mandates from *Sprawa Robotnicza,* and Marchlewski had one from a group of workers as well). Luxemburg and Marchlewski appealed to the congress's central office, which confirmed their mandates. The PPS then took the matter to the congress' plenary session.

Plekhanov, the Russian Marxist, spoke against Luxemburg; and Ignacy Daszyński, leader of Polish socialists in Austria, claimed that he had never heard of Luxemburg and Marchlewski, nor of *Sprawa Robotnicza*. Adolf Warszawski then telegraphed the congress, stating that he was the editor of *Sprawa Robotnicza*, and reaffirming that "his" newspaper had granted the mandates. The PPS then raised the stakes once again, claiming that Warszawski was suspected of being an agent. The issue was put to a vote of the congress. Luxemburg's mandate was denied, and Marchlewski was allowed to stay on the strength of his other mandate.[131]

The strategy had succeeded in 1893, but not without certain costs. Polish dirty laundry had been aired before the International, and PPS members at home (such as Strożecki, who demanded, and got, the resignation of Stanisław Mendelson from the Union) had been outraged by the rough treatment of Marchlewski and Luxemburg. In Geneva, Kelles-Krauz proposed that the SDKP be denied mandates for ethical, rather than formal reasons. He reasoned that since the SDKP no longer existed as a political party, it could not be represented at a congress of the Second International. In his view, the PPS should put the matter before the congress's central office as a moral protest, and leave it at that. This view was probably based upon his belief that no Pole would dare to publicly oppose his resolution, and his certainty of its passage.[132] Jodko and Jędrzejowski were more cautious. As Jędrzejowski put it, "We must not only make sure the motion passes, we must be sure to avoid the scandal that would follow if other Poles spoke against it." "The question of rejecting the *Sprawa* group," he wrote Kelles-Krauz, "becomes one of life and death."[133] Their view prevailed, and the Union resolved not only to deny the mandates of the group, but to take the issue to the plenary session of the congress if necessary.[134]

Before passing on to the steps taken by Kelles-Krauz and London to prepare European socialist parties for the resolution, it is worth pausing to consider just why such a resolution was presented in 1896, rather than earlier or later. As Jędrzejowski assured Kelles-Krauz, the idea had been raised several times before, but had not seemed timely.[135] Jan Lorentowicz had proposed such a measure to his fellow Polish delegates at the 1893 Zurich Congress; his idea was voted down by a majority of two at a beer hall gathering, and a resolution stating that "the time is not yet right to raise the issue at a Congress" was passed instead.[136] But by 1896, the PPS was in a much stronger position. Its leadership, in the Russian partition and in London, was united behind the idea of national independence. The PPS no longer (it might hope) had to fear accusations of unorthodoxy from a competing Polish socialist party. Piłsudski's *Robotnik* announced the merger of the SDKP with the PPS in January 1896,[137] and Luxemburg's *Sprawa Robotnicza* had not appeared since April 1895.[138] Jodko and Jędrzejowski had cultivated good relations with the SPD, and the Union now had an energetic representative in Paris.

It was to these German connections that London turned first. As Jędrzejowski wrote to Kelles-Krauz, " . . . we must be sure about the Germans . . . Then, and only then, will we ask you to take care of the French."[139] London submitted the resolution to Wilhelm Liebknecht (1826–1900), who along with August Bebel (1840–1913) had founded the German party. The text of the resolution that they showed him read:

> Considering, that the oppression of one nation by another can only lie in the interests of capitalists, and harms equally the working people of both Polish nationality and within the oppressing state; That in particular Russian tsarism, drawing its internal and external strength from the submission and division of Poland, is a constant threat to the international development of the working class movement; The Congress declares, that the independence of Poland is a political demand equally necessary for the whole international working class as it is for the Polish working class itself.[140]

That the resolution specified Russia, and not Germany and Austria, was no accident.[141] Liebknecht endorsed the resolution.[142]

Liebknecht was of an older generation of German socialists, and his views on Polish independence had been formed by personal contact with Marx and Engels.[143] Much has been written about Marx's and Engels's views on Poland, so a few lines of summary should suffice here.[144] Marx understood Polish independence chiefly as an issue of international politics. He agreed with Bismarck that Poland and Prussia could not exist side by side, and hoped to destroy Prussia in order to save Germany for democracy.[145] Poland should also be rebuilt to serve as a barrier to Russia, whose power slowed the progress of Europe.[146] Poles were up to the task, for unlike smaller Slavic nationalities, they were a "historic nation," with a political tradition and revolutionary consciousness.[147]

Marx and Engels also thought Polish independence necessary to the advancement of socialism, for two reasons. First, workers of a nation that oppressed others could be distracted from their class interests by nationalist propaganda.[148] Second, independence was a basic precondition to meaningful political change in Poland, and thus for Poland to play its progressive role in international politics. Engels compared Polish socialists who opposed Polish independence to German socialists so foolish as to oppose the repeal of Bismarck's anti-socialist law.[149] According to Engels, the foreign policy of the proletariat should be expressed "in two words: rebuild Poland."[150] The First Socialist International had been founded, in part, as a protest against Russian suppression of the 1863 Polish rising, and Marx and Engels had seen to it that the First International officially supported Polish independence.[151]

There is no hint of materialism in these arguments, and there was thus a certain tension between Marx's and Engels's recommendations about Poland, and the method of materialist analysis which socialist theorists of the 1890s took to be Marx's most important legacy. His arguments concerning Poland could therefore be interpreted in at least four ways. First, socialists could (as Liebknecht did) simply take them at face value. A German, Liebknecht was more alert to the Russian danger than to the Prussian, and understood Polish independence as a way to weaken the tsar. In fairness, Marx and (especially) Engels wavered on the question as to whether an independent Poland should include German territory. Toward the end of his life, Engels advised the SPD not to allow Polish independence to weaken Germany.[152] Second, socialists could decide that Marx's conclusions about Poland were simply out-dated, without coming to any strongly held position based upon Marx's methods of analysis (which is not to say that they did not have opinions about Poland drawn from other sources). With the exception of Liebknecht, this was the position of most leading German socialists.[153] Third, socialists could choose to use Marx's methods against the master's conclusions. Rosa Luxemburg wrote to Jogiches that she wished to "out-Marx Marx" on the Polish question, arguing that trends in economic history guaranteed Poland's demise.[154] Fourth, Kelles-Krauz thought it possible to accept Marx's conclusions about the independence of Poland, bolstering them with "Marxist" arguments.

London thought that Marx's legacy, embodied in Liebknecht, would suffice to get the support of the SPD, and thus of the International. With Liebknecht on board, London sent Kelles-Krauz among the French, where (according to his own understanding of the issue) he would try to explain the class character of the PPS program. Kelles-Krauz's efforts set off an international debate in which all four of these positions were represented.

Sommes-nous patriotes?

Confident of German support, London and Kelles-Krauz agreed upon a two-part approach to the French. First, the occasion of the tenth anniversary of the execution of four members of Proletariat (28 January 1896) was to be used to portray the PPS as the sole inheritor of Proletariat's legacy, and to propagate the PPS program of Polish independence.[155] This effort turned into a fiasco even before it began.

The Paris Section, as foreigners, could not legally sponsor a public political meeting, and so turned to a group of Guesdists for help. At the last preparatory meeting held by the Paris Section and these Guesdists, Warszawski and Urbach (both loyal to the SDKP) appeared, and Warszawski demanded that he be allowed to speak at the meeting the following day. The French replied that the gathering was to be public, that anyone could speak. Warszawski answered that he had wanted to be reassured, because he feared that the PPS would try to prevent him from taking the floor. Kelles-Krauz replied that Warszawski represented a fictional party, which made his charges that the PPS was the usurper all the worse. Warszawski replied that the PPS were "patriots." One of the French replied that the PPS were evidently "internationalists," for they had sent a telegram to the last Guesdist congress in Ramilly. Kelles-Krauz had indeed sent such a telegram, expressly thanking the Guesdists for supporting the cause of an independent Poland as in the interest of the international working class.[156]

Kelles-Krauz's diplomacy seemed to have worked. But then Warszawski stunned Kelles-Krauz: he asked the Guesdists if they knew that the Paris Section had published a pamphlet which condemned Guesde for not accepting the tactics of Allemane and Nieuwenhuis. Kelles-Krauz responded that members of the Union may have various views about various parts of the Guesdist program, casually mentioning that he himself opposed the Guesdist agrarian program, but that the Union as such does not take positions on internal French questions. The French accepted this explanation, and preparations for the meeting continued.[157] Kelles-Krauz escaped by a hair. Warszawski did not have a copy of "Class Character," so he could not point to the words "published with the approval of the Paris Section of the Union of Polish Socialists Abroad." He had asked for one from a member of the Paris Section earlier in the day,[158] so he must have been planning this line of attack: but not planning it far enough in advance to get a copy from Luxemburg, Jogiches, or Marchlewski. It was Kelles-Krauz's good fortune that of the four most important intellectuals associated with the former SDKP, the one who happened to be in Paris was also the one without a copy of "Class Character."

Still, Kelles-Krauz was confronted with the danger he had brought to his own party by so freely criticizing European socialist parties. He had chosen to identify himself—repeatedly, and in no uncertain terms—with the Allemanists in "Class Character"; that is, with one of the many fractions of French socialism. Without venturing too far into the thicket of nineteenth-century French socialist politics, we may note that Allemane and his followers joined Paul Brousse when the latter broke with Guesde's Parti Ouvrier in 1882 to form the "possibilists." Then, in 1890 Allemane broke with Brousse to found his own Parti Ouvrier Socialiste Révolutionnaire.[159] Allemane, though accepting the need for some political action, was best known as an advocate of the general strike. The Guesdists opposed the general strike, and this was one of the main programmatic divides between the two groups. The two parties got along very poorly: as Kelles-Krauz noted, Allemane would not speak at a meeting sponsored by the Guesdists, as a result of the "cat and dog" relations between the two groups.[160]

The Paris Section clearly needed the Guesdists' help—for the gathering planned for the next day, to take the example at hand. In general, if Kelles-Krauz was to have any hope of convincing French Marxists to support the PPS resolution on Polish independence, he would have to start with Guesde himself. Guesde was not only the leader of the largest French socialist party, but also one of the founders of French Marxism as such.[161] Faced with the enormity of the political damage that his pamphlet might have caused, Kelles-Krauz admitted his mistake. He accepted that the language of the pamphlet had been too strong, and treated the whole issue as historical. A year before, Kelles-Krauz's major goal had been to publicize "Class Character"; he now accepted that "Class Character" should never see the light of day. Warszawski's behavior, in publicizing a document that he knew that Union wished kept secret, infuriated Kelles-Krauz, who considered it a violation of the ethical principles obligating socialists.[162] The episode thus turned Kelles-Krauz toward London in two distinct ways: the "Class Character" issue was buried for good, and Kelles-Krauz's suspicion that the Luxemburg and her cohorts were ethically suspect was confirmed.

The meeting itself, held 28 January, was also a failure. None of the non-Polish socialists explicitly supported Polish independence. Warszawski, as promised, rose to speak, and claimed that Polish workers did not want independence, and that the SDKP was the legitimate inheritor of the

Proletariat legacy. In the protests that ensued, the French socialist Gerault-Richaud tried to restore order by calling out that "we all know that there are two Polish socialist fractions."[163] The Blanquist Édouard Vaillant, in his speech, alluded to the need of Polish socialists to make peace with one another. As the purpose of the meeting had been to publicise the PPS as the sole legitimate Polish socialist party, Kelles-Krauz could only understand these remarks by French socialists to mean that the meeting had failed.

In effect, Warszawski had singlehandedly countered all of the Paris Section's careful planning by a single speech in bad French, and had almost succeeded the day prior in discrediting the Paris Section before the Guesdists. Kelles-Krauz wanted to call Warszawski before a court of honor, before realizing that no Pole could objectively judge the case, and that no non-Pole could understand it. (Motz did him one better, challenging Warszawski to a duel.) Kelles-Krauz ended up breaking with Warszawski in a formal letter, "which our hitherto cordial relations demanded,"[164] and condemning him in the next issue of Przedświt. In that same article, he roundly criticized the French: though they called themselves internationalists, they knew little about political conditions in other countries, and were therefore unable to judge the claims of the PPS and SDKP.[165]

Despite this failure in Paris, the PPS did make some use of the tenth anniversary of the Proletariat executions elsewhere. At a meeting in Zurich, Plekhanov spoke for Polish independence, and in London a group of leading British and German socialists (including Eduard Bernstein) endorsed the PPS's proposed resolution.[166] London and Kelles-Krauz thus had some reason to hope that the second phase of their plan to gain French support might bear fruit.

London planned to publish a special May Day pamphlet, containing endorsements of Polish independence from leaders of other European socialist parties. To Kelles-Krauz fell the task of collecting articles from French socialists. In January, Kelles-Krauz (using the pseudonym Louis Radian) contacted Jean Allemane, Jean Jaurès, Jules Guesde, Alexandre Millerand, and Gustave Rouanet.[167] "Radian" repeatedly visited these five and other prominent French socialists in January and February, and made slow progress.[168] When Kelles-Krauz presented the project to socialists whom he knew personally, such as Dubreuilh and Vaillant, he learned that Rosa Luxemburg had been intriguing against him and the PPS. Kelles-Krauz regularly sent the Bulletin to Vaillant, and had always found him to support the PPS program.[169] On this occasion, however, Kelles-Krauz had to undo the damage caused by Luxemburg, who had told Vaillant that the PPS only represented a handful of Poles.[170]

On 15 March, unnerved by Guesde's long silence, Kelles-Krauz paid him a visit. The leader of France's largest socialist party surprised Kelles-Krauz by declaring that under no circumstances would he write anything for the May Day pamphlet. In 1893, Kelles-Krauz's social democrats had organized a meeting in which Guesde had spoken publicly for Polish independence,[171] but in 1896 Guesde was exasperated and baffled by the quarrel between the SDKP and the PPS, and had decided to opt out. As he explained to Kelles-Krauz, his party organ had printed articles by the PPS, and the SDKP had demanded a reply. Guesde decided not to allow a polemic. Then, after *Petite République* covered the Proletariat commemoration of 28 January,[172] Cezaryna Wojnarowska of the SDKP gave him a scolding.[173] She told him that he should at least be neutral in his coverage, and that the PPS were just patriots. Guesde had decided that he would not once more side with the PPS by writing for the May Day pamphlet.

Kelles-Krauz told Guesde that he would have to take a stand on Polish independence soon anyway, since the PPS were going to present a resolution about it at the London Congress. Guesde had not known this, as Alexandre Zévaès, entrusted to present the resolution to the directing council of the *Parti Ouvrier Français*, had not done so. Guesde's first reaction was astonishment: "But that's impossible! The International cannot pass anything like that, cannot remake the map of Europe. If governments took the resolution seriously, it would only have one result: a renewal of the holy alliance of three emperors against Poland, which we consider to be extremely dangerous for European socialism."[174] (Such a "renewal of the holy alliance" would also have meant the end of the Franco-Russian alliance.)

Guesde's other concern was that the PPS would mount a national revolt immediately after the resolution's passage, and be crushed. Kelles-Krauz assured Guesde that the PPS would only start a rising when the time was right: when Russia was reforming, or when revolutions in more westerly countries prepared the way. Kelles-Krauz also emphasized that the new independent state was for the workers, not the other way around. After this meeting, Kelles-Krauz wrote London that he was surprised to learn that Wojnarowska held such sway over Guesde and Paul Lafargue.[175] Jędrzejowski responded that Kelles-Krauz's Allemanist orientation (as revealed in "Class Consciousness") was the main cause of Guesde's reluctance.[176] Here Golde came to Kelles-Krauz's defense, saying that if that had been the reason, Guesde would have said so, as he does not mince words; that Guesde knew nothing about "Class Character"; and that Wojnarowska was a family friend of Guesde's, especially close to his wife.[177]

In the end Guesde wrote a short letter for the May Day pamphlet, though it said not a word about the PPS or its program. Other letters from French socialists were also disappointing. Allemane likewise made no mention of Polish independence. Louis Dubreuilh mentioned the cruelty of the partitions, but the main thrust of his article was the international unity of socialist parties. Jaurès went slightly further, writing that the PPS was right to "strive for national goals while giving evidence of [its] international character." Vaillant wrote that he did not know if independence and socialism were consistent goals, but that he hoped that they were. The Russian Petr Lavrov wrote that the existence of separate programs for separate socialist parties hurt the movement overall. Pavel Axelrod, another Russian, wrote that the role of Russian and Polish workers was to prevent tsarist reaction after a revolution in western Europe. London did get very supportive letters from two older German socialists, Liebknecht and the "red postman" Jules Motteler. The Italian Marxist Antonio Labriola wrote the best (for the PPS's purposes) letter of all, endorsing the PPS as the only Polish socialist party, and supporting its goal of Polish independence.[178]

The May Day pamphlet was thus a mild success. Though London did not intend this result, it also began a multisided debate over the issue of Polish independence in the European socialist press. London and Kelles-Krauz, though they had arranged for the resolution to be presented to various party leaders and directing bodies, had intended to publicize it only after propaganda based on the May Day pamphlet had created the perception of general support among socialists for Polish independence. But just as Warszawski had caused the Proletariat commemoration in January to fail, and Wojnarowska reduced the usefulness for the PPS of French socialists' contributions to the May Day pamphlet, Luxemburg brought the resolution into the public eye. She had read the text of the PPS resolution in the 14 February 1896 edition of Allemane's journal *Parti Ouvrier*.[179] (Kelles-Krauz had given Allemane the resolution when asking him to write for the May Day pamphlet, specifically asking him not to publish it. Allemane forgot, and did.[180]) Once again, work of Kelles-Krauz's had become known to Luxemburg in an unexpected way, and this time she exploited the opportunity.

On April 29 and 6 May, she published in two parts a long article on Polish independence in *Die Neue Zeit*, edited by Karl Kautsky and thought to express the SPD line.[181] The article was ostensibly a reply to a short note in the first number of the *Bulletin*, which had stated that the German and Austrian branches of Polish socialism supported the PPS program of independence. She claimed that they did not, pointing out that Polish independence does not appear in either party's program.[182] Writing that she would not "consider here in depth" the *Bulletin's* justifications for Polish independence in a socialist program she dismissed them summarily: "One note should suffice: they are based on purely utopian grounds and have nothing at all in common with social democracy." Luxemburg could read French and write German, but here she was taking advantage of the fact that few readers of *Die Neue Zeit* would also know the *Bulletin*. She added a now familiar argument: that if Polish workers were strong enough to gain independence, they would be strong enough to start a revolution. She cleverly appealed to German national pride: support of Polish national independence could only weaken the international movement, because a united Poland would weaken the German and Austrian parties.[183]

Polendebatten

The gauntlet had been thrown down. Jędrzejowskfs plan to avoid the "scandal" that would arise if a Polish socialist spoke out against the resolution had already failed—three months before the London congress. Because the Union and PPS had not expected Luxemburg's article, and had not known that she had access to *Die Neue Zeit*, they were already on the defensive. Fortunately for the PPS, the May Day pamphlet also gained a dedicated friend for the PPS program in Antonio Labriola. Labriola (1843–1904), a professor at Rome from 1874, had introduced Marxism to Italy, and helped to found the Italian Socialist Party in 1892.[184] He was old enough to recall Marx's and Engels' support of Polish independence. Unlike most Marxists of his day, he considered the nation to be an irreducible historical reality, and thus had his own reasons for believing that socialism would be achieved by nation-states.[185]

Labriola's enthusiastic letter for the May Day pamphlet encouraged Jędrzejowski to write to him for help on 28 April. That was a day prior to the appearance of the first Luxemburg article, and at first Jędrzejowski simply wanted Labriola's help in gaining the support of Italian socialists.[186] Luxemburg's article altered the situation, and Labriola's offer to use his connections among the Austrians and French was much appreciated. The tepid and uncomprehending response that his sincere and devoted efforts elicited from the Italians, French, and Austrians was a further reason for pessimism in London.

Labriola warned London that the Italians, a young Marxist party, were utopian internationalists.[187] When Labriola wrote to Filippo Turati, the leader of Italian socialism, he received the discouraging reply that Turati knew nothing about Poland.[188] Worse, Italian socialists had seen the Luxemburg article, and had simply accepted it as the view of *Die Neue Zeit,* and thus of orthodox Marxism.[189] Only five or six Italian socialists read German, noted Labriola, and they all took *Die Neue Zeit* as gospel.[190] He did not give up: he sent an article of his own in favor of the resolution to *Critica Sociale,* the Italian socialist organ. He wrote that argument in favor of the resolution should be unnecessary, as all socialists remembered Marx's and the First International's advocacy of Polish independence, and understood the danger posed by tsarist Russia. He endorsed the PPS as the unified Polish socialist party, and the only one with domestic support.[191] The editors of *Critica Sociale* placed the article, but included their own commentary. They compared Russian imperialism to Italian revanchism over Trieste (!): socialists have a position on the matter, but it is not an issue of the first importance. They appealed to an argument in Luxemburg's article: when the proletariat is strong enough to gain independence, it will also be strong enough to start the revolution. They closed with a call for Polish socialists to join the parties of the partitioning states,[192] and invited Luxemburg to comment on Labriola's article.[193]

Noting this unfavorable reaction, Labriola told London on 19 May to write a letter explaining the PPS resolution in French to Gregario Agnini, cofounder of the Italian Socialist party and secretary of the socialist fraction in parliament.[194] This task was delegated to Kelles-Krauz.[195] Kelles-Krauz sent a project for the letter back to London on 26 May. In the draft letter, Kelles-Krauz assures Italian socialists that Polish workers want independence, and that those Poles who oppose independence are émigrés, out of touch with domestic realities. He argues that socialism can only advance when Poles have their own republic, and adds that a Polish bulwark against tsarism will help socialism's cause in the rest of Europe. He concludes by saying that Polish socialists' first desire is that their program be acclaimed as internationalist and for the workers of Europe to demand a free Poland. "After all this has been cleared up," he writes,

> how splendid and inspiring will be the moment when the work-
> ers of all countries of the world will proclaim: "Vive la République

Polonaise indépendante!" For that will mean that the socialist proletariat is the defender of freedom, justice, and human dignity;
that the blood of all the Polish revolutionaries who have struggled
throughout the century for the freedom of Europe has created solidarity among the oppressed; but most of all it will mean a declaration of war upon the tsar . . . [196]

Whether this would have changed Agnini's mind is unknown, as London
did not comment on the project, and no letter was ever sent to Agnini.[197]
The Italians had been given up for lost.

Labriola had no better luck with the French; from the very beginning he had warned London that they were Russophiles.[198] He explained
the issue in early May to his friend Georges Sorel in Paris,[199] who was
then engaged in explaining his own version of Marxism on the pages of
Devenir Social.[200] Sorel agreed to do his best, and London arranged for him
to meet with Kelles-Krauz.[201] But Sorel's reports back to Rome were not
encouraging. His first view was that it was unlikely that the French would
understand the resolution.[202] After some work, he reported that French
socialists thought that there were already too many Slavic groups in Paris,
and that the resolution would only increase their number.[203] By the end
of May, Sorel concluded that the resolution would have no chance among
the French, and passed on the advice of Gabriel Deville not to present the
resolution at the London congress.[204]

Labriola likewise made no progress with the Austrians. He had written
to Viktor Adler in early May, asking him to write in favor of the Polish resolution.[205] Unlike the French and Italians, Adler knew something about
the Polish question. Polish socialists in Austria, led by his friend Ignacy
Daszyński, constituted an important part of his own party—and power
base. Both Adler and Daszyński thus had dual loyalties, which Kelles-
Krauz's resolution revealed.[206] The fate of the resolution at the congress
of Austrian social democracy in Prague in April 1896 is a case in point.
Daszyński did present the PPS resolution at the Austrian party congress
in April in Prague, as requested by London; but did so on the last day of
the congress, when there was no time left for discussion. The resolution
was thus neither discussed nor voted, and Austrian social democracy took
no official position. Daszyński had asked Adler to raise the question himself, but apparently took the hint when Adler declined. To have put the
issue to discussion would have raised the question—in principle—as to
whether Austrian social democracy supported national independence for

nationalities within multinational empires. Adler surely did not want that discussion to take place.

Adler's control of his multinational and increasingly decentralized party was based partly on Daszyński's loyalty. At the same time, given rising Czech separatism, he did not want to officially grant the Poles something he might later wish to deny the Czechs.[207] Still, Adler led a party whose very uniting principle was the autonomy of its constituent national parties, and he would go some distance to satisfy his Polish client. At Daszyński's request, he wrote to Kautsky to protest the Luxemburg article. With Daszyński, he also responded to it in his *Arbeiter-Zeitung*. When the article appeared, however, it was under the byline of a prominent member of Daszyński's party (and editor of its organ *Naprzód*), Emil Haecker.[208] Moreover, the article was more of a diplomatic effort than a direct polemic against Luxemburg: it noted that the PPS was now the only Polish socialist party; assured readers that the PPS had always cooperated with other European socialist parties; and claimed that the resolution had international support, without actually giving substantial reasons why any non-Pole should support it.[209] Adler wrote nothing further on the resolution, and declined to print Labriola's article, motivating his response by his assessment that the Polish resolution had taken on a complicated ("verwickelt") character.[210] His own attitude is revealed in the letter he wrote to Kautsky, on 13 May. He called Luxemburg's article "extremely untimely" and her views "doctrinaire," and asked Kautsky to let him vet her articles before they were published in *Die Neue Zeit*, because they were fragmenting his party. He feared that "the unnecessary but harmless Polish resolution in London may, thanks to her, blow up into an affair . . . "[211]

The lukewarm response to the May pamphlet and Labriola's discouraging letters pushed London back to its German patron. In early June, Liebknecht agreed to write an article for *Vorwärts*, the Berlin daily that served as an SPD organ; to speak in favor of the resolution at the forthcoming congress; and to try to sway the French during a coming trip to Paris. He said that the German party was intent on passing the resolution as a protest against the Franco-Russian alliance.[212] But just as Liebknecht arrived in Paris, Luxemburg complicated the state of play by presenting a "counter-resolution" in her *Sprawa Robotnicza*. She had come to Paris to publish two issues of the journal (which had not appeared for over a year), in order to ensure herself a mandate at the coming congress; and to work against the PPS resolution. Her counter-resolution issue of *Sprawa Robotnicza* thus killed two birds with one stone, and gave her friends in

Paris, Warszawski, and Wojnarowska a clear focus for their efforts to persuade French socialists to vote against the PPS motion.

Rosa Luxemburg's resolution, which was distributed to French socialists in the first half of June, stated that national oppression would only
disappear with the collapse of capitalism, that emphasizing national differences could only weaken the international solidarity of the proletariat,
and that naming Polish independence as a goal of international socialism
would draw the world's workers into a series of hopeless national battles.
Kelles-Krauz was unable to get articles opposing the counter-resolution
published in French journals. Guesde, who had promised to take Kelles-
Krauz to the national council of his party, neglected to do so. Kelles-Krauz
wrote to London at the end of June that Liebknecht's visit seemed not to have
had any effect. He added that the PPS had enemies among the Guesdists,
and could hope for no support from the internationalist Allemanists and
Blanquists.[213] Luxemburg agreed: "All of France is ours!"[214]

The SDKP even tried to win Liebknecht over to its counter-resolution.
Instead of responding with, "Noch ist Polen nicht verloren," his toast a few
days before in London,[215] he told Warszawski that he "did not want to get
involved in our [intra-Polish] affairs."[216] Though a far cry from the support
of the PPS resolution he had promised in London, this was also not the
response the SDKP wanted. As the congress neared, the SDKP got almost
exactly the same response from Vaillant. Luxemburg had reason to expect
his full support, and had come with a copy of the counter-resolution ready
for him to sign. Instead of doing so, he warned that he wanted to "avoid a
Polish discussion at the congress."[217] Vaillant was a left-wing French socialist from the syndicalist tradition; Liebknecht had been a friend and dis-
ciple of Marx and one of the founders of the SPD. But both were to sit on
the political commission at the London congress, and thus were to have
the job of submitting political resolutions that the congress could pass
unanimously. For all their disagreements, Luxemburg and Kelles-Krauz
both assumed that the issue of Polish independence was of crucial importance to international socialism, and that it would be decided on its merits. Neither took into account that congresses of the Second International
were more spectacle than substance, and that spectacles require careful
choreography. Liebknecht and Vaillant, feeling their responsibility, were
practicing their steps.

In July Kelles-Krauz rejoined the press debate he had begun. Though
he had been working furiously on the *Bulletin*, publishing five issues in
the ten months prior to the congress, his articles did not respond directly

to Luxemburg's. In Paris, cut off from *Die Neue Zeit*, he only read the
Luxemburg and "Haecker" articles on 19 July.[218] At this point in his life,
he read German but could not write it. Anything he had tried to write for
a major European socialist journal would have been reviewed by London,
which would have made timely responses even more difficult. In any event,
London did not ask him to write against Luxemburg. Piłsudski, then staying in London in preparation for the congress, appreciated that the appeal
of Luxemburg's articles was that they spoke the language of socialism,[219]
but it apparently did not occur him to ask the PPS's leading Marxist to try
a reply. Kelles-Krauz had difficulty enough getting London's permission
to print articles in his own journal. Since March,[220] he had been planning
to respond to French doubts about the resolution in a long article for the
Bulletin, entitled "Sommes-nous patriotes au sens propre du mot?," but
could not persuade Piłsudski that it should be published.[221]

The article presents the PPS program quite simply, "because we have
not been sufficiently understood by some of our friends abroad." It first
argues, following Engels, that one of the proletariat's first needs is political
rights. It then claims, following Lassalle, that the constitution of a given
country flows from the distribution of social forces in that country. Poland
is more industrially advanced than Russia, and thus when tsarism col-
lapses would be best served by its own constitution. The PPS supports
the Russians in their efforts to gain a constitution, but understands that
effort as preparation for its own claim to independence. If, he continues,
revolution in western Europe were to precede the fall of the tsar, the PPS
would become a barrier to tsarist reaction. He accepts that the program of
independence has drawn a few non-socialists into the party, but points out
that non-socialists are to be found in French parties as well.[222]

Polish independence is thus analogous to demands for a republic in
Germany and Italy, and for general suffrage in Belgium or Austria. It is
the political program which best meets the necessary uncertainty of all
politics. Here Kelles-Krauz is once again responding to Luxemburg's
argument, which he no doubt heard repeated in Paris, that a working
class strong enough to gain national independence would also be strong
enough to start a revolution. He argues that no Pole can be certain when
independence will come, just as no Austrian can know when his party will
win national elections. Political programs are not simply what we desire,
but also a means of preparing for all eventualities. Naming national independence as a goal of Polish socialism is the best way for Polish workers
to prepare themselves to make the most of independence.[223] London did

not allow this text to be published, perhaps fearing that even the mention of a Russian constitution could only divide the party. Jędrzejowski (though not Jodko, as we shall see) also believed that the strike of 40,000 Russian textile workers in Petersburg in June had undermined arguments about Polish exceptionalism within the Russian Empire.[224]

Kelles-Krauz ended up publishing an amended version of the article in July. By then, his frustration with French "internationalism" and French ignorance of Polish political reality showed clearly through his appeal:

> The socialists of every country often declare that if their country were suddenly to be invaded, they would resolutely defend its independence. Suppose that France were divided up between England, Germany, and Italy, victorious invaders—is there any doubt that the first objective of French socialists would be the reconstitution of France, and that in the absence of that reconstitution the progress of socialism would be stopped, or at least slowed in the annexed provinces? Many socialists proudly declare their sympathy for Cretans and Cubans, for people who, without waiting for the complete collapse of capitalism, are taking advantage of favorable circumstances to end their oppression and exploitation under a foreign conqueror. And yet when the PPS declares in its program that the first goal of its political struggle is the constitution of an Independent Democratic Polish Republic, there are people—unlikely as it may seem—who fail to understand, and call it the patriotism of the antisocialist and contrary to internationalism.[225]

He repeated the arguments about Poland's superiority to Russia, and about how a Polish proletariat prepared for independence would be best able to shape the constitution of a future Poland.[226]

Unlike Kelles-Krauz, Luxemburg could write in German, and was subordinate to no party. She could quickly counter whatever the PPS could place in German journals. By 1 July she had responded to the weak "Haecker" article with a second effort of her own in *Die Neue Zeit*.[227] Unlike her first, this article made no pretensions of concerning anything but Kelles-Krauz's resolution. It demolished the "Haecker" article, pointing out that it had not answered her arguments about the impossibility of creating new nation-states before the revolution, and about the risk of attracting patriots into socialist parties. (These arguments had been answered by Kelles-Krauz, but in French in the *Bulletin*, rather than in German in *Die Neue*

Zeit.) She then attacked the resolution sentence by sentence. Against the resolution's first claim ("Considering, that the oppression of one nation by another can only lie in the interests of capitalists and despots, and harms equally the working people of both Polish nationality and within the oppressing state"), she argued that noting that something is bad does not mean it can be changed. As to the second ("That in particular Russian tsarism, drawing its internal and external strength from the submission and division of Poland, is a constant threat to the international development of the working class movement"), she claimed that Russia's strength came from elsewhere. Against the resolution's conclusion ("The Congress declares, that the independence and autonomy of Poland is a political demand equally necessary for the whole international working class as it is for the Polish working class itself"), she argued that workers could not gain independence, and that the congress would lose credibility if it chose to support Polish independence. The kind of thinking which so frustrated Kelles-Krauz, and which seemed to work so well among European socialists, is evident. Political change is understood as sudden and radical, and there is thus no need to point out intermediate goals (such as national independence) or to emphasize any suffering aside from economic woe (such as tsarist national and political oppression).

From London, Jodko tried and failed to place a reply in Kautsky's *Die Neue Zeit*. While Luxemburg and Kautsky were on good terms, the PPS had to rely on the mediation of Liebknecht. But Kautsky and Liebknecht had never been particularly friendly, and Kautsky thought that the older man had nothing to offer on theoretical questions.[228] Jodko did eventually place the article in *Vorwärts*, with Liebknecht's help.[229] It focused on the history of the Polish movement, explaining that Polish socialists had opted for independence after the Russian movement had collapsed. Luxemburg was able to place a reply in *Vorwärts* at the end of July, just before the congress. What was worse for the PPS, Jodko's article provoked the Russian Marxist Georgii Plekhanov, heretofore a friend of the PPS, to an angry response. His article, which appeared in *Vorwärts* on 23 July, was an expression of national defensiveness.[230] Plekhanov took the side of Russian workers against Polish workers, pointing to the recent strike. Without seeming to notice that he was doing so, he judged the strengths of socialist movements according to their patriotism, arguing that Russian workers had national feelings as strong or stronger than those of the Poles. This article dealt yet another powerful blow to PPS hopes: the PPS had unintentionally yielded Plekhanov's influence to Luxemburg.[231] Plekhanov was not only influential among the Russians, but among the French as well. As Kelles-Krauz had written to London, the French understood support by Germans and Austrians for the resolution as emanating from a desire to embarrass French socialists about the Franco-Russian alliance, but support from the leading Russian socialist thinker had been persuasive.[232]

Finis Poloniae?

Though PPS attempts to counter Luxemburg in *Die Neue Zeit* failed or backfired, she did not have the last word on its pages. Kautsky did not publish Jodko's reply to Luxemburg, but he was preparing his own. From letters he had received from Labriola and Adler he knew that he had allowed Luxemburg to create an "affair" by giving her access to his journal. The arguments that had been raging since April had guaranteed that the PPS resolution could no longer be seen as "unnecessary but harmless." Its passage would indeed send a clear signal, if not to "the whole civilized world" (as Kelles-Krauz had foreseen), then at least to European socialists.

For European socialists, Polish independence was a troublesome topic. The cream of the SPD, the writers of its program, Bernstein and Kautsky, and its founders, Liebknecht and Bebel, had all at one time or another shown some support, in some (usually very attenuated) form, for an independent Poland. But they were a decided minority amongst party activists and workers.[233] Ignaz Auer (who, like Bebel and Liebknecht, was a member of the SPD's directing council, or Vorstand), spoke for the majority when he identified Polish independence with the loss of German territory.[234]

When a Polish socialist asked Bebel in 1892 for an article supporting Polish independence, he had replied: I support Polish independence, the European proletariat will bring it, but please do not print this letter as I do not wish to start arguments within the SPD.[235] Since the mid-1880s his attitude toward the Polish question had been determined by his fear of war with Russia. He hoped to ensure the loyalty of Poles in such a war by preserving their rights within the Second Empire, but could not counsel the loss of the Reich's buffer zone in the east.[236] By the mid-1890s, he was concerned to protect the integrity of the Austrian Empire as a barrier to Russian expansion, which gave him another reason to oppose Polish independence before the advent of socialism.[237] In 1896 his main goal was to avoid a Polish debate,[238] and he was unresponsive from the first to PPS overtures.[239]

Eduard Bernstein demonstrated the path that a German socialist might follow as the Polish resolution changed from a gesture to a serious matter. In February 1896 he had signed the PPS resolution in London,[240] but in July he rejected it in Paris.[241] Even Liebknecht, the PPS's best hope, followed a similar road: though in June he had promised London to write for *Vorwärts,* speak for the resolution at the congress, and try to persuade the French, he failed to do the first two,[242] and in all likelihood the third as well.

The Austrian case is similar, with the additional complication that the Austrian party was itself effectively a federation of national parties. Though Adler had presented himself as a friend to Poland since the founding of the PPS, he had other constituents against whose separatism he had to be on guard.[243] At the same time, he had no desire to take a firm stand against self-determination, partly on principle, and partly so as not to anger Daszyński and the Poles. But once again, of the Germans within the Austrian party, Adler was among the most supportive of Poland; most others, like German workers in Austria, were openly patriotic.

France is a different case, partly because geography lent French reflections about Poland a certain abstract character; partly because the Franco-Russian alliance was a relief to a political class (even on the left) frightened by the loss of Alsace and Lorraine; partly because Marxism was a newer implant;[244] partly because no Marxist party had subdued the trade unions;[245] and partly because French socialism was divided. Most French socialists most of the time did not understand the Polish resolution, for they were ostentatiously anti-patriotic and generally anti-parliamentarian. For Polish socialists like Kelles-Krauz, living under Russian tsarism, bourgeois democracy looked like a stage on the way to socialism. French socialists, living within a bourgeois democracy, were inclined to see their present political system as the antithesis of the future socialist order, and to regard all "bourgeois" political issues with indifference. (A few years later, Guesde and Lafargue were to abstain in the Dreyfus affair.) Ignorance of political conditions in other countries, combined with abstract internationalism, allowed French national interest to be confused with the interest of the international working class. As one Polish socialist then living in Paris remembered, after the Franco-Russian alliance was signed in 1891, French socialists had even more difficulty distinguishing between the political situation of Russians and Poles.[246] Guesde understood the resolution chiefly as a threat to the existing European order, to "stability" as we might say today.

Even so, no important European socialist leader or major socialist party had an interest in seeing the PPS resolution fail completely, or in seeing Luxemburg's counter-resolution pass. The PPS was a small party, and not internationally prominent. Nonetheless, Russian, German, and Austrian (if not French) socialists knew full well that it was the representative of socialism within the Russian partition of Poland. Without some good reason, they were not inclined to declare the program of a fraternal party illegitimate, which an outright rejection of the resolution would have signified. Luxemburg had all of the advantages of a lone intellectual while campaigning against Keiles-Krauz's resolution; but in the end the PPS was a party, and counted as such. Moreover, Luxemburg was not yet an important figure in the SPD, and she was openly disliked by Bebel, Adler, and Plekhanov.[247] Bebel and Adler blamed Luxemburg for beginning the *Polendebatten,* and had no wish to encourage her. In a word, some kind of compromise was needed, a compromise that could cover party leaders' previous verbal and moral commitments to Poland (and in Adler's case, responsibility to Polish clients) without obligating them to offend their constituents; a compromise which could save the PPS from an embarrassing defeat, without obligating the Second International to endorse the PPS program.

Kautsky's "Finis Poloniae?" is an attempt, by the most influential socialist theorist of the day, to find such a compromise.[248] Appearing a single week after Luxemburg's second article in *Die Neue Zeit,* and two weeks before the beginning of the London congress, it was in effect (if not quite in fact) the last word in the debate. Kautsky began by pointing out areas of agreement with Luxemburg. He agreed that Poland had lost the international importance it once had. It was no longer Europe's revolutionary country *par excellence,* nor was it the only bulwark against tsarism. Writing shortly after the strike of Russian workers, he believed Petersburg to be more important than Warsaw. Russian workers were also suffering and struggling under tsarism, so naming the Poles as victims of tsarist oppression (as the PPS resolution did) was unfair to the Russians. More, singling out the Poles as deserving national independence would set an unfair precedent for special treatment.

At the same time, Kautsky continued, the fact that Polish independence was not a task of the first importance for the international working class did not mean that it could not be part of the program of a Polish socialist party. Here he disagreed with Luxemburg, and leaned toward Kelles-Krauz's understanding of politics: political programs are not what we expect from a given social order, but what we demand. He also agreed with Kelles-Krauz that there was some chance that Poland would gain its independence before the socialist revolution. In Kautsky's model, Polish independence was a likely result of revolution in Russia, and was therefore tactically subordinate to the revolutionary efforts of parties within the Russian state. Thus his conclusion: Polish independence should be supported, insofar as doing so does not conflict with the interests of the international proletariat. There is no natural harmony between the two, nor is there any necessary discord. He thus opposed both the Kelles-Krauz and the Luxemburg resolutions, while supporting the right of the PPS to strive for Polish independence. This was the compromise position available when the congress began on 27 July.[249]

The London Congress

It would be a mistake, however, to tie the London congress's verdict on Polish independence too closely to argumentation carried out beforehand. The congress was dominated by the struggle between parliamentarians on one side, and anarchists and syndicalists on the other. It was indeed a struggle: voices were raised, chairs were hurled, delegates were expelled, a translator threw a speaker down a flight of stairs. On the very first day, the Englishman presiding threatened to call the police to restore order.[250] The British press amused its readers with accounts of the inability of aspirants to European power to run a trilingual conference. Also, none of the three great protagonists of the *Polendebatten*, Kautsky, Luxemburg, and Kelles-Krauz, played any significant role in the congress's proceedings. Neither Kautsky nor Kelles-Krauz attended. Kelles-Krauz had begged off from the very beginning, despite invitations from London. He gave two reasons. First, travelling to London would reveal his identity to the agents sure to be present there, and thus foreclose any opportunity to return to Poland.[251] Unaware that he had been known to the Okhrana for three years, he meant to keep his socialist activities secret. Second, he pleaded poverty: he was indeed having trouble making rent payments,[252] and Maria was writing correspondence for newspapers to help make ends meet.[253] Luxemburg went to London straight from Paris, confident that her own motion would pass. "It will be a victory, such as we shall need no greater!" she wrote to Jogiches.[254] But the PPS voted to deny her mandate, sending her to sit with the Germans or the Austrians. At the request of the congress's central office, they accepted her into the Polish delegation. One of her allies, Warszawski, was expelled successfully;[255] and the other, Julian Marchlewski, refused to vocally support her resolution.[256] She would make no grand speeches, and was (not surprisingly) not chosen by her delegation to sit on any of the commissions.

The little business that was done at the London congress was carried out in commissions. While the first three mornings and afternoons of plenary sessions were exhausted by quarrels over mandates, the commissions worked busily in the evenings to summarize resolutions into reports that could be approved unanimously by the congress as a whole (voting by national delegations). The political commission, which considered the Polish motions, was chaired by George Lansbury of the (British) Social-Democratic Federation.[257] As it happened, a branch of Lansbury's party had submitted a third motion concerning Polish independence, much to the surprise of the PPS. Impressed by the commemoration of the martyrs of Proletariat in London, the Kentish Town Branch (which had 75 members) had decided (by a 6–3 vote)[258] to move that freeing Poland from the "thralldom of Russia, Prussia, and Austria" be considered to be in the interest of "all civilized peoples."[259] Thus of the thirteen resolutions that Lansbury and his commission had to consider, three concerned Poland, and two were in favor of its independence. His job was to find a formula upon which his commission, and the congress as a whole, could agree.[260]

The Polish question was resolved at the first sitting of the commission: it was got out of the way, because Lansbury expected that the resolution asking the congress to define "political action" would take most of the commission's energy. The Polish delegates to the commission, Jodko and Daszyński, were at first unable to find their way to the proper room,[261] and when they did, they found that the commission had already agreed upon a formula:

> The Congress declares in favor of the full autonomy of all nationalities, and its sympathy with the workers of any country at present suffering under the yoke of military, national, or other despotisms; and calls upon the workers of all such countries to fall into line, side by side with the class-conscious workers of the world, to organize for the overthrow of international capitalism and the establishment of International Social-Democracy.[262]

That wording drew something from all three resolutions concerning Poland, and already had been accepted unanimously when the two Poles walked into the room. Given the business still before the commission, the issue was effectively decided: the Poles did not reopen the question. The Poles may also have felt a certain relief that Luxemburg's resolution had not passed in their absence. As Jędrzejowski mused, "Sometimes history is made in this way as well."[263]

Thus, no mention was made of Poland in particular. As Lansbury was to explain to the plenary, "In respect to resolutions 11 and 12 on the Agenda referring to the position of Poland, the Commission was in favor of the complete autonomy of that country and indeed, as paragraph four of the Report shows, in favor of the full autonomy of all nationalities."[264] We may surmise the issue turned not so much on the commission's desire to defend all nationalities, as it did on the pressures not to single out any particular government as an oppressor. None of the resolutions passed by the commission singled out any government by name for condemnation. (The Briton Lansbury himself suggested a resolution opposing colonialism—in principle.) No minutes of the debate within the commission were kept, but we may speculate that this pattern, evident in this congress and in others, held true. Facing real or expected pressure from Germans, Austrians, Frenchmen, or Russians, Lansbury may have decided to remove the word "Poland" from the commission's version of the resolution. (Any pressure from Germans, Austrians, or Russians must have been anticipated, as only Frenchmen, Englishmen, and Danes were in the room when the wording was chosen!)[265] Even an outsider could see the problem *vis-à-vis* Germany and Austria. As to Russia, the recent strike in Petersburg may have played a role. The Swiss delegation had passed in the plenary a resolution congratulating the Russians;[266] sympathy for the efforts of Russian workers may have worked against singling out the Poles as victims of the tsar.[267] Sympathy for the tsar might have had the same effect: the innocent Swiss motion had been objected to by a French delegate, who preferred a motion directed against "every government in the world" to one singling out the tsar.[268] Guesde, during a break between sessions, had repeated his argument that the PPS resolution would revive the Holy Alliance to Aleksander Dębski, a member of the *Centralizacja* in London. Dębski coolly responded: "You would prefer the Franco-Russian alliance, I see."[269] It is worth recalling that one of the French members of the political action commission was Vaillant, who had previously expressed his hope of avoiding a "Polish debate" at the congress.

In this way, a compromise resembling Kautsky's emerged, though it is unknown what role (if any) Kautsky's article played in the commission's deliberations.[270] Polish socialists (along with socialists of every other nationality in the world) were granted the right to include national autonomy (which could be interpreted various ways) within a party program, but Poland's special importance to international socialism was implicitly denied. In the plenary, the resolution in this form passed unanimously. No one spoke either for it or against it: all of the discussion on the political commission's report concerned the nature of political action itself, an issue at the heart of the dispute between parliamentarists and syndicalists which defined the congress. The PPS had lined up a speaker to point out that the committee's report contained its resolution, but that speaker— along with eleven others—was denied the floor after discussion about the definition of political action had consumed much of the plenary's allotted time.[271]

Kelles-Krauz and Luxemburg assumed that Polish independence was an important issue for the Second International. As it happened, both of their resolutions were lost in the flurry of debate between parliamentarists and syndicalists—a distinctly west and central European debate, for neither parliamentary reform nor a strike organized by trade unions was possible in the Russian Empire of the day. Yet even if the PPS motion had passed unscathed, it would not have carried the weight that Kelles-Krauz expected. Polish independence was for the major parties of the Second International a debate best avoided. Adler (and perhaps also Bebel) might have allowed a resolution on Polish independence to pass, but only as a "harmless" nod to the PPS. Luxemburg made this outcome impossible. Her role was not so much to convince leading socialists that the PPS resolution represented a positive danger or a Marxist heresy, as to attract attention to the issue, to turn it into an "affair." German and Austrian socialists had good reasons not to want Polish independence seriously understood as a demand of the international working class, and Kautsky had closed the debate with a compromise solution. It was this compromise, accepting national autonomy as desirable in principle, but denying Poland any special importance, which Lansbury found as well.

Luxemburg had thought that the PPS faced an irresolvable dilemma. If they wanted international socialism to endorse their demand for national independence, they had to prove their own internationalism. But to prove their own internationalism, they had to renounce their demand for independence. This may have been the case with the French. For the Austrians and Germans, the dilemma was quite real, but of another logic than the one Luxemburg imagined. If the PPS wanted Germans and Austrians to endorse their program of Polish independence, they would do so, as long as that endorsement took the form of a "harmless" resolution. If the resolution was taken seriously and widely noticed, so that it might require them to change the policies of their own parties, they would not.

The events of 1896 did much to strengthen PPS leaders' detestation of Luxemburg. They suspected her of some connection, witting or unwitting, with Poland's oppressors: Kelles-Krauz pointed out that her argument about Poland's organic incorporation into Russia was used by tsarist officials to mock socialism and encourage conservatives to support the Empire;[272] Jędrzejowski intimated that she was an agent of the Okhrana.[273] This latter charge is absurd, and the former must be seen in the light of Luxemburg's political strategy. The example of her reaction to Kelles-Krauz's resolution does, however, provide some evidence of a link between Luxemburg's own (unquestionable) internationalism and the nationalism of her allies. In her articles, she combined Marxist arguments about economic centralization with political arguments that appealed to German national pride. She was not so outspoken as her ally Alexander Helphand, who equated the working class movement with Germany and Austria, and warned Germans and Austrians that the formation of a new Poland would cripple their countries;[274] but the gambit is unmistakable. The Marxist arguments are for the leaders, the nationalist arguments are for the rest of the party—though, of course, leaders could also use her Marxist arguments as a veil for their own nationalism. Luxemburg was probably carried away by her own tactical sense, and never realized just how strange were her bedfellows. In any case, the use of internationalist language to hide national interest was fast becoming a habit within the Second International. The lack of resistance to nationalism in the more powerful socialist movements, allowed by this semantic tradition, was one source of the Second International's helplessness, so surprising to Luxemburg, in 1914.

Her behavior certainly helped to bring Kelles-Krauz closer to PPS leaders. Even if London had frustrated Kelles-Krauz's efforts to publish some of his own articles, for months he, Piłsudski, Jodko, and Jędrzejowski had not only a common project, but a common enemy. The London congress also taught Kelles-Krauz (and reconfirmed the belief of the others) that the party would have to rely on its own resources in the struggle for independence. It ended for good Kelles-Krauz's belief that the SDKP was a positive force with a misguided program. Kelles-Krauz's attempts to justify the PPS program to European socialists in Marxist terms had not worked. More, his prized exemplars of "scientific socialism," Allemane and Nieuwenhuis, had failed him completely and spectacularly.

Kancewicz has characterized the young Kelles-Krauz as an Allemanist, an advocate of purely economic struggle.[275] This is not quite right. From at least the time of "Class Character," Kelles-Krauz had taken the general strike to be a kind of political practice, rather than a *beau geste* or a way to substitute economics for politics. He thought that a program of national independence could replace the general strike in the territory of the Russian partition, could serve as a minimum program, and could raise the consciousness of workers. Allemane and Nieuwenhuis thought otherwise. Allemane had never understood the PPS program, and was among Luxemburg's most fervent admirers in July of 1896.[276] Nieuwenhuis led his Dutch party out of the London congress, minutes before Lansbury was to present the resolution on national autonomy for discussion. Nieuwenhuis had no use for political action of any kind, and left to protest the parliamentarian character of the congress: Kelles-Krauz wanted his country to have a parliament.[277]

Kelles-Krauz's syndicalist models did not understand Marxism as he did, and he had never put much stock in orthodox Marxists such as Bebel and Guesde. In 1896, Kelles-Krauz learned the hard way that an internationalist Marxist who wants to create new states had no constituency. The experience liberated Kelles-Krauz from his models, freeing him to create a new Marxism that took national issues into account. The path to independence did not pass through Marx, as Kelles-Krauz had expected; but neither did it pass through Germany, as London had hoped. London's strategy of winning the SPD through Liebknecht, and European socialism through the SPD, had also failed. As Jędrzejowski complained to Kelles-Krauz, no one had understood the resolution except "a few old Germans."[278] Kelles-Krauz and Jędrzejowski could agree that the Second International's leading parties considered the present interests of their own states more important than the possibility of future international solidarity.[279]

3

Sociology and Socialism, 1897–1900

THE YEARS 1897–1900 were the most settled of the Kelles-Krauzes' life. Kazimierz and Maria had adapted to life in Paris, even speaking French at home to their daughter Janina, born in November 1898.[1] They remained very much in love, and both helped in raising their child. Like other Parisian families, they tried to vacation each summer (though their travel included Kazimierz's flights from Paris before visits of the tsar). In 1898 they went to Concarneau with friends. Maria was able to take their daughter home to Radom in 1899.[2] The family spent the summer of 1900 in Antony, a small town outside Paris, having rented their flat to tourists in for the World's Fair.[3] Kazimierz and Maria spent their weekends and shorter holidays in galleries and museums.[4] Both had artists as friends, and Kazimierz not only wrote with competence and care about French literature, painting, and sculpture,[5] but was one of the founders of the Polish literary and artistic circle in Paris.[6] The couple was popular, and Kazimierz was often chosen to be the godfather of the children of friends.[7] Marie Curie remembered him as an old-fashioned gentleman, who would graciously dance with unaccompanied women at parties.[8] The Kelles-Krauzes often met Polish friends in two popular Polish restaurants in Paris, Koch's and Terbach's.[9] Comfortably integrated into Parisian life, they were also very much part of the Polish émigré community.

Kelles-Krauz was the leading figure among one part of that community, the socialists. He edited the *Bulletin* until its discontinuation in 1899, and his Paris Section was by far the most active of the Union's groups abroad.[10] The Paris Section was influential among Polish émigrés and especially among students, and Kelles-Krauz was an elder statesman of sorts within the association of Polish students in Paris.[11] He played a leading role, for example, in the group's campaign to move the Polish romantic poet Juliusz Słowacki's remains from Paris to Poland.[12] From 1897 Kelles-Krauz was also the secretary of the "Red Cross," a Polish émigré organization which sent money to imprisoned students and socialists.[13] London also expected him to keep watch over the Association of Polish Workers in Paris.[14] In all of these various capacities, Kelles-Krauz sought to identify the PPS with Polish socialism in general, and to ensure that the PPS was considered an ethical, as well as an effective, party.

Even with the perspective of time, a distinction between his personal and political life is somewhat artificial. Life in immigration tends to crowd personal friendships and political loyalties, and Kelles-Krauz's was an extreme case. His wife Maria was an active member of the Paris Section, and wrote for organs of Polish socialism in Germany and Austria.[15] Evening meetings of the Paris Section were followed by nights of drinking near the Observatory, where political discussions and maneuvering continued into the late hours.[16] When the bars closed, Kelles-Krauz strolled home along boulevard Arago with his wife—and with other members of the Section as well. The house on 42, boulevard Arago became a colony of Polish socialism in Paris. Ignacy Daum, who took Motz's place as treasurer of the Paris Section, lived on the same floor as the Kelles-Krauzes.[17] He was a close friend, and watched over Maria's health while Kazimierz was away.[18] Polish socialists who were not attached to the PPS also felt at home. Though supporters of the SDKP program, Kazimierz Kasperski and Zygmunt Gąsiorowski also lived on the same floor of the same building and enjoyed Kelles-Krauz's friendship.[19] Cezaryna Wojnarowska, the most active Polish social democrat in Paris after Luxemburg's last visit in May 1897,[20] was also on good terms with Kelles-Krauz.[21] Kelles-Krauz's flat was thus not only the headquarters of the Paris Section, but a gathering point for Polish socialists in Paris.

Kelles-Krauz and his Paris Section still lived within the same complex and confusing political context, defined by the tension between the possibilities created by French political freedom and the risks resulting from the Franco-Russian alliance. A powerful reminder of the latter were the tsar's visits to Paris, before which the French police would preventively arrest suspect Poles.[22] The continuing case of Ludwik Sawicki (whose suicide in 1893 was mentioned in chapter one) also illustrates this tension. For more than three years after Sawicki's death, Polish and Russian socialists contested the right to his personal papers with the Russian embassy in French judicial and political forums. Sawicki was a Russian subject, so the French government was bound by treaty convention to turn over his possessions to the Russian government.

In the spring of 1893, Bolesław Limanowski went to see Georges Clemenceau for help. Without rising from his game of billiards, Clemenceau promised to keep Sawicki's papers out of Russian hands, but soon thereafter he was distracted by accusations of being an English agent. Limanowski and other Polish socialists held public meetings in summer 1893 to explain the issue to the French public, and Parisians marched in the streets in support of the cause. Edouard Vaillant, leader of the Blanquists, also spread the alarm. Two of his followers, called Julien and Zimmer, broke into Sawicki's flat in order to further arouse public opinion, and were caught and imprisoned. The independent socialist Alexandre Millerand agreed in his capacity as a lawyer to represent the socialists in the pending case against the Russian consulate. After several appeals, he won in May 1896 as favorable a ruling as could be expected: a court in Orleans ruled that the treaty convention bound the French government to give Sawicki's possessions to the Russian government, but that friends of Sawicki had a right to examine the papers as they were recovered.[23]

The case of Sawicki demonstrates how Polish and Russian émigré socialists could limit (at the margin) the effects of the Franco-Russian alliance on their own freedom by way of spirited appeals to the French left and general population. Millerand would shortly endorse the Franco-Russian alliance, and Vaillant had no particular sympathy for Poland or Polish socialists. But they understood the issue in terms of basic rights, and both (not to speak of average Parisians, nor of Julien and Zimmer, who spent several weeks in prison for their trouble) helped as they could. Appeals to public opinion were made in the name of the rights of an individual who had chosen Paris as the place of his death.[24]

The Sawicki case was unusual, in that Polish socialists knew in advance of the nature of the threat from the Okhrana. The case of Bolesław Malankiewicz, the Okhrana's agent among Polish socialists in Paris, was in this sense much more difficult. Though Kelles-Krauz had known since 1895 that Malankiewicz was suspected of spying, the charge was never proven to his satisfaction.[25] As a result of the continuing division between socialists loyal to the PPS and to the SDKP, Ignacy Urbach's continuing friendship with Malankiewicz, and the flow of gossip among Poles in Paris, Malankiewicz's access to PPS secrets continued. Only his madness and eventual suicide stopped his reports.

In May 1896, his material and mental conditions steadily worsening, Malankiewicz checked into the cheapest hotel he could find. There he found Walery Wróblewski (1836–1908), hero of the 1863 rising and the Paris Commune, then a friend of Marx and Engels, living alone in poverty and poor health. Malankiewicz confessed to Wróblewski that he was suspected of being a spy by Kelles-Krauz and Golde, and Wróblewski persuaded him to meet Kelles-Krauz personally.[26] Such a meeting seems never to have taken place. Malankiewicz's health steadily worsened; his last reports to the Okhrana, in autumn 1896, are full of paranoid fantasy.[27] In August 1897 Malankiewicz sought help in a shelter for Polish veterans and orphans, run by Sisters of Charity.[28] There, elderly Poles called him an agent of the Okhrana, whereupon he pulled a revolver from his pocket and shot himself. This suicide, on the site of the poet Cyprian Norwid's death twenty years before, cleansed Malankiewicz in Kelles-Krauz's eyes. Kelles-Krauz wrote to London that agents rarely defend themselves by suicide, and suggested that Malankiewicz had been driven to his death by unfounded rumors.[29] Kelles-Krauz's memory of his friend Ludwik Sawicki, who had killed himself in a question of honor, may have affected his judgment.

By the time of Malankiewicz's suicide, the Okhrana knew enough about Kelles-Krauz to order his arrest at the Russian border. Though Kelles-Krauz never knew just who the informer had been, he began to realize that he could not safely return home to Poland. He left Paris before the tsar's visit in October 1896, and returned to the news that the French police had asked after him.[30] Other members of the Paris Section (in particular Estera Golde, who was imprisoned yet again in March 1898) had been arrested while attempting to return to the Russian Empire, and Kelles-Krauz must have suspected that his fate would be the same. In 1899 he began to make efforts to obtain Austrian citizenship, in the hope of gaining more direct influence over events in Russian Poland from Vienna or Galicia than he had from Paris.[31] Kelles-Krauz knew from the experience of others that Russian subjects with bad reputations could not expect to remain in Austria, and thus meant to keep his name as clean as possible.[32]

He therefore continued to divide his writing between legal and illegal publications, writing under his own name and under pseudonyms. He remained the Paris correspondent of *Kurier Warszawski*, and wrote for *Prawda* and *Przegląd Tygodniowy*. *Przegląd Tygodniowy* had been but was no longer an organ of Warsaw positivists; *Prawda*, founded in 1881 by

Aleksander Świętochowski, continued its traditions. Kelles-Krauz supplemented this income by translation work, some of which was anonymous. He translated a book by the Polish sociologist Ludwik Gumplowicz from German to French, but asked not to have his name mentioned in the French edition for fear of associating himself publicly with Gumplowicz's anti-Russian views.[33] Although Kelles-Krauz was one of the very few Polish émigré socialists able to live by his pen, much of his writing was scholarly, and often unpaid.[34] Kelles-Krauz was an indefatigable worker. His only weakness was his vision, and when he lit the candles that his doctor recommended he use for his work and placed his heavy blue-lensed glasses upon his brow,[35] the chances were as good as not that he was preparing to write sociology.

Sociology

By 1897, Kelles-Krauz was well known in Parisian sociology circles. Though there were then a few men in Paris who called themselves sociologists, there were no faculties or university chairs. The youthful informality of the discipline worked to Kelles-Krauz's advantage. He was apparently on good terms with the young French sociologist René Worms (1869–1926), who was then organizing an Institut International de Sociologie (hereafter: "Institute") based in Paris.[36] Worms, the editor of the *Revue Internationale de Sociologie*, shortly attracted many of the scholars interested in the new field. Though Kelles-Krauz's only experience in sociology was by way of secret circles in Radom and private study in the Bibliothèque Nationale, Worms offered him an associate membership in the Institute in the summer of 1894.[37] Kelles-Krauz made the most of this opportunity, participating actively in the Institute's congresses and using the Institute as a forum for his own further education. From the first, he was quite confident of his own knowledge and abilities, and certain that his own Marxist sociology would be of great benefit to the discipline.

The Institute was indeed international: the presidency rotated among nationalities, and only 16 of 77 members in 1894 were French.[38] Still, Kelles-Krauz had difficulty registering himself as a Pole at its first congress in October 1894. He was told at first that he could not represent a country that did not exist, but the Russian-French sociologist Jacques Novicov came to his rescue, explaining the distinction between nation and state to the Frenchman in charge of registration.[39] This logistical problem settled, Kelles-Krauz was able to present a paper for discussion on Max Nordau's theory of degeneracy.[40] Though ostensibly a reply to Nordau, the paper was in large part a summary of one of Kelles-Krauz's own theories, which he called "revolutionary retrospection." At the Institute's second congress in October 1895, Kelles-Krauz used a similar tactic, this time opposing the system of the French sociologist Gabriel Tarde, but in the main using Tarde's views as a foil for his own.[41]

Revolutionary Retrospection

These two papers, which began the first significant discussion between Marxist and non-Marxist sociologists,[42] constitute a single whole.[43] Kelles-Krauz's theory of revolutionary retrospection, as presented in 1894 and 1895, amounted to a schematic explanation of historical progress. In seeking the source of revolutionary ideals, Kelles-Krauz was drawn into an attempt to explain social change.

From the very first attempts of human beings to master nature, he argues, changes in the means of production have brought one class or another to political power.[44] In changing the existing political structure to facilitate the satisfaction of its own needs, the class in power identifies itself with society as a whole, and its needs with those of society.[45] (Kelles-Krauz defines the word "need" extremely broadly. It ranges from biological necessities to the most peripheral desires.) This "social apperception" guarantees that each ruling class will think of its own rise to power as the end of history.[46] But political revolutions do not halt changes in the means of production, and new classes with different needs emerge. At the same time, the very continuity of a certain political structure is alienating, for as the system ossifies, the means of satisfying certain needs come to be considered as ends in themselves.[47]

Unmet needs are not the immediate cause of revolution. Politics changes more slowly than economics, and thus "content" (the economic base) outruns "form" (the political superstructure). Dissatisfaction leads individuals to long for previous social orders, and to seek models for change in the real or imagined past.[48] As time passes, these historico-imaginary models provide a common language and ideal, allowing dissatisfied individuals to coalesce into groups with political goals.[49] Not all individuals seek revolutionary change: one group—the majority—simply longs for the past. A second group are reformers, who are too attached by self-interest to the present political system to imagine its fundamental transformation. The third are revolutionaries, who seek to synthesize ideals drawn from the past with the economic system of the present to create the political order of the future.[50] Because the function of the past is to supply the aesthetic ideal of revolution, the "tissue of dreams," those whose aesthetic sense is most violated by the present order become revolutionaries.[51]

Socialists are the revolutionaries of the era. Like all revolutionaries, they see themselves in the middle of a three-stage historical process, between a past golden age and a utopian future. Their golden age is the "primeval communalism" described by Lewis Henry Morgan, who is thus the "Erasmus of socialism"; their utopia is the synthesis of this primeval communalism with the economic achievements of capitalism.[52] According to Kelles-Krauz, with the addition of his own theory and Morgan's findings, Marxism becomes a complete explanation of social change as well as an inspiring call for revolution. But like all social theories, Marxism is a creature of its time. The socialist revolution will not end history: like all revolutions, it will satisfy some needs and not others, the cycle will begin anew, and a new theory of change and revolution will arise to take Marxism's place.[53]

This extraordinary theory of social progress obviously rejected Spencerian faith in continuous progress by way of adaptations made by rational individuals bent on satisfying their biological demands.[54] Yet it also had little in common with the orthodoxy of Second International Marxism. Marxist theorists in the 1890s generally understood Marx in the light of Darwin's theory of evolution, rather than in the light of Hegel's dialectic.[55] Their leading light Karl Kautsky "regarded the Hegelian origins of Marxism as a historical accident of small importance."[56] The understanding of Marxism in positivist categories was a general phenomenon—one historian has even claimed that: "No radicals were Hegelians any longer by the 1890s."[57]

Kelles-Krauz was. Rather than believing with Kautsky that man is a kind of animal, Kelles-Krauz considered that progress is a result of alienated human spirits turning to the past. The future, in his view, is the synthesis of a dialectic between thesis (the present) and antithesis (the past). This dialectic takes place within the minds of human beings, and the laws that characterize it were thus sociological rather than biological. Ideas, in particular, play a crucial role: "aesthetic elements of the past" are "necessary for every revolution."[58] A correct apprehension of social change must therefore recognize ideas "as real forces," rather than seeing them as "secondary or epiphenomenal."[59] Kelles-Krauz certainly believed that his view of progress is consistent with Marxism, and indeed wrote that he had explained the functioning of the Hegelian dialectic in Marxist terms.[60]

H. Stuart Hughes has written that the defining characteristic of the great social thinkers of the 1890s was a rebellion against positivism, understood as the explanation of human behavior in terms of analogies drawn from natural sciences.[61] This characterization fits Kelles-Krauz[62] (as well as other Polish Marxist sociologists), but not Kautsky (nor Mehring, nor any of their German comrades).[63] In the period between 1878 and 1890, while the SPD was illegal, it developed its own institutions, culture, and intellectual leaders. It defined itself as a permanent opposition to the legal world outside, and this opposition extended to the emerging study of sociology. But, as we have seen, Kautsky and his peers understood Marxism in the light of a certain determinist misreading of Darwin, in 1878 the fashionable premise for social science. Ironically, the SPD's isolation thus left them defending, in the name of Marxism, an older bourgeois premise for social science (Darwinism) against the more sophisticated possibilities that emerged. Even after the party was legalized in 1890, the Darwinism of its theorists was protected by Kautsky's belief that Marxism (by which he meant Marxism understood in the Darwinist categories of his youth) was a self-contained, all-embracing system.

For Poles in the Russian partition, there could be no question of self-isolation from legal sociology, because sociology as such was neither recognized nor taught as a discipline, and Darwin, Spencer, and Comte had to be read in secret circles. Likewise, there was never an identification of Marxism with Darwinism. Biological analogies had been one of the theoretical bases of Warsaw positivism, and the first generation of Polish Marxists sociologists had defined Polish Marxism in opposition to them. The Warsaw positivists had accepted Spencer's vision of society as a single organism, and the Marxists had replied that society was instead riven by the class struggle. But at the same time, the Marxists also developed methodological critiques which apply to any use of biological analogies in sociology. They retained the belief that science could guide politics, but could not believe in a simple correspondence between the laws of natural science and those of society. Once this distinction was made, deterministic understandings of Marxism grounded in the authority of biology or other sciences were harder to accept.[64]

So while German Marxism was a species of positivism, Polish Marxists were usually anti-Positivists. Such a comparison may explain in part why Polish Marxist sociologists rejected evolutionist conceptions of progress, but does not explain why progress was so often understood as a three-step process, with the present stage of history seen as a necessary transition between a golden past and a utopian future. To note that Polish socialists understood Marx in the light of Morgan rather than Darwin raises the question: why was Morgan's passage predicting the return of primeval communalism on a higher level of material development so influential? Morgan's appeal reached beyond these sociologists: even Luxemburg called Morgan the "high priest of the social democratic church," and believed that "the noble tradition of the past grants to the revolutionary his demands for the future."[65]

Morgan's work (as interpreted by Engels, and popularized by Polish sociologists in the 1880s) found a fertile place in the Polish political imagination—a place that was already well-tilled. Limanowski had been claiming since the 1870s that Poland's past of peasant communes would serve as a model for future socialist communities.[66] He continued the tradition of the historian Joachim Lelewel (1786–1861), who glorified Poland's past of free, democratic peasant communes.[67] Lelewel's contemporary, the first Polish ethnographer Adam Czarnocki (1784–1825), had sought remnants of a communal culture among peasants in what is now Ukraine and Belarus.[68] Between the 1830 and 1863 risings, the philosopher August Cieszkowski (1814–1894) had been the most prominent of a group of Polish Hegelians who prophesied a "third era" of human rebirth.[69] History, anthropology, and philosophy so understood could play a role similar to that of Adam Mickiewicz's (1798–1855) poetry: inspiring Poles to act for a better future in the name of a beautiful but tragically lost past.[70]

Kelles-Krauz thought that Mickiewicz prefigured socialism in his romantic longing for a primitive past.[71] Kelles-Krauz also believed that the more radical a social movement, the further back it would seek its models:[72] in the case of the Polish left, the less radical could dream, as Józef Piłsudski did, of the noble Republic rather than of the peasant or prehistorical communes that supposedly antedated it. A full discussion of the account of historical progress given by the Polish left in the nineteenth century would exceed the scope of this work, but it seems clear that the experience of the partitions inclined progressive Poles to look back into history in the name of the future, and that a triadic reading of history as paradise, fall, and redemption (or life, crucifixion, and resurrection) could inspire even the most agnostic of Polish radicals as late as the *fin de siècle*.

Organicism

Kelles-Krauz modified and defended his conception of progress for the rest of his life. In the process, he had to come to terms with the major currents of sociological thinking of his day, and define his own position in relation to them. This meant above all a confrontation with organicist theories of sociology. The use of organic models by philosophers seeking to explain social change can be traced back at least as far as Fichte and Hegel, but at the end of the nineteenth century Herbert Spencer seemed to have connected this appealing metaphor to biology's recent advances.

Spencer was variously interpreted. Among members of the Institute, organicism in the 1890s meant the assumption that human societies were best understood as organisms, their members as cells, and their institutions as organs. ("Organicism" is thus to be distinguished from "evolutionism," also associated with Spencer, which equates human beings with individual animals, society with a species, and evolution with progress.) Though later histories of sociology often have little to say about organicism, it was the dominant paradigm among the scholars who considered themselves sociologists in the 1890s.[73] The last volume of Spencer's *Synthetic Philosophy* was published in 1896, and though Spencer had declined the honorary presidency of the Institute,[74] his shadow loomed large over its congress on organicism in July 1897.

This congress was chaired by the "extreme, literal" organicist Paul Lilienfeld.[75] The remarks by which Kelles-Krauz introduced his own paper recall the prevailing intellectual atmosphere: "In a congress pre-sided over by Lilienfeld and Espinas, of an organization of which René Worms is secretary, to speak after Novicov against the organic theory of society [. . .] is sure to arouse a bit of disfavor."[76] Kelles-Krauz had prepared himself thoroughly. In the months before the congress he wrote about organicism in several forums: in a long letter to Tarde, in an article for *Prawda,* and in a paper for the Société de Sociologie de Paris (formed in 1895).[77] Together with Kelles-Krauz's intervention at the congress itself, these writings suffice to give the outlines of his thought on this matter.[78]

Polish positivists had been defending organicist models of society for a generation, and Polish Marxists had been opposing them for more than a decade. A summary of this debate gave Kelles-Krauz the occasion to review the contributions of Polish sociologists (of all political loyalties) in general.[79] This Polish controversy had prepared Kelles-Krauz for the debate to come in France—in particular, he drew some of his own arguments from the Marxist sociologist Stanisław Krusiński, whose body of work had been published by Ludwik Krzywicki in 1891.[80] In 1897, Kelles-Krauz chose as his polemical targets René Worms and Gabriel Tarde, two of the most prominent French sociologists of the day.

Kelles-Krauz's arguments against organicism can be divided into two categories: methodological and substantial. In his view, the task of building a method for the young discipline of sociology is only confused by premature analogies with biology. Analogies must be the fruit of long empirical research, rather than assumptions. There is no *prima facie* reason to believe that individual humans are like the cells of an organism, or that the behavior of individuals naturally tends toward "organic unity" in society in all circumstances. In any case, it is not known which kinds of societies would "match" which kinds of organisms. Further, even if society were an organism, we know too little about physiology to draw conclusions, so it is best to leave biology to the biologists, and begin the labor of sociology as such. This labor should begin from the assumption that man's natural state is society, and that this social nature is qualitatively different from the nature studied by biologists.[81] Kelles-Krauz advances the notion that sociology is only possible as a participatory act in society, that the study of society is only possible because of our intuitive ability to identify with other social beings, and that this sympathetic understanding is wasted on cells.[82]

These methodological objections justify Kelles-Krauz's seemingly categorical rejection of organicism in sociology: "The organic analogy explains nothing in society, and is completely sterile as a generator of sociological method."[83] But the substantial objections he raises, following Krusiński, undermine this conclusion. Krusiński's basic claim, which Kelles-Krauz finds tempting, is that in present conditions society is not an organism, but that primeval communalism was characterized by organic unity.[84] This unity was destroyed by the division of labor, and in conditions of capitalism any talk of organicism must be understood as the attempt by one class to identify society's interests with its own.[85] However, when private property is abolished we may expect organic unity to return, at a higher level of material development.[86] Kelles-Krauz does not seem to realize that these two lines of criticism sit ill with one another. It is one thing to claim that sociology must find its own method, because human society as such is qualitatively different than nature; and another to state that under present conditions talk of organic unity is class manipulation, but that it describes correctly both future and past societies. This tension in Kelles-Krauz's thought is unresolved.

The thinly veiled utopianism of these latter arguments reveals something further about the peculiar conditions under which sociology began in Russian Poland, and about the attractiveness of Morgan to Polish sociologists. Polish sociologists, be they Marxist or liberal, had been well-prepared to debate positivism by their own experience. In the 1890s the number of Polish sociologists and their tendency to identify with socialism were quite remarkable. Young Poles saw research in sociology as a way to fulfill their national duty, as a hope for some rescue from Poland's political fate.[87] Recall the role of books in secret circles: a refuge from an oppressive public life and a promise of an eventual escape. The young Ludwik Krzywicki put the matter quite clearly: "The purpose of sociology is to see which system will make us poor, suffering mortals the happiest."[88] Like Kelles-Krauz and Krusiński, Krzywicki was inclined to believe in primeval communalism, and to draw political conclusions from this historical premise. Straining toward utopia, these sociologists found its seeds in the past.[89]

The political agenda of French sociologists such as Tarde and Worms was more modest: to strengthen a Republic which already existed. Whether or not this was an attainable task, it was considerably less demanding than the one before Polish sociologists. Compare Krzywicki's definition of the goal of sociology to Dürkheim's: "the philosophy B which would contribute to giving the Republic a basis and inspiring in it B rational reforms while giving the nation a principle of order and a moral doctrine."[90] More, because France's educational system was not dictated by Russian policy, the division between politics and scholarship, and thus between socialism and sociology, was necessarily greater. Jaurès's recollection that during his years at university he "did not know that there were Socialist groups in France"[91] would have been quite unthinkable in Polish conditions. Even before attending university, Polish students in school secret circles devoured socialism and sociology together: both were forbidden and seductive. To choose to study sociology in France was a political act of a different order than to choose to study sociology in the Russian partition of Poland.

Kelles-Krauz was certainly right to point to political context as one factor determining whether or not a given paradigm seems like a plausible basis for social science. In this connection, it should be noted that the methodological arguments Kelles-Krauz advanced against the organicism of his French sociologist colleagues would have served just as well against the evolutionism of his German Marxist comrades. Kelles-Krauz also held by 1897 that human beings have a flexible nature, and that different social systems generate different sets of felt needs.[92] It is thus fruitless to imagine human beings struggling against a natural environment that can be described by scientific laws, for in the main they struggle within an "incessantly" changing social environment of their own making, and what they demand of that environment is not static, but changes as the struggle continues.[93] At this early point in his career, Kelles-Krauz did not explicitly criticize orthodox Marxists on these grounds; this would come later.

Comte and Vico

By the Institute's third congress in 1897, Kelles-Krauz had returned to university. He had enrolled in autumn 1896 in the École Libre des Sciences Politiques in Paris.[94] The École Libre was a private, "free" institution of social studies and history. Its courses were intended to broaden the education of lawyers, civil servants, and diplomats, and its lectures were given by politicians as well as scholars. The program of studies lasted two years, and ended with the award of a diploma—private universities in France could not confer degrees. At this time, the École Libre's faculty included its director Émile Boutmy and Louis Renault in law, Pierre-Paul Leroy-Beaulieu in economics, Albert Sorel and Albert Vandal in history, Theophile Funck-Brentano in philosophy and sociology, Gabriel Tarde in sociology, and Lucien Lévy-Brühl in the history of philosophy.[95]

Kelles-Krauz's course of general and legal history included five to six hours of daily lectures[96] in the subjects of comparative constitutional history, diplomatic history, the history of parliament in France, political economy, finance, geography and ethnography, law, and political ideas and public spirit in Germany.[97] He passed exams in these eight subjects in June 1898, and received a diploma with distinction on 28 June.[98] He also won third prize for his thesis ("L'age d'or de Vico au Marxisme"), to which he had dedicated most of his labor.[99] Given Kelles-Krauz's interest in sociology, it seems surprising that Tarde did not supervise this thesis. We might surmise that Tarde did not because Kelles-Krauz had vociferously criticized the older man's theories at the second congress of the Institute in 1895[100] and in private communication just three weeks before Kelles-Krauz began his studies.[101] In any event, Kelles-Krauz was supervised by Lucien Lévy-Brühl (1857–1939).[102]

Lévy-Brühl was later to gain world renown as a sociologist, but had been trained as a philosopher, and at this point in his life considered himself as such. He had been lecturing since 1886 at the École Libre on the history of German political thought, and had just (in 1896) been appointed lecturer in philosophy at the Sorbonne. Lévy-Brühl was sympathetic to socialism without belonging to a socialist party.[103] Kelles-Krauz's main influence upon his mentor seems to have been an interest in traditional societies, later to be the subject of Lévy-Brühl's most famous work.[104] In this small way, Kelles-Krauz played a role in the French social sciences similar to that played by Bronisław Malinowski in the British social sciences.[105] In 1898, when Kelles-Krauz began his thesis, Lévy-Brühl was principally occupied with the philosophy of August Comte,[106] and this interest was his main influence upon Kelles-Krauz. In later discussions of Comte,[107] Kelles-Krauz expressly acknowledged his own debts to Lévy-Brühl's interpretations.[108]

Kelles-Krauz came to believe that Marxist sociology was the inheritor of Comte's philosophy.[109] In his analysis of organicist theories of society, Kelles-Krauz certainly followed Comte's dictum that if sociology was to be a science of its own, it must have its own laws and methods, not deducible from the laws and methods of other disciplines. Kelles-Krauz chose Comte over Spencer as the forerunner of Marxist sociology for precisely this reason.[110] He also accepted Comte's view that, although scholarly work must result from human needs, the scholar should set objectivity as the goal of his will.[111] Kelles-Krauz was thus able to work with equanimity as a sociologist while all the time believing that all academic endeavors are conditioned by the class struggle. Comte's notion that human history can be divided into three stages (religious, metaphysical, and positive) may have confirmed Kelles-Krauz's own tripartite conception of historical progress.

Kelles-Krauz's two years in the École Libre certainly improved his knowledge of the history of philosophy. He sought and found dialectical thinking and the longing for a golden age throughout the history of western thought,[112] and in his thesis discussed examples of revolutionary retrospection in Italian, French, and German philosophy.[113] His studies inclined him to the view that the act of retrospection is characteristic of human history, and that the content of the imagined past and the desired future varies according to the historical circumstances of the thinker at hand. Socialism is simply the latest contribution to a rich tradition, unique only insofar as its longings for the past have a scientific basis in the work of Marx and Morgan.[114]

Kelles-Krauz became interested in the Italian philosopher Giovanni Battista Vico (1668–1744), and argued that Marxism should take into account certain aspects of Vico's philosophy. Like Kelles-Krauz, Vico had believed in a cyclical view of history, and in the possibility of *ricorsi* to earlier stages (though he regarded this as a threat to feckless progressives,

not a promise for revolutionaries).[115] Taking his cue from Vico's principle that we understand that which we have created (*verum quia factum*),
Kelles-Krauz hinted at an epistemology which would break down the distance between observer and observed by understanding science and perception as activities.[116]

This was precocious: though Vico was widely understood in this fashion by Western Marxists after the First World War, he was seen by Marxists
during the Second International as a proponent of determinism.[117] Still,
Kelles-Krauz's intention of treating Marx as susceptible to improvement
by reference to eighteenth-century Catholic conservatives, or for that matter by reference to any kind of pre-Marxist tradition, constituted the more
serious deviancy from the Kautskian orthodoxy. Kautsky "opposed all
attempts to enrich or supplement Marxist theory by elements from any
other source, except Darwinism."[118]

The Family

Kelles-Krauz's reputation at the École Libre and in the Institute probably
earned him a position in another Parisian "free" university, the Collège
Libre des Sciences Sociales. He took up a professorship of general sociology there in autumn 1897, just as he was beginning his second year as
a student at the École Libre.[119] The Collège Libre had been founded in
1895 to unite all schools of sociology within a single institution. Though
students were awarded only a Certificat d'Études Sociales after completion of a two-year course, the institution was subsidized by the French
government, and could thus rent a building on rue Danton.[120] The list of
lecturers changed yearly, and each lecturer was given full responsibility
for the content of his or her course.[121] During Kelles-Krauz's four years on
the faculty (1897–1901),[122] he lectured alongside scholars such as Tarde,
Maxime Kovalewskii, Henri Ferri, and Charles Seignobos.[123]

Kelles-Krauz's new post brought him work, but not income. Developing
a ten-lecture course on "Marxist Sociology" did force him to organize his
own thoughts, and he produced a series of publishable manuscripts. His
very first lecture in his first term on "Economics and Music" was praised
by the socialist historian Max Beer, who convinced Kelles-Krauz to offer it
to *Die Neue Zeit*.[124] (Kelles-Krauz and Beer spoke French, neither realizing
that the other was Polish.) The lectures also brought Kelles-Krauz a series
of book offers.[125] Kelles-Krauz considered his teaching an integral part of
his political life, but the juxtaposition of his academic and conspiratorial

roles could create problems. One of Kelles-Krauz's students once visited him at home to ask for a recommendation to the Alliance Juive. The student asked his professor to sign the letter with his full name and title (Baron), and Kelles-Krauz reluctantly agreed. The student then promptly sold the signature to the SDKP. Kazimierz greeted this news with equanimity, but Maria announced that she would throw the student down the stairs should he appear again.[126] Luxemburg and her lover Jogiches thereafter referred to Kelles-Krauz as "the baron."

Kelles-Krauz applied for a post at the university in Fribourg (Switzerland) in 1898, but apparently failed to get it.[127] In early 1901 he did parlay his experience as a lecturer at the Collège Libre into an offer to join the faculty of yet another "free" university, the Université Nouvelle in Brussels.[128] This leftist institution had been founded as a result of an anarchist attack. After August Vaillant bombed the French Chamber of Deputies, Belgium banned anarchists, including the gentle geographer Élisée Reclus, from teaching in state institutions. So the Université Nouvelle was founded to give Reclus a forum.[129] Unlike its French counterparts, it was in all official respects equal to state universities. As Kelles-Krauz recalled, it was also "a center of free, and often quite radical thought, a place for professors who wander from country to country ... "[130] In January and February 1901 Kelles-Krauz gave a series of twelve lectures on "The Social Dialectic" to about forty enthusiastic Russian and Belgian students.[131] He publicly defended the series of lectures as a doctoral dissertation, and was awarded a doctorate in March.[132]

During his course of lectures in Brussels, Kelles-Krauz returned to a theme he had raised during his lectures in Paris and in discussions within the Société de Sociologie de Paris: the history of the family.[133] He wished to demonstrate the existence of a primeval communalism characterized by equal rights between the genders, and prove its relevance to the present and future.[134] He argued that primeval communalism is possible not because it corresponds to human nature, but because it corresponds to certain kinds of economic activity;[135] he postulated a stage of communal agriculture in which the role of the genders is effectively equal.[136] He wished to rescue Marxist sociology from Engels's view that Marxism could not be applied to primitive societies without taking into account another kind of production, the production of human beings.[137] According to Kelles-Krauz, Marxism is applicable to all forms of human social existence, not just to class societies. Human society begins with tool-making and the division of labor, and from this point onward the explanation of human behavior requires sociological, rather than biological, tools of investigation. The division of labor, even among hunting and primitive agricultural societies, determines the place of men and women in society.

Following Bebel's *Die Frau und der Sozialismus*, Kelles-Krauz believed that socialism would restore to women their lost equality.[138] Also like Bebel, Kelles-Krauz preferred to believe that this equality would not take the form of a return to a matriarchy or to the orgies that both believed characterized primeval communalism, but would rather consist in equal rights and an equal place within monogamous marriage.[139] Kelles-Krauz was demonstratively supportive of socialist declarations on the equality of women.[140] He also tried to live according to the ethic of gender relations he had ascribed in his youth to the socialist future: equality, honesty, compromise, boundless love between lovers, and the possibility for non-sexual friendship between men and women.[141] This was of course a romantic and liberal ideal,[142] rather than a peculiarly socialist one, but Kelles-Krauz lived in accordance with it to a remarkable degree. He also wrote a great deal over the years about the effects of capitalism upon the family.[143] He regarded the family as a vitally important conduit of tradition and of moral values, and considered its weakening one of the dangers of capitalist development.[144] At the same time, he regarded the bond between men and women as capable of surviving the most dramatic of social changes,[145] and admired its resilience among the lumpenproletariat of Paris.[146]

Though Kelles-Krauz never formed these attitudes about gender relations and arguments about the primitive family into a coherent whole, their expression does betray a consistent interest in the social role of the family. Kelles-Krauz was fortunate enough to have had two very loving families, and this might have inclined him to presume that future society would include the perfection, rather than the dissolution or transformation, of this particular social form. If Kelles-Krauz's marriage served him as an opportunity to demonstrate a socialist ethic of gender equality, his father and grandfather had allowed him to take part in the tradition of retrospection among the Polish gentry. As a student in Radom he could see and write about the uses to which Poland's history was put by conservatives, positivists, and Marxists,[147] and in his papers on retrospection he would again distinguish three types of attitudes to the past: reactionary, reformist, and revolutionary.

In Kelles-Krauz's view, the revolutionary has as much need of inherited tradition as his rivals, and it may be that the particular role of Polish noble families such as Kelles-Krauz's in passing down Polish traditions inclined him toward his sympathetic lifelong interest in the family as a conduit of tradition as such.[148] The death of his mother during his own childhood may also have heightened his sensitivity to the role played by women in this process, and breathed the note of longing into his discussions of the role played by women in the prehistoric past.

Socialism and Sociology

Kelles-Krauz considered Marxism to be the proper form of sociology, and thus sociology, rightly conceived, to be another name for Marxism. In addition to calling his own sociological views "Marxist," he played the Hegelian trick of pointing out to bourgeois sociologists how their theories were consistent with, subsumed by, or contributed to "economic materialism." He believed that understanding Marxism as a sociology insulated it from the philosophical criticisms which, collectively, caused the "crisis" of Marxism at the end of the nineteenth century. In 1900, he had the opportunity to express in full his conception of a Marxist sociology. Because his critique of organicism had been outstanding at the Institute's congress in 1897, he was given the honor of presenting the opening paper at the Institute's September 1900 congress, which was devoted to Marxism.[149] Throughout the 1890s, there had been little interaction between socialism and sociology, despite the fact that each was a kind of academic counterculture, and that each considered itself a science of society.[150] Kelles-Krauz had been one of the few bridges, and the 1900 congress provides some evidence as to why the connections were not deeper and stronger.[151]

Kelles-Krauz explained at the outset that he intended to present his own understanding of economic materialism.[152] He began from the now familiar premise that economic materialism concerns human beings, rather than nature broadly understood. When humans began to use tools, they became something qualitatively different than other animals. Tools serve as an extension of man's natural abilities, and determine the course of his interaction with his natural environment. The progress of technology spurs changes in the organization of society, and society becomes an "artificial nature," mediating the individual's apprehension of and interaction with the nature of biologists and physicists. Society is thus man's "natural state," and economic materialism is exclusively concerned with man's "second nature" (in Lukács's later term), with society only. Society is not the whole of reality: but since the discovery of tools, the nature studied by biologists and physicists has remained more or less static, and changes in the human condition have had social, and thus technological, causes.[153]

The means of production are thus the "base" of society, and the super-structure may be divided into ethics and law, which are closely tied to economic changes, and knowledge, art, and philosophy, whose connections to the economic are more indirect. But there is no easily observable or predictable relationship between a particular change in the base and changes in the superstructure. Further, each element of the superstructure is rife with autonomous traditions, which continue independently of the economic base. In addition, the chain of causation is downward as well as upward, for the superstructure can also affect the base. At this point, the primacy of economics is much attenuated.[154]

But in Kelles-Krauz's conception, "economics," like "law" and "art" are only useful fictions, or "ideal types" (in Weber's later phrase). Society is an interdependent whole, and sociologists may consider certain aspects of certain kinds of relationships between individuals as "parts" of society (such as "economics," "law," or "art") "only at the level of purest abstraction."[155] Such terms serve as tools which allow the social scientist to work. Marxists must regard these labels as tools, for Marxists take a "fully phe-nomenological" stance, understand that phenomena are the result of the simultaneous action of multiple factors, and seek to understand events as they are understood by their participants. Economic materialism thus boils down to social psychology.[156]

The primacy of economics, in this conception, is a result of the fact that the impulses that we call "economic" constitute an unchanging part of human nature: individuals always try to satisfy their needs as efficiently as possible. The base is thus not the sum of actual changes in the means of production, but a tendency of the human mind. But if the tendency is fixed, its object is not: humans also strive to most efficiently satisfy needs, but what they perceive those needs to be changes as society changes. Indeed, the very act of satisfying, or attempting to satisfy, needs creates new ones.[157] Human nature is thus both fixed and extremely flexible: fixed in its eternal striving to efficiently satisfy needs, flexible in that these needs unceasingly change.[158]

Class societies, in particular, build needs that they cannot satisfy. The division of labor separates individuals from the fruits of their labor, leading them to confuse the means of satisfying a need with the need itself. As capitalism advances, the number of intermediary steps required to satisfy a given need increases, and each of these intermediary steps can create its own felt needs. At the same time, capitalism creates new kinds of needs by teaching consumption as a way of life.[159] This alienation is exacerbated by what Kelles-Krauz called class apperception. Members of any particular class, though striving to fulfill their own collective needs, tend to see themselves as objective observers and as representative of society as a whole.[160] Ruling classes are thus insensitive to changes in the needs of other classes. Political form falls behind economic content, the dissatisfaction of individuals becomes the progressive ideology of groups, and the reforms pressed by these groups, in sufficient number, may become revolution.[161]

According to Kelles-Krauz, economic materialism does not consist in Marx's, or anyone else's, conclusions. It does not amount to a set of statements about the nature of capitalism, or about anything else. To say that Marxism is a doctrine which is susceptible to critique and change understates the case: it is not a doctrine at all, but the "research approach" most appropriate to the study of society.[162] It is not vulnerable to the methodological critique of neo-Kantians, since it does not seek after "things in themselves," but is concerned with the relations between the individual and the external world, understood as phenomena.

Kelles-Krauz took the opportunity to set out his own position on Kant's notion of *a priori* knowledge, writing that he did not

> expect great things from the much-heralded "return to Kant." In any event we would understand this return somewhat differently: we would like to translate this standpoint into social terms. We would like to recall that the larger group, or the class, to which an individual belongs, imprints a certain stamp on his consciousness, forces upon him *a priori* a certain understanding of society and of the world, from which the individual may no more free himself than he can see otherwise than through his iris. As a result, the proletariat also must have a certain class apperception, thus its system of philosophy, like all previous ones, is in its essence relative and transitory; and it too will stop being (that is, seeming) true, when the social apperception of a future classless society replaces that of the class struggle. The philosophy of this future society, though it will derive from Marxism, must in the nature of things be different from and in some respects opposed to Marxism. Just how it will differ we cannot today know. This cannot be deduced from the present or the past: all of our predictions are subject to one of the class apperceptions of today.[163]

Economic materialism applies to itself, and its practitioners recognize the limits to knowledge that this implies.[164]

Kelles-Krauz then turned to a second aspect of the Kantian revival. By 1900, some Marxists in Germany and Austria were turning to Kant in an attempt to create an ethical socialism.[165] In Kant they attempted to resolve a basic moral vacuity within Marxism: though it may be the case that socialism is inevitable, that fact constitutes no moral reason to endorse it. Kelles-Krauz offers two responses. First, he believed that the argument is inapplicable to Marxist social science, which treats both values and facts as psychological phenomena.[166] This reply is correct, as far as it goes, but it dodges the basic question as to the ethical justification of socialism as politics. Kelles-Krauz then appealed to his Hegelian theory of revolutionary retrospection to explain the origins of socialist ideals. He located the source of the ideals of today's revolutionaries in their mystified recollection of the primeval communalism of the distant past, and concluded his paper to the congress with the words: "The dead overcome the living, in order to lead the living forward."[167]

Did Kelles-Krauz mean that his theory of revolutionary retrospection explains the genesis of revolutionary ideals? If so, he still has not addressed the ethical question, for the fact that certain social conditions bring certain ideals to mind is no moral argument. Or did he mean that retrospection is the means by which people catch a glimpse, however mystified, of their own essence, and that this goads them forward to the revolution which will restore to them their species-nature (in Marx's term)? This would contradict his earlier criticism of Engels for introducing the notion of an original human nature into socialist debates, but it is consistent with his plea to Tarde: "The goal toward which socialists strive is precisely returning man to himself, returning him to his own dignity."[168]

The debate which followed Kelles-Krauz's opening paper at the 1900 congress of the Institute did not much deal with the eschatological possibility of the union of human subject and object. Kelles-Krauz's Hegelianism, which one might suspect would attract criticism or astonishment, was passed over without a word. In fact, his entire paper was virtually ignored. The speakers that followed "expressed long-held opinions as if the paper did not exist."[169] Tarde said that all materialism is utilitarianism, that all utilitarianism is flawed by its assumption that people always act rationally, and that Marxists are mistaken in believing in objective historical laws.[170] Worms called Marxism a simplistic theory of causation,[171] and Alfred Fouillée noted that the theory "speaks incessantly about determinism."[172] Nicolas Abrikossof noted that there are non-material needs,[173] and Tönnies said that Marxism was not sufficiently psychological.[174] The list could be extended: with the single exception of Novicov,[175] the sociologists present did not respond to Kelles-Krauz, but to their own understanding of Marxism. Charles Limousin admitted as much: "This is not the way in which Kelles-Krauz has explained the Marxist system, but it is the way in which I understand the system . . . "[176] Kelles-Krauz attributed this absence of debate to the class apperception of his colleagues,[177] though he must surely share the blame for underplaying the differences between his own Marxism and the positivist Marxism of European party leaders and Kautsky's *Die Neue Zeit*.

As Hughes has noted, "to come to terms with Marxism was the first and most obvious task confronting the intellectual innovators of the 1890s."[178] By 1900, when Kelles-Krauz gave his paper, innovators and mediocrities alike had generally taken a position. Sociologists approached Marxism in two ways, which might be called Weberian and Durkheimian. Weber took Marxism as an attempt at a science of society, and polemicized with "the 'vulgar' Marxists who found a home in German social democracy."[179] Like Weber, most of the members of the Institute knew Marx through the interpretations of these disciples. Durkheim, on the other hand, did not at this time treat Marxism "as a scientific theory or a 'sociology in miniature,'" to be evaluated for its truth or plausibility, but rather as a "practical" doctrine, a "plan for the reconstruction of present-day societies," and a "cry of anguish, and, sometimes, of anger, uttered by the men who feel most keenly our collective malaise."[180]

Had Durkheim known of Kelles-Krauz, he might have modified his view, but Durkheim moved from Bordeaux to Paris in 1902, a year after Kelles-Krauz had left. Kelles-Krauz's paper addresses several of Weber's objections to Marxism, but the two men never met.[181] The founders of modern French and German sociology were out of reach, and the sociologists who made up Kelles-Krauz's international audience in Paris in 1900 had already made up their minds. Kelles-Krauz's attempt to unite sociology and Marxism had failed, and further attempts along these lines would have to wait until after the First World War.

Politics

Kelles-Krauz's dual identity as "Casimir de Kellès-Krauz," Parisian sociologist, and "Michał Luśnia," Polish revolutionary, reflected a certain gap between theory and practice in his own life. It is certainly possible to draw political implications from his sociological views: revolutionary retrospection, for example, justifies socialism in backward countries, and its corollary that some souls are more sensitive than others to the call of the past justifies a special role for the intelligentsia in politics. But Kelles-Krauz was rarely in a position to test these implications. This is not to suggest that he was not fully immersed in the PPS and in the Paris Section, but simply that this conspiratorial life had little connection with his sociological writings.

The Union of Polish Socialists Abroad

Kelles-Krauz could advance only so far as leader of the Paris Section and as a member of the *Centralizacja*. Wojciechowski and Piłsudski led the PPS in the Russian partition of Poland, and close personal ties as well as common political goals linked them with Jodko and Jędrze-jowski in London. From the development of Kelles-Krauz's career within the Union between 1897 and 1901, we may see that it was friendship and trust, rather than formal position within the Union, that ultimately determined his influence.

Despite the Union's centralization, its component sections had some say in its direction so long as the Union was formally distinct from the PPS. This was most evident at the Union congress of December 1897. Members of the Union had grown dissatisfied with the irregularity of *Przedświt* and its editor Jodko's long absences from London. The Zurich Section planned to take over the *Centralizacja* and to replace Jodko with Leon Wasilewski.[182] The Zurich initiative was supported by the majority of Union members, and a new *Centralizacja* of Leon Wasilewski (from the Union section in Vienna), Bolesław Miklaszewski (Zurich), Władysław Studnicki (Vienna), and Kelles-Krauz was elected. Piłsudski was present at the congress, but was powerless to change the outcome. He was angered by the fate of Jodko and Jędrzejowski, and he told Wasilewski that he was not up to the job of editing *Przedświt*.[183] The result of this change was a split within the foreign representation of the PPS. The directing committee of the PPS immediately separated the "conspiratorial committee," in charge of relations between the party and the Union, from the *Centralizacja*.[184] The new committee's leadership and the editorship of a second theoretical journal (*Światło*) were entrusted to Jędrzejowski.[185]

Like Piłsudski, Kelles-Krauz had voted against the change,[186] but his reaction to it was fundamentally different. Kelles-Krauz found himself, as a member of the past and present *Centralizacja*, as an element of stability. In the belief that "people of good will can always come to an understanding,"[187] he took on the role of mediator, urging the new *Centralizacja* to communicate with Jodko and Jędrzejowski, and vice-versa.[188] As the year passed, trust began to increase on all sides.[189] By October 1898, Kelles-Krauz was trying with Wasilewski's approval to co-opt Jędrzejowski back into the *Centralizacja*, but Jędrzejowski refused.[190] He knew already that Piłsudski and the PPS were planning to dissolve the Union entirely, and re-create it as a subordinate part of the party. Kelles-Krauz was surprised and angered when he learned of this in December: "What has the Union done to deserve this?"[191] But representatives of the PPS were unable to attend the next congress of the Union, held in January 1899 in Kelles-Krauz's flat, so this threat was temporarily averted.[192]

Kelles-Krauz and his Paris Section tried without success to find a compromise that would satisfy the PPS without destroying the Union.[193] In November 1899, the PPS once again proposed its dissolution of the Union,[194] and the Paris Section responded with an alternative motion.[195] But this time the party was able to send representatives to the Union's sixth congress, held in December 1899, and won the debate and the vote. Kelles-Krauz argued for the Union's continued utility. He believed that the Union ensured continuity of leadership if party leaders in the Russian partition were arrested, that the Union was capable of the kind of theoretical debate that was impossible in the conditions of the Russian partition, and that the PPS's fears of irresponsible student politicking within the Union were groundless.[196] In the end, though, he voted for the PPS motion.[197] A fellow member of the Paris Section was surprised at how easily he gave in.[198]

Piłsudski and Russia

The Union, after all, had been created to support the PPS, and it must have been difficult to resist the PPS's wishes in this instance. Kelles-Krauz knew that his own position was not seriously threatened: he was the natural leader of the Paris Section of the PPS, and he was given a place in the PPS Foreign Committee which replaced the Union.[199] Piłsudski's personal authority probably ended Kelles-Krauz's resistance. The two were on friendly terms—having met only once previously, they wrote to each other using the Polish familiar form of address "ty," and used diminutive forms of each others' names. Though the two men sometimes disagreed on political questions, Kelles-Krauz trusted Piłsudski's judgement on party strategy.

Their acquaintance had grown from their discussions of Russian social-ism, initiated by the formation of the Russian Social-Democratic Workers' Party in March 1898. Anticipating this possibility, Piłsudski had led the party to delineate conditions for cooperation with Russian socialist parties at the party's fourth congress in November 1897.[200] In order to cooperate with the PPS, a Russian party would have to recognize the right of Poland to independence, promise not to enter into relations with other Polish par-ties without the permission of the PPS, and acknowledge the right of all non-Russian peoples to define the nature of their own relations with the Russian party.[201]

Kelles-Krauz decided to set out his own position on cooperation with Russian socialists. Although it took him nearly a year to get the pamphlet published, the disagreements with Piłsudski that caused the delay had nothing to do with these three conditions. In fact, "Socialistes polonais et russes" was above all an attempt to persuade Russian socialists to sup-port the PPS program. As in "Class Character," Kelles-Krauz opposes his notion of political progress in stages to the expectation that a sudden revo-lution will resolve all present political problems.[202] The next logical stage for Polish and Russian socialists alike is the support of separatist move-ments within the Empire. The dissolution of the Empire is a precondi-tion for democracy, which is inconceivable in a unitary state of so many nationalities.[203]

Polish patriotism is thus by nature progressive, and Russian patriotism must be reactionary. Russian socialists must be very careful not to yield to the temptation of identifying Russia's present borders with Russia's just borders.[204] If they do so, they will be unable to prevent the tsar from using Russian nationalism as a weapon against socialism in Poland and elsewhere.[205] Likewise, Russian socialists deceive themselves by speaking of a democratic, federalist constitution instead of the destruction of the Empire. If the constitution were fully federalist, then the subject peoples would secede, so there is no need to speak of it as a discrete goal. The PPS has openly stated that a future Poland will give its neighbors the right to self-determination, and Russian socialists should do the same.[206]

Piłsudski thought that the pamphlet contained too many suppositions to serve as effective agitation, and did not want it placed in *Robotnik*. He also wanted Kelles-Krauz not to mention words such as "constitution" and "federation," for fear that discussion of these ideas would be read as

endorsement of them. But Piłsudski wrote that the pamphlet "is interesting, and I would be happy to see it in a monthly, and as a separate
pamphlet I would gladly distribute it among the Russians and other sav-
age folk."[207] Kelles-Krauz and Piłsudski met in March 1899, and probably
then came to a compromise on the details.[208] "Socialistes" was published
in *Humanité Nouvelle* in April, and the PPS paid for its publication as a
pamphlet.[209] Though Kelles-Krauz found the delay very frustrating, it is
difficult to speak of substantial differences of opinion between him and
Piłsudski. At most, we see a difference of attitude: Kelles-Krauz thought it
worthwhile to keep lines of communication open with Russian socialists,
in the hopes of eventually persuading them by argument to endorse Polish
independence.

Kelles-Krauz accepted invitations to speak at meetings of Russian
socialists in Paris, and patiently tried to explain the PPS program.[210]
At the same time, he was not unduly optimistic. Having seen the first
issue (December 1900) of Lenin's journal *Iskra*, he correctly predicted
that Lenin meant to impose the organ on all socialists of the Russian
Empire.[211] He also expected that Lenin would manipulate the issue of
Polish independence rather than take a clear stand. In his only encounter
with Lenin, Kelles-Krauz criticized him for not supporting Polish independence on the pages of *Iskra*.[212]

The PPS and France

If the differences between Kelles-Krauz and Piłsudski on Russian socialism were minimal, differences between Kelles-Krauz and PPS leaders on
French socialism were negligible. After the London congress, Kelles-Krauz
rarely distinguished among French parties according to their Marxist status, and his appreciation for Allemane's syndicalism vanished. Given
Kelles-Krauz's inability to gain French support for the PPS motion in
1896, the tasks for PPS agitation in Paris were obvious. Kelles-Krauz had to
reply to several characteristic French responses to the PPS program: 1) the
conflation of the French national interest with the progress of socialism;
2) and closely related, the conflation of the interests of socialists with the
interests of rulers within the Russian Empire; 3) indifference to national
issues; and, 4) indifference to foreign policy in the belief that the revolution would settle all outstanding political questions. (The fifth characteristic response was the conflation of Polish and Russian socialists, which was
addressed in "Socialistes Polonais et Russes," discussed above). Though

Kelles-Krauz devoted a good deal of energy to counteracting the lingering influence of Rosa Luxemburg,[213] most of his efforts were devoted to these French attitudes. Indeed, as Luxemburg had done much to fortify some of these attitudes, these goals were in harmony.

(1) *French national interest/European socialism.* Kelles-Krauz and London agreed that the most pressing need was for the official renunciation of the Franco-Russian alliance by all leading French socialists.[214] Kelles-Krauz devoted the first 1897 number of the *Bulletin* to an "Open Letter from the Polish Socialist Party to French Socialists" on the alliance, which rebuked Alexandre Millerand and Paul Brousse for their "socialist Russophilia." Millerand had written rather uncritically of the tsar, and Brousse had argued that Russia was a natural ally for France, just as Poland had been in the past.[215] Kelles-Krauz also criticized French socialists for distinguishing sharply between foreign and domestic policy, knowing from his own experience that the alliance did indeed reduce the level of political freedom within the Republic.[216] He also argued that the alliance buttressed the tsar's domestic power, and that French socialist Russophiles weakened the position of their Russian comrades.[217] Neither Millerand nor Brousse chose to reply,[218] and Kelles-Krauz could only note with dismay that Millerand's "Russophilia" was increasing.[219]

(2) *Rulers/Subjects in the Russian Empire.* The tsar's visit to Warsaw in September 1897 served Kelles-Krauz as an occasion to explain to his French readership the realities of politics within the Russian Empire. The third number of the *Bulletin* in 1897 was an effort to expose the "Polish-Russian Compromise" as a sham of the tsar and the most conservative of Poles.[220] During his visit, the tsar had accepted a gift of one million rubles from Polish conservatives, decreed that the money be used to build a polytechnic in Warsaw, and authorized a memorial to the romantic poet Adam Mickiewicz.[221] As Kelles-Krauz described these events, "the nobles and bourgeois prostrated themselves, the self-proclaimed patriots kept a restrained silence, and only the PPS protested . . . "[222] In the view of Polish socialists, "today there is no longer compromise, only submission pure and simple."[223] Attempts at compromise in Warsaw only allowed the tsar to act with more resolve in the Far East, and removed one cause of his unpopularity in western Europe.[224] French socialists should not allow themselves to be duped.

In early 1898, the PPS had the spectacular good luck to obtain a copy of a memo from the governor-general of Warsaw, expressing his contempt for the weakness of Polish conservatives in the former Congress Kingdom.[225] Through his friend Lucien Herr (1864–1926), Kelles-Krauz placed an article about the memo in the *Revue de Paris*. Herr was the librarian at the École Normale Superieure, and was enormously influential among socialist *normaliens*, most of whom he had converted.[226] He was in favor of Polish independence, and could even read Polish with difficulty. Kelles-Krauz's cultivation of Herr in 1898 and 1899 was one of his few successes in his attempt to persuade Frenchmen to endorse the PPS program.[227]

(3) *Indifference to national issues*. Polish and French socialists in Paris commemorated the centenary of Mickiewicz's birth, on 29 December 1898.[228] The literary editor of *Petite République*, Camille de Saint-Croix, denounced the involvement of socialists on the grounds that Mickiewicz had been a patriot. Kelles-Krauz seized on this occasion to explain the progressive character of Polish patriotism, in an open letter to her, which was printed in the *Bulletin*:[229] " 'Mickiewicz,' you say, 'was not a man who strove to redeem society in liberty, equality, and brotherhood, but simply a patriot.' But, Citizen, are these values so irresolvably contradictory? In your opinion, is it impossible for patriotism to be revolutionary? The French Revolution, one could say, created modern patriotism ..." He then argued that French socialists ask something of Poles that they would not think of asking themselves. "We consider it far too early to resign from our Polish identity and become simple human beings without further definition ... At present socialists of all nations, and above all French socialists, from Millerand and Jaurès all the way to Guesde, do not miss a chance to display their own patriotism ..." Polish socialists are also not alone in expecting political gains before the revolution: "In terms of gaining political freedom, you must only—still!—abolish the Senate, we still have to gain that precondition to all other rights, national freedom. How can you not perceive the shocking contradiction of denying the right to independence to twenty million Poles, while insisting on it for 300,000 Cretans?"[230]

(4) *Indifference to foreign policy*. The allusion is to one in a series of crises in the Balkans in the late 1890s, during which French socialists tended to support the right to self-determination of national groups within the Ottoman Empire. Kelles-Krauz was forced to respond to the position that Cretans had a right to national independence, while Poles had denationalized themselves and therefore had no such right.[231] Kelles-Krauz used the occasion of crises in the Balkans to set out a new position: that the socialist

parties of Europe should have a common policy on issues of international relations. He chose a new pseudonym for his writings on foreign affairs (Elehard Esse), arranged still another book contract,[232] and set to work persuading French socialists that it was in their interest to draw up such a proletarian international policy. In 1898 he set out to give a comprehensive shape to his idea of socialist foreign policy in a long article in *Devenir Social*.[233]

Kelles-Krauz believed that socialists, lacking an international policy of their own, would respond at crucial moments with patriotic formulas.[234] He noted that very few socialists have had the courage, even in times of calm, to renounce their own state's imperial gains.[235] Socialists tend to take positions on far-away conflicts which do not touch upon their own states' interests, and do not ground even these occasional statements in a socialist framework. Kelles-Krauz argued that the organizing principle of such a framework must be his notion of stages. The revolution is ongoing, and each gain toward democracy or socialism anywhere in the world must be considered as part of the revolution. Socialists must therefore consider the political stages of other nations, and draw up a foreign policy that will best facilitate the political progress of Europe considered as a whole.[236]

He drew a few practical conclusions. Socialists should accept that some boundary arrangements are better than others, and not stop at the assertion that the revolution is international.[237] Socialists cannot take a fixed position on "war," as some armed conflicts can be justified in the name of the struggle.[238] (Talk of "peace" is not always in the interest of socialism: the disarmament negotiations sponsored by the Russian foreign minister in 1898, for example, should be seen as a calculated move to sanctify existing borders.)[239] Above all, socialists should strive to weaken Russia at every turn, and support England and the possibility of an Anglo-French alliance wherever possible.[240]

Independence

Aside from French socialists, Kelles-Krauz had to defend the PPS program to Polish socialists who supported the SDKP program. Although the remnants of the SDKP in Russian Poland had joined the PPS in 1895, the intellectuals who had helped lead the party from abroad did not. Rosa Luxemburg moved to Berlin in 1898 and began to make her name within the SPD.[241] Other intellectuals, such as Cezaryna Wojnarowska in Paris and Julian Marchlewski in Munich, continued to propagate the SDKP

program, and represented themselves as the foreign branch of Polish
social democracy. Wojnarowska was on friendly terms with Guesde and
other French socialists, and had a voice in editorial decisions on articles
concerning Poland in *Petite République*.[242] Though there was no rival to
the PPS's *Robotnik* within Russian Poland, debate among Polish socialists
over the national independence continued in French socialist journals. As
Kelles-Krauz knew, Wojnarowska's influence extended beyond her French
friends to a sizable group of workers and students in Paris, among them
his housemates Gąsiorowski and Kasperski.[243]

In 1899 Kelles-Krauz set out to justify the PPS program in Polish, both
to attract émigrés loyal to the SDKP program, and to ground national independence in socialist terms for PPS members. His position had shifted
subtly, but significantly, since the days of "Class Character." Unlike in
1895, when Kelles-Krauz was concerned to keep (in his term) "patriots" out
of the PPS, he was now trying to ensure that the PPS program was attractive to young patriotic socialists who might otherwise join the National
League. In 1895, he had understood independence as a means to an end;
by 1900 we find him treating it as an end in itself, as well as a means to the
end of socialism. Michał Sokolnicki, who knew Kelles-Krauz in Paris from
1898 but not earlier, recalled him in this way:

> Despite the cool and calculating gaze with which his young eyes took
> in the world around him, despite the coarseness which he affected
> in the struggle for power, one felt in him above all an inborn bright-
> ness, a good and noble heart not bearing slavery or oppression, and
> even characteristically Polish impulses and prejudices. Despite all
> of his efforts, national independence was never for him a category
> of reason.[244]

Kelles-Krauz had moved toward the center of the party: he wholeheartedly
endorsed, for example, the official history of the PPS published in 1900.[245]
Unlike previous articles, his case for "Polish Independence in a Socialist
Program" was published as a pamphlet and entirely without changes. (Its
sequel, "The Latest Misunderstanding," was also published without difficulty.) Kelles-Krauz was even allowed to keep some of the proceeds from
its sale.[246]

In the article, Kelles-Krauz claims that socialism's ideals are given by
revolutionary retrospection and the pitiable sight of the exploitation of
workers. Early Marxists believed that programs could concern economics

exclusively, leaving open a gap between economic reforms and the final goal of systemic change.[247] Kelles-Krauz argues that experience has taught socialists to think in political terms, to close this gap between reform and revolution by thinking of tactics in terms of stages. In politics, as in nature, "progress" amounts to a chain of small advances.[248] As he puts it, "we are divided from the socialist system not by a single explosion, but by a series of legal and economic changes; if we cannot from our point of view make out the entirety of the road before us, we may with sufficient probability predict the next steps."[249] Marxism consists in the constant dialogue between means and ends, with the ethical ideal of socialism serving to light the path from one step to the next. The very idea of a sudden revolution that transforms society completely is thus not only false, but exerts a harmful influence on tactics. To wait for a cataclysm is to abandon present possibilities for real change, retard class consciousness, and delay the progress of socialism.[250]

For all European socialist parties, approaching stages include political rights and institutions not won by the national bourgeoisie. The fight for general suffrage, for example, is expected to bear fruit before the final revolution.[251] Poland's socialists have inherited the struggle for national independence. A republic would provide socialists immeasurably better conditions under which to work for socialism.[252] (Kelles-Krauz maintains (as he did in 1895) that the prospect of a Russian constitution that could substitute for Polish independence is a mirage. No constitution granted by the tsar to the Russian bourgeoisie would grant Poles the right to secede, and so Polish national aspirations would remain unsatisfied).[253] "Minimum programs" such as national independence, which articulate the next stage as the immediate goal of socialists, are necessary for effective agitation.[254] Kelles-Krauz now views the PPS program's appeal to non-socialists as an advantage.[255] He believes that it will maximize Polish "revolutionary energy,"[256] though he advises Polish socialists always to keep their final goal in mind.[257]

Kelles-Krauz advances other arguments for Polish independence. He calls Poland part of west European civilization, and argues that the restoration of Poland would strengthen European democracy.[258] He claims that the division of nations among empires hinders the progress of democracy and socialism, by allowing tyrants to play national majorities against national minorities.[259] The appeal of nationalism is so strong that the class struggle is best played out within nation-states.[260] He also suggests that national consciousness is an intrinsic part of the political consciousness of every worker,[261] and that national liberation is part of the socialist ideal.[262] These new ideas would await development in later writings.

The first of Kelles-Krauz's two programmatic articles, "Poland's Independence," was not polemical in character, though it did briefly address Luxemburg's organic incorporation thesis. As against Luxemburg's claim that independence would hinder Poland's economic development by cutting off its eastern markets, Kelles-Krauz argues that Russia's Polish territories are now subject to protectionism at the whim of the Russian government, and that an independent Poland could better defend its trade rights. To Luxemburg's argument that the Polish bourgeoisie, fearing such a trade collapse, opposes independence, Kelles-Krauz responds that Polish socialists should not base their goals upon the wishes of the bourgeoisie.[263]

The second article, "Misunderstanding," had a more polemical tone. Kelles-Krauz had learned of Luxemburg's attempts to identify the PPS with Bernsteinian revisionism.[264] Even more, he was responding to articles by Marchlewski and others in the French socialist press in early 1900[265] arguing that Polish national independence would be achieved after socialism.[266] This new position (not Luxemburgian, for it mentioned independence, but not that of the PPS, for it put socialism before independence) heralded the rise of a new Polish socialist formation. Although Kelles-Krauz answered the arguments, he did not expect the arrival of a new party.

The SDKPiL and Luxemburg

Kelles-Krauz did not know that Marchlewski (who had never agreed with Luxemburg's organic incorporation thesis) was writing in support of the new Social-Democracy of the Kingdom of Poland and Lithuania (hereafter "SDKPiL").[267] The initiators of this new party were two members of Lithuanian Social-Democracy, a group of Polish-speaking socialists in Lithuania who had resisted merger with the PPS. In 1899 they had accepted a few workers from Warsaw into their organization, and had changed its name and geographical scope.[268] The first congress of the SDKPiL in December 1899 had not renounced Polish independence, but anticipated that Polish independence would follow a Russian constitution. The new party did not distribute Luxemburg's 1895 pamphlet, "An Independent Poland and the Worker's Cause."[269] After Feliks Dzierżyński was arrested in January 1900, Cezaryna Wojnarowska took the leading role in the SDKPiL. She favored a softer line than Luxemburg's on independence.[270]

Luxemburg was not one of the initiators of this new party, and played no role in the SDKPiL in 1899 and 1900. She did however take up the Polish question in the summer of 1900, in preparation for the Paris congress of the Second International to be held that September. In an article for the SPD organ *Vorwärts* she called the PPS a nationalist group, and claimed that its recently published history of Polish socialism exploited German naïveté.[271] Kelles-Krauz had expected such a move in the run-up to the Paris congress,[272] and favored denying Luxemburg a place in the Polish delegation on the grounds that the SDKP had done nothing in Poland for five years.[273] After reading her article, he wrote to London:

> Now I am of the opinion that if Rosa appears in a Polish delega-
> tion it is our sacred duty to throw her out, even if she were to have
> a thousand mandates. If the commission then confirms her man-
> dates, we should threaten to walk out, which, in view of Daszyński,
> will force the commission to yield. We should publicly state that no
> honest Polish socialist would shake hands with Rosa, and that if
> she weren't a woman, the appropriate course would be to box her
> snout.[274]

Kelles-Krauz heard of the foundation of the SDKPiL shortly before the article appeared, and assumed that the two events were related.[275] He seems to have considered the SDKPiL a pre-congress gambit of Luxemburg's, similar to her revival of *Sprawa Robotnicza* just before the London congress in 1896.

Kelles-Krauz was not at all eager to attend the Paris congress. By 1900 he agreed with Jędrzejowski and Piłsudski that congresses of the Second International were "farces."[276] His experience at a preparatory conference in Brussels in May 1899 was hardly encouraging: "Among those who were present, I've known Vaillant, Brenton and Dubreuilh for a long time, and they know me. In theory, they support us, but in practice they want us to leave them alone."[277] Kelles-Krauz also feared that he would be recognized if he attended the Paris congress.[278] Russian subjects with conspiratorial lives had good reason to fear unintentional exposure by their west European comrades. In Brussels, a socialist journal had printed Kelles-Krauz's true name, even though he had appeared as Elehard Esse.[279] But in the end, because there was no adequate French-speaking substitute, Kelles-Krauz acceded. The only attraction was the chance to meet PPS members before his planned move to Vienna in 1901.

The Paris Congress

The first order of business at the Paris congress, held in the Salle Wagram from 23–27 September 1900,[280] was the confirmation of mandates. As leader of the Polish delegation (in the absence of Piłsudski and Jędrzejowski), Kelles-Krauz found himself with the unenviable task of deciding whether or not to accept mandates from the new SDKPiL. Kelles-Krauz was surprised by the arrival of representatives of the new party, and telegraphed London for guidance.[281] London had no great respect for Lithuanian Social-Democracy, but also no cause to deny their mandates. At the same time, the PPS did not intend to accept mandates from the SDKP, because that party was completely defunct. The SDKPiL was seen as the merger of a legitimate and a nonexistent party.[282]

Kelles-Krauz proposed that mandates from Lithuanian Social-Democracy be accepted, because the party did exist and had carried out some activity. Mandates from émigré social democrats like Wojnarowska, he argued, had been accepted in London, and should therefore be accepted here as well. Only the three mandates from the SDKP were rejected, as were Luxemburg's two from workers in Poznań and Silesia (one was adjudged "German," the other "fictional"). Kelles-Krauz's compromise admitted both leading groups of the new SDKPiL, the Lithuanians and Wojnarowska's émigrés, but excluded Rosa Luxemburg. Luxemburg did not attend this meeting, and Wojnarowska did not defend Luxemburg's mandates.[283]

When Kelles-Krauz and Limanowski told the congress's bureau of Luxemburg's expulsion from the Polish delegation, they were met with the surprise of Paul Singer, an SPD leader. Limanowski explained that Polish socialists denied that Luxemburg represented any Polish group, and understood that she might join the German delegation. Singer agreed that the German delegation would give her a place.[284] Singer presided the following day over the congress's plenary session, and granted Luxemburg an unusually long opportunity to defend her mandate,[285] which she exploited to attack the PPS. She called the PPS program a "harmful utopia," because "the proletariat cannot change political geography," and claimed that she "and her friends" (not mentioning a Polish party) opposed "all such utopias" in the name of an international socialist republic. She then proudly claimed her place in the German delegation: "There I am and there I will remain!"[286]

Though Viktor Adler, the leader of Austrian social democracy, defended PPS leaders from Luxemburg's charge that they were "nationalists,"[287] she had turned the denial of her mandate into a political victory. This outcome was predictable enough: by 1900, Luxemburg was a major figure in German social democracy, having made her name in polemics against Bernstein.[288] As Nettl points out, she was strong in the suits that mattered in the Second International, intellectual respectability and personal connections.[289] This respectability was a result of articles in German for *Die Neue Zeit*, and her most important personal connection was to Kautsky. The PPS had hoped to register a symbolic protest by denying her a place among Poles, but Luxemburg's prominence within the SPD guaranteed that even this move backfired.

Kelles-Krauz had rejected in advance the use of any morally compromising means against Luxemburg at the congress;[290] it seems likely that Luxemburg planned in advance to use the occasion of her rejected mandate to denounce the PPS. Kelles-Krauz was "outraged by Luxemburg's speech," and after the congress prepared a resolution stating that Luxemburg was unfit to take part in any Polish socialist organization until she formally apologized for her slanders. This declaration was signed by all of the PPS delegates, and four of the six SDKPiL delegates from Paris; two of these four were Kelles-Krauz's housemates Gąsiorowski and Kasperski. It was published shortly thereafter in *Petite République*.[291]

Even if Kelles-Krauz could hope to limit Luxemburg's venues within Polish socialism, he could do nothing to slow her rising international prominence, so evident during the remainder of the congress. Delegated by the SPD to one of the congress's political committees, she co-authored a resolution on militarism. Like Kelles-Krauz, she had been writing on international issues for the last several years, and so was well prepared to present the resolution to the plenary session.[292] That appearance was the first substantial speech by a Pole during a congress of the Second International, and was well received.[293] The resolution, which called specifically for the education of youth against militarism, the organization of peace marches, and a pledge by socialist deputies to vote against declarations of war, then passed.[294] It fit well into the traditions of the Second International's international policy. Like Lansbury's resolution against "colonialism" in 1896, it condemned a group of practices under a general heading without specifying policies of particular states.

Though Kelles-Krauz had opposed Luxemburg's positions on questions of socialist foreign policy before,[295] the character of Luxemburg's resolution brings most clearly to light the fundamental difference in their understandings of internationalism. At the 1899 preparatory conference in Brussels, Kelles-Krauz had advocated that socialist parties take up questions of international relations one by one, rather than denouncing categories such as "militarism" and "colonialism." He was able to pass a resolution at this preparatory conference condemning the tsar's latest disarmament conference at the Hague. But his attempt to place other questions of international politics (such as Alsace and Lorraine, the partition of Poland, and the future of the Balkans) on the congress's agenda failed. As he wrote to London, "This is just one more piece of evidence that the internationalism of the proletariat is still in its infancy."[296]

For Kelles-Krauz, "internationalism" meant a solidarity among socialists that would allow them to design a common policy to further European progress as against the interests of particular European states. Such a policy would demand criticism by socialists of particular acts of particular states, and would give socialists the knowledge to respond firmly to general calls for "peace," such as the tsar's at the Hague.[297] For Luxemburg, on the other hand, internationalism meant treating particular questions of international politics as manifestations of the international class struggle. "Militarism," a stage of "capitalism," was a threat to "peace," which must be the highest goal of the proletariat in international relations.

Luxemburg's devotion to the general value of "peace" reveals another difference between them. As we have seen, Kelles-Krauz did not support a general renunciation of war by socialists: this was typical within the PPS. Even leaders who did not speak of an armed uprising or hope for a European war found the notion of socialism as pacifism alien. In Limanowski's words:

> Socialist pacifism, so popular in countries which have political freedom, is for us undesirable, and even difficult to understand. We understand that war [...] is a relic of barbarism, and that as the spiritualization of human relations proceeds, it must become ever rarer and more localized. But we also understand that peaceful slavery is a hundred times worse. Armed struggle, even when unsuccessful, instills the spirit of agitation and revolt into a nation [...] whereas peaceful slavery brings a meek endurance of every indignity, every wrong, and every humiliation.[298]

Unlike Luxemburg, Kelles-Krauz linked disarmament to foreign policies, rather than to capitalism. He argued that the Polish question was the key to disarmament, because the occupation of Poland forced Germany, Austria, and Russia to spend more on arms than they would otherwise.[299]

Luxemburg could offer the Second International a seductive "peace" which did not require changes in "political geography."

Kelles-Krauz had predicted that the Paris congress would lay to rest the tsar's manipulation of public opinion by way of appeals for "peace,"[300] but it was Luxemburg's version of internationalism that won the day. In the approach to "militarism" endorsed by the Paris congress, we may see three commonalities with the tsar's favored conception of peace: the understanding of peace as the simple absence of war, the implicit endorsement of existing borders between states, and the notion that peace was attainable not by changes in the foreign policies of individual states, but by international action such as conferences and negotiations.

Luxemburg's triumph in Paris meant that she had the credentials to propose the resolution on war passed by the Stuttgart congress in 1907; its general line was followed at Copenhagen in 1910 and Basel in 1912. The debate at these three congresses concerned what the European proletariat should do to prevent war in general, rather than how national proletariats might affect the foreign policy of their states so as to resolve problems that might lead to war.[301] As Kautsky recalled, only war itself forced socialists to think in the terms that Kelles-Krauz had advocated: in July and August 1914 each socialist party was forced to judge the policy of its own state, in order to determine whether its goals were aggressive or defensive.[302] Their lack of practice in such critical appraisal, and the SPD's consequent belief that the Reich was fighting a defensive war, was in some measure a result of the parameters of debate which Luxemburg established over Kelles-Krauz's objections.[303] The SPD's rejection of self-determination for Alsace-Lorraine in the Stockholm Memorandum of June 1917 likewise lends support to Kelles-Krauz's view that particular problems of international relations should be discussed openly at international meetings of socialists.[304]

Imprisoned during the war, Luxemburg pilloried the SPD, not realizing that her own sincerely felt pacifist internationalism had helped to perpetuate socialists' ignorance of foreign affairs and to mystify socialists' patriotism. If the SPD had become (in her words) a "stinking corpse" by voting for war credits in August 1914, Luxemburg had been an accomplice—unwitting, to be sure—in the murder.

Politics and Science

The fourth congress of the Second International (Paris, 23–27 September 1900) overlapped with the fourth congress of the Institut International de Sociologie (Paris, 25–29 September 1900). The day after being called a nationalist by Rosa Luxemburg before an international audience of socialists at the Salle Wagram, Kelles-Krauz gave the opening paper on economic materialism to an international audience of sociologists at the University of Paris. Kelles-Krauz was exhausted after the two congresses, and accepted Jędrzejowski's invitation to rest for a few days in London at the party's expense. This short break gave Kelles-Krauz a chance to reflect on the events of the preceding days, and to discuss with Jędrzejowski his plans for Vienna.[305] The contemporaneity of Kelles-Krauz's most important appearances within international sociology and international socialism gives us a nice occasion to reflect upon his understanding of the relationship between science and politics.

Such a reflection might begin with the main issue before the Paris congress: the participation of socialists in bourgeois governments. Millerand had accepted Waldeck-Rousseau's offer to become minister of commerce in June 1899, forcing French socialists to face squarely the issue of the reformability of capitalism. The pitch of the debate was heightened by the fact that the minister of war in this government was Gallifet, who had crushed the Paris Commune. Millerand was supported by independent socialist deputies such as Jaurès and Briand, as well as less orthodox leaders of parties, such as Brousse. But the left wing of French socialism, led by Guesde, won the argument at the Paris congress, and Millerand's act was condemned by the Second International.[306]

Given Kelles-Krauz's advocacy of the principle of stages, and his belief that the revolution was a continuous process rather than a sudden and complete break with the past, one might suspect that he would have supported Millerand. In fact, Kelles-Krauz agreed with Guesde that the principal result of Millerand's participation was the dilution of class consciousness.[307] It is worth recalling, however, that in accepting a ministerial portfolio Millerand obliged himself to defend the Franco-Russian alliance, and that Kelles-Krauz considered Millerand a Russophile. This may well have stood behind Kelles-Krauz's judgement.[308] Kelles-Krauz was alert to the possibilities for reform presented by Millerand's choice, and noted Millerand's modest success in changing labor laws.[309]

For the most part, French socialist leaders who rebuked Millerand were indifferent to the Dreyfus Affair as a quarrel among capitalists, while those who supported Millerand were Dreyfusards, believing that the Republic's principles were worth defending. Even before Zola's "J'accuse" appeared in January 1898, Jaurès had been arguing for Dreyfus's innocence in *Petite*

République. As Jaurès had been urged to do so by Kelles-Krauz's friend Lucien Herr and by Kelles-Krauz's academic advisor Lucien Levy-Brühl, it is perhaps not surprising that Kelles-Krauz agreed that the Dreyfus case deserved the attention of socialists.[310] Kelles-Krauz criticized Guesde for ignoring the affair,[311] did his part to bring the issue to the attention of the public,[312] and was moved by the importance of the questions at stake.[313] The fact that Kelles-Krauz did not support Millerand, but was a Dreyfusard, betrays no contradiction. A socialist might consistently believe that social-ists should support the Republic without believing that the time was ripe for socialists to govern. Yet few did—and Kelles-Krauz's unusual position must be seen as a result of his own political and moral judgement, rather than of the application of a science of politics.

This banal statement is of great importance, if we wish to place Casimir de Kellès-Krauz, sociologist, and Michał Luśnia, socialist, in their proper relation to one another. Kelles-Krauz regarded Marxism as sociology and sociology as Marxism—and he certainly believed that his scholarly work, in some sense, stood behind his political writings. In fact, Kelles-Krauz's references to sociology in his political writings of this period usually amounted to little more than appeals to common sense. Just as sociolo-gists must participate in society to study it, so socialist theorists must take part in the movement to write about it, and so on. Kelles-Krauz's belief that political gains are made one step at a time also seems sensible enough, though hardly scientific. But Kelles-Krauz justified it as such:

> First of all we shall define the general principle upon which the approach of all socialist parties is based, and from which flows the position of the PPS in the matter of an independent Poland. To characterise this principle, we have used the expressions "social democratic," "stages," and "class possibilism." This is the only posi-tion which deserves the name "scientific socialism," because it takes into account the laws of real social development.[314]

Kelles-Krauz's point that socialist parties cannot make predictions about the distant future, but can plan their next step in the light of an ethical goal, seems sensible. But it is striking that Kelles-Krauz wrote as though socialists looked only backwards and forwards: into the past for values via revolutionary retrospection, and into the near future for immediate goals via his notion of stages. Missing in his "scientific" view of socialist tac-tics as "class possibilism" is an account of parties looking side to side, any recognition of the fact that socialist parties of various nations influenced each other, or that socialism might take on a national character as a result of international politics. Though Kelles-Krauz did advise taking into account "local conditions" and the design of a "proletarian international policy," these concerns do not yet undermine his belief in the scientific character of his theory of stages.

One example should suffice to illustrate the importance of this flaw. Kelles-Krauz borrowed the term "possibilism" from Paul Brousse, a French socialist. But in Brousse's (defensible) view, possibilism implied the endorsement of the Franco-Russian alliance as a necessary means of protecting the Republic. Kelles-Krauz (justifiably) thought that possibilism implied that socialists should take up foreign policy in the interests of European progress, and that this implied opposition to the Franco-Russian alliance. It is doubtful that either could have convinced the other by argument, and certain that no application of Kelles-Krauz's "science" of politics could clear up their dispute. If two people, with avowedly the same goal (socialism), considering the same stage (the French Republic in the 1890s), using the same method (possibilism) disagree about tactics, no appeal to "science" will resolve their essentially political disagreement.

The main reason for their different assessments is obviously national loyalty, which Kelles-Krauz's "scientific socialism"—despite mentions of national identity as part of worker consciousness, and of national rights as part of the socialist ideal—did not yet take into account. Although Kelles-Krauz believed that all scholarly judgements were conditioned by the class position of the scholar, he did not yet consider other possible sources of bias, such as national loyalty. There was as yet no category of "national apperception" to supplement his notion of "class apperception." A similar tension is evident in his theory of revolutionary retrospection, which sometimes posits a generic source for the ideals of socialists (the prenational primitive past), but sometimes assumes that each society (nation) would have its own historio-mythical founts of political inspiration. Are socialists immune to the allure of national myths because their retrospect is the primitive past, or will that immunity only come with the advent of socialism itself? Kelles-Krauz's sociological writings give some support to the first view, but his political writings and experience decidedly support the latter. As he wrote to Camille St. Croix: "We're still waiting for socialists in nations which are free from national oppression to give us an inspiring example of the renunciation of national identity. It will not be our fault, or theirs for that matter, if we have to wait until there are no longer classes or national boundaries anywhere, and perhaps until there is a single universal language."[315] Only in Vienna would Kelles-Krauz begin to consider the nation as a historical entity equal in importance to the class, and face directly the relationship between national consciousness and socialist politics. In doing so, he would confront anew the pretense that his political judgements were identical to science.

4

Central Europe, 1901–1905

THE KELLES-KRAUZES ARRIVED in Vienna on 6 April 1901. Because Kazimierz no longer believed he could return to Russian Poland, he intended Vienna to be a way station to Austrian Galicia. Once the family had settled in (first at 2 Hebragasse, then 130 Gentzgasse), Kazimierz continued his efforts to gain Austrian citizenship.[1] With his surname and title of Baron, he hoped to be taken for a German noble from the eastern marches rather than a Polish political refugee.[2] He enrolled in law at the University of Vienna on 27 April[3] in order to gain a degree which would allow him to teach in Austria, preferably in Cracow.[4] A decade after his expulsion from school in Radom, his goals were much the same: to gain a chair at a Polish university and to work as a socialist agitator.

As in Paris, Kelles-Krauz was engaged in an extraordinary number of ventures. He was a full-time student of law, although he often missed lectures, and had to take weeks to study for examinations at the end the academic year.[5] Kelles-Krauz's old Radom friend Władysław Bukowiński arranged for him to become the Vienna correspondent of *Prawda*.[6] During Kelles-Krauz's first ninety days in Austria, he published more than thirty articles, in *Prawda* and elsewhere, amounting to more than 360 printed pages.[7] He supplemented his journalist's commissions by translating books. All the while, he was working on two books in French based on his Brussels dissertation,[8] as well as several other book-length projects for publishers in Warsaw.[9] The Université Nouvelle continued to demand his services,[10] and he lectured in Brussels one last time in 1902.[11] He was offered full membership in the Institut International de Sociologie during that trip.[12] (At one point it appeared that his credentials would win him a chair in sociology at the Jagiellionian University in Cracow, but in the end it was awarded to a priest.[13]) Kelles-Krauz's interest in pedagogy extended to participation in worker and popular education groups in Vienna,[14] and to the founding of a "free university" in 1904 in Zakopane.

Kelles-Krauz worked remarkably hard. On one occasion, it is reported, while reading as he walked down a Vienna boulevard, he collided so violently with a lamppost that his hat went flying, and a lady passerby screamed. Without removing his nose from the book, he picked up his hat, apologized to the lamppost, and continued on his way.[15] Yet much of the activity that led to such distraction was not remunerative, and Kelles-Krauz had tuition to pay. Because his family relied on Kazimierz's writing for income, their fortune varied with his productivity. Springtime, which found Kazimierz studying for exams, was particularly difficult. Maria translated from French to Polish to try to help make ends meet, and their combined income sufficed so long as Kazimierz was healthy.[16]

All of Kelles-Krauz's work from 1903 onwards was carried out under more than usually adverse conditions. In February 1903 he had fallen ill with what he took to be influenza,[17] but may well have been the first attack of tuberculosis. In July of that year he fell so ill he could not stand without help, and the family retired for three months to Tyrol for the mountain air.[18] Kelles-Krauz relapsed at the beginning of 1904, and departed on in February for another sanatorium in Tyrol.[19] There he spent two months waiting in vain for the sun and being subjected to creams, compresses, punctures, and the "electric bath"—a mirrored closet blanketed with light bulbs.[20] He missed Maria terribly, and passed the time in quadrilingual conversation with the furniture.[21] In April he returned to Vienna, only to spend the summer at another sanatorium in Kosiv (Kossów pod Kołomyją), Galicia.[22] The family could ill afford to pay for these cures,[23] and Maria tried in vain to gain a stipend for Kazimierz.[24] He began to ask the PPS in London to be paid for his articles.[25] All the while Kelles-Krauz displayed an "unconquered sense of optimism,"[26] and his accomplishments during these years are almost beyond belief.

The Kelles-Krauz family remained close and loving despite its troubles, and took immediately to the challenges of a new city. Kazimierz and Maria did their best to speak Polish to Janina at home. The move to Vienna allowed Maria to take her daughter to Poland a second time;[27] but the summer vacations the family had enjoyed in France gave way to Kazimierz's stays at sanatoria. Kazimierz spent a good deal of time with his daughter, who played at his feet as he wrote at his desk.[28] Kazimierz's brother Stanisław (1883–1965), expelled from the school in Radom for distributing materials from a secret library, joined them in Vienna in 1902.[29]

Kazimierz moved quickly into progressive Vienna intellectual and political circles, meeting Tomáš Masaryk within a week of his arrival,[30] and making the acquaintance of Viktor Adler, leader of Austrian socialist democracy, soon thereafter. Estera Golde, who (when not in prison) was then living in Katowice and Cracow, remained a close friend of the family.[31] Kelles-Krauz also grew to be friends with Max Zetterbaum, the Galician Jewish socialist.

Most notably, Kelles-Krauz's years in Vienna brought him closer to Józef Piłsudski. Piłsudski had been arrested in February 1900 and imprisoned in the Warsaw Citadel. He feigned madness until December, when he was sent to a mental hospital in Petersburg. In a daring and well-planned maneuver, he escaped in May 1901. Exhausted from this episode, Piłsudski left the Russian partition and withdrew somewhat from party work, settling in Galicia just weeks after Kelles-Krauz had moved to Vienna. Piłsudski and his wife Maria were frequent guests of the Kelles-Krauzes; the two men also met in Cracow. Piłsudski would relax with Kelles-Krauz over chess. Each found the other's foibles amusing—Piłsudski called Kelles-Krauz "the aristocrat"—but one also senses mutual affection and respect. Despite differences in style and politics, these two sons of declassé noble families from the east appreciated each others' company and talents.[32]

These friendships reveal the major directions of Kelles-Krauz's political work during his four years in Vienna. With Estera Golde, he worked to support Polish socialism in Germany. Arguments with Viktor Adler formed the background of his critique of the program of Austrian social democracy. Discussions with Max Zetterbaum helped him to set out his own position on the Jewish question. His last major political article attempted to frame the issue of Polish independence in a way that could unite Piłsudski's PPS. At the height of his intellectual powers, unleashed from the organizational responsibilities he had in Paris, and on ever better terms with the PPS leadership, Kelles-Krauz was to engage himself during the last years of his life in the national question in central Europe.

Poles in Germany (1901–1903)

Kelles-Krauz's attention was drawn first to the plight of Polish socialism in Germany. The PPSzp (Polish Socialist Party of the Prussian Partition), founded in 1893, gathered the small groups of Polish socialists then working in Berlin and Poznań (Posen).[33] Although its organ *Gazeta Robotnicza* was edited briefly by outstanding figures such as Stanisław Grabski and the outstanding modernist writer Stanisław Przybyszewski, the party suffered from a shortage of intellectuals.[34] It also faced competition from the German Catholic *Zentrum* party, the Polish Christian Democratic Movement, and Catholic labor unions, rivals aided by the especially conservative character of Silesia and Poznania.[35] The PPSzp also had difficulty drawing Polish workers away from Dmowski's National League, which could present a more "Polish" image.[36] The PPSzp adopted the SPD program and published *Gazeta Robotnicza* with the help of a subsidy from the SPD: as we shall see, this affiliation tied the PPSzp's hands on the question of Polish independence.

Polish socialists in Germany complained that their sponsor paid too little attention to Polish national rights, and turned a blind eye to ongoing Germanization.[37] From 1896, PPSzp activists based an open advocacy of Polish independence on the resolution passed by the Second International in London, but were deterred from changing their program by fear of losing SPD financial support.[38] From 1897, as PPSzp activists began to work in earnest to win Upper Silesia's largely Polish[39] worker population from the *Zentrum* in the 1898 elections, open conflict with the SPD over the allocation of candidates began. The SPD insisted that the PPSzp put forward a candidate in no more than one electoral district. When the SPD threatened to end its subsidy, the PPSzp yielded.[40]

The SPD showed little support for the idea of a Polish socialist organization on German soil. The subsidy of *Gazeta Robotnicza* was seen as a means to contain Polish energies and prevent the advent of an independent Polish organization.[41] SPD leaders regarded the PPSzp as a group of comrades who could be of especial use with Polish-speaking populations.[42] But when the moment arrived to choose candidates to stand for the Reichstag in districts where the majority of the population spoke Polish (as in Upper Silesia), the SPD preferred to support trusted Germans. Although some SPD elites spoke out occasionally against Germanization, others were its open advocates: and the latter were supported by the vast majority of the party.[43] After Liebknecht's death in 1900, no important German socialist made an issue of Polish independence, and certainly none imagined that a future Poland might include lands presently German.[44] German socialists had trouble coming to terms with Polish interest in Upper Silesia, which although ethnically Polish had not been part of a Polish state for six hundred years.[45] Liebknecht had personified the tradition of 1848, and was loyal to his friend Marx's heritage on the Polish question. But even in 1848, the attitude of German liberals had been at best ambiguous; and in his later years even Engels had weakened his support of Poland.[46] As the

SPD grew into a mass party concerned chiefly with winning elections, the German left's thin tradition of support for Polish aspirations fell by the wayside.[47]

German socialists at the beginning of the twentieth century simply did not give the national question (and in particular the Polish question) very much thought.[48] It had no role whatsoever in the ongoing revisionism controversy, which set the tone of intraparty debate.[49] Lacking a reasoned position, German activists fell back onto prejudices and fears. Their greatest fear was that the party would be once again outlawed, for open advocacy of Polish independence might well have opened the SPD to charges of treason.[50] Short of formal charges, SPD leaders had to be ever on their guard against accusations of being *vaterlandslose Gesellen*.[51] On a different level, much of the SPD leadership feared a Russian invasion of Germany, and thus valued Polish lands as a buffer.[52]

After Rosa Luxemburg moved to Berlin in 1898, she became the SPD's link to Polish socialism in Germany. Between 1898 and 1901, when Kelles-Krauz arrived in Vienna, she endeavored at every turn to bury the PPSzp as a separate organization. She first joined the PPSzp and proposed resolutions condemning "PPS nationalism."[53] She then urged the party to dissolve itself. Failing that, she joined its press commission, hoping to gain control of *Gazeta Robotnicza*.[54] Despite these clearly destructive efforts, the PPSzp was forced to endure Luxemburg's continued participation. Although Luxemburg was formally banned from the PPS in 1900 for calling the party "nationalists," the SPD in effect overruled the ban, instructing the PPSzp to accept her into its ranks.[55] In the end, Luxemburg persuaded SPD leaders that *Gazeta Robotnicza* was endangering the SPD by advocating Polish independence, and the SPD withdrew its subsidy in April 1901.[56] This left the PPSzp independent, but without means.

Luxemburg campaigned for the SPD in Poznań and Upper Silesia, and wrote of winning back "our people" from Estera Golde and the PPS.[57] She tried to persuade Polish workers that a Polish state would be of no use to them, arguing that German comrades could be trusted to reverse Germanization once they gained power.[58] She claimed that there were no Germanizing tendencies within the SPD, though she knew full well that this was false. Party Secretary Ignaz Auer told her in May 1898 that the SPD "couldn't do Polish workers a better favor than to Germanize them."[59] Her SPD comrade in Upper Silesia, August Winter, was known for his opinions that the border of Germany and the Russian Empire was the border of civilization and barbarism; that good Polish socialists spoke

German to their children; that Polish workers really understood German, but were merely less intelligent than their German comrades; and so on.[60] Luxemburg's dissembling can be explained by reference to her sense of tactics. She was in fact sensitive to the importance of national culture, and felt happily at home among Polish workers in Germany. But she believed that the socialist project could be most effectively carried out within existing states, and that advocacy of Polish independence was a trojan horse for the petty bourgeoisie.

Remarks of Winter's at the 1897 Hamburg SPD congress had excited Kelles-Krauz's interest in the PPSzp. In response, Kelles-Krauz had divided socialists who opposed Polish independence into two categories: those who "were possessed of a simpleminded radicalism, skip over present reality, and relegate national emancipation to a time after the socialist revolution" and those who, "using the sophistic theory of historical necessity of the superiority of the civilization of the conquerer, demand that we renounce our national goals, without taking the trouble to combat the aggressive chauvinism" of their own governments and bourgeoisies.[61] Kelles-Krauz's views were diametrically opposed to Luxemburg's: he believed that socialism would be achieved within democratic nation-states, and that the proletariat should be taught that it needed a republic to pursue its own interests. The PPSzp had to be protected precisely because of its weak position, for it formed part of a movement that must win a Polish republic in the name of socialism. National chauvinism in German comrades was to be unmasked, rather than denied in the name of international solidarity.

From Paris, Kelles-Krauz could do little to aid the PPSzp. From Vienna he could try to harden the party's resolve, and provide some theoretical support for the party's stance toward the SPD. Kelles-Krauz arrived in Vienna shortly after the PPS had decided to replace the lost subsidy of *Gazeta Robotnicza*, move the journal to Katowice, and lend Estera Golde to the PPSzp as an editor and agitator.[62] Kelles-Krauz suggested in May 1902 a new draft program for the party, which emphasized political and cultural autonomy for Polish lands until such time as Poland is reunited. Kelles-Krauz did not hide that he expected a future Poland to be formed from territories taken from all three partitioning powers.[63] In the event, no new program was adopted, and the more contact Kelles-Krauz had with the SPD, the less he strayed from the simple line of Polish independence. In July, just after the first issue of the new *Gazeta Robotnicza* had appeared,[64] Kelles-Krauz visited Golde in Katowice, and probably became acquainted with other PPSzp activists then.[65]

Kelles-Krauz discussed the PPSzp's new position with Viktor Adler, himself the head of a confederal party with a Polish branch. The occasion for their conversations was usually an excessively diplomatic (in Kelles-Krauz's view) response by Adler to German heavy-handedness toward Poles. In June 1901 Luxemburg persuaded the Poznań section of the SPD to pass a resolution stating that the PPSzp was no longer considered to be a socialist party. When the Austrian party's *Arbeiter-Zeitung* noted this without comment, Kelles-Krauz protested. Kelles-Krauz told Adler that the PPS had once been so naive as to care what other parties wrote about Polish affairs, but now knows to expect no support. He explained to Adler that the SPD wanted to win as many parliamentary seats as possible, and would not allow the PPSzp to run even a single candidate. Adler agreed that the Poles should have deputies of their own. (Though Friedrich Austerlitz, then editing the *Arbeiter-Zeitung,* voiced his opinion that the Poles in Germany must be Germanized). Adler then went on to remark that his party cooperates well with its Poles, but is having problems with its Czechs because they stubbornly refuse to Germanize. (The implication is not that the Poles had Germanized already, but that Adler following Engels and Kautsky considered the Czechs an unhistoric nation.) He found it ironic that the progress of socialism seemed to run in train with the slavicization of the Empire. Kelles-Krauz began to reply that the increase in national feeling was a historical necessity rooted in economic and social moderni-zation. Adler interrupted: "If so, let me say that I consider the necessity to be a bitter one."[66]

The next occasion for a talk with Adler was the SPD party congress in Lübeck of September 1901, where Luxemburg succeeded in quelch-ing efforts by Georg Ledebour to restart negotiations with the PPSzp.[67] Kelles-Krauz found Adler's response to the conference overly restrained, and urged Adler to support Ledebour.[68] Adler replied that Ledebour car-ried no weight in the German party, because romantic ideas about Poland brought no votes. Ledebour considered himself Liebknecht's heir, and Adler pointed out that the German party had seen even Liebknecht's support for Poland as "the folly of an old man." Adler argued that Polish socialism was no less opportunist, in that it took into account the popular desire for independence. Kelles-Krauz replied that the partitions forced this demand upon Polish socialism, and that at least Polish "opportunism" was revolutionary. Adler asked Kelles-Krauz to keep him informed, and agreed to pass a letter of Kelles-Krauz's to Paul Singer of the SPD *Vorstand.* The letter argued that the PPSzp would be a unified organization if not for

Luxemburg and Winter; that the three million Poles in Germany would not be Germanized; and that although the PPSzp wished to cooperate with the SPD, Polish socialists in Germany would print their own organ, run their own candidates, and preserve their own organization, even if this led to a long period of struggle between the two sides.[69]

Adler arranged for Kelles-Krauz to meet with SPD leaders who were to take part as guests in the November 1901 conference of Austrian social democracy in Vienna. Kelles-Krauz and Ignacy Daszyński agreed upon a list of demands to be raised during the meeting: that Polish independence be accepted as part of the PPSzp program; that the PPSzp be considered an autonomous part of the SPD; that Polish candidates run for parliament in Polish lands; and that Luxemburg be excluded from the party. In the event, the meeting of 4 November 1901 with Bebel, Kurt Eisner, and Adler served as a forum for the exchange of views, and nothing more. Kelles-Krauz argued that the PPS had remained faithful to the old revolutionary character of socialism, while the rest of European socialism had grown opportunist and passive. Bebel, who carried with him Kelles-Krauz's letter to Singer, replied that the PPSzp had been given numerous chances, and that the SPD could not risk charges of treason for the sake of *Gazeta Robotnicza*. Kelles-Krauz repeated that the PPSzp would survive with or without German help, and that in a decade the Germans would come to terms. Bebel gently counseled him not to threaten the SPD, and Kelles-Krauz and Adler assured him that it was a "prophecy" rather than a threat. In parting, Adler told Bebel that he had half a mind to send fifty thousand Czechs to Berlin to show him what a real national problem was.[70]

After the PPSzp announced in July 1902 that it would run its own candidates in the 1903 elections, and the two sides failed to find a compromise at the September 1902 SPD congress, an SPD-PPSzp conference was scheduled for 19 October 1902 in Berlin. Kelles-Krauz (like Piłsudski) hoped for an agreement, but not at the cost of concessions on key issues.[71] The PPSzp made three demands: complete internal autonomy, meaning acquiescence to SPD congress decisions but a decisive voice on Polish matters; control of *Gazeta Robotnicza* with a subsidy; and bilingual candidates in regions of mixed national character. Dusting off an old tactic, Luxemburg came prepared with a list of counter-demands: that the PPSzp change its name to "Polish Social-Democracy in Germany"; that the goal of Polish independence be renounced and no longer mentioned in *Gazeta Robotnicza*; and that the journal's editorial content be controlled by the SPD (that is, by her). This drew a sharp response from Daszyński, and Bebel said that he understood the Polish demand for independence, but that the SPD could not risk subsidizing a patriotic journal. The SPD claimed that it could not sanction an autonomous organization without calling a party congress, effectively suppressing that demand. While accepting in principle the idea of bilingual candidates, the Germans demanded that all candidates be nominated by local SPD organizations.

The PPSzp agreed to these terms: autonomy was to be informal only, there would be no subsidy for *Gazeta Robotnicza*, but bilingual candidates would stand in districts of mixed populations. An agreement appeared to have been reached. Then the SPD changed its position, demanding that the monolingual August Winter stand for election in Upper Silesia. The Poles accepted this. The SPD then demanded that PPSzp congresses agree not to pass resolutions of fundamental importance for Polish workers in Germany. The Poles felt obliged to accept this as well. In the end, the SPD decided that the PPSzp could select the designated party candidate in Katowice only.[72] Despite Kelles-Krauz's urgings, the PPSzp officially accepted these conditions in its party congress in December 1902.[73]

Under pressure from Luxemburg and Winter, the SPD continued to add conditions. In late January 1903 the SPD demanded that Luxemburg be accepted as a member of the PPSzp. The PPSzp reminded the SPD that she had been banned from Polish socialism by the PPS in 1900, but Bebel again urged toleration. The PPSzp once again yielded. On 3 February, the PPSzp received a letter from the SPD containing another condition: that the name PPS be abandoned in favor of "Polish Social-Democracy." Appended to the letter was a protocol, meant to be kept secret, stating that Polish socialists in Germany had no distinct program, and that the Erfurt program was silent about Polish independence. The PPSzp, scandalized by the secret protocol and supported by the Kelles-Krauz and PPS leaders in London, refused to sign.[74] Kelles-Krauz was so angry at the SPD and Luxemburg that he complained in a letter to Leon Wasilewski that he could not sleep.

In the same letter to Wasilewski, he proposed to write an "Offener Brief" (open letter) to the SPD, chronicling its own acts and setting out the PPS position.[75] Its purpose would be to change the terms of the debate by granting the PPSzp a vehicle to make accusations against its former patron. The "Offener Brief" was printed in September 1903, in time for the SPD congress in Dresden. It argued that the PPSzp had made an inordinate number of compromises, and still could not find reconciliation with the SPD. It mocked the secret protocol, comparing it to agreements between colonizing powers.[76] Although its tone was moderated by PPSzp activists, the stir that followed its publication forced Paul Singer to add the Polish question to the congress agenda on 16 September. Although some German socialists were upset by the secret protocol, the only motion passed was Luxemburg's: that the congress endorse the SPD's present negotiating position and move on to the order of the day.[77] The congress was absorbed by fraternal bloodletting over the issues of whether social-ists could write for bourgeois journals and whether the SPD could accept a vice-presidency in the Reich.[78]

Kelles-Krauz was unable to take direct part in these congresses, as he was seriously ill. He had been bedridden all summer, and it was from his sickbed in Tyrol that he had written Karl Kautsky on 11 September, implor-ing him (in vain) to raise his voice on the Polish question at Dresden. "For the love of God," he wrote, "the SPD already has 81 mandates. How could it be hurt by a few Polish mandates, which for us would be of tremen-dous importance?" He attributed the SPD attitude in part to Luxemburg's influence. Probably not realizing that Kautsky and Luxemburg were on good terms, Kelles-Krauz called her a "limited person and a stubborn fanatic." At the same time, he believed that the SPD itself was yielding to undesirable changes. "Perhaps I'm wrong, but it seems to me that the new position, so worthy of regret, of German social democracy toward the Polish question and the PPSzp is also a result of the crisis of Marxism, of revision, of a small-minded and short-sighted revision of the elevated and daring principles of revolutionary social democracy."[79] After the Dresden conference, Kelles-Krauz wrote to Kautsky again. He regretted that rela-tions between German and Polish socialists could not be based upon "jus-tice and revolutionary principles," and called the SPD's attitude toward the PPSzp "the worst kind of revisionism."[80]

Kautsky

Since the Dresden congress was generally seen as a rout of the revision-ists, this choice of terms seems odd at first glance. Indeed, Kelles-Krauz himself praised the SPD publicly for bringing the revisionists to heel, yet wrote privately to Piłsudski that "that German filth at Dresden was revolting."[81] If we examine his single press polemic with Kautsky in 1904 and his approach to revisionism, spelled out in several articles between 1901 and 1905, we find that Kelles-Krauz thought that both sides in the German revisionism debate were misguided, and we can reconstruct his own unusual but coherent conception of "revisionism." In his debate with Kautsky in *Die Neue Zeit*, Kelles-Krauz faulted the SPD for having no clear idea as to the form a revolution would take in Germany, and Kautsky in particular for his vagueness on this point.[82] Kautsky answered that the impossibility of predicting exactly the nature of the revolution meant that concerns of guns, armies, and strikes were not of immediate importance. Kautsky accused Kelles-Krauz of misunderstanding Germany's special political situation, and of overestimating the chances that a European revolution would begin in Germany.[83] As Plekhanov pointed out, Kautsky was unable to meet Kelles-Krauz's challenge to provide a credible scenario for socialist revolution in Germany.[84] In suggesting that the SPD support Polish independence, as well as in proposing that the SPD actually consider scenarios for taking power, Kelles-Krauz was trying to force Kautsky to consider concrete steps toward revolution.

The polemic was unusual, in that Kautsky's *Die Neue Zeit* very rarely published articles on the means to revolution.[85] The strength of the SPD was at the ballot box, rather than in its revolutionary tactics: in the May 1903 Reichstag elections the party had garnered more than 30% of votes cast, and won 81 mandates.[86] But because the Reichstag had very little power, in practice the SPD had almost no voice in imperial policy. A telling anecdote concerns August Bebel, the party's leader. He served in the Reichstag from its foundation in 1868 until 1913, yet was never addressed by a minister of government outside of proceedings until just before his death in 1913.[87] The SPD created its own political world, full of press organs, worker education classes, choirs, self-help circles, feminist groups, sports teams, glee clubs, and festivals.[88] Within this subculture, party leaders "acquired a mythical status reserved, in England at least, for the royal family."[89] Kautsky was the "the pope of socialism," Bebel the "red emperor."

The habit of isolation, born of exclusion under Bismarck, and nurtured by political impotence after his fall, was given ideological cover by Kautsky's Marxism.[90] Since the revolution was predetermined by scientific laws, so long as the party's electoral results were improving and its membership lists bulging, there was no reason to think in very specific terms about just how the existing system would be displaced. Kautsky thought that the task of socialist parties was to "complete" the proletariat, "apart from the revolution, before the revolution."[91]

One might compare the effect of the doctrine of "inevitable revolution" upon the SPD to that of the doctrine of "predestination" upon Calvinists. In both cases, a certain outcome is thought to be preordained: socialist revolution in the one case, salvation or damnation in the other. An expected response of both groups might be indifference and quietism: the future of society, or the fate of the soul, are beyond the reach of human action. The actual response of each group was quite different: just as Calvinists engaged in good (or at least prosperity-inducing) acts to demonstrate that they were among the elect, Kautsky endorsed all kinds of practical activity designed to show that the revolution was coming (if not to bring the revolution about). The Calvinist had his increasing earnings; the SPD its improving electoral results. Yet neither Calvinists nor Kautskyites could in any sensible fashion close the gap between theory and practice. In his "socialist catechism," Kautsky famously wrote that the SPD was a "revolutionary," but not a "revolution-making" party.[92] Calvinism is equally "salvationary," but not "salvation-making."

As we have seen, Kelles-Krauz had little patience for understandings of "scientific socialism" which did not carefully plot the stages necessary to attain the socialist ideal. From the very beginning of his career in Paris, he had criticized the SPD on this point. Though he supported the German party in articles for the Polish public, his writings for *Przedświt* reveal his frustration. In his view, the SPD should come to terms with the fact that its accession to power by peaceful means in Wilhelmine Germany was unlikely, and should begin to consider practical steps toward a revolution, such as recruiting within the army, awakening its labor unions to the political possibilities of strikes, or supporting Polish socialism.[93] He thought Kautsky placed far too much hope in the possibility of a Russian democratic revolution.[94] His polemic against Kautsky should be seen as a provocation and a challenge.

Luxemburg

Rosa Luxemburg seized the occasion of this debate to attack Kelles-Krauz for the first time. By this time, she and her allies had gained control of the SDKPiL, and she chose its organ *Przegląd Socjalistyczny* as her forum. In her own inimitable style:

. . . this "professor" of "retrospective sociology," "doctor," baron, knight of three titles, having striven vainly for years with the help of two pseudonyms to gain a name for himself, has finally attained his goal. He has received for his troubles a few kicks in the back from Kautsky, but that's how it goes, that's just part of the European acclaim that in Mr. Elehard Esse's opinion Mr. Michał Luśnia has now gained . . . One has to hand it to the social patriots: they have indeed nationalized Polish socialism in the full sense of the word. For such Luśnias are the incarnation, in the world of socialism, of our own particular type of Warsaw publicist, who gains his notoriety by stomping on the corns of the famous in the street.[95]

Luxemburg, who during the entirety of her prolific career had never once addressed Kelles-Krauz's arguments, failed again to do so here. Kelles-Krauz was an oddity: a Marxist who made Marxist arguments in favor of an independent Poland. His first political article in *Die Neue Zeit* thus signalled the coming of a most unwelcome rival, with whom Luxemburg had never known quite how to deal. She chose to attack the man—and there is a wild and ramshackle character to the *ad hominem* barrage. Does one really seek fame by writing under pseudonyms? Might the famous sometimes deserve to have their weak spots revealed (especially as Luxemburg herself was less than inspired by Kautsky's revolutionary spirit)?[96] Is not a kick in the back worse than a stomp on the foot? Most strikingly, Luxemburg published the pseudonyms of a socialist comrade in a public forum, indeed in a journal that she knew was read carefully by the Okhrana. Of course, she was at no risk of any sanction from the SPD: most of her German comrades did not even realize that she was a member of another socialist organization, and it is safe to assume that none of them read *Przegląd Socjalistyczny*. (When Luxemburg included this article in a collection on the Polish question she published in 1905, she deleted this passage. Naturally, she also failed to place any articles by Kelles-Krauz in this volume.)[97] As for Kelles-Krauz, he wrote that he had been waiting for the axe to fall, having expected that Luxemburg would be jealous. He took the attack as confirmation that he should continue to try to gain Austrian citizenship, and play an ever larger role in the German-language socialist debate.[98] Wasilewski consoled him in typical PPS style: "Only beating them to death could have any effect. Lately they've been overcome by a madness born of desperation, and simply don't know what they are doing."[99]

Bernstein

In urging Kautsky to be practical, Kelles-Krauz was not endorsing Bernsteinian revisionism.[100] Indeed, Kelles-Krauz agreed with Kautsky that Bernstein was mistaken in believing that the class struggle was growing less severe. In his rare forays into economics, he supported the orthodox line.[101] At the same time, Kelles-Krauz thought that Bernstein's argument had the merit of opposing "empty revolutionary phraseology" and agreed that the SPD should not count on "a sudden leap from capitalist to socialist society."[102] Like Bernstein, Kelles-Krauz found a basic discontinuity between SPD theory and practice: but he could not agree with Bernstein's dictum that the "the end is nothing, the means everything," for he believed that the means were ascertainable only in light of the end.

Kelles-Krauz saw Bernsteinian revisionism as moral weakness, rationalized by philosophical error. In his understanding, Bernstein's main line of argument was that progress depended upon short, pragmatic steps based upon scientific (that is, economic) knowledge, rather than upon a determinist understanding of history linked to ideals that exist only in the minds of the individual. Bernstein believed that it was Marx's misfortune to have been influenced by Hegel, and opposed an empiricist pragmatism to Kautsky's determinist materialism.[103] Kelles-Krauz found this a false choice, which revealed errors about both the character of science, and the relation between socialist practice and the socialist ideal.

Kelles-Krauz blamed Bernstein's ignorance of philosophy for his inability to distinguish between "natural science" and Marxian "applied science."[104] Social scientists, unlike natural scientists, are indissolubly connected to the object of their study. We have seen that Kelles-Krauz believed that the sociologist forfeits the advantage of his intuition about his fellow beings by treating them as equivalent to animals, cells, or simple objects of natural laws. He continued to believe that social science is only possible through participation in society. Accepting Labriola's term *praxis* and relating the concept to Vico's principle that *verum* is *factum*, Kelles-Krauz claimed that we may only know that which we have acted upon.[105] Also, the object of study is different. Bernstein (on the attack) and Kautsky (in the defense) both assume that Marxism amounts to a set of determinist laws about the relationship between the natural world and human action. For Kelles-Krauz, historical materialism "limits itself instead to the research of human society, in which all relations are from the nature of things psychic, and of these relations considers one to be decisive: the economy."[106] Socialists who do not accept this view have misunderstood Marx.[107]

The primacy of the economic base reduces to the general psychological tendency in each individual to produce more with less effort. The belief in a determining "economic factor" as the ultimate cause of social change carries no more explanatory power than phrases like "the logic of events."

In fact, "man himself makes his own history, not forces or factors standing beyond him." The individual's common-sense belief in such forces or factors is a mystification: what appear to be objective barriers to his or her will are in fact the consequences of the actions of a large number of other individuals. Society takes on the form of an "artificial environment,"[108] but apparent "laws" of society, unlike laws of nature, may be altered if understood. The task of Marxist applied science is to understand these social relations, gaining knowledge which liberates the individual. By placing man rather than nature as the object of its study, and by assuming that knowledge about society is only possible through participation in society, Marxist applied science has a methodological advantage over all of its rivals in gaining such knowledge.[109]

Kelles-Krauz suggests that one of the tasks of such an applied science is to suggest social systems that speak to the ideals of the day. Ideals emerge as a result of adverse material conditions, but research is needed to determine how material conditions might best be improved.[110] For example, it is possible to foresee that the ideal of equality between the sexes will become general in the twentieth century, and it is the task of social research to prepare the ground so that this ideal may take on political and social forms with a minimum of conflict.[111] Social science mediates between the world as it is and the world as it is desired.

Theory and Practice

Marxist social science is thus neither an empiricist pragmatism skeptical of ideals (Bernstein), nor a passive observation of natural laws (Kautsky). The former attitude privileges the category of "reform," the latter the category of "revolution," but neither offers a satisfactory manner of relating the two. The debate over revisionism is carried out as if reform and revolution were opposites, when in fact they are mutually complementary. In Kelles-Krauz's view, a party must be revolutionary to be reformist, and reformist to be revolutionary.[112] Kelles-Krauz shared the prevalent view within the Second International that the purpose of reforms is to prepare worker consciousness for revolution,[113] but his understanding of the relationship between reform and revolution was grounded more deeply in his understanding of Marxism as applied science.

If we imagine the attainment of socialism on the analogy of crossing a river, Kelles-Krauz's view presents itself as follows. Kautsky stands on one bank, satisfied that he will one day stand on the other. Various enterprises flourish on his side of the river, but his "science" obviates the question as to whether any of them are building boats or bridges. Bernstein, by contrast, hops onto the first stone that rises visibly above the water, then to the next that he sees, and so on. He faces downward, ever seeking the next step, so his direction is dictated by the arrangement of the stones rather than the goal of attaining the opposite bank. He can continue to "progress" indefinitely without ever attaining his goal. His "science" limits him to the facts at hand, denies him the ability to interpret them in any light except that of their apparent utility at the given moment, and inclines him to opportunism.

Kelles-Krauz argues that a socialist must move forward, his path across the river drawn for him by the goal of attaining the other side. The task is at once empirical and idealist, for it conceives the relations among the stones in light of the bank at the other side. This is his familiar theory of "class possibilism": a sequence of attainable "stages," chosen one at a time, revealed by the ideal of socialism (which emerges in capitalist societies as a result of "retrospection"). This view of strategy is refined by Kelles-Krauz's discussion of Marxism as applied science. Sociology, or applied science, becomes the tool by which the socialist makes judgments about stages, both as to their attainability and as to their desirability in relation to the ideal. Sociology also eases the transition from stage to stage by explaining changes as they come.

Yet even with the best of research some stones will not offer an easy path to the next. These occasions call for a leap forward, for a moral courage based on "purity of consciousness."[114] In Kelles-Krauz's view, the SPD must take such a courageous stand in its relations with the PPSzp. Despite all the difficulties involved, German socialists should have recognized that support of Polish independence is a necessary step toward the European revolution.[115] But whence the "consciousness" that would have inclined German socialists to understand the issue in this way? It is all very well to argue that social science mediates between experiences of the present and ideals for the future, but these ideals must be shared within the social movement in question.

In calling the SPD's lack of support of the PPSzp "revisionism," Kelles-Krauz therefore had in mind a betrayal of (putatively) formerly shared ideals. Attempting to undermine this "revisionism" by way of argument, Kelles-Krauz forced Kautsky to think about practical questions of the revolution, and attacked Bernstein at the level of philosophy. But just as he could do little to change SPD attitudes about Poles in Germany, he had no success in changing the course of the SPD debate over theory and practice. Given that Kelles-Krauz continued to insist on the point that Marxism could offer no goals, but only a set of priorities for research,[116] this should not have surprised him. If Marxism did not offer comrades of different nations a common understanding of ends, then what could? On Kelles-Krauz's view, ideals come not from Marxist analysis, but from revolutionary retrospection. Kelles-Krauz had not yet answered the question as to whether all socialists shared a single retrospective ideal, or whether ideals varied from nation to nation. Kelles-Krauz's contact with German socialism proved to be one impetus toward the latter understanding of the theory.

Austrians in Austria (1903)

Kelles-Krauz's contact with Austrian socialism also influenced the evolution of his thinking on the nation, though on a different set of questions reflecting the different character of the Polish question in Austria. Unlike Germany, Austria was a multinational empire, within which Poles were a major nationality.[117] The landholding Polish nobility, well represented in the parliament thanks to the curia system, had gained a good measure of autonomy for Galicia. Though in 1896 the franchise had been extended to all adult males, the curia system ensured that the upper classes were disproportionately represented in the Reichstag.[118] Nonetheless, socialists of Viktor Adler's federal party, including the leader of the Polish PPSD Ignacy Daszyński, held seats in parliament.

As a Russian subject, and as a representative of the foreign organization of the PPS, Kelles-Krauz was an observer rather than a participant in Austrian social democracy. Because he was trying to gain Austrian citizenship, he may have intentionally kept a low profile. In any case, there was no place in Austrian socialism that would have satisfied him. The leadership of Polish socialism in Austria was firmly in the hands of Daszyński, leader of the socialists in parliament after Adler lost his seat in 1902, and one of the parliament's outstanding orators. Daszyński was the most prominent Polish political figure anywhere, and received requests for interpolation from Poles of all three partitions.[119]

Kelles-Krauz was particularly interested in the Austrian party's approach to the national question. In 1897 in Vienna, the party had declared itself a federal organization, constituted of German, Czech, Polish, and Slovene branches (soon joined by Ukrainian and Italian ones).[120] In practice, the branches drifted apart.[121] In 1899 in Brno, the party had declared its goal to be a democratic and federal Austria. The project envisioned autonomous territories with borders based upon language; education and cultural ministries at the level of these districts; a general law protecting the rights of minorities everywhere; and no official state language.[122] Daszyński's Polish socialists read aloud to the congress a declaration to the effect that their long term goal was Polish independence.[123]

Kelles-Krauz was a student of national problems in Austria-Hungary. He wrote about the national conflicts of the day: the desire of Italians (and thus that of almost every other nationality) for a university; the difficulty of achieving an economic agreement between the Austrian and Hungarian parts of the Empire; the rising voices in Budapest for a Hungarian army; the achievements of Czech patriots in Prague; the government of Galicia by Polish nobles; and so on.[124] During Kelles-Krauz's stay in Vienna, national issues regularly caused parliamentary obstructions which halted legislative work. Also, Vienna's mayor was Karl Lueger, who had won the office by the astute use of anti-semitism. Without having yet systematized his thoughts about the origins of modern nationalism, Kelles-Krauz had concluded by 1903 that Austria-Hungary was doomed to fragment.

An occasion soon arose for Kelles-Krauz to criticize the program of Austrian socialism on the basis of his observations. In 1902 the Austro-German socialist theorist Karl Renner published a work which emphasized the cultural rather than the territorial side of national demands, while insisting upon a strong central state.[125] According to Kelles-Krauz, because Renner identified himself with the Austrian state rather than the peoples fated to live under it,[126] he was incapable of believing that any nation might wish to secede, or of imagining a world in which the Austrian Empire no longer existed.[127] This national bias prevented Renner from understanding the national aspirations of non-Germans, and explained his overestimation of cultural autonomy.[128] Kelles-Krauz argued that the character of nationalism is such that its attendant aspirations may never be satisfied simply by the protection of individual rights, no matter how broadly adumbrated to include cultural rights. National identity is not an individual right in the traditional sense, for it can only be fulfilled by the formation of institutions of power.[129] "Fully developed nationalities cannot be purely unions of people, but must rule territory."[130]

In then turning his attention from cultural autonomy to democracy, Kelles-Krauz was criticizing not only Renner's position, but an article of faith of Adler and of Austro-German socialists generally. They believed that Austria must become more "European" by abolishing the curia system and thereby installing true universal suffrage.[131] According to the conventional wisdom, such democratic reform would end national conflicts by sweeping away the reactionary feudal elements now in power. As Kelles-Krauz noted, Austrian socialists emerged as defenders of the territorial integrity of the imperial lands.[132] Kelles-Krauz was convinced that democracy would have the opposite effect. Democracy may in the short term ease national conflicts by opening channels of communication,[133] but would soon after midwife the Empire's dissolution. "[Austrian socialists] believe that one of the basic arguments for universal suffrage is that it will unite the various nationalities, and paralyze the centrifugal forces that are breaking apart the state. This view still rattles around in many heads, but I must repeat that it is wrong through and through." National feeling is an authentic mass phenomenon, rather than a mystification forced upon the people: "the working classes are at least as interested in the fate of their nations as are the upper classes."[134] Unlike Adler, who thought that socialism could survive "until separatism outlived itself,"[135] Kelles-Krauz recognized that national feeling in Austria would proceed in train with modernization. Kelles-Krauz believed that a democratic Austria was very unlikely,[136] and predicted that the Empire would collapse during an international crisis.[137] Kelles-Krauz thought that Austrian socialists should therefore complement their demand for democracy with an affirmation of the right of the nationalities of the Empire to secede, thereby rendering their program consistent with that of the PPS.[138]

Jews in Poland (1902–1904)

At the end of his long article on the Austrian socialists' program, Kelles-Krauz noted that Jewish socialists, lacking a territory, were naturally attracted to cultural rather than territorial autonomy. Kelles-Krauz had begun his own reflections on the Jewish question, which would bear final fruit in 1904. Jan Kancewicz believes that Kelles-Krauz's most exceptional characteristic was his "political imagination,"[139] a trait most evident in his writings on this subject. In order to appreciate their originality, however, we must first examine briefly the PPS attitude toward Jews and Jewish socialism.

Polish and Jewish Socialism, 1893–1901

The Jewish question had been an unsolved riddle for the PPS since its foundation. The pale of settlement included the territories of the

Polish-Lithuanian Commonwealth just before the partitions (as well as lands known as New Russia), and Piłsudski and the PPS leadership believed that Jews as well as Poles had an interest in severing these lands from Russia.[140] Piłsudski's hope was that Russian oppression would turn Jewish workers in Vilnius toward Poland and the PPS,[141] but the response from the emerging Jewish socialist intelligentsia to his agitation there was hostile.[142] Although in the 1890s Poles (about 38%) outnumbered Russians (about 12%) in Vilnius, the city's Jews (about 45%) were turning toward Russian culture.[143] Since the closing of the Polish university and schools in Vilnius in 1832, Russian language and culture had crowded out Polish among Vilnius's Jewish intelligentsia.[144] The young intellectuals who were to lead Jewish socialism in Vilnius regarded their education in Russian as a window onto a wider world, which signals just how different their attitudes about Russian culture were from Piłsudski's.[145] The early PPS was more understanding of Jewish concerns than socialist parties in western Europe, but the experience of Jews as Russifiers was embittering.[146] In the first number of *Robotnik* (April 1893), Piłsudski demanded that Jewish socialists agitate in Yiddish rather than Russian, which some of them began to do.[147]

Jews also made up nearly two-fifths of the urban population in the former Congress Kingdom at this time, and Warsaw was the largest Jewish city in the world.[148] Traditionally, the Warsaw Jewish intelligentsia was Polonophone, though workers and others spoke Yiddish.[149] Jewish immigrants from Lithuania, whose second language after Yiddish was Russian rather than Polish, were beginning to affect this picture. The PPS (like the SDKP and Jewish and Polish progressive intellectuals generally) saw Jewish culture as backward and reactionary, believed that Jewish workers would soon assimilate, and hesitated to agitate in Yiddish for fear of slowing the process.[150] At a more practical level, although there were many assimilated Jews in the party leadership, very few of them could write in Yiddish.[151] When the Jewish socialist John Mill arrived from Vilnius with Yiddish materials in 1895, he was able to split the PPS's Jewish organization and start his own.[152]

The true challenge to the PPS's hold on its Jewish membership arrived in 1897 with the foundation of the Bund. Mill's Warsaw group joined the new party, which was also soon active in Białystok and Hrodna (Grodno).[153] Functioning in Yiddish, claiming as its geographic scope the Russian Empire, and advocating a pure internationalism, the Bund quickly became the PPS's *bête noire*. The PPS condemned the Bund for dividing Jews from the Polish and Lithuanian nations and for its willingness to deal with the existing Russian state, and set about trying to publish its own Yiddish journal.[154] Max Horwitz (the only PPS intellectual able to write, if weakly, in Yiddish) edited two numbers of *Der Arbeyter* in 1898 and 1899 before being arrested. Leon Wasilewski then taught himself Yiddish in order to continue the journal.[155]

For its part, the Bund opposed Polish independence on the grounds that it would divide the largest Jewish community in the world.[156] Mill argued that Jews would be wasting their effort in working for an independent Poland, for they would have to begin socialist agitation all over again in the new Polish state.[157] In conditions of democracy, Poles might well vote to deny rights to the Jewish minority.[158] At the Bund's founding congress, a resolution was passed favouring contacts with Russian socialists, but no mention was made of the PPS.[159] Several members of the Bund took part in first congress of the RSDRP in Minsk in 1898, to which despite its "all-Russian" character the PPS was not invited.[160] In the years 1898–1900, the Bund was on very good terms with Rosa Luxemburg, and reprinted her articles in its organ *Der Yidisher Arbeyter*.[161] At the time of Kelles-Krauz's arrival in Vienna, the Bund and the PPS had very poor relations and very little contact, and the PPS was engaged in a desperate struggle not to lose its Jewish members.

Vienna

Kelles-Krauz's own interest in this problem had been manifest in Paris. He had followed the struggle for Warsaw's Jewish proletariat as closely as he could, and had advocated the publication of agitation material in Yiddish. Upon meeting Jews from Warsaw, he tried to learn something of their attitudes about their own national status.[162] In 1899 he wrote a long letter to Maria, providing her with arguments to use against an acquaintance who termed Jews natural usurers. Kelles-Krauz explained that no trait inheres in any nation, and that throughout history typical Jewish vocations have varied enormously.[163] Yet despite his interest in the Jewish question, he had little reason to take up the issue in any comprehensive manner from Paris.

In Vienna, it was absolutely unavoidable. The city was in the midst of one of European history's most magnificent flowerings of science and culture, led by people of Jewish descent. The majority of Viennese doctors and lawyers were of Jewish origin, and the same was probably true of journalists.[164] Jews were very prominent in industry, and the Empire relied upon Jewish financiers. At the same time, about a third of the Jewish population of Vienna was working class, and the Jews pouring into the capital each year from Galicia were usually quite poor. Nevertheless, the stereotype of "Jew as capitalist" ruled the age, and the age was one in which capitalism was very unpopular.

The Jews lacked the traditional prestige of old landholders, and their association with the calamitous instability of early capitalism was consciously encouraged by almost every major political force, save the liberals and the socialists.[165] Karl Lueger, leader of the Christian Socials, was a political calculator rather than an anti-semite by conviction. Understanding that anti-semitism had become the lowest common denominator of Viennese politics, he tailored his electoral message around the theme that the common man's problems were a result of Jewish capital.[166] He was elected mayor in 1895, though the emperor refused to sanction his election. Freud smoked a cigar to celebrate Franz Jozef's (Emperor) decision.[167] But the continuing rise of the Christian Socials forced the emperor's hand in 1897,[168] and Lueger governed Vienna during the entirety of Kelles-Krauz's stay there. (He was still in office when Adolf Hitler arrived in 1910.) Lueger's party grew to be the dominant political force at the national level as well, sending the largest number of deputies to parliament in the elections of 1902.[169]

Austro-German[170] socialists were ill equipped to meet the challenge of an anti-semitic rival on the left. Competing with the Christian Socials for the Catholic German working class, the socialists did little to undermine the popular association of Jewish wickedness with the crises of capitalism. In the prevailing political climate, the debate between the socialists and the Christian Socials often amounted to each party claiming that the other was the real tool of Jewish capital. Because almost the entire leadership of Austrian social democracy was of Jewish descent, it began this contest at a disadvantage.

Moreover, Austro-German socialists assumed that the Jewish problem would eventually solve itself. In an argument that harmonized with the lives of Marx and numerous socialist leaders to follow, Hegel had claimed that Jews were a non-historical relic. For Marxists of the Second International, Jews were a caste, a religion, a medieval curiosity, but certainly not a nationality. Assimilation was as inevitable as it was desirable. Pogroms were regrettable, but the only progressive response was to encourage assimilation, for the organization of Jews could only prolong the death throes.[171] Following this reasoning, Austrian socialists actually

welcomed the success of the Christian Socials, in a peculiar Hegelian fashion. As the Christian Socials had buried the liberals in 1902, the socialists
were now the leading force of the opposition. Since socialists believed that
anti-semitism was an intermediary step toward opposition to capitalism as
such, and that the Jewish question would soon be resolved by history, they
took their defeat at the hands of an anti-semitic party as a signal of their
eventual victory. Anti-semitism was the socialism of the dolt (Otto Bauer),
and the Christian Socials were doing the socialists' work (Viktor Adler).[172]

Although far from the worst culprits, socialists contributed to a political atmosphere more and more suffocating to Austria's Jews. The traditional political options available to Jews were ever less viable. Assimilation
had traditionally meant an acceptance of German culture, but as German
culture itself became ever more associated with anti-semitism, this option
lost much of its appeal.[173] The political direction that corresponded to
assimilation, liberalism, was in radical decline.[174] The opposite path, assertion of a Jewish nationality, was also blocked. While increasing anti-semitism and the example of the Czechs and others catalyzed Jewish national
self-identification,[175] Jewish demands for national autonomy and a Jewish
curia in parliament went unheeded.[176] It was in this environment of political encirclement and frustration that the least expected and most con-
troversial option of all took shape: Zionism. Until Herzl's death in 1904,
Vienna was an international center of the Zionist movement,[177] and it was
Zionism which prompted Kelles-Krauz's first published reflections on the
Jewish question in April 1902.

Zionism (1902)

Kelles-Krauz was impressed not only by Zionism's attainments, but by its
resemblance to other national movements.[178] A speech of Martin Buber's
reminded him, in content and especially in tone, of Polish patriotism. This
may have been a key to Kelles-Krauz's intuition about Zionism: that it signified a qualitative change in the character of Jewish identity toward that
of a modern nation.

> So I ask, what is this common goal, uniting artist and economist?
> Why do people of such different political convictions in other spheres
> feel that they have something essential in common? Nationality.
> It suffices to look at the Zionist movement without prejudice to
> see that from Jews, scattered about the globe, speaking different

languages, from populations which for ages have had nothing in common except religion and tradition, is being formed a modern nationality.

At this point Kelles-Krauz hinted at a general analysis of the causes of modern national identity:

> I call the Jews a modern nationality because the Jewish nationality is being formed under the influence of these same factors that have strengthened or revived nationalities: French, German, Italian, Slovene—up to and including the Serbo-Lusatian revival, and not least under the influence of the most important of these factors, that great historical current, the point of exit of which is the French Revolution: the democratization of culture, the accessibility of cultural goods to the people, allowing the masses to master and further develop culture.[179]

Although in Kelles-Krauz's view Zionism's goals were unachievable, its existence as a movement signalled the arrival of a Jewish nationality, deserving of the "universal, and for us the most profitable, principles of tolerance, respect, and equal rights."[180]

Max Zetterbaum and the Bund (1902–1903)

For the general Polish public, the Jewish question was most startlingly put by Zionism; for the PPS, it was represented by the Bund. Kelles-Krauz's insight that Jews had become a modern nationality informed his own attitude toward the Bund, and distinguished him from his peers. Though he agreed with the PPS leadership that the Bund's program was misguided, he was unusual in his willingness to try to understand the Bund's point of view, and never underestimated the Jewish party. He began to teach himself Yiddish,[181] and through the good offices of his friend Max Zetterbaum attempted to resolve the dispute between the two parties.

Zetterbaum was a natural link between Polish and Jewish socialism. A Galician Jew raised in poverty, he finished law at the University of Lviv. He then returned home to Kolomyia (Kołomyja), and agitated among local Jews. He organized a strike of tallith weavers in which chasidim took to the barricades, and rabbis urged the strikers to persevere.[182] Zetterbaum was a founding member of Daszyński's PPSD in 1892, and consistently supported the goal of an independent Poland. Much of his efforts were directed toward preventing Jewish separatism within the PPSD.[183] He also wrote on various questions of socialist theory for *Przedświt, Arbeiter-Zeitung,* and *Die Neue Zeit,* where he discussed his "friend" Kelles-Krauz's conception of Marxism as sociology.[184] Zetterbaum wrote a good deal about the Jewish question, though his position was quite different from Kelles-Krauz's.

Kelles-Krauz met Zetterbaum shortly after his arrival in Vienna, and kept him company during his recovery from the amputation of a leg.[185] At the end of 1901 Zetterbaum revealed to Kelles-Krauz his dream of convincing the Bund to accept the PPS program.[186] In response to a query from Kelles-Krauz, Jędrzejowski indicated that London was willing to let Zetterbaum try, though they were convinced that the Bund's activities were on balance harmful, and fairly sure that the Bund would reject any overture from the PPS side. Jędrzejowski characterized the mood of PPS leaders as "*Judenmüde.*"[187]

In February 1902 Zetterbaum reported back to Kelles-Krauz that the Bund was preoccupied with the organizational form a merger might take. Kelles-Krauz replied that the PPS's *sine qua non* was the Bund's agreement to propagate Polish independence on Polish lands. If the Bund agreed to that, as well as to cooperate with Polish, Lithuanian, and Ukrainian rather than Russian socialists, the PPS would grant the Bund complete autonomy on Jewish matters on Polish lands.[188] Piłsudski was of the same mind, writing Kelles-Krauz that "you responded so beautifully to Zetterbaum that I want to hug you." Piłsudski added that:

> In time we'll have to put something in the program guaranteeing certain rights of Jews in the Polish paradise to come. [. . .] *A propos* "certain rights," don't think that I'm trying to oppress them, I mean that in a section of the party program we could specifically indicate that Jews in a future Poland will have the right to remain Jews if they wish, and that we will defend their rights as a nationality. But that's the future.[189]

Piłsudski's proposal spoke to an important change in the Bund program, approved at its fourth congress in Białystok in April 1901. Ending its previous indifference to national questions, the Bund declared that it supported the transformation of Russia into a federation of nations, with cultural autonomy guaranteed to all nationalities—including the Jews.[190]

The Bund's leaders were agreed, however, that socialists could not support territorial resolutions to national problems.[191] The next PPS congress, in June 1902 in Lublin, continued to condemn the Bund, but offered the following concession on the question of Jewish rights: "A [Polish] republic would assure the Jews complete equal rights as citizens, would give Jews the possibility of free development and sufficient influence on public affairs [...] in our country, which is at the same time their country."[192] Although relations between the Bund and the PPS were still very tenuous, Kelles-Krauz saw this as a ray of hope. From 1901, the Bund's close ties with the Russian socialists and Luxemburg's SDKPiL began to unravel. As the Bund adopted national goals (and as its use of Yiddish material awakened the national identity of Jewish workers), the SDKPiL began to regard the party as patriotic.[193] Lenin's *Iskra* attacked the Bund for its independence on programmatic issues, and Plekhanov also voiced his hostility. In the months preceding the second congress of the RSDRP of July 1903, Lenin used the SDKPiL as an instrument to attack the Bund's right to autonomy within the Russian party.[194] That congress, best known for the Bolshevik-Menshevik split, also witnessed the withdrawal of the Bund from the RSDRP.[195]

In 1903, Kelles-Krauz seems to have perceived a window of opportunity for a rapprochement with the Bund. He kept up contacts with Bundists through Zetterbaum, though with little result.[196] As Zetterbaum pointed out, no Bundist could understand the advantages that Polish independence might have for Jews.[197] Kelles-Krauz tried to advance a more attractive deal in the conclusion of his long article on the Austrian socialists' program (July 1903). There he noted that unlike Russian comrades, the PPS understood and accepted the Bund's goal of autonomy.[198] In any case, he argued, the Bund will never manage to win national rights for the Jews in any multinational state ruled from Moscow. The PPS, on the other hand, promises full autonomy within a future Polish republic. The Bund should therefore realize that its proper partner is the PPS, and accept the PPS program.[199] In the same spirit, hoping to find the formula that might break the ice between the Bund and the PPS, Kelles-Krauz decided in late 1903 to give voice to his personal views on the Jewish question.

Narodowość Żydowska

Kelles-Krauz's most significant article of the Jewish question, "On the Question of Jewish Nationality," was published in the January and

February 1904 numbers of Wilhelm Feldman's influential Cracow monthly *Krytyka*.[200] It was not an explanation of the PPS position on the Jewish question to the general Polish public, but the call by an individual to both his party and the progressive public to take a fresh look at the issue.[201] He grants the typical Polish objection that Zionism's goals are utopian, but argues that the "historical content" of Zionism is not exhausted by its program. Its significance must be sought in the factor, standing beyond its plans and personalities, that has made such a seemingly unlikely organization successful: the idea of Jewish nationality.[202]

At this point, Kelles-Krauz stops to define terms. Nationality is a new and modern social category, qualitatively different from religious or state affiliations inherited from feudalism. The nineteenth century has proven the forge of nations, in that groups of people speaking a similar language and having something like a common history have concluded that they constitute a distinct body. Each nation believes that it is of equal worth to all others, and that it must decide upon all questions of its fate. Kelles-Krauz stresses that this transformation is characteristic not only of nations which achieved unified statehood in the nineteenth century (Germany and Italy), or of states with proud state traditions (Hungary and Poland), but also of "nationalities, which, one might say, no one expected": the Czechs, the Ukrainians, the Croatio-Slovenes, the Lusatian Sorbs, the Lithuanians.[203]

Whence this new form of consciousness? Kelles-Krauz's answer is unequivocal: "modern capitalism directly forms nationalities." Capitalism transforms a static feudal economic order into numerous, mobile, and overlapping classes. The individual, uprooted from his traditional economic and social position, finds a single constant in the new capitalist economy: his native language. At the same time, the qualitatively more complex relationships created by capitalism demand an effective form of communication. Producers and consumers speaking the same language are more likely to trade than those who do not, and entrepreneurs speaking the same language are more likely to cooperate against the foreigner. The consolidation of this national identification is hastened by mass culture. Capitalism demands an educated population, and thus traditional national myths "in the very interest of capitalism" will reach the nation as a whole, rather than its elites only. Here intellectuals catalyze "retrospection." Although modern nationalism is a genuinely new form of social consciousness, its advocates traditionally present their beliefs and goals as the revival of an eternal tradition. The formation of modern nationalities always takes on the "external form" of a "renaissance." Mass culture also allows for the transmission of the liberating ideas of "equality and democracy" to the oppressed. Since the French Revolution began the process of spreading these ideas throughout Europe, they need not be formulated anew by each awakening nation.[204]

In setting forth a general descriptive model of the rise of the modern nation, Kelles-Krauz created criteria by which recent Jewish history might be judged. Given the power of traditional stereotypes, this was in itself no small accomplishment. Kelles-Krauz found that Jews were manifesting the same signs of nation formation as other European peoples. The idea of "equality" served an important function: Jews observed the arrival of modern nationalism around them, and applied the same set of ideas to themselves. The very fact the Jewish political formations, such as the Bund, now demanded to be treated as a nationality was of key importance. The idea must also be found in larger masses, however, and a mass culture demands a mass language. The distribution of Yiddish socialist materials by the Bund and the PPS allowed workers a sense of their own worth as part of a larger community. Despite the intentions of both parties, this self-identification took on a national form. Kelles-Krauz calls the Zionist program (with its return to Zion and the associated revival of Hebrew) a characteristic example of retrospection.[205]

Kelles-Krauz then draws the political conclusions. He distinguishes between the Zionist program and the idea of Jewish nationality, noting that arguments against the feasibility of the first rarely speak to the reality of second. He takes careful aim at a popular argument of the Polish left: that if Jews organize rather than assimilate, they should not be surprised if anti-semitism increases. He argues that this can only sound like a threat, and further increase the tension between Poles and Jews. Against the claim that Jewish organizations will tend to be reactionary, he cited the Bund.[206]

Because every nation considers itself to be an end in itself, Poles and Jews will find common ground only if progressive Poles search for arguments that speak to the interests of Jews. Kelles-Krauz argues that the interests of both nations would be best served in a Polish republic that offered extensive national rights and cultural autonomy to its Jewish citizens. Given that Jews will not leave Poland *en masse* for Palestine, that Jews have no territorial solution in Europe, and that large-scale assimilation has become highly improbable, a future Polish republic should recognize the national rights and autonomy of its Jewish population. (Here Kelles-Krauz once again addresses the Bund to argue that its program of cultural autonomy would be much more feasible if it turned its attention from a future constitutional Russia to a future independent Poland.) Kelles-Krauz imagined a Poland in which Polish and Jewish cultures freely intermingle, and in which Polish citizens considering themselves to be of both Polish and Jewish nationality provide links between the two. In such a republic, each individual would have the right to choose his own national identity.[207]

Motives

Kelles-Krauz hoped for cooperation between the PPS and the Bund. He knew that the Bund could not see the advantage of a Polish republic, and so advanced the idea of a Polish state which more than met the demands of the Bund's program. Unlike the majority of the PPS leadership, Kelles-Krauz did not think that the Bund would splinter and weaken of its own accord, and his argument that the Jews constituted a nationality was intended to provoke thought in that quarter as well. Even as anti-semitism increased, the small Polish Jewish assimilationist movement dissolved,[208] Zionism made inroads into the Russian Empire, and the Bund overtook the PPS among Warsaw's Jews around 1904,[209] most PPS leaders stood by their belief in the inevitability of assimilation.[210] Piłsudski was willing to entertain the idea that Jews were a nationality if it served a political purpose; Kelles-Krauz became convinced that it was genuinely so.

Central European Marxists were usually even less flexible than the PPS on the Jewish question. Kelles-Krauz's position, although based upon what he understood to be Marxist premises, could scarcely have differed more from the consensus among his Marxist comrades.[211] Rather than believing that capitalism would necessitate a general assimilation that would obviate the Jewish question, Kelles-Krauz believed that it had transformed Jewry into a modern nation, and that central European socialists were in need of a new and creative political response.

Kelles-Krauz may have been motivated by another political goal. In Vienna, he was confronted with the reality of a popularly-elected, economically leftist, anti-semitic mayor. Critical of capitalism and armed with a scapegoat ideology, leftist anti-semitism had succeeded in attracting the working class.[212] Roman Dmowski's National Democrats, then embracing an ever more exclusionary and biological view of nationality, offered a similar message to Poles.[213] Because Kelles-Krauz believed neither that assimilation was inevitable nor that anti-semitism would naturally lead to simple anti-capitalism, he sought to safeguard a future Polish republic from Dmowski.

Kelles-Krauz did temporarily convert Wilhelm Feldman (of *Krytyka*) from ardent assimilationism to his own position, and apparently exerted some influence over Aleksander Świętochowski (of *Prawda*) as well.[214]

For Kelles-Krauz the Jewish question was an object of personal concern as well as political import. He was a lifelong opponent of anti-semitism, and had intended to write on the Jewish question well before his arrival in Vienna. Moreover, from a research point of view the Jewish question was even more fruitful than the Polish question. The Polish question had allowed him to reflect on the relationship between the nation and the state, while the Jewish question allowed him to create a general theory of the rise of modern nationalism. Indeed, some of the arguments he developed in this context would find use shortly in defense of the PPS program.

Poles in Europe (1904–1905)

The Bund was not the PPS's only competitor for the allegiance of workers. Whereas for much of the 1890s the PPS had been the only underground political party within Russian Poland, it now faced a number of rivals: the Bund, the SDKPiL, and the RSDRP on the left, and the National Democrats and Christian Democrats on the right. The PPS's fame had been based upon spectacular successes: most notably, the continuous publication of *Robotnik* between 1894 and 1900, and the theft and publication of the Imeretynskii memo in 1898. As the century turned, Piłsudski believed that the PPS needed to change the character of its activity in order to shake itself out of a growing lethargy.[215]

Rivals to Piłsudski and London were also emerging within the PPS. After Piłsudski and his ally Aleksander Malinowski were arrested in 1900, a large number of young left-wing PPS activists resisted control by Piłsudski's emigrant allies.[216] London managed to keep hold of the party leadership, and used its control of the press to try to keep the views of these young activists from gaining further support.[217] The result between 1901 and 1904 was a continuity of formal leadership by Piłsudski, Wojciechowski, Jędrzejowski, Jodko, and Wasilewski, but a growing gap between these older men and a new generation of activists within the Russian partition.[218] Following a turn of phrase of Piłsudski's, Polish historiography traditionally refers to Piłsudski and the London leadership as the "old ones," and to the left opposition in Poland as the "young ones"— indeed, a number of their disagreements can be traced to generational differences.

First, this new generation had not experienced the birthing pangs of Polish socialism, and was therefore less inclined to accept the party's traditional emphasis on conspiracy over open agitation. Their own first experience with socialism had often been leading strikes in the late 1890s,[219] and they were more inclined to believe in the masses than in the need for careful plans and secrecy. Second, these younger activists had no memory of the 1892 strike in Łódź, which had brought the men and women who were to lead the PPS to the conclusion that a Polish socialist program must include national independence. Their attachment to the program of national independence was therefore less firm. In this connection, it bears mention that a far higher proportion of the "young ones" than the "old ones" were assimilated Jews.

Third, while the PPS had been founded at a time when Russian socialism was extremely weak, these activists had come of age at a time when the Russian movement was reasserting itself. They were thus more likely to favor cooperation with Russians, and to believe that a Russian constitution would allow for the development of socialism in Poland. Fourth, these younger activists had started their careers at a time when Luxemburg was in Germany and the SDKP was non-existent. Having not experienced the first competition with the SDKP, they were more likely to see its revival as a neutral or positive development, and to urge cooperation. Fifth, they had a different perspective on PPS history. Piłsudski, looking back at his decade in the party, came to the conclusion that the PPS was stagnating, and should begin a revival by extending a hand to other layers of society besides the working class.[220] From the left of the PPS, Kelles-Krauz was coming around to the same view. But younger activists in Warsaw were more likely to see the PPS's task as agitating within a growing working class that was just beginning to be politicized. Sixth, the left opposition had little experience with the leaders of foreign socialist parties, and thus had not been disabused of its simple internationalism.

Kelles-Krauz stood between the two groups. In many respects, the younger activists' views resembled his own, ten years previous. Like the most outspoken members of the left opposition, he had been (and remained) a Marxist. His first pamphlet, "The Class Character of our Program," aimed to decentralize the Union of Polish Socialists Abroad in 1894, just as younger Warsaw activists wished to decentralize the party itself in 1904. His advocacy of a general strike had been based upon the same trust in the working class. In 1894, Kelles-Krauz had also been optimistic about cooperation with Russian socialists, and considered the

SDKP a positive force with a misguided program. In 1894, while critical of the programs of leading international parties, Kelles-Krauz had assumed that they would cooperate with Poland in its struggle for independence and socialism.

As the years passed, Kelles-Krauz's views grew closer to, while still differing in several important respects from, those of Piłsudski and London. By 1904, his disgust with Luxemburg and her SDKPiL was unsurpassed. (Although he was unusual in believing that some of its members might be simply mistaken, rather than acting in bad faith.) His experience with French, German, Austrian, and Russian socialists had persuaded him that the PPS could count on little help from other parties. But perhaps more important than changes of mind was a certain change in attitude. Kelles-Krauz was now on the inside of the party leadership. In a subtle process that stretched over years, he grew to be friends with those who set the party line, notably Jędrzejowski and Piłsudski. By the time he moved to Vienna, he used the "ty" form of address with Jędrzejowski, Jodko, and Wasilewski, as well as with Piłsudski. By 1904 he spoke of the Union of Polish Socialists Abroad—the organization to which he had dedicated himself in Paris—as a mistake that had lasted too long,[221] and presumed for London in its disputes with his former Paris Section.[222]

Kelles-Krauz was trusted by the PPS leadership because his devotion to the cause of independence had proven true. He was the only Marxist among the leading figures of the PPS, and one of only a handful of Marxists in Europe, to argue a strong case for the independence of Poland. His Marxism had made him a suspect quantity from the first, but eventually came to be accepted—if only as a personal foible.[223] By 1904 Kelles-Krauz found his London colleagues' opposition to Marxism amusing, but it no longer provoked serious arguments between them.[224] Aside from his Marxism, his major differences with Piłsudski and London were two: he believed that the best opportunity to gain independence would follow a German or Austrian revolution[225] (although he grew less and less convinced that German and Austrian socialists were capable of leading revolutions), and he did not exclude the possibility of cooperation with Russian socialists or the Bund.[226]

Marxism and National Independence

Kelles-Krauz's last important article on the national question in central Europe, "Polish Independence and the Materialist Understanding of

History,"[227] was intended to justify the party program to PPS members who considered themselves Marxists, and were tempted by Luxemburg's arguments on the national question.[228] From 1901, Luxemburg had taken direction of the SDKPiL, and from 1902 its two party organs, *Przegląd Socjalistyczny* and *Czerwony Sztandar,* were propagating her theory of organic incorporation.[229] Kelles-Krauz was prompted to write the article by the desire expressed by some members of Daszyński's PPSD for cooperation with the SDKPiL.[230]

Kelles-Krauz had been opposing his understanding of the national question to Luxemburg's for ten years. Most recently, he had produced a long pamphlet for workers, in the form of a dialogue between two workers on the programs of the two parties.[231] The novelty of the new "Materialist Understanding" article was that Kelles-Krauz supported his criticisms of the Luxemburg position with his own conception of the rise of the modern nation.

He begins from the generally accepted socialist view that capitalism demands a strong, centralized state. But Kelles-Krauz argues, against Luxemburg's view, that it also demands a national state. He brings to bear the arguments he developed while considering the Jewish question. Nations are formed by capitalism; capitalism's ability to unite various groups into nationalities is determined by the geography of language. Before the arrival of capitalism, groups which spoke similar dialects had little contact and little reason to identify with one another. Capitalism brings an extraordinary and unprecedented mobility of populations, and thus teaches which dialects are mutually intelligible and which are not. It likewise heralds the arrival of a mass culture, which unifies mutually comprehensible dialects into a single language. Production and exchange are most successful within areas of a single language, and the development of capitalism and of national consciousness continues in train. Nations will always seek to govern themselves, and sometimes succeed. But modern nations may also meet the resistance of pre-modern dynasties, such as the Romanovs and Habsburgs. Their empires did not arise as a result of capitalism (and should not thus be justified as the kinds of states which will best catalyze its development), and exist in a state of tension with the nationalities arising within and across their borders.[232]

Multinational empires do not in practice seek to "organically incorporate" their various national regions. The dominant nationality will develop its industry at the expense of others. Industry in the Congress Kingdom is discriminated against within the Russian Empire;[233] Galicia is kept in a state of backwardness by Vienna. These regions will remain vulnerable so long as they lack a national government to protect them and a national market to serve.[234] Nation-states can negotiate trade with their neighbors, so the existence of a Polish state would not end its commerce with Russia. Luxemburg may well be correct to argue that the Polish bourgeoisie opposes independence, but that is for fear of revolution rather than out of rational economic calculation.[235] The power of existing empires in eastern Europe has prevented the bourgeoisie from playing its historic state-building role. The desires of the Polish bourgeoisie should not, however, determine the strategy of the Polish proletariat, which must itself build a national state.[236]

The proletariat needs the democratic nation-state in order to win the class struggle. Only democracy can assure the free exchange of ideas, the unbiased education, and the spread of culture that are necessary to build a strong workers' movement. Further, the democratic nation-state is the only political system within which the proletariat can build socialism. The social direction of the economy will be an enormously complex task, possible only within the discrete area of a single nation-state. Moreover, every socialist reform must have the legitimacy of an electoral majority in order to succeed. This legitimacy is impossible if minorities are (or believe themselves to be) discriminated against in economic or other matters.[237]

The nation-state is also necessary for the socialist project because national and class consciousness arrive simultaneously. When workers awaken to their own human worth, they identify not only with people facing the same economic conditions, but also with those of the same nationality. "There is no anational proletariat, there are only Polish, Russian, German working classes."[238] Each participant in the class struggle is thus motivated by national as well as class goals. "The proletariat must say: I am the nation, nothing which is national is foreign to me."[239] In democratic conditions, shared national identity and language permit the formation of commonly accepted norms and regimes based upon a shared understanding of the common good. These norms and regimes form the boundaries of the class struggle.[240]

Kelles-Krauz concludes by arguing that the SDKPiL and the PPS correspond to immature and mature working class consciousness. In the first years of its self-awareness, the proletariat is weak and isolated. It asserts its independence from the bourgeoisie by a simple negation of all bourgeois values, including national values. It conceives the revolution as a sudden and complete transformation of society. Later, as the proletariat gains strength and experience, it asserts its own point of view, rather than simply opposing the society that exists. It begins to understand that all parts of society are mutually interdependent, and that there is no such thing as a clean break with the past. The party "becomes national, comes to terms with all elemental problems of its particular country, accounts for its distinct character, understands its needs."[241] (In Gramsci's later term, it seeks "hegemony.") Instead of rejecting all national values, the proletariat asserts its opposition to the status quo by endowing national goals with a revolutionary character.[242] This argument, addressed to a group whose views were much like the young Kelles-Krauz's, and with its explicit evocation of maturity, has an unmistakably autobiographical air.

Science, Politics, and the Nation

Kelles-Krauz did not live to reconceive his general approach to Marxism in light of his conclusions about the national question. Nevertheless, with some effort we may piece together answers to the questions raised at the end of chapter three about his understanding of the relationship between politics and science. Kelles-Krauz's understanding of the unity of sociology and socialism found its greatest difficulties with regard to the national question. The major problems were his ambiguity about whether the retrospective ideals which inspire revolutionaries are universal, or instead take on varying forms according to national traditions; and his lack of a concept of national bias to complement the notion of "social apperception."

From his work on the Jewish question, we cannot judge what he would have argued about the relationship between the retrospect of primeval communalism, and the retrospect toward national historical myths. What is certain is that he grew to believe by 1904 that retrospection applied to emerging national as well as class consciousness, inspiring intellectuals leading national as well as class movements. Similarly, though Kelles-Krauz never used the term "national apperception," he began to collect examples of the phenomenon. Time after time, he argued that the French and Germans were blinded by the fact that they were citizens of nation-states from seeing the importance of the nation-state to Poles.[243] Preparing for negotiations with Bebel on the PPSzp, he expressed the view that all European socialist parties were "nationally predatory."[244] His arguments with Adler provide further evidence that he regarded national bias, even on the left, as inevitable.[245] In his polemic with Renner, he argued that the national bias of Austro-German socialists prevented them from

understanding the national aspirations of others and inclined them to identify themselves with the existing Austrian state. Mocking the arrogance of
his fellow sociologists, he wrote that theories assuming the supremacy of
whites served only to show that each race will always consider itself superior.[246] His final political writings amplify a conclusion long before drawn:
majorities will oppress minorities in the belief they are doing right, and
minorities will assume they are repressed even when they are not. Such
national bias is so powerful that it will resist even the free flow of information and mass culture facilitated by democracy, and can render socialism
impossible.

In light of his growing appreciation of national identity as a source of
ideals as well as of bias, did Kelles-Krauz still identify his political views as
science? In Paris, he had claimed that his strategy of "class possibilism"
or "stages" was itself constitutive of "scientific socialism." He believed that
intellectuals, most sensitive to the calls of the past, would be inspired by
visions of primeval communalism to plot a methodical course to international socialism. It was possible to foresee that the independence of
Poland would be a necessary stage on this journey. Yet, his view of Marxist
sociology expressed in Vienna as "applied science" is substantially more
modest. He no longer claimed that the simple effort by intellectuals of
identifying stages in light of ideals is "scientific," but instead advocated
sociological research in order to determine how popular ideals might best
be realized. Crucially, this is a much more democratic vision.

The category of democratic pluralist politics was emerging clearly in
Kelles-Krauz's political thought. The two most common topics of his articles in the legal press were the constitutions of existing states and the
progress of social reform by way of parliamentary legislation.[247] A frequent
critical tool was his own definition of democracy: the rule of law rather
than of bureaucracy; division of powers between a sovereign parliament
(with final control over budgets and immune from dissolution) and a
purely executive government; elections by universal suffrage on the principle of one-person, one-vote.[248] As Kelles-Krauz pointed out, no such system existed anywhere in the world at the time.[249] (But he was also at pains
to explain that flawed democracy was better than none.)[250] Similarly, in his
sociological work, he now wrote of anthropological evidence of "primitive
democracy," and of socialism as its revival.[251] This heightened attention
to democracy dovetailed with Kelles-Krauz's work in the Polish socialist
press: his advocacy of democracy in his 1905 "Polish Independence" article
extended beyond its instrumental value as a stage on the way to socialism.

Kelles-Krauz now presented democracy as the form of government which most flexibly and effectively deals with the inevitable conflicts of interest of a complex modern society. In a formulation with a remarkable Karl Marx-meets-Karl Popper flavor, Kelles-Krauz argued that:

> Society develops, and must develop, because it yields to the unceas-ing pressure of mankind, striving for ever greater productivity and ever fewer hours of work. As a result, economic forms change, and the state and its law must change as well, sooner or later. But on the other hand, we also know that the state and the law must resist every transformation. And when this resistance lasts too long and is too stubborn, society falls into a state of illness . . . One could argue that democracy is the form of government, at least in this era, which allows for the execution of greater and smaller changes, as we might put it, painlessly, and at the proper time—not too early, thus avoiding reaction, and not too late, thus avoiding revolution. The essence of the theoretical, sociological justification of democracy, which would now have to be translated into the language of law, is that it guaran-tees society the possibility of full and peaceful evolution . . .[252]

In another work of 1905, Kelles-Krauz argued that fully-developed democ-racy could "gradually adapt itself to new demands of social life, to today's call for a rebirth [of socialism]."[253]

This justification of democracy is striking in its resemblance to Kelles-Krauz's definition of the role of "applied science." Both enterprises serve the purpose of easing transitions while speeding change, smoothing con-flicts of interest while sharpening debate. Neither directs social change, both are means of allowing it to take place peacefully. This provides a signal that Kelles-Krauz's strengthening belief in pluralist democracy is related to the new modesty of his claims about the possibility of a science of politics. Applied science allows intellectuals to catalyze social progress to some extent, but is unable to resolve the inevitable and unceasing con-flicts among interests. This is democracy's role.

Yet, the national question could render even fully democratic repub-lics dysfunctional, and even intellectuals of the left are distressingly susceptible to national chauvinism's siren song. This further limits the reach of science into politics, for no intellectual is capable of engaging in an applied science that was not compromised by national bias. As far as geography permits, democracy must take place within a nation-state.

In that way, national consciousness may unify citizens and thus provide the boundaries of the class struggle, rather than divide them and prevent social progress. The "science" of politics becomes politics itself, politics as practiced under the conditions of far-reaching democracy and within the confines of the nation-state. Sociology no longer stands in for politics; at most there is a "sociological justification" for democracy, within which "applied science" allows intellectuals their modest place. The democratic nation-state is a norm toward which Poland must strive.

At the same time, Kelles-Krauz's justification of democracy weakened not at all his belief that a revolution would be needed to free Poland from Russia.[254] In his view, the most likely scenario for Polish independence was: (1) social revolutions in Austria and Germany, (2) an attempt by the tsar to restore the *anciens régimes* by military force, (3) revolution in the Russian Empire, including a decisive blow by the PPS.[255] The likelihood of this prediction's fulfillment depended on the revolutionary spirit and practice of the German and Austrian parties. The character of his interest in these parties reveals Kelles-Krauz's own national bias. While in Vienna, he came to see the violent revolution as the struggle by Poles to gain national independence, which would allow democracy and the gradual attainment of socialism. At the same time, he urged German and Austrian comrades on toward a violent social revolution, which he did not foresee for Poland. He must have assumed that these revolutions would bring socialists to power, for he counted on help for the PPS from Germany and Austria. This is obviously not a contradiction, for one could certainly hold the view that Imperial Germany (if not Imperial Austria) had proven unsusceptible to peaceful methods of change, while a newly independent Poland would be a true democracy. Even so, it is clear that Kelles-Krauz saw European politics through the prism of Polish independence.

Sociology, Pedagogy, and Revolution (1904–1905)

In its various forms, the national question in central Europe was Kelles-Krauz's main concern during his time in Vienna, and it, rather than the discipline of sociology, inspired most of his new ideas. Kelles-Krauz was studying law rather than sociology, and could no longer attend conferences in Paris. He nevertheless continued to write a good deal on sociological subjects, often defending his own view of sociology (as we have seen in the context of the SPD), polemicizing against organic analogies, and defending the existence of primeval communalism.

A sociological work published shortly after his arrival in Vienna was "A Glance at the Development of 19th Century Sociology," which provided a Hegelian scheme of the history of the discipline. Kelles-Krauz considered sociology as a reaction against eighteenth-century rationalism, whose retrospective ideal was classical antiquity. Sociology began as an attempt to return attention to the organic links between concrete events, and longed for the imagined harmony of the middle ages. Saint-Simon exemplifies this tendency. While retaining the best of Saint-Simon, Comte escaped his fascination with feudalism, and thus opened the way for a truly progressive sociology. The eighteenth-century enlightenment restrospect of Greece had to meet the nineteenth-century sociologists' historicist retrospect of the middle ages to allow for a retrospect of primeval communalism.[256] The dialectical logic here is almost unmanageable. What is of interest is Kelles-Krauz's general appreciation that the history of a discipline is not a steady march forward, and his more specific appreciation that the modern academic division of labor does not flow simply from the principles of the enlightenment, but that disciplines such as history and sociology are rooted to a certain extent in reactions against it.

Kelles-Krauz returned to his theory of revolutionary retrospection in 1903, in an article about "The Social Movement in Antiquity"—a work even more entangled in Hegelian reasoning than the previous. He argues that the source of feudal ideals was the Roman Empire; the source of bourgeois ideals the Roman and Greek republics; and the source of socialist ideals the primeval communalism which preceded Greece. He makes the historical claim that the first retrospection was the Greek idea of a golden age, which reflected dim but existing historical memories of the primeval communalism which preceded Greek civilization. In an argument which seems to justify a passage to socialism by way of democracy, Kelles-Krauz now claims that consistent bourgeois democrats who long wholeheartedly for Greek antiquity also began to long for what the Greeks themselves longed for: primeval communalism. Kelles-Krauz sees all of this as an argument for further research and education on antiquity and prehistory, for he believes that knowledge about the past allows retrospective longings to find their proper object. Interestingly, he argues that belief in God is a result of historical ignorance, in that retrospective longings which can find no object settle on an abstraction. He thus explains the success of

Christianity in the early middle ages by the sudden break with tradition that followed the fall of Rome.[257]

One of Kelles-Krauz's two major sociological projects in 1904 and 1905 was *Portraits of Deceased Sociologists* (published in 1906, after his own death). Kelles-Krauz defends familiar views here, although he adds a few interesting notes. He makes a convincing case for different national styles in sociology, noting that Poles tend to resist biological analogies, Germans to start from the premise of the existence of the state, and Frenchmen to proceed logically from *a priori* grounds.[258] He correctly predicts that Spencer, the greatest sociologist of his time, would be nearly forgotten within a generation.[259] He calls Spencer the "protoplast" of the organicist schools of sociology, and notes that Spencer's influence has been such as to prevent the enactment of labor laws.[260] He criticizes Spencer for failing to notice that as society becomes more complex, the labor of individuals becomes increasingly specialized and dull.[261] This is one example of a growing concern for the spiritual effects of capitalism.

Art and Alienation

This concern is central to his second major academic project of 1904 and 1905, "Some Major Principles of the Development of Art." From his days of reciting love poetry in student circles in Radom, art had played a consistently important role in Kelles-Krauz's life, and Kelles-Krauz had always in some general sense connected art with social change. He remained devoted to Polish romantic poetry, with its political aspirations, throughout his life. In Paris, the Kelles-Krauzes had artists as friends, and often spent their weekends in art museums. In Brussels, Kelles-Krauz was pleased to find artists and revolutionaries on good terms, and to find social concern in the work of Young Belgium.[262] In Vienna, however, Kelles-Krauz would find the slogan "art for art's sake" accepted far more widely than in Paris and Brussels, and connected to political indifference and mysticism by a large part of the bourgeoisie as well as by the artistic intelligentsia.[263] The confrontation between this credo and his own long-held beliefs pushed him to at last systematize his thinking on the social role of art.[264]

Kelles-Krauz began from two assumptions: first, humans are instinctively aesthetic;[265] second, humans are tool-making animals, and adapt to their environment by technical rather than biological changes.[266] Among primitive peoples, tools serve clear functions such as gathering food, defense, or attracting a mate. But tools satisfy aesthetic needs as well, and assert the individuality of their creators. Because the creation and use of tools was itself pleasurable, primitive peoples expended far more energy than would have been necessary simply to satisfy their physical needs. This expenditure of energy was not work in our understanding of the term, for the joy of making and using tools prevented the gap between means and ends from emerging.[267] Although tools were at first clearly linked to tasks, they soon took on social meanings as well. The warrior's weapons began to stand for leadership, and so on. These meanings often came to dominate the original purpose of the tool.[268] Here we find art's special trait: although initially connected to the satisfaction of needs, its relationship to these needs can be mystified in such a way as to communicate social norms.[269]

In slightly more complex societies, labor is cooperative. Fishing, farming, and hunting all require some means to organize the activity of several individuals. The key to many collective tasks is simple rhythm, which is created by chanting and singing, or by drums and other instruments.[270] While facilitating cooperation, rhythm also gives rise to a feeling of unity. Singing, dancing, and the playing of instruments grow from coordinated labor, become arts in their own right, and allow for this feeling of harmony even when separated from their productive purpose.[271] They also come to be rites, associated with the hope for a fruitful result of agricultural labor.[272] (Kelles-Krauz notes that singing is usually associated with women, to whom in primitive societies are consigned the most repetitive tasks. This stands behind the myth of female secret knowledge, of witches chanting while stirring cauldrons.)[273]

As societies modernize, the connection between the satisfaction of basic needs and art grows ever more attenuated and imperceptible, but continues to exist. At the simplest level, technology determines what kinds of artistic enterprises are possible, and by the same token limits our own aesthetic sensibilities. The ability to distinguish between notes, for example, demands musical instruments.[274] Just as simple tools designed to meet needs become art by degrees, so do more complex technologies eventually take on an aesthetic character. The techniques needed for basketweaving suggest geometrical patterns which then appear in other products.[275] Architectural styles responded to certain building materials, yet survive these materials' obsolescence.[276] Social organizations can play a similar role, as when mediaeval musical guilds stifled innovation.[277] At the most general level, our aesthetic sense depends upon prevailing moral practice and beliefs, which are in turn connected to economic and social changes.[278]

The more developed a society, the more intermediary links there are between art and "economics, or 'life.'"[279] Art is thus a particular case of a general principle Kelles-Krauz had elucidated in his sociological work in Paris. A characteristic of capitalism, he had argued, was that it complicates the satisfaction of needs, widely construed. As the division of labor progresses, ever more steps are necessary to accomplish the goal of satisfying a need. This leads to a confusion between ends and means, for the means become so numerous, complex, and difficult that they must be treated as ends in themselves simply in order to be attained. The connection between an individual's effort and the satisfaction of his needs becomes increasingly thin and elusive. Purely physical needs continue to be satisfied, though at the price of psychic exhaustion and division.

The division of labor also alienates us from our aesthetic selves, as creation is slowly removed from the occupations and becomes the preserve of professional artists. Instead of hunting for game with handmade tools, planting crops to the rhythm of the songs of the village, or even producing crafts at a loom or forge, modern workers spend lives making holes in needles or springs for watches.[280] Only the small minority of artists has retained from primitive peoples what most have lost: the simple pleasure of creating for its own sake.[281] For everyone else, the result is dire: a complete atrophy of a need, alienation from a natural and vital part of the soul.[282] Dreams are deferred, and dry up like raisins in the sun.

Even the position of professional artists is tenuous and uncertain. They are assailed from all sides under capitalism, for all classes have accepted that the good is the same as the useful, and that good deeds spring from obligations rather than inclinations.[283] Artists have responded by elevating themselves to the level of mystical prophets, and calling for an art for its own sake.[284] While this isolation and this credo are historically explicable, they carry with them the danger of decadence. Kelles-Krauz supports this claim with a specific prediction. As artists try to liberate themselves from society, art for its own sake will become identified with a concentration on form. This will reduce art to technique: instead of lofty ideas, its subject will becomes its materials. No exercise in *l'art pour l'art* should thus be understood as a challenge to the existing order.[285]

In fact, the slogan of art for its own sake often serves as cover for cowardice and servitude.[286] The notion is a sociological absurdity: the people who make art are products of their times, and thus no art that people produce can be separated from history. It does not follow, however, that socialists should call upon artists to serve their progressive cause.[287] The credo of art for art's sake is a result of a division of labor which has grown so monstrously complex, and the cultural crisis it signals demands a radical remedy. For art and life to be reunited, the social purpose of art as a transmitter of ideals must once again become apparent; but at the same time art must be pursued for its own sake, rather than conceived in terms of utility. This seeming paradox can be resolved only by ending the division of labor. Schiller's ideal of art as a mediator between the individual and society, between freedom and obligation, was possible in primitive societies, and will be possible again under socialism.[288]

Kelles-Krauz wrote these last paragraphs of his work on art with a kind of critical sympathy. His own life shared much with those of the artists he addressed: at the most terrible level, it is no coincidence that tuberculosis has been called "a disease of revolutionaries" as well as "a disease of artists." Like avant-garde artists, Kelles-Krauz was an antipositivist in an age of positivism, and sensitive to the cultural transformations of capitalism. Like Nietzsche (whom he cites), Kelles-Krauz believed that civilization had been won at the price of the suppression of the valors of primitive man. Kelles-Krauz saw the problem of aesthetic alienation as part of man's alienation from his own nature. The understanding is Hegelian, and although later Marxists (notably Lukács) would devote much attention to art and alienation, it bears little resemblance to Marxist thinking of the era.

Kelles-Krauz had once criticized Engels for adding reproductive drives to the Marxist schema. In his discussion of art, Kelles-Krauz not only postulated the existence of aesthetic needs alongside material needs, but assigned an autonomous role to tradition, creativity, the human capacity to draw meaning from ambiguous signs, and the ability of societies to unite their members around a group of shared symbols. Yet, Kelles-Krauz's own view of himself as a Marxist was unchanged. He considered his work on art to be within the tradition of historical materialism; and in a set of lectures given in August 1904 at a "free university" Kelles-Krauz helped to found in Zakopane, he presented himself, as ever, as an orthodox Marxist.

Nauka Polska

From autumn 1903, Kelles-Krauz from Vienna and Wilhelm Feldman from Cracow planned a Polish "free university" ("Uniwersytet Wakacyjny") in Zakopane.[289] Having taught at independent universities in Paris and Brussels, and interested in other private universities such as the London School of Economics,[290] Kelles-Krauz was convinced that such institutions were a necessary complement to state education. They allowed for the teaching of novel fields, such as sociology, as well as inconvenient ideas, such as socialism. As the level of state education available to Poles was generally far lower than that available to the French, the Belgians or the British, such an institution would be all the more desirable on Polish lands. The needs of Poles from the Russian partition were greatest, and the university was planned with them in mind. For Kelles-Krauz, the task of a free university was to instill in its students the critical attitude and cult of knowledge that would allow them to draw their own conclusions on social and political questions.

The courses were scheduled for August 1904, so during vacation, and in Zakopane, an attractive Galician location where Poles from all three partitions and elsewhere could gather. It was to be a united national endeavor.[291] "*Nauka Polska*," as the enterprise was called, was to be an opportunity for Polish academics as well as the Polish public. Kelles-Krauz aimed to give qualified Poles from the Russian partition (first of all Bolesław Limanowski) the opportunity to lecture they had been denied for political reasons.[292] Limanowski would describe Kelles-Krauz leading him into a room of famous Polish academics;[293] Kelles-Krauz was pleased to act as a mediator between these two worlds. The university was also a forum for Polish scholars of European renown, such as the linguist Jan Baudouin de Courtenay, to gather in Poland. Other lecturers included outstanding Polish intellectuals who were not academics, such as Feldman and Stanisław Witkiewicz. Socialists were well represented by Krzywicki, Limanowski, and Kelles-Krauz, among others. The foreign organization of the PPS supported the venture, after some persuasion by Kelles-Krauz, and sent along its own representatives.[294] Ignacy Daszyński and other leading Polish socialists gave informal lectures on current political events.[295]

From Vienna and his various sickbeds in 1903 and 1904, Kelles-Krauz filled out forms,[296] sent out course announcements to newspapers,[297] wrote to prospective lecturers,[298] and discussed with Feldman the concept of a free university.[299] In late July, Kelles-Krauz left his sanatorium in Kosiv (Kossów), and traveled straight to Zakopane to prepare for the university's opening.[300] He saw to the inevitable logistical details, and on 31 July delivered an inaugural lecture on the purposes of free universities. The following day he gave the first lecture in a series on "The Modern Social Movement as a Second Renaissance." At his first mention of the word "socialism" a chorus of whispers followed: "He admits it!" The lectures seem to have been generally well-received, although National Democrats took advantage of seminars following each lecture to accuse him of spreading propaganda rather than knowledge.[301]

Zakopane was a stronghold of the National Democrats,[302] so some such response was to be expected. Although Limanowski was generally treated with great respect, he was insulted and snubbed by National Democrats. At a stocktaking session midway through the month-long course, a group of students led by a priest called the university a propaganda center. Kelles-Krauz responded that in free universities points of view such as socialism are not excluded from the outset, but judged on their merits.[303] The National Democrats also tried to take control of the future of the "free university" by gaining a majority within its governing body; this threat was also turned aside.[304]

On balance, it appears that Kelles-Krauz's enterprise transformed Zakopane for the month of August 1904 from a sleepy, conservative resort town into a progressive outpost of education. 456 registered students, mainly under thirty and from the Russian partition, joined a larger number of unregistered attenders from nearby.[305] An Okhrana informer estimated the total of students and attenders at 2400, and claimed that as many as 400 students were present at certain lectures.[306] Despite the strife brought by National Democrats, most students were satisfied with their unique opportunity to meet the cream of Poland's intelligentsia. "Nauka Polska" was also an tremendous financial success, and its organizers planned to build a proper lecture hall for the next year's course.[307] For socialists, it was an unparalleled opportunity to become acquainted with the youth of Russian Poland. Kelles-Krauz wrote Maria that he was very happy that he had chosen to come, for something special had been accomplished in Zakopane.[308]

Rewolucja

The gathering of socialists and progressive intellectuals from all three partitions and abroad provided an exceptional opportunity for much-needed political discussion. The Russo-Japanese War, which had begun in February 1904, had enlivened both wings of the PPS. Rising unemployment and fear of the draft brought thousands of new members to the party. During the spring and summer of 1904, young activists in Poland had led large demonstrations of workers. The reaction of Piłsudski and the émigré leadership (now moved to Cracow) was different. Piłsudski went to Tokyo in May, and offered the Japanese diversionary action and intelligence in exchange for arms and a promise to raise the Polish question at peace talks. The Japanese, already winning the war, had no reason to add a European front. They did agree to exchange arms for intelligence, which helped Piłsudski supply new PPS armed squads.[309] The right of the PPS also sought contacts with the Polish middle classes, and tried to find some arrangement with the National Democrats.[310]

Younger PPS activists within Russian Poland hoped to exploit the war to provoke a revolution in cooperation with Russian comrades and the Bund, while older leaders feared a spontaneous, elemental rising, and aimed to exploit the war to organize disciplined armed units. In the spring and summer of 1904, Kelles-Krauz expected little from the war,[311] but his contact in Zakopane with arrivals from Warsaw seems to have raised his hopes somewhat. In Zakopane on 25 August, Kelles-Krauz and his comrades Wasilewski and Jędrzejowski from the foreign organization of the PPS met with representatives of the PPS from Warsaw, members of the PPSD, and independent intellectuals to discuss the war. A number of Warsaw intellectuals, represented here by Ludwik Krzywicki, believed that the PPS was underestimating the Russian bourgeoisie, and that a constitution in Russia was indeed possible. Kelles-Krauz attempted to co-opt this feeling by proposing that the PPS, while standing by its program of independence, announce that in the case of the promulgation of a Russian constitution its goal would be a parliament in Warsaw with full political authority (by which he meant the right to declare independence).[312]

Kelles-Krauz returned to Vienna at the end of August, but he found no rest. Russia continued to boil in late 1904, and the PPS leadership relied on Kelles-Krauz both in international negotiations, and to keep the peace within the party itself. Between 30 September and 9 October, Kelles-Krauz served as one of the PPS delegates to a conference in Paris of eight opposition parties within the Russian Empire, including the National Democrats, but not the Bund, the SDKPiL, or the Russian social democrats. Russian groups and the National Democrats successfully opposed including Polish independence within a general list of common goals.[313] Later in October, a conference of PPS leaders in Cracow failed to define a common response to the war. Piłsudski and the left agreed that there should be armed units, at least to protect workers during demonstrations.[314] On 13 November, fifty armed PPS members opened fire on Cossacks who had arrived to crush a workers' demonstration in Warsaw. It was the first time that Poles had fired on Russians since 1864.[315] In late December, Kelles-Krauz was called to Geneva to take part in a conference of the PPS foreign organization.

He asked to be allowed to stay home as a result of his continuing illness, but his presence was demanded.[316] As the year closed, he found himself defending and explaining the actions of the older leadership to younger activists.[317]

On 22 January 1905, revolution began in Petersburg. A peaceful procession led by Father G. A. Gapon was fired upon by the Russian army, and about a thousand marchers perished. On 27 January, workers in Warsaw began a general strike, which spread throughout Russian Poland. The Warsaw committee of the PPS dashed off a "political declaration," in which it demanded political, national, and economic rights without explicitly demanding Polish independence. Its aim was cooperation with Russian workers and socialists to bring about the fall of the tsar. Kelles-Krauz reversed his earlier opinion, and decided that the moment for a national rising had arrived. His newfound decisiveness may have been due to causes besides the changing political situation. At around the time of the Petersburg massacre, Kelles-Krauz's illness was first diagnosed as tuberculosis.[318] All of his political judgments of the next several months must be read in the knowledge that Kelles-Krauz had learned that his own death was probably imminent.

On Adler's advice, Kelles-Krauz sent an article to *Die Neue Zeit* at the end of January on the events in Warsaw, arguing that the slogan of 1831, "for your freedom and ours," now meant cooperation among all socialist parties within the Russian Empire in the fight to topple the tsar. He did suggest the possibility that the revolution might bring an independent democratic Poland, but not a fully democratic Russia. Kautsky rejected the article for that reason,[319] and Adler agreed with Kelles-Krauz that Kautsky had behaved foolishly.[320] In an article of February in *Krytyka*, Kelles-Krauz appealed to the Polish martyrological tradition, and indicated that he now believed that Polish independence might be won.[321] In a March article in the same journal, Kelles-Krauz again recalled the Polish tradition of national risings, calling the "revolution" of today of greater significance than the rising of 1863. Not only are more people involved, but the participants are workers and intellectuals, instead of nobles. He endorsed the "political declaration" of the Warsaw PPS, with its demand of a parliament for Warsaw (and another for Vilnius) with full political powers. He wrote with a wink to the right wing of the PPS: he expected that such parliaments would immediately vote for independence, and aimed to keep the left of the party and independent intellectuals on board by accepting this tactic.[322]

On the ground, the split between the left and the right of the PPS widened. The strikes forced quick decisions, undermining the remaining
authority of the émigrés (and of Piłsudski, who was in Cracow). As party
membership grew to the tens of thousands,[323] plans to organize tightly
disciplined units seemed absurd to activists in Warsaw. The revolution
exacerbated the key disagreements about goals and tactics to the point
where the party effectively split.[324] The Warsaw party organization called
a party conference for 5 March, and then voted itself the authority of a
party congress. It resolved that although the party's eventual goal would
remain Polish independence, its immediate goal should be parliaments in
Warsaw and Vilnius. Armed units would be used to protect mass demonstrations, and would not be the centerpiece of party strategy. Cooperation
with Russian parties, the Bund, and the SDKPiL was to be sought. Party
authority would be devolved downward to local organizations. A new
directing committee was called, including Piłsudski (providing that he
return to Russian Poland). Wasilewski was expelled from the foreign organization of the PPS.[325]

Jędrzejowski and Jodko, the bastions of the party's émigré right wing,
resigned from the Foreign Committee of the PPS, though Jodko wrote to
Kelles-Krauz with a request to mediate. Kelles-Krauz went to Cracow on 19
March to talk to young party leaders, and found that he sympathized with
many of their complaints. After talking to both sides, Kelles-Krauz arranged
a compromise on 23 March. Max Horwitz and Jan Strożecki (the man who
had introduced Kelles-Krauz to the PPS back in 1894) would keep the positions of authority they had won at the congress, but Wasilewski's expulsion would be withdrawn and the resignations of Jodko and Jędrzejowski
would be forgotten.[326] Trusted by Piłsudski[327] and the right as an old comrade in arms, and trusted by the left for his ideas and his evident good
faith, Kelles-Krauz was the only individual in a position to bring off such
an agreement.

In its aftermath, Kelles-Krauz wrote his last letter to Piłsudski. Kelles-
Krauz maintained that Piłsudski and the émigrés had failed to take
seriously the legitimate complaints of younger activists, and had underestimated the importance of the events of January. Since the March party
congress had united the most serious activists in Russian Poland, it must
be accepted as legitimate. He urged Piłsudski to become directly involved
in the party's operations, for in the absence of experienced leadership the
left would commit serious errors. Confident that Piłsudski would find an
exit from the quarrel, Kelles-Krauz closed with his own recommendation:

I consider the slogan of a parliament in Warsaw with theoretically unlimited powers as excellent and as corresponding to the present situation in the best possible way, but I am fundamentally opposed to limiting in advance its achievements to autonomy instead of independence. As to means, even though at the beginning I was one of those counseling the greatest caution, I now consider that we must retreat before nothing. We must strive for an armed revolution.[328]

In April, Kelles-Krauz then wrote a third article for *Krytyka*, in which he admitted he had been mistaken to place his hopes in a revolution in Austria or Germany.[329] But by the end of the month, he was forced to withdraw to a sanatorium near Pernitz, where he continued to read, write, and plan his books.[330] From letters from friends, he learned that Russian soldiers fired into a workers' march in Warsaw on May 1, and that the PPS replied by bornbing Cossacks.[331] He must have been disappointed to learn that despite the effectiveness of its armed units, and the new wave of strikes that followed, the PPS could not find lasting agreement about its tactics. From his sickbed, Kelles-Krauz could do little to help.

In a congress near Warsaw beginning 15 June, the left wing of the PPS effectively took over the party. The key disagreement was over priorities: the left thought that all efforts must be directed toward dethroning the tsar, while the right thought that independence should be seized if the opportunity presented itself. Growling that no soldier had ever been killed by Marx, Piłsudski urged the creation of larger militias. The role of armed units was clarified to include terror as well as protection of demonstrations. But the party's directing committee was dominated by five members of the left,[332] and Piłsudski chose not to run for a spot.[333] In Kelles-Krauz's absence, no further compromise between the left and right wings of the party would be found. On the last day of the congress, 18 June, five more Polish workers were killed during a march of five thousand in Łódź. Around twenty thousand workers attended the funerals on 20 June. Official figures give 70,000 as the number of workers demonstrating the following day. On the morning of 23 June, all factories stood still, barricades went up all around Łódź, and workers battled police. That day another general strike was declared, and the tsar announced a state of war in Łódź.[334]

Polish historians describe 1831 and 1863 as "powstania," or risings. The word "rewolucja" enters Polish history with the events of 1905: this struggle for national freedom crossed class lines and created the first mass parties in Polish history. The PPS had done more than any other organization to prepare the ground for a revolution. Even so, it was overtaken by events, and it frayed and split as it was transformed—for a brief moment—from a conspiracy to a mass party. The cause to which Kelles-Krauz had devoted his life was in its ascendance, and the party which he had served was at once in triumph and in tatters. The next day, 24 June 1905, Kazimierz Kelles-Krauz died of tuberculosis at five o'clock in the afternoon.

Conclusion

EUROPEAN LITERATURE OF the end of the nineteenth and the beginning of the twentieth centuries abounds in coming-of-age stories that explore the theme of a generation which finds traditional authority inadequate to a new world. Yet the portrayals of generational rift (to take three rather different examples) in Ward's *Robert Elsmere* (1888), Alain-Fournier's *Le Grand Meaulnes* (1913), and even Musil's *Die Verwirrungen des Zöglings Törless* (1906), all pale in comparison to the trials of Polish youth recalled by Żeromski in his *Syzyfowe prace* (1897). By illustrating the problems and concerns of a generation of educated Poles in the Russian Empire, Kelles-Krauz's life helps us to understand why this is so.

His political education, like that of most of his fellows, began in the home. Like many of his peers, Kelles-Krauz sought to transcend the romantic and patriotic values of his father, which seemed to offer no exit from the verdict of 1863. His generation's formal education was humiliating and difficult, for Kelles-Krauz and his fellows reached adolescence at the height of the Russification of schools. They were beaten for the smallest infractions, forced to speak a foreign language in classes and in the schoolyard, had to parade through the churches of another religion, and were told to despise the values taught by their families. Yet sharp as this break between school and home was, these students were not content to retreat to traditional Polish values. The self-education circles they organized were a kind of self-defense before the Russian state, and provided the background for early tests of ingenuity, loyalty, and organization. But they were also a place of learning, where young people absorbed ideas which were new and alien to their parents. Students reached enthusiastically for western books and western ideas, which offered the promise of a radical transformation of backward, partitioned Poland into social and political modernity. This formed in some of them an enduring fascination with ideas, as though the dedication of a few individuals to the correct studies could change the fate of a nation.

Youthful experience of oppression either broke or reinforced individuality, aspirations, and dreams. Students who managed to finish school with their loyalties to political ideas intact were then often forced into an even more unsettled adult life. Here Kelles-Krauz was typical of young political intellectuals: denied the possibility of a university education in the Russian Empire, he chose to live and study in Paris. He was relatively fortunate, in that he was able live by his pen, and even had an academic career of sorts. His French was superb and his German was good, and he was well integrated into Parisian and Viennese social and political life. Most prosaic and most important, he had a very happy marriage and family life. He preserved a stable sense of optimism and an impressive work ethic, while many of his comrades alternated between fits of feverish work and long spells of inactivity and depression. Still, he could not escape the constraints and disappointments of émigré life. He lived in an atmosphere of gossip and paranoia, but also in a world of necessary conspiracy and justified fears. He wrote under pseudonyms, knowing that the whole of his work would not be appreciated until after his death. As the years passed, he had to accept that he would probably never be able to return home.

Kelles-Krauz was typical of Polish political émigrés in believing that Poland was important to Europe, and typical in his frustration with Europeans who were indifferent to or ignorant of Poland. The position of Polish political intellectuals was incomparably weaker than that of the western intellectuals and politicians they met in emigration, and yet their tasks were immeasurably more demanding: they had to win national freedom, rebuild a state, and design a modern economy. Devoted to this cause, but separated from hearth and homeland, they substituted ideas and imagined bonds with the people for the emotional and cultural ties they lacked. As they aged, as their failures mounted, as their parties remained tiny, as the slender possibility of an academic career vanished, as the revolution failed to come, as Poland remained resolutely backward, as Russian repression continued, and as comrades, friends, and lovers vanished behind bars or to Siberia, they had little more than hope and work for the cause to sustain them. Poverty conspired with politics to deny the comforts of a normal life.

Kelles-Krauz's unceasing work brought him and his family a measure of financial, social, and psychological stability, but at a price. In the words of his best friend from Radom, Władysław Bukowiński:

In other conditions, society would have assured him work, would have contributed to the development, in some small part, of the rich stores of his soul. In our conditions, it is otherwise. Pushed away from the gates of the university, he wandered through the world, supporting himself for many years by newspaper correspondence and scholarly articles. His entire life he wore himself out with excessive work, exhausting his frail organism, and the only institute in Warsaw whose goal is to support the work of scholars refused him aid for purely formal reasons when he turned to it in time of illness. A mediocrity with better finances could have counted on help, but throughout his life Krauz [...] had to struggle with circumstances, uncertain of the nearest future. In his last months he received help only from his closest comrades of the Idea, who now weep after his passing.[1]

Another of these comrades added, "We won't speak of Luśnia's personal life, of his difficult material conditions. For who doesn't know the position of the socialist Polish intelligentsia?"[2] Kelles-Krauz's youthful death of tuberculosis was a not uncommon fate among his contemporaries, and especially among his socialist comrades. It denied him the political future which awaited friends who survived to see the Second Polish Republic. He would have been 46 in 1918, and 54 in 1926.

Politics

Kelles-Krauz's life illustrates, within limits, the kinds of choices which awaited young Polish intellectuals who chose to practice politics. Despite poverty, emigration, and dedication to scholarly work, Kelles-Krauz was an exceptional political activist, both in terms of the scope of his accomplishments, and the manner in which he treated his comrades and rivals. For the most part, he avoided the petty personal quarrels and doctrinaire absurdities so endemic to émigré life. He went out of his way to dispel unfounded rumors, and believed that patience and good faith could resolve most disputes. Surprisingly often, he was on good and even friendly terms with SDKP activists. Although he was a sharp polemicist, he treated the arguments of opponents fairly, and usually avoided *ad hominem* attacks. At the same time, this tolerance had nothing to do with moral laxity, and he was quick to condemn fellow socialists who violated the ethical norms which he believed bound comrades. Even political opponents acknowledged his moral authority.

Kelles-Krauz was typical of Polish political intellectuals in his preoccupation with the relation between national liberation and social revolution, but he was unusual in his patience in seeking some resolution of the two. Although Polish socialists were more sophisticated than their west European counterparts on the relationship between the national question and the class revolution, they nevertheless tended to wish one of the two problems away. In the SDKP and on the left of the PPS, most activists favored Polish national independence in principle, but believed that the class revolution would in some fashion resolve this problem. Luxemburg's belief that Polish lands had been "organically incorporated" into the Russian Empire was extreme rather than representative, even in her own party. On the center and right of the PPS, Piłsudski and others believed that independence was necessary to resolve social problems but they rarely moved beyond this simple assertion. They tended to see in Marx what Marx had seen in Poles: fighting spirit. Kelles-Krauz spoke the language of the Marxists, but supported the conclusions of the patriots.

According to Kelles-Krauz, the very power of nationalism means that the goals of socialism can be achieved only within democratic nation-states. The nation-state is an end in itself as a resolution of national aspirations, although its boundaries and constitution must be drawn up in such a way as not to thwart the national aspirations of others. The democratic nation-state is also a necessary condition for socialism, as it is for all reforms which concern a politically aware populace divided into groups with divergent interests. Democracy is the political system best suited to the demands of modernity, and best suited to resolve social tensions while avoiding the extremes of open class war or reactionary *coups d'état*. Kelles-Krauz's extraordinary political achievement was thus to transcend the apparent conflict between the national and social questions, justifying democracy as the closest thing to their resolution.

He provided the PPS with the center position it needed, and during the revolution of 1905 Kelles-Krauz was the only activist in a position to hold the party together. His ideas, force of personality, and simple good will provided a bridge between the "old ones" and the "young ones." As

Jędrzejowski wrote to Limanowski, "He died at the worst possible time, both for him and for us."[3] Even had he lived, he might not have been able to prevent the final division of the PPS in 1906. In any case, his death left an opening in the Polish left which remained unfilled. Whereas Kelles-Krauz had come to see democracy as the necessary mediator between national and class issues, neither of the two parties which emerged from the PPS was especially democratic. The PPS-Left was organized along fairly democratic lines, but like Luxemburg's SDKPiL assumed that the question of democracy would be resolved within the framework of a constitutional Russia (or of some international socialist organism). Piłsudski and other leaders of the PPS Revolutionary Fraction had their eyes firmly fixed on independence, which they came to view almost exclusively as an end in itself. The Revolutionary Fraction was run as a military hierarchy, organized around Piłsudski's personal authority.[4]

Luxemburg and Piłsudski, though both democrats in some sense, lacked the kind of reasoned justification for democracy which Kelles-Krauz had achieved by 1905. Luxemburg is known for her doctrine that revolution must come from the masses, but she also regarded the legitimation of social reform by majority vote as "parliamentary cretinism." Her famous criticism of the Bolsheviks is muddled on this key point: she praised the October Revolution, but wanted immediate elections, which the Bolsheviks surely would have lost. In 1926, Piłsudski effectively ended democracy in interwar Poland, which was compromised by (among other things) its inability to come to terms with the national question within its borders. In fairness to Luxemburg and Piłsudski, one should say that Kelles-Krauz did not live to face the choices of 1917 and 1926.

Sociology

Kelles-Krauz was also an exceptional thinker within the Marxist tradition. Although he called himself orthodox, his understanding of the character of Marxism was profoundly different from that of mainstream theorists of the day. While Karl Kautsky regarded Marxism as a closed system, Kelles-Krauz considered Marx to have been simply the greatest in a line of social thinkers. He traced Marx' s lineage back to the Greeks, and supplemented his work by reference to Morgan, Comte, Hegel, and Vico. (Orthodox Marxists did allow the Marxist canon to be interpreted in light of the writings of Engels and Darwin, but Kelles-Krauz was hostile to the influence of both.) He treated the Marxian legacy as "open" (in Hochfeld's phrase)

to continuing improvement and amendment. Indeed, Kelles-Krauz considered Marxism as a manner of posing questions, rather than as a set of
given answers. Far from believing that Marxism provided the natural laws
through which social change could be explained and predicted, he was
convinced that it supplied the best guidelines for social research.

Although his version of Marxism may appear modest, Kelles-Krauz in a
certain sense expected much more from historical materialism than did his
orthodox peers. In the first place, his Marxism was eminently political. He
never substituted determinism or economics for politics, and considered
that the task of "scientific socialism" was to provide an "applied science"
which could inform political choices. He never ceased to remind socialists, especially German Marxists, that politics is almost always a question
of small gains won by hard work and detailed knowledge. At the same
time, Kelles-Krauz's vision of the ultimate goal of these "stages" was a total
remaking of civilization. For him, revolution was brought about by human
longings, rather than measurable economic changes; and he believed that
socialism would bring a new kind of culture, as well as economic justice.
Capitalism is necessary for this transformation, in that it brings economic
development and modernization. But its division of labor alienates man
from his own nature, and thus brings about the demands for a total social
transformation which were best articulated by Marx. These take the form
of a longing for the real and imagined past—the revolution must also be
a restoration.

Although other socialist writers considered the past as a fount of values, Kelles-Krauz was alone in developing a theory of progress which was
based upon tradition. Hobsbawm writes that "a general hostility to irra-
tionalism, superstition, and customary practices reminiscent of the dark
past, if not actually descended from it, made impassioned believers of the
verities of the enlightenment, such as liberals, socialists, and communists,
unreceptive to traditions old or novel."[5] This is the crucial point: Kelles-
Krauz was amenable to traditions both authentic and invented because he
was ambivalent about the enlightenment itself. He saw both socialism and
sociology as reactions to the enlightenment: they absorbed its rationalism
and empiricism, then transcended it by recognizing the force of tradition
and the necessity of treating society as irreducible to the individual or the
natural world. Progress achieved by understanding nature has its limits,
which socialists and sociologists perceive and seek to surpass.

Kelles-Krauz's more academic sociological work was also exceptional
in its day, for some of the same reasons. He was typical of a generation

of Polish sociologists who were at once anti-positivist and utopian—wary of analogies of society with nature, they nevertheless believed that sociology could hold the key to radical social change. They tended to assume a tripartite model of history, in which knowledge gained in the present could link the glories of the past with a modern national future. Critical of contemporary notions of gradual or evolutionary progress, they tended to draw attention to the continuity and autonomy of tradition. Of these sociologists, Kelles-Krauz was most successful in opposing the biological analogies then dominant in European sociology, arguing convincingly that the study of society must find methods other than those of the natural sciences. He proposed that the sociologist must exploit a sympathetic understanding of his subject which is not available to the natural scientist, and that he must participate in a given society in order to understand it. He considered "things in themselves" as well as "single causes" to be mystifications, and asked sociologists to treat the objects of their investigations as phenomena with multiple causes.

Before Max Weber (1864–1920), Kelles-Krauz articulated the need for a distinct methodology appropriate to the study of society, and was urging sociologists to treat such terms as "the economy" as ideal types (in Weber's term) useful for research, rather than as discrete realities. Unlike Weber, he never believed in the desirability or possibility of a "value-free" *Wissenschaft*, insisting that the methods, concepts, theories, problems, professional ethos, and simple existence of academic disciplines were historically conditioned. Sociology is itself a legitimate and necessary subject of sociology; historical materialism applies to itself. According to Kelles-Krauz, researchers must treat both "facts" and "values" as phenomena, and include their own conditions and persons within their investigations. They should strive to understand the historical causes of their own biases, and then set objectivity as the unattainable goal of their wills. Kelles-Krauz's insistence on this point made him aware of his own biases, most notably allowing him to see his own nationalism as typical of larger trends in European social history. Weber's different approach on the question of "fact" and "value," despite its undoubted success on other fronts, freed him from the obligation of personal or scholarly critique of his own nationalism.[6] Strict separation of "fact" and "value" can justify (as in Weber's own case) the individual's choice of *both* the "vocation" of politics and the "vocation" of science, while freeing him from any need to critique his political actions by way of his scholarly work. Kelles-Krauz did not believe (as Weber would) that politics and science are distinct "vocations," opting instead to outline a specific set of tasks which constitute the "applied science" of the political intellectual.

This careful demarcation of the uses of science in politics distinguishes Kelles-Krauz from Weber's pupil György Lukács (1885-1971), although in other respects these two Marxists had much in common. If we follow convention and date the beginning of Western Marxism from Lukács's *History and Class Consciousness* (1923), it becomes clear that Kelles-Krauz anticipated some of that tradition's major concerns. Lukács defined Marxism as a method, which was precisely Kelles-Krauz's understanding. Lukács[7] preferred Marx to Engels, as did Kelles-Krauz. Both Lukács and Kelles-Krauz thought that determinism was a characteristically bourgeois error, and both believed that the natural sciences had nothing to do with Marxism properly understood. Marxism concerned society: man's "artificial environment" (Kelles-Krauz), or "second nature" (Lukács). Lukács used the term "reification" to describe the process which Kelles-Krauz discussed as the confusion of means and ends brought on by the division of labor; both believed that a task of Marxism was to allow people to understand that apparently immutable social forms are in fact the results of human labor. Lukács rediscovered Marxism's Hegelian roots and placed the notion of alienation at the center of his thought, as had Kelles-Krauz. For both, Marxism was neither a description of the world as it is, nor an ideal of the world as it should be, but an expression of history in which the proletariat takes part. But while Lukács thought that the "totality" of the historical process could be understood by identification with the proletariat, Kelles-Krauz took the view that this impression of "totality" was characteristic of every rising social group—the proletariat would be one in a long series of classes to believe that its rise signaled the end of history. Kelles-Krauz's Hegelianism was psychological rather than teleological: he was inclined to see man's search for totality, rather than the emergence of totality itself, as a motive force of history. He did not believe that history employed men in a particular way so as to achieve its own ends, but rather that men are such that they think in certain historical terms. Kelles-Krauz was thus self-referential in a way that Lukács was not, and denied that the proletarian viewpoint allowed any objective knowledge about history.

Given their common emphasis on alienation, it is perhaps not surprising that both Lukács and Kelles-Krauz had strong ties to art. Lukács had been a prominent literary critic before a sudden conversion to Marxism in adulthood; Kelles-Krauz had kept a foot in both worlds from his student days as romantic poet and materialist.[8] Some of the better-known works of each concern the place of art in capitalist societies, and both men tended to define intellectuals in terms of sensibilities rather than knowledge or attainments. Nevertheless, their different understandings of the historical character of "alienation" and "totality" led them to different conclusions about the role of party intellectuals. Lukács granted a party elite authority over the masses due to its putatively proletarian understanding of history. In his youth Kelles-Krauz had proposed a view of intellectuals that could have supported such a conclusion, but in his later years he was careful to define an "applied science" which would help to foresee, explain, and ease change, but not to dictate its course.

Nations and Nationalism

Kelles-Krauz's most important contribution to scholarship was his work on the national question. Here he is outstanding when compared to socialists and scholars not only of his day, but down to our times.[9] More than any other aspect of his thought, his analysis of nationalism deserves a restatement here.

Kelles-Krauz believed that nationalism was a child of capitalism. Capitalist development creates a new set of fluid, complex, and impersonal relationships, which put greater demands on language. In the first place, industrialization brings an unprecedented mobility of populations and goods, and thus increases the importance of previously existing linguistic borders. Trade is more likely among populations which can understand each other, and producers who speak a single language are more likely to build oligopolies and join forces to seek the support and protection of the state. At the same time, capitalism brings a mass culture which tends to unify mutually intelligible dialects into a single language. The advent of mass education, demanded by capitalism, brings an official version of a given language into the schoolroom. All the while, ever-increasing contact between people of various dialects will tend to erode their differences. At a certain point, mastery of a "high" or "literary" language will become obligatory among intellectuals, but this is a stage rather than a precondition of national development. Where there is a popular language and capitalist development, a literary language will soon be created. Ukrainian and Yiddish, he predicted, will at some point become literary languages.

The individual who has been cast from his traditional social and economic position by the new capitalist division of labor will seek after some kind of stability, and will find it in the national language. He or she will come to feel a kind of solidarity with others who speak this language, whether he or she has met them before or not. This impersonal solidarity (which Anderson would later call the "imagined community") takes the form of a belief in a shared fate, articulated with reference to a mythical national past. Although the national identity is a genuinely new form of consciousness, it is invariably expressed in the language of eternal tradition. The creation of a national idiom of the mythicized past is one of the main tasks of nationally-oriented intellectuals. Although historical memory is rather weak, the use of "invented traditions" (in Hobsbawm's later term) has a powerful consolidating effect. Historical myths will inevitably conspire to justify a nation's demand for sovereignty and independence. Indeed, this will to state-building is the signal of the arrival of a modern nationality. The model of the democratic nation-state has been available in Europe since the French revolution, and has been seized upon by each emerging nation. Also, nations which are oppressed by multinational empires cannot help but realize the importance of controlling the state apparatus. This national awakening and its demands are a crucial part of a larger process of the entrance of the masses into politics. Thus, national solidarity by no means excludes other forms of solidarity, such as that of economic classes. In practice workers tend to become aware of their national and social identities simultaneously, and attempts to awaken their class consciousness also arouse their national awareness.

The modern nation is a historically new form of social consciousness; its loyalties and aspirations are qualitatively different from those of religions, or of status groups within feudal systems. Because the modern nation is new, there is no fundamental difference among nations which have had more or less national states for hundreds of years (the English, the French), nations which have recently acquired them (the Italians, the Germans), stateless nations with state traditions (the Poles, the Hungarians), and nations with neither states nor traditions of states in modern times (the Jews, the Ukrainians, and so on). The traditional distinction between historical and unhistorical nations is illusory: fulfilled or not, the aims of all nations are the same.[10] Because national identity is a form of consciousness, it cannot be decided by "objective" criteria such as blood, geography, or language. Although particular national identities are clearly related to particular national histories, the choice between competing and viable identities must be left to the individual. This choice criterion for national identity, though it has since become conventional wisdom in some western states, was very unusual at the time.

Kelles-Krauz predicted the end of the multinational empires of his day, believing that the emerging nations of the Ottoman, Austrian, and Russian domains would seek to build their own states. He argued that multinational democracy, the remedy proposed by Austrian socialists, was neither ethical nor effective. It fails in practice, for it does nothing to slow the inevitable secessions and disintegration. It is ethically insufficient because national identity is not a right which may be protected by a just state, but an aspiration which may be fulfilled only by identification with the state. Democracy may allow the process of nation-building to take place without violence, so long as it is coupled with the right of each nation to secede. No multinational state which does not respect this right should be considered democratic.

Likewise, socialism could be justified in practical and moral terms only within the democratic nation-state. Only in conditions of free expression can socialist ideas find their natural constituents. More, the process of radical social reform must be democratic, for the economic choices involved are so complex and difficult that they must be sanctioned by a majority. But even democracies can only succeed in this task if there are not large ethnic minorities, for minorities will inevitably feel themselves to be discriminated against in economic matters. Kelles-Krauz concluded that the will of the majority is a moral and practical justification for political action only when the minority is of the same nationality as the majority. So long as this is true, commonality of language, agreement about basic national interests, and protection of freedom of expression will allow for dialogue and compromise. The democratic nation-state can thus keep the class struggle within reasonable and desirable political boundaries. Rule by socialists is no substitute for the democratic nation-state, for socialists are equally imbued with national consciousness, and socialists of the largest nationality will seek to dominate the others.

Writing on behalf of both Poles and Jews, Kelles-Krauz considered the problems of national minorities. He began from the premise that every nation has a certain dignity, such that it deserves to be treated as an end in itself. Every nationality will demand to be treated as an equal to all others, and to be allowed to decide on all questions of its fate; the normal historical outcome of these demands is the creation of a national state. When a territorial solution to national aspirations is impossible (as in the case of Jews in a future Polish republic), it is in the interest of the majority to recall that the minority's national identity and aspirations are of the same quality as its own. In seeking to win the minority's loyalty to the state, the majority must seek arguments which appeal to the minority's interests as a national group. The minority should be granted the use of its language in schools, courts, and local government. Similarly, if the majority wishes assimilation to take place, it should not arrogantly press its claims to cultural superiority. Its members should instead turn their energies to a "competition" of cultures, rendering their culture as attractive as possible for newcomers. Individuals who assimilate should be welcomed, for they are uniquely qualified to contribute to solidarity between the groups and to the culture of all. Minorities and majorities alike should respect the right of each individual to choose his or her nationality.

These views are remarkable for their vivid contrast to the consensus about national questions then prevailing within the Second International, or within the European left generally. Kelles-Krauz opposed the traditional distinction between historic and unhistoric nations, believed that capitalism created nations and languages rather than destroyed them, emphasized the importance of popular over literary languages, argued that ideas (from the past, or borrowed from other nations) played a crucial role in social change, maintained that class and national consciousness were integrally connected rather than opposed, thought that the Jews would become a nationality rather than assimilate, thought that democracy would destroy Austria rather than save it, was certain that every nation would seek a state rather than be satisfied with the protection of cultural rights, and concluded that socialism could only be built within a democratic nation-state rather than in some future international structure."[11]

Kelles-Krauz's predictions were generally correct. His claim that every attempt to unite a nation will rely on historical mythology proved accurate and prescient. He was right about the end of Austria-Hungary and multinational empires in Europe generally, right that Jews would come to be considered a nationality, and right that the "unhistorical nations" of central, eastern, and southeastern Europe would gain their own states. He correctly foresaw the necessity for some approach to the problem of minorities within a Europe of nation-states. His concern that the combination of anti-semitism and some form of planned economics could crowd out social democracy in central European republics proved justified in the interwar years. His insight that class consciousness and national consciousness were integrally connected seems confirmed not only by socialism in Europe (an apatriotic proletariat has never emerged, even in communist states), but by the character of anti-colonialist movements in the third world. The success of socialism in multinational empires is before our eyes to judge.

Kelles-Krauz

Kelles-Krauz's political and intellectual work has not yet received its due. The record of his life has been obscured by his pseudonyms, his division of labor between politics and scholarship, his emigration and travels, and his mastery of languages. Most of his work was in Polish, which has probably sufficed to keep him from western histories of sociology and Marxism. At the same time, satisfactory Polish accounts have been prevented by politics. He died at the height of the Revolution of 1905, which distracted the friends who might have written the first biographies. His PPS split in 1906, and his Marxist patriotism was a troubling legacy for both new parties. Much of his thought, on nationalism for example, was so pioneering that it was effectively ignored in Poland during the interwar period. Finally, the Second World War brought a People's Poland which treated Kelles-Krauz's legacy in terms of the political goals of the day. Wittgenstein said that if someone is ahead of his time, time will eventually catch up with him. This is perhaps true; but by then he may be dead and forgotten, or, if remembered, badly misunderstood.

The brief comparisons to four other central European political intellectuals (Piłsudski, Luxemburg, Lukács, and Weber) presented here are a first step toward placing Kelles-Krauz within the history of the Polish patriotism, the history of Polish socialism, the history of Marxism, and the history of social thought. It is striking that these four figures are best known for their accomplishments after 1905, the year of Kelles-Krauz's death. Of the four, only Lukacs was younger than Kelles-Krauz, and is considered to be of another generation; but this is largely due to the fact that Lukacs began his career as a Marxist thinker at 33, while Kelles-Krauz perished at that age. Still, such comparisons should not be taken to mean that Kelles-Krauz's thought is of historical interest only. His work on the relationship between the social sciences and the natural sciences, as well as that between the social sciences and politics, remains timely. His canny grasp of national issues, combined with his sophisticated internationalism and anti-pacifism, render him a typically East European check on inclinations of the Western left during this century. He offers to contemporary socialists innovative positions on the fundamental political questions of pluralist democracy and the nation-state, as well as pioneering work on the cultural questions which have dominated the Western Marxist tradition. He was at once and without reservation a socialist democrat, socialist patriot, and socialist theorist of alienation—a unique combination, and perhaps a useful example.

In his work on the national question, Kelles-Krauz far surpassed his contemporaries. He avoided the errors of his time: racial and Darwinist explanations of national differences;[12] the assurance of Marxists and liberals that social progress would eliminate national conflict;[13] and the general tendency within sociology to identify the nation with the state.[14] As Andrzej Walicki has noted, Kelles-Krauz deserves to be credited for anticipating now-established views about the origins of nationalism.[15] His body of writings proposed the explanations of the origins of modern nationalism which are central to the contemporary debate, and which are associated with the works of Anderson, Hobsbawm, and Gellner.[16] He anticipated Anderson's idea of the "imagined community," Hobsbawm's connection of modern nationalism to the process of "inventing traditions," and Gellner's argument that nationalism is a function of economic and social modernization. What is more, he united all three of these threads in a single body of work, eighty years before the publication of these three books in 1983. He did so without the benefit of the second look at the origins of nationalism which western scholars were afforded by decolonization, which to a great degree stands behind these books. Yet the most unlikely feature of Kelles-Krauz's accomplishment is that he was simultaneously observer and participant, that he was able to write dispassionately about the national question in general while taking passionate part in a particular national movement. When he wrote of intellectuals as bearers of traditions old and new, he was at once discussing a phenomenon, his party, and himself. He took seriously the precepts of his "applied science": among them that one must participate to know, and yet one must subject one's own biases to historical analysis.

Kelles-Krauz's achievement seems difficult almost to the point of paradox. At a time when Marxist theory was indifferent to nationalism, and sociology was hostile to Marxism, he created a Marxist sociology which anticipated today's scholarship on the national question; he did so as the leading theorist of a patriotic Polish party which was hostile to the national goals of Jews, and yet his basic intuitions about modern nationalism sprang from his perceptions of similarities between Jews and Poles. Kelles-Krauz tended to hold views which his contemporaries, political activists and scholars alike, found difficult to reconcile with one another.

Sometimes he was wildly wrong, but more often he was perspicacious and even prescient. To some extent, the sources of his unusual concerns and conclusions can be found in Poland's political predicament, and in related traditions of Polish scholarship. But in the end, the best if imperfect means to appreciate his work is to treat it as the fruit of a single life.

Julian Barnes asks, "What chance would the craftiest biographer stand against the subject who saw him coming and decided to amuse himself?"[17] Although an exemplar of modernity in other senses, Kelles-Krauz was not a modern figure in this sense of ironical reference to an uncertain identity. Indeed, a key to his achievements was that he was self-critical without being self-conscious. Although he lived in conditions of extreme difficulty and undertook intellectual projects of extreme complexity, his life records (to take the examples at hand) no psychological crises which mark important intellectual shifts (Weber), and no sudden conversions to new political views (Lukács). Unlike his peers Luxemburg and Piłsudski, he did not dodge difficult ethical questions, and did not succumb to the temptation of believing that one political problem (be it independence or socialism) underlay all others. He attained what F. Scott Fitzgerald, in a reflective moment, defined as success: the ability to act decisively while holding several difficult ideas in mind at once. He did see biographers coming, but the traces he left behind are of a very fertile mind, astoundingly abundant work, an admirable sense of public and private ethics, and extraordinary dedication and endurance. The task of writing his life has not been one of untangling confused aspects of a personality, but of relating difficult and complex ideas and choices to a rather consistent individuality.

APPENDIX I

Biographical Sketches

Edward Abramowski (1868–1918). Philosopher, psychologist, and theorist of the Polish anarcho-cooperativist movement. In his youth a socialist activist. In 1891, while Kelles-Krauz was attending the University of Warsaw, attempted to unify the fragmented Polish socialist movement. In 1898, reviewed Kelles-Krauz's theory of revolutionary retrospection. During the revolution of 1905, an important ideologist of the populist movement in Russian Poland.*

Viktor Adler (1852–1918). Leader of Austrian socialism, 1889–1918. In 1896, took a middle position on Kelles-Krauz's Second International resolution. Defended the PPS from Luxemburg's charges of nationalism at the International's Paris Congress of 1900. In 1901 befriended Kelles-Krauz in Vienna, and arranged for Kelles-Krauz to meet leaders of German social democracy. Disapproved of Kelles-Krauz's idea that national awareness and industrialization would proceed in train. Cooperated with the Austrian government in 1914, briefly foreign minister of Austria's provincial government in 1918.

Zygmunt Balicki (1858–1916). Theorist of Polish integral nationalism, political organizer, sociologist. Founder of the Union of Polish Youth (Zet); from its formation in 1893, one of the leaders of the National League. In 1894 and 1895, Kelles-Krauz sought to have Balicki expelled from the Union of Polish Socialists Abroad,

---

* These sketches are intended to serve two purposes. First, they are meant as a reference for the reader adrift in unfamiliar names. For this reason, greater attention is devoted to the Poles than to other Europeans. Second, they are intended to suggest the variety of fates of Kelles-Krauz's peers after his death in 1905. To take a dramatic example, four of his acquaintances became heads of state of European republics, while another four were brutally executed (two by German nationalists and two by the Soviet secret police).

and in 1898 their differences led to a press polemic. Author of *Egoizm narodowy wobec etyki* (1902), one of the most important documents of National Democracy.

Stanisław Barański (1859–1891). Polish patriotic socialist. Barański had lived in the house on 20, rue de la Glacière in Paris until his death in summer 1891, and his ideas were shared by the Polish students who lived in the house when Kelles-Krauz arrived in December 1891.

August Bebel (1840–1913). One of the founders of German socialism, leader of the SPD. His one theoretical work, *Die Frau und der Sozialismus* (1883), probably influenced Kelles-Krauz's view of the history of women and their role in socialist society. In 1894, Kelles-Krauz singled out Bebel's orthodoxy as a mistaken and passive conception of Marxism. In 1901, Bebel met with Kelles-Krauz to discuss the future of the PPS in Germany. Kelles-Krauz found his lack of support for an autonomous Polish organization infuriating.

Eduard Bernstein (1850–1932). German socialist theorist, co-author of the SPD's Erfurt program of 1890, the first revisionist. In 1896, Bernstein first supported, and then opposed, Kelles-Krauz's Second International resolution. From 1901, Kelles-Krauz opposed his own understanding of Marxism as applied science to Bernstein's pragmatism. Bernstein served as Reichsrat deputy, 1902-1907, 1912-1918, 1920-1928. After supporting the German declaration of war in 1914, became one of the war's most prominent critics. One of the drafters of the SPD's revised Görlitz program in 1921.

Bronisław Białobłocki (1861–1888). Polish Marxist sociologist. Along with Stanisław Krusiński and Ludwik Krusiński, one of the most important critics of Warsaw positivism in the 1880s.

Stanisław Brzozowski (1878–1911). Polish philosopher, novelist, and literary critic. Brzozowski never met Kelles-Krauz, but regarded him as an important influence. His belief that individuals could only apprehend their social environment through the prism of national identity, as well as his understanding of Marxism as a philosophy of action, resemble Kelles-Krauz's views.

Władysław Bukowiński (1871–1927). Polish poet, critic, and teacher. Kelles-Krauz's best friend in Radom, Bukowiński helped him to become Vienna correspondent for *Prawda* in 1901. Bukowiński wrote Kelles-Krauz's obituary for *Prawda* in 1905.

Ignacy Daszyński (1866–1936). Leader of Polish socialism in Austria, Austrian and then Polish parliamentarian. Tactfully supported Kelles-Krauz's resolution in

1896, in 1901 worked with Kelles-Krauz to support Polish socialism in Germany, and in 1904 lectured at the free university in Zakopane. Chairman of the PPS in independent Poland, 1921–1928 and 1931–1934. As Marshal of the Sejm, refused to begin its 1930 session after his former comrade Piłsudski had packed the chamber with armed military men.

Ignacy Daum (1869–1932). Polish socialist activist. Daum was Kelles-Krauz's close friend in Paris until 1900, when Daum returned to Warsaw. After working as a PPS organizer and activist in Russian Poland and Galicia, Daum returned to Paris in 1907. He worked as a medical doctor in France for the rest of his life.

Aleksander Dębski (1867–1939). Polish socialist, leader of the Union of Polish Socialists Abroad until its dissolution in 1899. He then emigrated to the United States, where he organized Polish workers. He returned to Europe to support Piłsudski during the First World War, but opposed Piłsudski's seizure of power in 1926. Elected senator in 1930.

Roman Dmowski (1864–1939). Leading theorist and activist of Polish integral nationalism. In 1893 transformed the Polish League into the National League, which eventually forced a clear split between Polish nationalism and Polish socialism. In 1894 and 1895 Kelles-Krauz sought to expel members of Dmowski's organization from the Union of Polish Socialists Abroad. In the late 1890s Dmowski's National Democracy movement worked to establish itself in all three Polish partitions, and initiated numerous programs of popular education. In 1903 Dmowski published *Myśli nowoczesnego Polaka*, the bible of Polish ethnic nationalism. Polish representative at the Paris peace talks following the First World War, and in 1919–1923 minister in the government of Wincenty Witos. In interwar Poland undisputed leader of National Democracy and the major opponent of Piłsudski.

Feliks Dzierżyński (1877–1926). Polish socialist and Soviet head of secret police. The founder of the SDKPiL in 1899. Kelles-Krauz was faced with the problem of whether or not to allow members of this new party to participate in the Paris congress of the Second International in 1900. Between 1900 and 1905, Kelles-Krauz wrote several articles justifying Polish independence in Marxist terms in order to keep young activists from abandoning the PPS for the new organization. Dzierżyński remained one of the leaders of the SDKPiL, opposing Polish independence and advocating cooperation with the Bolsheviks. The revolutions of 1917 found him in Moscow. He was the founding leader of the Cheka, a position he held until his death. He died of a heart attack after a speech denouncing intra-party fractions.

Wilhelm Feldman (1868–1919). Polish critic and historian. Broke with his orthodox Jewish community in 1886, and in the 1890s established himself as a leading exponent of moderate socialism and Jewish assimilationism in politics and the Young Poland movement in culture. Edited *Krytyka* (1901–1914), where Kelles-Krauz published his "On the Question of Jewish Nationality" in 1904. Feldman briefly wavered in his belief in the inevitability of assimilation while confronting Kelles-Krauz's ideas. In 1903–1904 collaborated with Kelles-Krauz in the planning of the free university in Zakopane. From 1905 associated with Piłsudski's PPS-Revolutionary Fraction, and in 1914 joined Piłsudski's Legions. Between 1914-1920 published his *Dzieje polskiej myśli politycznej w okresie porozbiorowym*, which included an informed discussion of Kelles-Krauz. This work remains the most useful history of Polish political thought.

Estera Golde (1872–1938). Polish socialist and communist activist, pediatrician and organizer of charity. Golde was a member of Kelles-Krauz's social democrats in Paris in 1893, and one of his best friends. From 1901 Kelles-Krauz tried to support her efforts to win Polish workers to the PPS in Silesia. In 1905 and 1906 one of the leaders of the leftist Warsaw organization of the PPS. Left Poland in 1906, married Jan Strożecki, and lived with him in Paris until his death. Returned to Poland in 1919 as an activist of the Polish Communist Party. 1934–1936 in the USSR, 1936 returned to France.

Stanisław Grabski (1871–1949). Polish politician, diplomat, and economist. A member of Kelles-Krauz's Paris social democrats in 1893, one of the group of *Przegląd Socjalistyczny* writers brought into the PPS with Kelles-Krauz's help in 1894. As Grabski moved to the right, criticized Kelles-Krauz as doctrinaire. In 1901 he and Kelles-Krauz published *Rzut oka nà rozwój ekonomii i socjologii w XIX wieku*. Left the PPS in 1902, joined the National League in 1905. Developed a pro-Russian orientation, elected to the Russian Duma. From 1905–1926 one of the leading ideologues of National Democracy, parliamentary deputy and twice minister of religion and public education in the 1920s. As negotiator at Riga after the Polish-Soviet War of 1919–1920, took less territory than the Soviets offered, thereby splitting Ukrainian and Belarusian lands between Poland and Soviet Russia. Broke with National Democracy in 1926. In 1944 accompanied Mikołajczyk to Moscow for negotiations with Stalin, in 1945 returned to Poland and joined the Polish communists' Homeland National Council.

Władysław Grabski (1874–1938). Polish politician and economist. A member of Kelles-Krauz's Paris social democrats in 1893, he returned to Poland and devoted himself to agrarian reform. Took part in the Paris Peace Conference (1919), and served several times as minister in Polish governments. Best known for economic reforms carried out 1923–1925 while he served as prime minister and finance minister.

Jules Guesde (1845–1922). French Marxist and leader of the Parti Ouvrier Français. Kelles-Krauz rejected Guesde's orthodoxy as passive in 1894. In 1896 Guesde opposed

Kelles-Krauz's resolution at the London congress of the Second International, treating the struggle for Polish independence as a threat to European order. In 1898 Kelles-Krauz criticized Guesde for his indifference to the Dreyfus affair.

Ludwik Gumplowicz (1838–1909). Polish sociologist, professor at Graz, author of *Der Rassenkampf* (1883). In 1896 Kelles-Krauz translated one of his books from German to French, and after Kelles-Krauz moved to Vienna in 1901 the two corresponded.

Lucien Herr (1864–1926). French socialist. Librarian of the École Normale Supérieure in Paris, where he converted numerous *normaliens* to socialism. Favorable to Polish independence, he was cultivated by Kelles-Krauz in Paris 1898–1899.

Max Horwitz (1877–1937?). Polish socialist and communist activist. Occasionally helped Kelles-Krauz edit the *Bulletin Officiel du Parti Socialiste Polonais*. As the only PPS activist able to write in Yiddish, edited *Der Arbeyter* 1898–1899. In 1905 one of the leaders of the left's revolt within the PPS; Kelles-Krauz mediated between the party's left and right wings. From 1906 a leader the PPS-Left; in 1918 instrumental in the unification of the PPS-Left and the SDKPiL and the formation of the Polish Communist Party. By Stalin's decision forced from the leadership of the Party in 1924, thereafter lived in Moscow and worked for the Comintern. Arrested in 1937 and executed.

Jean Jaurès (1859–1914). Founding father of French socialism, philosopher and parliamentarian. In 1896 persuaded by Kelles-Krauz to write a favorable article for the PPS's May Day pamphlet. In 1898 like Kelles-Krauz and mutual friends a determined Dreyfusard. From 1905 a leader of the united French socialist party. A capable leader in parliament and an eloquent speaker, regarded by many as the conscience of the Republic. Shot dead in a Paris café by a nationalist fanatic on 31 July 1914.

Bolesław Antoni Jędrzejowski (1867–1914). Polish socialist. A founding member of the PPS in 1892, a leader of the Union of Polish Socialists Abroad from London, editor of *Przedświt* through 1897. Along with Jodko, Piłsudski, and Wojciechowski, one of the most important figures within the PPS before 1905. First Kelles-Krauz's adversary, and then his friend, within the party. After the split of the PPS in 1906, a leading activist of Piłsudski's PPS-Revolutionary Fraction. Died of tuberculosis.

Witold Jodko-Narkiewicz (1864–1924). Polish socialist and diplomat. A founding member of the PPS in 1892, and with his friend Jędrzejowski leader from London of the Union of Polish Socialists Abroad. Before 1905 one of the most important figures within the PPS, along with Jędrzejowski, Piłsudski, and Wojciechowski. After the party divided in 1906, an ideologist and leader of Piłsudski's PPS-Revolutionary Fraction. After the First World War, Polish ambassador to Turkey and Latvia.

Leon Jogiches (1867–1919). Socialist conspirator. Friend, comrade, and lover of Rosa Luxemburg. Referred to Kelles-Krauz as "the baron" in correspondence with Luxemburg, and urged her to attack him with greater force. Played a significant and underestimated role in the organization of the SDKP, the Polish revolution of 1905, and the Spartakus uprising in Germany. Murdered by the German police.

Karl Kautsky (1854–1938). German Marxist. Co-author of the SPD's Erfurt program of 1890, leading Marxist thinker of the Second International, and editor of *Die Neue Zeit,* 1883–1917. In 1896 provided a compromise position in the debate over Kelles-Krauz's resolution. In 1903 Kelles-Krauz wrote Kautsky bemoaning the SPD's attacks on Polish socialism in Germany. In 1903–1904 Kautsky debated Kelles-Krauz on the possibility of German revolution. In 1905 Kautsky rejected Kelles-Krauz's article on the Polish revolution because Kelles-Krauz suggested that it might bring democracy to Poland but not to Russia. On several occasions Kelles-Krauz opposed his understanding of Marxism as applied science to what he saw as Kautsky's division of theory from practice. Kautsky supported the vote for German war credits in 1914, but changed his mind in 1915. After 1917 a critic of Bolshevism.

Stanisław Krusiński (1857–1886). Polish socialist and sociologist. Along with Bronisław Białobłocki and Ludwik Krzywicki, participant in the Marxist turn against Warsaw positivism in the 1880s. In Paris, Kelles-Krauz drew on Krusiński's work in his own criticism of organicism in sociology.

Ludwik Krzywicki (1859–1941). Polish Marxist sociologist. With Bronisław Białobłocki and Stanisław Krusiński, one the major critics of Warsaw positivism from the left during the 1880s. Krzywicki did more than any other individual to introduce Marxist concepts to Poland, and his work and that of his friends did much to convince Kelles-Krauz and others of his generation of the scientific basis of socialism. Like Kelles-Krauz, Krzywicki was concerned with the sociology of primitive societies. Krzywicki hosted Kelles-Krauz in Berlin in November 1892, and took him to observe an SPD congress. In 1904 Krzywicki lectured at the free university in Zakopane. Krzywicki wrote the entry on Kelles-Krauz for the 1907 *Wielka Encyklopedia Powszechna Ilustrowana.* In independent Poland, directed the Institute of Social Economy, which published the first serious studies of social and economic life in Soviet Russia.

Ludwik Kulczycki (1866–1941). Polish socialist and sociologist. In the late 1880s leader of the Second Proletariat, a revival of the first Polish socialist party. In 1893 and 1894, the most prominent PPS advocate of including the struggle for a Russian constitution within the party program. Left the PPS in 1900 to found the Third Proletariat.

Antonio Labriola (1843–1904). Founding father of Marxism in Italy, unorthodox Marxist scholar. Believed that nationality was an independent historical reality, and in 1896 aided the PPS in its attempts to persuade European socialists to support Kelles-Krauz's resolution regarding Polish independence.

Lucien Lévy-Brühl (1857–1939). French philosopher and anthropologist. Supervised Kelles-Krauz's thesis "L'age d'or de Vico au Marxisme" at the École Libre des Sciences Politiques in 1898. Lévy-Brühl interested Kelles-Krauz in Comte; Kelles-Krauz may have turned his teacher toward the study of primitive societies that later made him famous.

Wilhelm Liebknecht (1826–1900). German socialist. With Bebel, a founder of German social democracy. A friend of the PPS program, he nevertheless failed to support Kelles-Krauz's resolution at the 1896 London congress of the Second International.

Bolesław Limanowski (1835–1935). Polish patriotic socialist, sociologist, and historian. In the 1880s, virtually alone among Polish socialists in opposing extreme internationalism. Throughout his long life he linked the cause of socialism to that of an independent Poland. In the 1890s, he was the most prominent thinker among Polish patriotic socialists in Paris. He was a founding member of the PPS in 1892, and like Kelles-Krauz took part in negotiations which brought a number of patriotic socialists in Paris to the PPS in 1894. In 1900, helped Kelles-Krauz lead the Polish delegation to the Paris congress of the Second International. In 1904, lectured at the free university in Zakopane. His idea that peasant communes prefigured socialism resembled Kelles-Krauz's theory of revolutionary retrospection. Senator in independent Poland, 1922–1935.

Jan Lorentowicz (1868?–1940). Polish literary critic. In his youth in Paris a leader of patriotic Polish socialists in Paris. Met Kelles-Krauz at the train station when Kelles-Krauz emigrated to Paris in 1891, and found him lodging at 20, rue de la Glacière.

Rosa Luxemburg (1871–1919). Socialist activist and theorist, leading theorist of the SDKP and the SDKPiL, as well as of the left wing of German social democracy. Considered the goal of Polish independence reactionary, and consistently sought to weaken the PPS. Never debated Kelles-Krauz directly, but worked hard to dissociate Polish independence from Marxism. In 1896 started the *Polendebatten* which ensured that Kelles-Krauz's resolution on Polish independence could not pass; from 1898 worked to end the autonomy of Polish socialists in Germany; in 1900 called the PPS "nationalists" at the Paris congress of the Second International; in 1904 attacked Kelles-Krauz in print and revealed his pseudonyms. During her lifetime best known for her *Die Akkumulation des Kapitals* (1912). Imprisoned during the First World War, she wrote *Die Krise der Sozialdemokratie*, effectively the founding program of German communism; and an unfinished analysis of the October Revolution which later gained her posthumous renown as a critic of Bolshevism. Murdered by *Freikorps* in January 1919.

Alexander Malinowski (1869–1922). Polish socialist, ally of Piłsudski in the PPS.

Julian Marchlewski (1866–1925). Polish socialist and Soviet diplomat. Leader of the SDKP. His articles in the French press in 1900 heralded the arrival of the SDKPiL, which briefly sought a middle ground between the Luxemburg position (Polish independence was impossible) and that of the PPS (Polish independence was necessary for socialism). Kelles-Krauz turned his attention to this new position in 1900 and 1901. Like Luxemburg, Marchlewski devoted most of his energy to German socialism. Imprisoned in Germany during the First World War, he reached Moscow as a result of a prisoner exchange. There he served the Bolsheviks after the October Revolution, working in the Soviet diplomatic corps and heading the "revolutionary committee" of Poles formed by the Bolsheviks during the Polish-Soviet war of 1919–1920.

Stanisław Mendelson (1858–1913). One of the first Polish socialists and a founding member of the PPS. Left the party at around the time Kelles-Krauz joined.

Bolesław Miklaszewski (1871–1941). Polish chemist. In his youth a socialist activist, and an acquaintance of Kelles-Krauz as leader of the Zurich section of the Union of Polish Socialists Abroad. From 1905 devoted himself to scholarly work. In independent Poland served in 1923–1924 as minister of religion and public education.

Zygmunt Miłkowski (1824–1915). Polish patriot, émigré political writer and organizer. In 1887 author of "On Active Defense and the National Treasury"; founder of the Polish League that same year. The Polish League inaugurated modem Polish patriotism and provided an alternative to socialism for Polish youth.

John Mill (1870–1952). Jewish socialist organizer. Mill brought Yiddish-language materials from Vilnius to Warsaw in 1895, weakening the PPS's position among Jewish workers. Helped found the Bund in 1897, and raised the issue of the national rights of Jews at the Bund's Third Congress in 1899. Kelles-Krauz's innovative position on the Jewish question, as well as his more general reflections on the character of modem nationalism, was spurred by the challenge of the Bund. Mill emigrated to the United States in 1915, where he organized Jewish laborers and worked as a dental assistant.

Alexandre Millerand (1859–1943). French politician. An independent socialist in the 1890s, in 1896 he helped Polish émigrés in their attempts to keep the private papers of Ludwik Sawicki from coming into the possession of Russian authorities.

Joined the government of Waldeck-Rousseau in 1899, and thereby split French and European socialism over the issue of whether socialists should join bourgeois governments. Kelles-Krauz opposed Millerand's choice, perhaps because he regarded Millerand as a friend of the Franco-Russian alliance. Grew steadily more conservative over a long political life, in which he served in several governments before being elected president of the Republic in 1920. Senator from 1925–1943.

Józef Piłsudski (1867–1935). Polish revolutionary and statesman. One of the most important PPS activists in Russian Poland until his arrest in 1900. He escaped to Galicia, where he befriended Kelles-Krauz. Although Piłsudski was indifferent to Marxism, he and Kelles-Krauz respected each others' talents. The two scions of déclassé noble families from the east played chess and enjoyed each others' company. After Kelles-Krauz's death in 1905 and the formal split of the PPS in 1906, Piłsudski led the PPS-Revolutionary Fraction. He placed independence as the preeminent goal of his party, and intended to win it by an appropriately timed armed uprising. Although he placed his Legions at the service of the losing side in the First World War, in 1918 he was the undisputed leader of Poland. He served as head of state until the election of Poland's first president in 1922. As head of independent Poland's armed forces, he sought to win eastern borders favorable to his idea of an East European federation. He withdrew formally from politics in 1923, only to return three years later by *coup d'etat*. He then ruled Poland until his death.

Stanisław Przybyszewski (1868–1927). Polish modernist writer. In his youth a socialist activist in Berlin, and for a time editor of *Gazeta Robotnicza*. Informed Kelles-Krauz in 1893 that their comrade Stanisław Grabski had been arrested.

Karl Renner (1870–1950). Austrian socialist and politician. His *Der Kampf der Österreichischen Nationen um den Staat* (1902) advocated national rights for individuals as a way to preserve and democratize Austria. Kelles-Krauz's criticism of this pamphlet clarified his own views on the relationship between nation and state. Renner was later a leader of the Austrian cooperative movement. Supported the Austrian government during the First World War, and named chancellor of the provisional government in 1919. Severed links with the socialist movement after the 1934 civil war, and supported Anschluss in 1938. Elected president of the Austrian republic in 1945.

Georges Sorel (1847–1922). French theorist of syndicalism, whose anti-rationalist Marxism found him admirers on the far right as well as the far left. In 1896 briefly helped Kelles-Krauz promote his Second International resolution in Paris.

Jan Stróżecki (1869–1918). Polish socialist. Recruited Kelles-Krauz to the PPS in 1894, helping him to found the party's Radom section. On the left wing of the PPS, he was one of the leaders of the revolt within the party in 1905, which Kelles-Krauz was able to momentarily resolve. Married Kelles-Krauz's close friend Estera Golde, then migrated to France in 1907. Perished attempting to rescue a drowning man.

Władysław Studnicki (1867–1953). Polish politician and writer. In his youth a socialist, led the Vienna section of the Union of Polish Socialists Abroad. As he began a shift to the right, accused Kelles-Krauz of dogmatism. Evolved toward extreme nationalism combined with Germanophilia. During the Second World War advocated cooperation with Nazi Germany in occupied Poland.

Aleksander Świętochowski (1849–1938). Polish critic and scholar. As an essayist in *Przegląd Tygodniowy,* and then as editor of *Prawda* (1881–1902), the leading light of Warsaw positivism. *Prawda* was read and respected by Kelles-Krauz and his peers in secret student circles in the 1880s; it was the main legal outlet for Polish Marxists. Kelles-Krauz wrote for *Prawda* on assignment in Paris and as regular correspondent in Vienna. Świętochowski was briefly influenced by Kelles-Krauz's view of the Jewish question in 1904. In 1905 he founded the Progressive-Democratic Union, a liberal party. In 1906 established the Society of Polish Culture. As his political influence declined, he concentrated on historical writing and literary criticism.

Gabriel Tarde (1843–1904). French sociologist. His theory of imitation served Kelles-Krauz as a foil for his own theory of revolutionary retrospection in 1895. Also known for his studies of criminology and mass behavior. In many respects represented the bourgeois positivist sociology which Kelles-Krauz sought to revolutionize. Perceptively portrayed in Kelles-Krauz's *Portrety zmarłych socjologów.*

Édouard Vaillant (1840–1915). French socialist. A founder of French socialism, Vaillant was *delegué* for education of the Paris Commune and then member of the General Council of the First International. After the death of Blanqui in 1881, leader of the Blanquist Revolutionary Central Committee. Vaillant straddled the radical republicanism of the Blanqui movement and the Marxism of Guesde and his followers, and sought to bridge the two ideas through syndicalism. In 1894 and 1895, Kelles-Krauz was an admirer of Vaillant, and saw Vaillant's syndicalism as a more correct understanding of Marxism than the orthodoxy of Bebel and Guesde. Kelles-Krauz was disillusioned by Vaillant's failure to support his resolution in 1896. Vaillant's organization (renamed the Revolutionary Socialist Party) gained popularity in the 1890s, and in 1905 he played an important role in the unification of French socialism. As a parliamentary deputy (1893–1915), Vaillant proposed numerous reforms, many of which became the basis of laws.

Adolf Warszawski (1868–1937?). Polish socialist and communist activist. One of the leaders of the SDKP, Warszawski while in Paris (1892–1896) opposed

Kelles-Krauz's attempts to gain French support for the PPS program. Prevented by the PPS-dominated Polish delegation from taking part in the 1896 London congress of the Second International. A leader of the SDKPiL after its foundation in 1899, in 1918 one of the initiators of the merger of the SDKPiL and the PPS-Left and the founding of the Polish Communist Party. Deputy to the Polish Sejm in the late 1920s, and leader of its communist fraction. Expelled from the Party in 1929 for "rightist deviations," emigrated that year to the Soviet Union were he worked in the Marx-Engels-Lenin Institute. Arrested in 1937 and executed.

Ludwik Waryński (1856–1889). Founder of the first Polish socialist party, Proletariat. An internationalist who rejected the struggle for Polish independence. Perished in prison.

Leon Wasilewski (1870–1936). Polish socialist, politician, and scholar. From 1896 active in the PPS, from 1897–1905 editor of *Przedświt*. Took part in a coup within the Union of Polish Socialists Abroad against Jodko and Jędrzejowski in late 1897. Though Piłsudski resented this move, Wasilewski eventually became one of his closest associates. After the PPS split in 1906, a leading activist of Piłsudski's PPS-Revolutionary Fraction. Foreign minister in independent Poland 1918–1919, director of the Institute for the Study of Contemporary Polish History from 1924. Advocate of a federal arrangement between Poland and its eastern neighbors and expert on nationality questions.

Stanisław Wojciechowski (1869–1953). Polish socialist, theorist of the cooperative movement, and president of the Second Polish Republic. While a student of Warsaw University with Kelles-Krauz in 1891, a member of Balicki's Zet and Abramowski's Unification. While Kelles-Krauz was then an internationalist, Wojciechowski regarded socialism as a philosophy of action and a means of restoring Polish independence. With Piłsudski and Strożecki established the PPS in Russian Poland in 1893; with Piłsudski edited *Robotnik*. Kelles-Krauz's approval of Wojciechowski's history of the party in 1900 signaled Kelles-Krauz's shift toward the party's center. 1905–1914 a leader of the cooperative movement. 1919–1920 interior minister of the Polish Republic; 1922–1926 president. Resigned the office after his former comrade Piłsudski's *coup d'etat* of May 1926.

Cezeryna Wojnarowska (1861–1911). Polish socialist. A member of Kelles-Krauz's group of Polish social democrats in Paris in early 1893, but joined that SDKP later that year. Opposed Kelles-Krauz's attempts to gain French support for the PPS program in Paris, though the two cooperated in raising financial aid for political prisoners in the Russian Empire. Just as Kelles-Krauz was the most important representative of the PPS in Paris from 1894, Wojnarowska was effectively the leader of Polish social democrats. From 1900 active in the SDKPiL, perhaps as a result of

Kelles-Krauz's influence favored a less dogmatic treatment of the national question than Luxemburg. Marginalized within the SDKPiL by Luxemburg, she turned her energies to French socialism in the years before her death.

René Worms (1869–1926). French sociologist. Founder of the Institut International de Sociologie, of which Kelles-Krauz was an early and active member. Kelles-Krauz presented his understanding of Marxist sociology to the Institute's annual congress in 1900.

Gabriela Zapolska (1857–1921). Polish actress and novelist, a friend of Kelles-Krauz's during his first years in Paris. Returned to Poland in 1895.

Max Zetterbaum (1871–1927). Socialist theorist and activist. Zetterbaum, a Jew from Galicia, was a prominent activist of the Polish socialist movement in Austria, and a lifelong supporter of the idea of Polish independence. Kelles-Krauz befriended Zetterbaum in Vienna in 1901, and used his good offices while attempting to persuade Jewish socialists to accept the PPS program. Zetterbaum discussed Kelles-Krauz's sociology in *Die Neue Zeit* in 1904.

APPENDIX 2

Kelles-Krauz and People's Poland

A simple problem of language stands behind the weakness of the literature concerning Kelles-Krauz. Three different editions of Kelles-Krauz's selected works have been published in Polish since 1962, and his collected letters were published in Polish in 1984. Some of the articles had to be translated from French, and many of the letters from French, German, or Russian. Although a good deal of Kelles-Krauz's work was published in other languages, no historian without knowledge of Polish could hope to undertake a study of his life or works.

No account of the Second International written in English mentions Kelles-Krauz's name. Leszek Kołakowski accords him a brief chapter in his *Główne nurty marksizmu*, the translation of which is the only introduction to Kelles-Krauz's life and works available in English. Accounts devoted to the attitude of socialists to the national question (Haupt, Avineri, Herod, Davis) or to the Jewish question (Wistrich, Frankel, Mendelson, Tobias) do not discuss Kelles-Krauz. The three exceptions are brief summaries of Kelles-Krauz's views in two papers devoted to other subjects by the Polish historian Andrzej Walicki, and a compact and competent article on Kelles-Krauz's attitude to the Jewish question by Michael Sobelman. Although Kelles-Krauz anticipated many of the concerns of Western Marxism, no work on that subject refers to him. Nettl's otherwise comprehensive biography of Rosa Luxemburg makes several passing references to Kelles-Krauz, but lacks a comparison of the two figures, an analysis of Kelles-Krauz's arguments, or mention of Luxemburg's harsh treatment of him. No other biography devoted to Luxemburg deals with Kelles-Krauz. Steenson refers once to Kelles-Krauz in his biography of Kautsky, but with this exception no work on the SPD (including Hans-Ulrich Wehler's work on German socialism and the nation-state) discusses Kelles-Krauz. To my knowledge, no history of French socialism makes more than a passing reference to him. No history of sociology written outside of Poland discusses Kelles-Krauz's scholarly work.

The postwar Polish historiography, while abundant, is fraught with politics. In 1947 Głowacki wrote articles praising Kelles-Krauz as a proper model for the PPS in that party's organ *Przegląd Socjalistyczny*. In 1949, after the PPS had been absorbed by the new Polish United Worker's Party, Adam Schaff and Bronisław Baczko attempted to discredit Kelles-Krauz (and thus the possibility of a Polish left aside from the communist party) in the "theoretical" party organ *Nowe Drogi*. He was portrayed as an imperialist in socialist guise, as hostile to Russia and Russian socialism, and as an incompetent sociologist misled by idealism and unable to appreciate Lenin's contributions to the field. These articles coincided with an attempt by the Polish communist party to impose Marxist-Leninist methods imported from the Soviet Union upon Polish historians. Schaff led this effort.

From about 1956, this attempt was abandoned. The party retained control of academic institutions, and subjects such as relations between Poland and Russia and the history of socialism remained subject to censorship. In 1962 Kelles-Krauz's selected works were published, though an introduction by Julian Hochfeld portraying Kelles-Krauz as a representative of "open Marxism" was removed. Henceforth Kelles-Krauz would be treated not as a representative of the PPS, but as a figure whose patriotic Marxism could be exploited to justify the existence and practices of People's Poland. Although Ciołkosz wrote of Kelles-Krauz and the PPS from London (exaggerating Kelles-Krauz's influence), the PPS was no longer a threat. Its traditions could be picked apart, carefully, for useful morsels.

Bieńkowski's biography of 1969, the first comprehensive study of Kelles-Krauz's life and work, reflected the new political conjuncture. Whereas two decades previous Kelles-Krauz had been condemned, here he was glorified. With a few exceptions such as his putative underestimation of Lenin and Russian socialism, Bieńkowski's Kelles-Krauz was practically infallible. Bieńkowski treated all of Kelles-Krauz's political and sociological claims as equally brilliant, and clothed them only scantily in historical context. Bieńkowski did not have access to the excellent scholarly apparatus of the 1984 edition of Kelles-Krauz's letters. Bieńkowski set the precedent of treating Kelles-Krauz's Marxism according to a pamphlet Kelles-Krauz wrote in 1894 at the age of 22, and judging his patriotism from his writings of a decade later, just prior to his death. Writing in a time and place where all judgments on the relationship between patriotism and socialism were highly risky, Bieńkowski did not explain Kelles-Krauz's Marxist justification for the nation-state. Kelles-Krauz was at once an orthodox Marxist and an ardent advocate of Polish independence, and that was that. Bieńkowski's Kelles-Krauz "brought the new wine of social revolution, but delivered it in the old bottle of national liberation."[1] Bieńkowski's work set a standard for qualified but enthusiastic acceptance of Kelles-Krauz, which we find in evaluations of Kelles-Krauz in the 1970s

---

1. Borrowing a phrase from Thomas W. Simons, Jr., "The Peasant Revolt of 1846 in Galicia. Recent Polish Historiography," *Slavic Review* 30(4) 1971: 815.

by Kasprzakowa, Ajnenkiel, and Markiewicz (who in large part reversed his earlier crit-icism). In 1969, the sociologist Wiatr defended Kelles-Krauz against the earlier charges of imperialism, nationalism, and hostility to Russia, and rehabilitated him as having "anticipated the route of the later development of the Polish working class movement."

If the Gomułka years saw a qualified rehabilitation of Kelles-Krauz, Gierek's and then Jaruzelski's rule saw the disentanglement of Kelles-Krauz's sociological legacy from thorny political questions. In 1973 Wiatr analysed Kelles-Krauz's sociology crea-tively, and this time without political comment. Throughout the 1970s and 1980s we find articles treating various aspects of Kelles-Krauz's thought (his attitude toward art, toward music, toward religion, and so on), similarly without any mention of poli-tics. Szacki devoted a few pages to Kelles-Krauz in his history of sociology, published in 1981. Walicki's 1983 edited volume on the history of Polish philosophy included a very useful chapter on Marxism, which discussed Kelles-Krauz. In 1987 Bębenek published a solid analysis of Kelles-Krauz's thought on the national question within the Marxist tradition. Though I have learned from this work and several others pub-lished in these decades, none of them constitutes anything like a comprehensive treatment of Kelles-Krauz's thought.

All the while, Kelles-Krauz's rehabilitation as a figure with a politically useful legacy continued. In 1984, to the accompanying endorsement of a long article in *Polityka*, a magnificent edition of Kelles-Krauz's letters was published. By the 1980s, even the taboos about Kelles-Krauz's politics had fallen away, and Kancewicz's 1984 treatise on the early PPS treats Kelles-Krauz's role in the party without the previously obligatory reservations. 1989 ended these dynamics, though the use of Kelles-Krauz for political ends by the Polish left continues. *Myśl Socjaldemokratyczna*, the organ of Social-Democracy of the Republic of Poland (the descendant of the Polish com-munist party), is published by the Kelles-Krauz Foundation. The days of political constraints on writing about Kelles-Krauz have now passed, but there is as yet no satisfying treatment of Kelles-Krauz's life or works.

APPENDIX 3

Sources

My methods of research were straightforward. I tried to read as much of Kelles-Krauz's work as possible: in published collections, in Polish newspapers and journals at the libraries of the Universities of Warsaw and Wrocław and at the Biblioteka Narodowa in Warsaw, in French socialist organs in the British Library in London and the Bibliothéque Nationale in Paris, and in manuscript at the Biblioteka Zakładu Narodowego im. Ossolińskich "Ossolineum" in Wrocław. I have in several instances sought the articles against which Kelles-Krauz directed his criticisms, in Polish, French, and German socialist journals, and within a collection of articles on the national question edited by Rosa Luxemburg. I have read both sides of the debates Kelles-Krauz instigated in the *Annales de l'Institut International de Sociologie*.

The most valuable source on Kelles-Krauz's quotidian life is the collection of his letters published in 1984. A few letters which escaped this collection are in the archives of the Paris Okhrana at the Hoover Institution in California. I have tried to read the other side of this correspondence when possible, in published collections of letters of Józef Piłsudski and Leon Wasilewski; in uncollected letters from the London Archive of the PPS, now to be found in the Archiwum Akt Nowych in Warsaw; and among Maria Kelles-Krauzowa's letters at the Ossolineum in Wrocław. I have also found letters concerning Kelles-Krauz among the published correspondence of Rosa Luxemburg, Gabriela Zapolska, and Antonio Labriola. Letters and documents concerning Kelles-Krauz's academic career are also among his personal papers at the Ossolineum, and documents concerning the Kelles-Krauz family history are in the Archiwum Główne Akt Dawnych.

I have also used PPS party documents in the Archiwum Akt Nowych in Warsaw; unpublished recollections of friends and relatives at Ossolineum in Wrocław and the Biblioteka Polska in Paris; and informers' reports in the Paris Okhrana archives at the Hoover Institution at Stanford, and the Archiwum Główne Akt Dawnych, Warsaw. (I looked without success for informers' reports in the archives of the

Préfecture de Police in Paris.) Some PPS records have been published, and I have also relied on the published reports of the 1896 and 1900 congresses of the Second International. I have reviewed the PPS organs *Przedświt, Robotnik,* and *Naprzód.* I have also had recourse to the memoirs of Stanisław Grabski, Bolesław Limanowski, Ignacy Daszyński, Ludwik Krzywicki, Jan Lorentowicz, Stanisław Koszutski, Stefan Żeromski, and others.

There are two avenues of primary source research which I have not pursued. First, I made no effort to systematically study Kelles-Krauz's correspondence from Paris for the Warsaw daily the *Kurier Warszawski* in the 1890s. Kelles-Krauz considered this work for a censored and (more importantly) increasingly conservative newspaper "literary prostitution," and saved his better analysis for the illegal socialist press and legal intellectual journals. Second, I did not go to Moscow to search for further Russian secret police reports on Kelles-Krauz. Kelles-Krauz lived in the Russian Empire for only the first eighteen years of his life. While it is possible that he was spied upon at the University of Warsaw before he emigrated to Paris, he was only a student there for a matter of weeks. The Okhrana's foreign branch, based in Paris, was charged with the task of "controlling" émigré in France, and I have used its archives.

Kelles-Krauz's life was such that I have had to attain some measure of competence in several secondary literatures in Polish, English, French, and (to a much lesser extent) German. Broadly speaking, they are the histories of: Poland under the partitions; politics in France, Germany, and Austria at the turn of the century; Polish socialism and its leaders and theorists; socialist theory and practice on the national question; Marxist thought, especially during the Second International; French, German, and Austrian socialist parties; Jewish nationalism and socialism in central and eastern Europe; the Polish intelligentsia; Warsaw positivism and positivism generally; Polish sociology, French sociology, and sociology as such. I have also tried to understand contemporary explanations of the origins of modern nationalism, and come to terms with the philosophies of Vico, Hegel, Comte, and Marx. Naturally, the available time was insufficient to master any of these considerable literatures.

Notes

1. Michał Kelles-Krauz, "Kazimierz Kelles-Krauz na tle historii rodziny," *Biuletyn Kwartalny Radomskiego Towarzystwa Naukowego* 22(2) 1988: 49–50, gives the family traditions. The information that the family hails from Bavaria comes from Jan Krauze and is cited by Teofil Głowacki, "Kazimierz Kelles-Krauz: Człowiek i dzieło," *Przegląd Socjalistyczny* 3(7–9) 1947: 15. A schoolmate of Kazimierz's in Radom confirms that the family descended from Knights of the Sword. [Józef Dąbrowski] J. Grabiec, "Wilhelm Feldman jako publicysta i działacz społeczny," in *Pamięci Wilhelma Feldmana* (Cracow, 1922), p. 74. For records of the confirmation of nobility of Elehard Krause, see Rewizja Inflant (tak zwana Metryka Litewska), signature IV B.28, p. 288; Sumariusz Metryki Litewskicj, signature IV, p. 163; and Metryka Koronna, signature ks. 131, p. 66; all in Archiwum Główne Akt Dawnych, Warsaw. Also Zygmunt Wdowiszewski, "Tytuły polskie nadawane cudzoziemcom," *Materiały do biografii, genealogii, i heraldyki polskiej* 1966 (3): 13. On Eginhard Krause, see Seweryn Uruski, *Rodzina: Herburz szlachty polskiej*, vol. 8 (Warsaw, 1911), p. 47. On Polish colonization of Livonia: Stanisław Herbst, *Wojna Inflancka 1600–1602* (Warsaw, 1937). For a German historical novel on the von Krause family around the years 1555–1575, see T. H. Pantenius, *Die von Kelles* (Bielefeld, 1885). The novel has it that the Krauses betrayed Livonia and fought for Russia, and that Baron von Krause and his son were killed in battle. The background is drawn from Norman Davies, *God's Playground: A History of Poland*, vol. 1 (New York, 1982).

2. On the appearance of Krauzes in Lithuania, Uruski, *Rodzina*, p. 47. For Jan and Michał's generations: Michał Kelles-Krauz, "Historia rodziny," p. 49. See also Gustaw Manteuffel, *O starodawnej szlachcie krzyżacko-rycerskiej na kresach inflanckich* (Lviv, 1912), pp. 7–12. On Różycki's troops, see Stefan Kieniewicz, *Powstanie styczniowe* (Warsaw, 1972), pp. 497–502.

3. Matylda's death is ignored in Wiesław Bieńkowski, *Kazimierz Kelles-Krauz. Życie i dzieło* (Wrocław, 1969). Bieńkowski calls Matylda Michał's "lifelong companion," which is only true if the life in question is hers; and neglects to mention the rather interesting fact that Michał later (October 1892) married an older sister of his son Kazimierz's girlfriend and future wife. Michał had six children by his first wife, and three more by his second. Janina Kelles-Krauz, "Mój ojciec— Kazimierz Kelles-Krauz," *Miesięcznik Literacki* 1972 (9): 89.

4. He also taught Kazimierz the family history. On a page of his datebook Kazimierz sketched a family tree, next to a note reading "Elehard 1585." It seems likely that in retrospect this date was of importance for the family as marking the beginning of its loyalty to Poland. See "Kalendarzyk Memorandum 1890," pages for 15–16 February, folder 18/89, unsorted materials, Department of Manuscripts. Biblioteka Zakładu Narodowego im. Ossolińskich *"Ossolineum,"* Wrocław. Hereafter *"Ossolineum,"* and where numbers are given in parenthesis, these are folder numbers of unsorted materials. For a loving and grateful letter from Kazimierz to his grandfather, see Kelles-Krauz in Orońsk to Jakub Daniewski in Radom, 24 July 1890, Kazimierz Kelles-Krauz, *Listy,* ed. Feliks Tych et al., vol. 1 (Warsaw, 1984), pp. 28–29. (Hereafter *Listy* I, and for volume 2, *Listy* II). See also Janina Kelles-Krauz, "Mój ojciec," p. 89.

5. Kelles-Krauz in Vilnius to Maria Goldsteynówna in Radom, 13 October 1890, *Listy* I, p. 44.

6. Kelles-Krauz in Vilnius to Goldsteynówna in Radom, 17 September 1890, *Listy* I, p. 33; "Kalendarzyk Memorandum 1890," *Ossolineum* (18/89).

7. See Peter Brock, "The Polish Identity," in W. J. Stankiewicz, ed., *The Tradition of Polish Ideals* (London, 1981), pp. 23–51.

8. Thomas W. Simons, Jr., *Eastern Europe in the Postwar World* (New York, 1991), pp. 9–10.

9. Gumplowicz: Jerzy Jedlicki, "Inteligencja," in Józef Bachórz and Alina Kowalczykowa, eds., *Słownik literatury polskiej XIX wieku* (Wrocław, 1991), p. 373; Libelt and Trentowski: Jerzy Jedlicki, "Szlachta," ibid., p. 923. See also Andrzej Walicki, *Philosophy and Romantic Nationalism: The Case of Poland* (Oxford, 1982), pp. 176–77.

10. To avoid awkwardness, I will occasionally use the term "Congress Kingdom" to refer to these lands during periods which extend past 1865.

11. Kieniewicz, *Historia,* pp. 299–300.

12. Konstanty Grzybowski, *Historia państwa i prawa Polski,* vol. 4, (Warsaw, 1982), pp. 129–33; Kieniewicz, *Historia,* p. 300; Piotr Wandycz, *The Lands of Partitioned Poland* (Seattle, 1974), p. 196.

13. Robert Blobaum, "The Revolution of 1905–1907 and the Crisis of Polish Catholicism," *Slavic Review* 37(4) 1988: 669.

14. Hugh Seton-Watson, *Nations and States* (London, 1977), pp. 85–86. Seton-Watson claims that Russification was turned "first" against the loyal Baltic Germans and

Armenians, though Russification of German and Armenian institutions started slightly later than that of Polish institutions.

15. Polish newspapers were legal, though preventatively censored. Yiddish newspapers were banned completely after 1868. Russian policy did not attempt to eliminate Polish and Yiddish, as it did Ukrainian and Belarusian. Stephen Corrsin, "Language Use in Cultural and Political Change in Pre-1914 Warsaw," *Slavonic and East European Review* 68(1) 1990: 78–80.

16. Stanislaus Blejwas, *Realism in Polish Politics* (New Haven, 1984), p. 57; Jerzy Jedlicki, "Kwestia nadprodukcji inteligencji w Królestwie Polskim po powstaniu styczniowym," in Ryszarda Czepulis-Rastenis, *ed.*, *Inteligencja polska pod zaborami* (Warsaw, 1978), p. 220; Wereszycki, *Historia polityczna*, p. 61.

17. Wandycz, *Lands*, p. 201.

18. Kieniewicz, *Historia*, pp. 271, 280; Wandycz, *Lands*, p. 199.

19. Kieniewicz, *Historia*, pp. 287–91; Wandycz, *Lands*, pp. 201–206.

20. Kieniewicz, *Historia*, pp. 335–36; Piotr Górski, *Socjalistyczno-niepodległościowa idea narodu polskiego* (Cracow, 1994), p. 30.

21. Jan Luboński, *Monografia historyczna miasta Radomia* (Radom, 1907), p. 337; Stefan Witkowski, "Struktura współczesnego przemysłu radomskiego," in Jerzy Jędrzejewicz, ed., *Radom: Szkice z dziejów miasta* (Warsaw, 1961), p. 137; Jan Boniecki, "Radom w okresie 1865–1918. Stosunki polityczno-społeczne," in Stefan Witkowski et al, eds., *Radom: Dzieje miasta w XIX i XX w.* (Warsaw, 1985), p. 81.

22. Boniecki, "Radom," p. 82. See also Anna Żarnowska, "Religion and politics. Polish workers c. 1900," *Social History* 16(3) 1991: 301.

23. Marek Gawlik, "Początki przemysłu garbarskiego w Radomiu," in Jędrzejewicz, *Radom*, pp. 129, 136; Luboński, *Monografia historyczna*, p. 338.

24. Kieniewicz, *Historia*, p. 302.

25. Testis, "Pamiętniki dyrektora gimnazjum radomskiego," in *Zwierciadło Polskie* (Warsaw, 1915), p. 78; Bohdan Cywiński, *Rodowody niepokornych* (Paris, 1985), p. 23; Blejwas, *Realism*, p. 58.

26. I cite after Norman Naimark, *The History of the "Proletariat"* (New York, 1979), p. 7.

27. Kieniewicz, *Historia*, p. 302; Edmund Staszyński, *Polityka oświatowa caratu w Królestwie Polskim* (Warsaw, 1968), pp. 21–24; Stanisław Koszutski, *Walka młodzieży polskiej o wielkie ideały* (Warsaw, 1928), p. 8; Jan Luboński, "Historja gimnazjum radomskiego," in *Jednodniówka Zjazdu Koleżeńskiego Radomiaków* (Warsaw, 1924), p. 56.

28. Kieniewicz, *Historia*, p. 351.

29. Cywiński, *Rodowody*, p. 28.

30. Blejwas, *Realism*, p. 58; Staszyński, *Polityka oświatowa*, p. 35, Cywiński, *Rodowody*, p. 23. Not all schools taught the classics, but only those that did gave diplomas that allowed students to attend university.

31. Wereszycki, *Historia polityczna*, p. 60; Staszyński, *Polityka oświatowa*, p. 29; Cywiński, *Rodowody*, p. 25.

32. Cywiński, *Rodowody*, p. 26.

33. Kieniewicz, *Historia*, p. 302; Cywiński, *Rodowody*, p. 28.

34. Andrzej Garlicki, *Józef Piłsudski, 1867–1935* (Warsaw, 1988), p. 9; Włodzimierz Suleja, *Polska Partia Socjalistyczna* (Warsaw, 1988), p. 41.

35. Luboński, "Historja gimnazjum radomskiego," p. 35.

36. Luboński, "Historja gimnazjum radomskiego," pp. 33–34; Testis, "Pamiętniki dyrektora," p. 72.

37. Stanisław Radwan, "Wspomnienia z życia koleżenskiego w latach 1889–1905," in *Jednodniówka*, p. 58.

38. Smorodinov's memoirs are in *Russkaia Starina* 1913 and 1914. They are summarized in Testis, "Pamiętniki dyrektora."

39. Testis, "Pamiętniki dyrektora," p. 76.

40. For these details, *Widoki Radomia* (Warsaw, 1899) and Maria Maj, "Kolegium Pijaiów," in Jędrzejewicz, *Radom*. The Radom gimnazjum had been built by the Piarists, and was finished in 1756.

41. Corrsin, "Language," p. 79.

42. Wereszycki, *Historia polityczna*, p. 91; Cywiński, *Rodowody*, p. 32.

43. Józef Dąbrowski, "Uczniowskie kółka tajne w Radomiu w latach 1889–1904," in *Jednodniówka*, p. 37; Cywiński, *Rodowody*, p. 32.

44. Kieniewicz, *Historia*, p. 322.

45. On this generational divide, Cywiński, *Rodowody*, p. 28 and *passim*. Stanisław Wojciechowski defined the difference as between those who were victims of social passivity and those who could not understand it. *Moje wspomnienia*, vol. 1 (Lviv-Warsaw, 1938), p. 23. See also Wereszycki, *Historia polityczna*, p. 11; Garlicki, *Piłsudski*, p. 10.

46. On Poles, socialism, and Russian universities, Naimark, *Proletariat*, pp. 56–59; Lucjan Blit, *The Origins of Polish Socialism* (Cambridge, 1971), p. 16.

47. Ludwik Krzywicki, *Wspomnienia*, vol. 2 (Warsaw, 1958), pp. 20, 41–47; Wereszycki, *Historia polityczna*, p. 118.

48. Leon Baumgarten, ed., *Krakowski komisarz policji na służbie carskiego wywiadu* (Cracow, 1967), p. 78; John-Paul Himka, *Socialism in Galicia* (Cambridge, Massachusetts, 1983), p. 95; Wereszycki, *Historia polityczna*, p. 82; Kieniewicz, *Historia*, p. 338.

49. Although, according to Wereszycki, a Polish worker had died in the Warsaw Citadel as early as 1879, *Historia polityczna*, p. 75.

50. r., "Kuno i War," *Przedświt* 1896 (1–3): 17. Kelles-Krauz's pseudonyms will be italicized in citation.

51. Jan Offenberg, *Stan umysłów wśród młodzieży akademickiej w latach 1885–1890* (Warsaw, 1929), p. 5. Miłkowski's "Rzecz o obronie czynnej i Skarbie Narodowym" called for clear thinking about when a rising might be possible, and for the collection of a national treasury to finance it when the time came. On its effect, see Wilhelm Feldman, *Dzieje polskiej myśli politycznej w okresie porozbiorowym*,

vol. 3 (Warsaw, 1920), p. 24. Stefan Żeromski called Colonel Miłkowski the only member of the older generation who called for resistance. See his *Dzienniki,* vol. 6 (Warsaw, 1965), p. 206. Another example of a link between 1863 and modern politics was Limanowski, whose *Patryotizm i socyalizm,* written in 1881 in Geneva, was popular among students.

52. Adam Hrebenda, "Miejsce Bolesława Limanowskiego w polskim ruchu robotniczym," in Stanisław Michalkiewicz and Zbigniew Żechowski, eds., *Nestor polskiego socjalizmu czy tylko demokrata?* (Katowice, 1987), pp. 52–53; Wereszycki, *Historia polityczna,* p. 83; Peter Nettl, *Rosa Luxemburg,* vol. 1 (London, 1966), p. 47.

53. Cywiński, *Rodowody,* p. 31; Wandycz, *Lands,* p. 93; Kieniewicz, *Historia,* p. 93.

54. Cywiński, *Rodowody,* p. 31.

55. Wojciechowski, *Wspomnienia,* p. 13.

56. This is the interpretation of Wojciech Modzelewski, *Naród i postęp* (Warsaw, 1977), p. 60.

57. Leszek Kołakowski, *The Alienation of Reason* (Garden City, 1968).

58. Modzelewski, *Naród i postęp,* pp. 17, 27.

59. Modzelewski, *Naród i postęp,* pp. 29–33.

60. Modzelewski, *Naród i postęp,* pp. 36–37.

61. Modzelewski, *Naród i postęp,* pp. 24–26.

62. Jedlicki, "Inteligencja," p. 376.

63. Jedlicki, "Nadprodukcja," p. 220; Marta Zahorska, "Spór o inteligencję w polskiej myśli społecznej do I wojny światowej," in Ryszarda Czepulis-Rastenis, ed., *Inteligencja polska pod zaborami* (Warsaw, 1978), p. 193.

64. Jedlicki, "Nadprodukcja," pp. 225–28, 249–50.

65. Alina Molska, "Wstęp" to Alina Molska, ed., *Pierwsze pokolenie marksistów polskich* (Warsaw, 1962).

66. Zahorska, "Spór," p. 215.

67. For a discussion of the Warsaw intelligentsia's self-definition, Zahorska, "Spór," pp. 188–215. For the vicissitudes of the term more generally, Jedlicki, "Inteligencja"; Jerzy Szacki, "Gdzież są ci nasi inteligenci," in *Dylematy historiografii idei* (Warsaw, 1991), pp. 364–72.

68. Dąbrowski, "Uczniowskie kółka," p. 37.

69. Dąbrowski, "Uczniowskie kółka," p. 38.

70. Wiesław Bieńkowski, *Listy* I, p. 39n2; Kelles-Krauz in Vilnius to Goldsteynówna in Radom, 25 September 1890, *Listy* I, p. 36.

71. *Michał Luśnia,* "Aryele," in "Majówka," supplement to *Naprzód* 14(97) 1 May 1905: 5–6.

72. For accounts by two of his fellows: Koszutski, *Walka młodzieży,* pp. 19–20; Dąbrowski, "Uczniowskie kółka," pp. 41–42. See also Ludwik Krzywicki, "Krauz Kazimierz Kelles," *Wielka Encyklopedia Powszechna Ilustrowana,* vol. 39–40 (Warsaw, 1907), p. 813.

73. On Pinko: Wiesław Bieńkowski, *Listy* I, p. 30nl.

74. The less flattering portrait in Testis, "Pamiętniki dyrektora," p. 75.
75. Kieniewicz, *Historia*, p. 331; Feldman, *Dzieje polskiej myśli*, p. 51.
76. Kieniewicz, *Historia*, p. 353.
77. Dąbrowski, "Uczniowskie kółka," pp. 41–42.
78. Students' writings in *Ossolineum* (19/89).
79. *Radosław*, "Trzeba walczyć," *Gazeta Radomska* 7(51) 1891, cited after Bieńkowski, *Kelles-Krauz*, p. 23nlo.
80. Dąbrowski, "Uczniowskie kółka," p. 39.
81. Cywiński, *Rodowody*, p. 35.
82. Wojciechowski, *Wspomnienia*, p. 5.
83. Luboński, *Monografia historyczna*, p. 33.
84. Kelles-Krauz's friend Władysław Bukowiński remembered Kelles-Krauz's years in Radom's school thus: "Passing from year to year with distinctions, in other conditions he would have been the pride and delight of the school." "Kazimierz Krauz," *Prawda* 25 (25) 1905: 293.
85. The account is compiled from: Cywiński, *Rodowody*, p. 35; Bukowiński, "Kazimierz Krauz," p. 293; Janina Kelles-Krauz, "Mój ojciec," p. 89; Bieńkowski, *Kelles-Krauz*, pp. 24–25 (although he makes the point that Kelles-Krauz took part in the scheme even though he was only in his seventh year, which is false: he registered in the fall of 1882, and his datebook shows that he was preparing for exams); "Kalendarzyk Memorandum 1890," *Ossolineum* (18/89).
86. Janina Kelles-Krauz, "Mój ojciec," p. 89.
87. Kelles-Krauz in Vilnius to Goldsteynówna in Radom, 8 October 1890, *Listy* I, p. 41.
88. He left on 14 July 1890. "Kalendarzyk Memorandum 1890," *Ossolineum* (18/89).
89. On Brandt see Włodzimiera Drewniewska, "Sylwetki malarzy radomskich," in Jędrzejewicz, *Radom*.
90. Kelles-Krauz in Vilnius to Goldsteynówna in *Radom*, 11 February 1891, *Listy* I, p. 73; Kelles-Krauz in Warsaw to Goldsteyówna in Radom, 23 January 1891, *Listy* I, p. 66.
91. *K. Radosławski*, "Poszukiwania. Odpowiedż z Orońska," *Wisła* 15 (4–5): 489–501, 619–33; *C. Halak*, "Próba agitacyi na wsi przed laty dziesięciu," *Przedświt* 1902(1): 21–24.
92. Kelles-Krauz in Paris to Centralizacja ZZSP in London, 28 March 1896, *Listy* I, p. 532. Hereafter "CZZSP" for "Centralizacja ZZSP."
93. Kelles-Krauz finished it in May 1892. Kelles-Krauz in Paris to Goldsteynówna in Radom, 1 June 1892, *Listy* I, p. 170. "Czy teraz nie ma pańszczyzny?" was published in 1897 by the PPS, and saw four further publications before the First World War. It was used first in Galicia, and eventually translated by a Ukrainian party. Walentyna Najdus, *Polska Partia Socjalno-Demokratyczna Galicji i Śląska* (Warsaw, 1983), pp. 279–80.
94. "Związek Robotników Polskich." Kelles-Krauz, "Próba," p. 21.

95. On the Second Proletariat, Feldman, *Dzieje polskiej myśli*, p. 24; Wereszycki, *Historia polityczna*, p. 84. On the Union of Polish Workers, Feliks Tych, *Związek Robotników Polskich* (Warsaw, 1974), pp. 171–220; Feldman, *Dzieje polskiej myśli*, pp. 24, 58; Krzywicki, *Wspomnienia*.

96. Kelles-Krauz, "Próba."

97. Janina Kelles-Krauz, "Mój ojciec," p. 89; "Kalendarzyk Memorandum 1890," *Ossolineum* (18/89).

98. Goldsteynówna in Radom to Kelles-Krauz in Vilnius, 30 October 1890, *Ossolineum* (19/89); Kelles-Krauz in Vilnius to Goldsteynówna in Radom, 28 October 1890, *Listy* I, p. 50.

99. Wiesław Bieńkowski, *Listy* I, p. 54nl.

100. Kelles-Krauz in Vilnius to Goldsteynówna in Radom, 10 December 1890, *Listy* I, p. 63.

101. Wiesław Bieńkowski, *Listy* I, p. 72nl.

102. Kelles-Krauz in Vilnius to Goldsteynówna in Radom, 18 October 1890, *Listy* I, p. 47. Maria's father was a military doctor. One day he treated a soldier who had lost his hearing after a beating by a superior. The soldier's cries of despair turned Maria to socialism. Janina Kelles-Krauz, "Mój ojciec," p. 90.

103. Kelles-Krauz in Vilnius to Goldsteynówna in Radom, 18 October 1890, *Listy* I. p. 46.

104. Kelles-Krauz in Vilnius to Goldsteynówna in Radom, 17 September 1890, *Listy* 1, pp. 31–32.

105. Kelles-Krauz in Vilnius to Goldsteynówna in Radom, 7 November 1890, *Listy* I, p. 55.

106. Kelles-Krauz in Vilnius to Goldsteynówna in Radom, 17 September 1890.*Listy* I, p. 32.

107. Kelles-Krauz in Vilnius to Goldsteynówna in Radom, 19 November 1890, *Listy* I, p. 60.

108. Kelles-Krauz in Vilnius to Goldsteynówna in Radom, 18 October 1890, *Listy* I, p. 47.

109. Kelles-Krauz in Vilnius to Goldsteynówna in Radom, 14 September 1890, *Listy* I, p. 30.

110. Kelles-Krauz in Vilnius to Goldsteynówna in Radom, 3 February 1891, *Listy* I, p. 71.

111. Kelles-Krauz in Warsaw to Goldsteynówna in Radom, 23 January 1891, *Listy* I, p. 66.

112. Kelles-Krauz finished *Looking Backward* on 18 September 1890, "Kalendarzyk Memorandum 1890," *Ossolineum* (18/89).

113. Kelles-Krauz in Vilnius to Goldsteynówna in Radom, 17 September 1890, *Listy* I, p. 33.

114. Edward Bellamy, *Looking Backward* (New York, 1986 [1888]), p. 65.

115. Bellamy, *Looking Backward*, p. 111.

116. "Think of a world in which there can be nothing but matches of pure love!" exclaims West. Bellamy, *Looking Backward,* p. 191.

117. Koszutski, *Walka młodzieży,* p. 25; Sokolnicki, *Czternaście lat,* p. 8. When Bellamy died in 1898, the PPS organ *Przedświt (Dawn)* published a long obituary and portrait. "Bellamy," *Przedświt* 1898 (7): 17. Bellamy served Polish socialists as a common point of reference. Kelles-Krauz later wrote of a polemical foe: "As I love God, I begin to think that this man didn't even understand Bellamy!" *Michał Luśnia,* "Sartor sarritus albo czy Ostoja ostoi?," *Przedświt* 1898 (11): 11–17, cited after Kazimierz Kelles-Krauz, *Pisma wybrane,* vol. 2 (Warsaw, 1962), p. 77. Henceforth *"Pisma I"* and *"Pisma II."* Where possible, I will cite after these volumes.

118. Kelles-Krauz in Vilnius to Goldsteynówna in Radom, 17 September 1890, *Listy* I, p. 33.

119. It was translated into Polish in 1887, but by then it was already familiar to Polish students, having been popularized by Ludwik Krzywicki during the first half of the 1880s. Krzywicki had introduced Morgan to Poles on his own initiative, before Engels had his say in *The Origin of the Family, Private Property, and the State* in 1884. See Andrzej Walicki, *Polska, Rosja, marksizm* (Warsaw, 1983), p. 7. Krzywicki then translated the Engels popularization: [Ludwik Krzywicki] J.F. Wolski, *Początki cywilizacji,* Paris 1885. We know Kelles-Krauz read Engels on Morgan: Entry for 27 May in "Kalendarzyk Memorandum 1890," *Ossolineum* (18/89). In Vilnius, he taught Morgan to Dowiatt's daughters, through another popularization, this time by Edward Abramowski in 1890. See [Edward Abramowski] Z. R. Walczewski, "Społeczeństwo rodowe" (Kraków 1890), in Edward Abramowski, *Pisma,* vol. 4 (Warsaw, 1928).

120. Lewis Henry Morgan, *Ancient Society* (Tucson, 1985 [1877]), pp. xxxii, 552–53.

121. Morgan, *Ancient Society,* pp. 10–12.

122. Morgan, *Ancient Society,* p. 505.

123. Morgan, *Ancient Society,* p. 552.

124. On Bernstein, Kautsky, and the "Anti-Dühring": see (respectively) Peter Gay, *The Dilemma of Democratic Socialism,* (New York 1962); and Gary Steenson, *Karl Kautsky* (Pittsburgh, 1978).

125. Friedrich Engels, "The Origin of the Family, Private Property, and the State," in Karl Marx and Friedrich Engels, *Selected Works in One Volume* (London, 1991), pp. 430, 433. Engels completed a work Marx had begun. Elisabeth Tooker, "Foreward" in Morgan, *Ancient Society,* p. xvi. Marx was convinced by Morgan, and Morgan's work was a major topic of discussion between Marx and Engels. Eric Hobsbawm, "Introduction" to Karl Marx, *Pre-capitalist Economic Formations* (London, 1978), pp. 24–25. On Engels's reading of Morgan, see Adam Kuper, *The Invention of Primitive Society* (London, 1991), pp. 72–73; Maurice Bloch, *Marxism and Anthropology* (Oxford, 1991), pp. 47–62.

126. Kelles-Krauz in Vilnius to Goldsteynówna in Radom, 10 March 1891, *Listy* 1, p. 80; Kelles-Krauz in Vilnius to Józef Goldsteyn in Radom, 17 March 1891, *Listy* I, p. 81; Kelles-Krauz in Vilnius to Goldsteynówna in Radom, 23 March 1891, *Listy* I, p. 84; Kelles-Krauz in Vilnius to Goldsteynówna in Radom, 2 April 1891, *Listy* I, p. 87.

127. Kelles-Krauz in Kielce to Goldsteynówna in Radom, 29 April 1891, *Listy* I, p. 89.

128. The earliest of his publications in these Warsaw journals that I have seen is K.Radosławski, "Trzy typy etyczne," *Głos* 6(2) 1891: 16–17.

129. On the Kielce circle, see Koszutski, *Walka młodzieży*, pp. 14–25.

130. Garlicki, *Piłsudski*, p. 36; "Les Socialistes polonais," *La Bataille*, 17 May 1891: 1.

131. Koszutski, *Walka młodzieży*, p. 27.

132. Kelles-Krauz in Kielce to Goldsteynówna in Radom, 8 June 1891, *Listy* I, pp. 90–91.

133. Kelles-Krauz in Orońsk to Goldsteynówna in Radom, 6 July 1891, *Listy* I, pp. 91–92; Kelles-Krauz in Orońsk to Goldsteynówna in Vilnius, 22 July 1891, *Listy* I, pp. 93–96.

134. Ireneusz Ihnatowicz, "Uniwersytet Warszawski w latach 1869–1899," in Stefan Kieniewicz, ed., *Dzieje Uniwersytetu Warszawskiego* (Warsaw, 1981), especially pp. 383, 414, 441; Koszutski, *Walka młodzieży*, pp. 40–41; Feldman, *Dziejepolskiej myśli*, p. 20.

135. Kieniewicz, *Historia*, p. 351.

136. Ihnatowicz, "Uniwersytet," p. 447.

137. Ihnatowicz, "Uniwersytet," pp. 418–19; Kieniewicz, *Historia*, p. 351.

138. Offenburg, *Stan umysłów*, pp. 7–8.

139. An organization called "Bratnia Pomoc" had existed on and off since the founding of the Akademia Medyko-Chirurgiczna, before 1863. Kieniewicz, *Historia*, p. 231. Its most recent incarnation arose in the school year 1889–1890. Ihnatowicz, "Uniwersytet," p. 472.

140. Ihnatowicz, "Uniwersytet," pp. 458, 464; Koszutski, *Walka młodzieży*, p. 37.

141. Offenburg, *Stan umysłów*, p. 14.

142. Koszutski, *Walka młodzieży*, pp. 6–7.

143. Ihnatowicz, "Uniwersytet," p. 494.

144. Ihnatowicz, "Uniwersytet," pp. 470–71.

145. Dated according to sp., "Wspomnienia z dwóch lat (1892–1893)," *Zpola walki* (London, 1904), p. 28. Student participation according to Koszutski, *Walka młodzieży*, 41; Offenburg, *Stan umysłów*, p. 13.

146. Krzywicki, *Wspomnienia*, p. 291; Wojciechowski, *Wspomnienia*, chapter 1. "Zjednoczenie."

147. Koszutski, *Walka młodzieży*, p. 50.

148. Kelles-Krauz in Vienna to KZPPS in London, 12 February 1902, *Listy* II, p. 600. "Centralne Koło Studenckie," "narodowcy," "międzynarodowcy."

149. Koszutski, *Walka młodzieży*, p. 37.

150. Koszutski, *Walka młodzieży*, pp. 22, 37, 41; Wojciechowski, *Wspomnienia*, pp. 5, 8.

151. Koszutski, *Walka młodzieży*, p. 13.

152. Koszutski, *Walka młodzieży*, pp. 13, 48. "Koło Młodych."

153. In the course of that autumn, Kelles-Krauz traveled to Radom to try to impose some kind of order on its various circles. Dąbrowski, "Uczniowskie kółka," pp. 39–40.

154. Bukowiński, *Wspomnienia*, p. 293; Kelles-Krauz in Vienna to Goldsteynówna in Warsaw, 17 December 1893, *Listy* I, pp. 100–103.

155. Goldsteynówna in Radom to Kelles-Krauz in Paris, undated, *Ossolineum* (19/89).

156. Kelles-Krauz in Vienna to Goldsteynówna in Warsaw, 17 December 1891, *Listy* I, p. 101.

157. Kelles-Krauz in Vienna to Goldsteynówna in Warsaw, 17 December 1891, *Listy* I, pp. 100–103; Kelles-Krauz in Munich to Goldsteynówna in Radom, 20 December 1891, *Listy* I, pp. 104–106.

158. Folder 2, Index Number XIX, Archive of the Paris Okhrana, Hoover Institution, Stanford University. Hereafter "*Hoover* (index number/folder)."

159. Jan Lorentowicz, *Spojrzenie wstecz* (Warsaw, 1935), p. 167. This estimate is consistent with Kieniewicz's count of 4,000 Polish political émigrés in France after 1863. *Historia*, p. 272.

160. Koszutski, *Walka młodzieży*, p. 145.

161. Michał Sokolnicki, *Czternaście lat* (Warsaw, 1936), p. 11.

162. Stanisław Grabski, *Pamiętniki*, vol. 1 (Warsaw, 1989), pp. 88–89.

163. Koszutski, *Walka młodzieży*, p. 145.

164. Grabski, *Pamiętniki*, p. 89.

165. Jedlicki, *Jakiej cywilizacji*, p. 243.

166. Kieniewicz gives 800 registered students from the Congress Kingom abroad, as compared to 2,000 within the Empire. *Historia*, p. 352. Some of this proportion is accounted for by political, or semipolitical, emigration: Kelles-Krauz arrived just after the latest wave of students expelled from the University of Warsaw by Apukhtin. Lorentowicz, *Spojrzenie*, p. 151.

167. Sokolnicki, *Czternaście lat*, p. 13.

168. Sokolnicki, *Czternaście lat*, p. 13.

169. Lorentowicz, *Spojrzenie*, p. 148.

170. Lorentowicz, *Spojrzenie*, pp. 151–52.

171. Lorentowicz, *Spojrzenie*, p. 152.

172. Kieniewicz, *Historia*, p. 352; Grabski, *Pamiętniki*, p. 89.

173. Lorentowicz, *Spojrzenie*, pp. 153–60.

174. Kelles-Krauz in Paris to Goldsteynówna in Radom, 7 February 1893, *Listy* I, p. 245.

175. Wiesław Bieńkowski, "Kelles-Krauz Kazimierz Radosław Elehard," in Feliks Tych, et al, eds., *Słownik biograficzny działaczy polskiego ruchu robotniczego*, vol. 3

(Warsaw, 1992), p. 139. The *Kurier Warszawski* (1821–1939) had two daily editions, and its volume in the 1890s was about 25,000.

176. Kelles-Krauz in Paris to Goldsteynówna in Radom, 29 February 1892, *Listy* I, p. 146. See also Kazimierz Krauz, "Indywidualizm w dziennikarstwie," *Prawda* 13(45) 1893: 535–36; in manuscript at *Ossolineum*, signatures 28/77, 291/78, 292/78. Aleksandra Garlicka nevertheless emphasizes that, despite all the necessary compromises, Kelles-Krauz's reportage clearly reflected different concerns that than of other correspondents. "Kazimierz Krauz: Dziennikarz Polski," *Kwartalnik Historii Prasy Polskiej* 26(2): 48.

177. Kelles-Krauz in Paris to Goldsteynówna in Radom, 8 January 1892, *Listy* I, p. 118; Kelles-Krauz in Paris to Goldsteynówna in Radom, 26 February 1892, *Listy* I, p. 138.

178. "Korespondencja Sekretarza Generalnego Akademii Umiętności z 1899 r.," *Ossolineum* (18/89).

179. Lorentowicz, *Spojrzenie*, p. 153.

180. Lorentowicz, *Spojrzenie*, p. 162. "Gmina narodowo-socjalistyczna."

181. Marian Żychowski, *Polska myśl socjalistyczna XIX i XX wieku* (Warsaw, 1976), pp. 175–77.

182. Feldman, *Dzieje polskiej myśli*, pp. 37, 51.

183. Lorentowicz, *Spojrzenie*, pp. 162–63; Żychowski, *Polska myśl*, p. 177.

184. Grabski, *Pamiętniki*, p. 92.

185. Goldsteynówna in Radom to Kelles-Krauz in Paris, 20 June 1892, *Ossolineum* (19/89); Kelles-Krauz in Paris to Goldsteynówna in Radom, 24 June 1892, *Listy* I, p. 179.

186. Jędrzejowski in Berlin to Mendelson in London, 11 July 1892, *Archiwum Akt Nowych, Oddział VI: Archiwum Lewicy*, 305/VII, volume 47, cards 15–16. Hereafter, *"Archiwum Lewicy."* For the content of this article, see "Kazimierz Kelles-Krauz," *Przedświt* 1905 (6-8): 230. It was not published, though seven others for *Gazeta Robotnicza* were. Walentyna Najdus, *Ignacy Daszyński* (Warsaw, 1988), p. 73.

187. Grabski, *Pamiętniki*, p. 94

188. Kelles-Krauz in Paris to Goldsteynówna in Radom, 27 July 1892, *Listy* I, p. 187.

189. Goldsteynówna in Radom to Kelles-Krauz in Paris, 2 January 1892; Goldsteynówna in Radom to Kelles-Krauz in Paris, 20 January 1892; Goldsteynówna in Radom to Kelles-Krauz in Paris, 25 January 1892, *Ossolineum* (19/89).

190. The circle was founded by Władysław Bukowiński, and included several other students from Radom. Wiesław Bieńkowski, *Listy* I, pp. 33–34n3.

191. Kelles-Krauz in Warsaw to Goldsteynówna in Warsaw, 29 October 1892, *Listy* J, p. 203 for his nomination; Kelles-Krauz in Warsaw to Goldsteynówna in Warsaw, i 8 October 1892, *Listy* I, p. 202 for time spent with Bukowiński.

192. Kelles-Krauz in Berlin to Goldsteynówna in Warsaw, 15 November 1892, *Listy* I, p. 214.

193. [Feliks Perl] Res, *Dzieje ruchu socjalistycznego w zaborze rosyjskim*, vol. 1 (Warsaw, 1910), pp. 361–62. Feliks Tych, *Socjalistyczna irredenta* (Cracow, 1982), pp. 27–28.

194. By November 1892, the Second Proletariat and the Union of Polish Workers had ceased to exist, and only Unification, which had never been very strong, remained. [Ludwik Kulczycki] Mieczysław Mazowiecki, *History a polskiego ruchu socjalistycznego w zaborze rosyjskim* (Cracow, 1903), p. 235.

195. Kelles-Krauz in Paris to Goldsteynówna in Radom, 17 November 1892, *Listy* I, p. 217.

196. Perl, *Dzieje ruchu*, p. 363.

197. James Joll, *The Second International* (London, 1955), pp. 48–55. Engels wrote that it would be "utterly insane" for German workers to strike, given that a May Day strike in Hamburg in 1890 had caused a traumatic lockout. Gary Steenson, *After Marx, Before Lenin* (Pittsburgh, 1991), pp. 33–34.

198. Wereszycki gives the estimate of "several thousand" workers on the street on the first May Day, in 1890; Garlicki says 8,000–10,000. Wereszycki, *Historia polityczna*, p. 118; Garlicki, *Piłsudski*, p. 36.

199. Witold Jodko-Narkiewicz, *Zarys dziejów P.P.S* (Warsaw, 1917), pp. 10–11. Feldman, *Dzieje polskiej myśli*, p. 38, remembers this as the first mass strike in Polish history. A major primary source on these events is Ł., "Bunt Łódzki w r. 1892," *Z pola walki* (London, 1904), pp. 25–28.

200. Leon Wasilewski, *Zarys dziejów Polskiej Partji Socjalistycznej* (Warsaw, 1925), pp. 26–27; Wereszycki, *Historia polityczna*, p. 129; Ryszard Michalski, *Socjalizm a niepodległość w polskiej myśli socjalistycnej* (Toruń, 1988), p. 48.

201. sp., "Wspomnienia," p. 29.

202. For individual recollections: Wojciechowski, *Wspomnienia*, pp. 34–35; Jodko-Narkiewicz, *Zarys*, p. 12; [Witold Jodko-Narkiewicz] A. W., "Kwestya niepodległości w programach socjalistów polskich" (Lviv, 1901); *Michał Luśnia*, "Rachunek," *Przedświt* 1896 (10-11): 11–15; *Michał Luśnia*, "Rozmowy towarzyszy o socyalizmie i patriotyzmie, konstytucyi i niepodległości" (London, 1904), p. 5. For a summary: Perl, *Dzieje ruchu*, pp. 366–67, 375.

203. From 1870 unions and strikes were outlawed. Kieniewicz, *Historia*, p. 336; Jedlicki, *Jakiej cywilizacji*, p. 362.

204. For an example of the last, see "Roma" in Zurich to Stanisław Grabski in Paris, 14 May 1893, *Hoover* (XIX/5).

205. Kieniewicz, *Historia*, p. 290.

206. Kieniewicz, *Historia*, p. 293; Jedlicki, *Jakiej cywilizacji*, p. 352.

207. Feldman, *Dzieje polskiej myśli*, p. 40.

208. Bolesław Limanowski, *Pamiętniki*, vol. 2 (Warsaw, 1958), p. 439.

209. Limanowski, *Pamiętniki*, p. 439.

210. One suspects that this rather odd appellation ("Centralization") was chosen as homage to the Towarzystwo Demokratów Polskich, a previous organization of Polish émigrés, whose directing body bore this name. For the participants and

agenda of this meeting, Garlicki, *Piłsudski*, p. 39; Wereszycki, *Historia polityczna*, pp. 121–22. Limanowski, *Pamiętniki*, pp. 439–43 gives the details of the arguments. Krzywicki, *Wspomnienia*, p. 292, explains why terrorism was an important question. "Związek Zagraniczny Socjalistów Polskich."

211. Bismarck's fall in 1890 was important in two ways (at least) for the future of the Second International. First, the SDP was legalized. Second, France, driven into the arms of Russia by the loss of Alsace and Lorraine, was finally able to seal an alliance. Bismarck had guarded against this outcome carefully. Even before the alliance had been signed, the French government cooperated with the Okhrana in the hope of speeding its progress. See Lorentowicz, *Spojrzenie*, p. 213. On French treatment of political crime during the Third Republic: Barton Ingraham, *Political Crime in Europe* (London, 1979), pp. 176–87.

212. An appeal was tabled in parliament, but public opinion was absorbed by Panama. Wojciechowski, *Wspomnienia*, pp. 53–54. Paris was usually the first choice of Polish exiles, and London a last resort—although England was far safer. Rosemary Ashton, *Little Germany* (Oxford, 1986), pp. 24–55.

213. Kaczyńska, *Ochrana*, p. 34.

214. Richard Johnson, "Zagranichnaia Agentura," in George L. Mosse, ed., *Police Forces in History* (London, 1975), pp. 22–24.

215. Brunet to Paris Okhrana, 15 January 1893, *Hoover* (XIX/2A).

216. Brunet to Paris Okhrana, 23 January 1893, *Hoover* (XIX/2A).

217. They met secretly, but also organized public gatherings to which they attracted figures as eminent as Jules Guesde. Kelles-Krauz in Paris to CZZSP in London, 27 July 1897, *Listy* I, p. 706.

218. Grabski, *Pamiętniki*, pp. 133–34.

219. K. Radosławski, "Proletariat uliczny i jego poezja miłosna," *Krytyka* 5(2–3) 1896: 61–71, 128–35. For the impression the Paris underworld made on Gabriela Zapolska during her visit with Kelles-Krauz to a "thieves' den," see Zapolska in Paris to Stefan Laurysiewicz, 6 April 1892, Gabriela Zapolska, *Listy*, vol. 1 (Warsaw, 1980), pp. 317–18.

220. On their friendship, see Kelles-Krauz in Radom to Goldsteynówna in Warsaw, 31 October 1892, *Listy* I, p. 205; Kelles-Krauz in Paris to Goldsteynówna in Warsaw, 17 November 1892, *Listy* I, p. 217; Kelles-Krauz in Paris to Goldsteynówna in Warsaw, 18 November 1892, *Listy* I, p. 219; Kelles-Krauz in Paris to Goldsteynówna in Warsaw, 6 December 1892, *Listy* I, p. 226. In Polish, SDKP stands for "Socjaldemokracja Królestwa Polskiego."

221. By December 1895, the actual informer, Malankiewicz, was reporting that Kuzimierz and Maria Kelles-Krauz and Estera Golde considered Urbach a dangerous leak. Bolesław Malankiewicz to Paris Okhrana, 12 December 1895, *Hoover* (XIX/4B). In November 1895, Kelles-Krauz asked the Centralizacja about Urbach's past, Kelles-Krauz in Paris to CZZSP in London, 17 November 1895, *Listy* I, pp. 463–64.

222. Himka, *Socialism in Galicia*, pp. 97–99, 208.

223. Aleksander Kochański, *Listy* I, p. 446nlo.

224. Johnson, "Agentura," p. 21.

225. Elżbieta Kaczyńska and Dariusz Drewniak, *Ochrana* (Warsaw, 1992), p. 34.

226. Aleksander Kochański, *Listy* I, p. 446nlo.

227. Malankiewicz to Paris Okhrana, 1 January 1894, *Hoover* (XIX/4B).

228. Malankiewicz to Paris Okhrana, 13 December 1894, *Hoover* (XIX/4B).

229. Malankiewicz to Paris Okhrana, 2 February 1896, *Hoover* (XIX/4B).

230. With Malankiewicz: Malankiewicz to Paris Okhrana, 7 December 1893, *Hoover* (XIX/4B). With Kelles-Krauz: Kelles-Krauz in Paris to Goldsteynówna in Warsaw, 17 November 1892, *Listy* I, p. 217; Kelles-Krauz in Paris to Goldsteynówna in Warsaw, 18 November 1892, *Listy* I, p. 219.

231. This account from: Kelles-Krauz in Paris to Goldsteynówna in Warsaw, 27 February 1893, *Listy* I, p. 249; Limanowski, *Pamiętniki;* Lorentowicz, *Spojrzenie*, pp. 195–210; "Sprawa Sawickiego," *Przedświt* 1896 (5): 18.

232. Kelles-Krauz in Paris to Goldsteynówna in Radom, 25 June 1893, *Listy* I, pp. 287–90.

233. Telegram from Julia Kelles-Krauzowa to Kelles-Krauz in Paris, 15 March 1893, *Ossolineum* (19/89).

234. Grabski, *Pamiętniki*, p. 134.

235. Kelles-Krauz in Berlin to Joachim Bartoszewicz in Paris, 9 June 1893, *Hoover* (XIX/5).

236. Stanisław Grabski to Władysław Grabski in Paris, 12 June 1893, *Hoover* (XIX/5).

237. Brunet to Paris Okhrana, 22 June 1893, *Hoover* (XIX/2A).

238. Jan Kancewicz, "Golde-Strożecka Estera," in Tych, *Słownik* II, pp. 286–87.

239. Kelles-Krauz in Paris to Goldsteynówna in Warsaw, 25 September 1892, *Listy* I, p. 222; Kelles-Krauz in Paris to Goldsteynówna in Warsaw, 6 December 1892, *Listy* I, p. 226; Kelles-Krauz in Paris to Goldsteynówna in Warsaw, 29 January 1893, *Listy* I, p. 241. See also Sokolnicki, *Czternaście lat*, pp. 21–22.

240. Kelles-Krauz in Paris to Goldsteynówna in Warsaw, 3 December 1892, *Listy* I, p. 296.

241. Note from the Secretary of the Faculté des Sciences Sociales de Paris *Ossolineum* (18/89).

242. Kelles-Krauz in Paris to CZZSP in London, 17 October 1894, *Listy* I, p. 217. Maria's father helped him regain the passport: Janina Kelles-Krauz, "Mój ojciec," p. 89.

243. Malankiewicz to Paris Okhrana, 16 January 1894, *Hoover* (XIX/4B).

244. Kelles-Krauz in Paris to CZZSP in London, 17 October 1894, *Listy* I, p. 217.

245. The PPS arose twice. First in March 1893, without knowledge of the November 1892 program, as a merger of the three older parties. This group was unable to cooperate with the Centralizacja, not having accepted the need for independence or for political action. It was offended by a 1 May pamphlet which used

the words "Orthodox beasts," and outraged by (unfounded) accusations by the Centralizacja that one of its members was an informer. After the split a second PPS arose under the guidance of a new man from Vilnius, Józef Piłsudski, and a caretaker from the Centralizacja, Stanisław Wojciechowski. Jan Kancewicz, *Polska Partia Socjalistyczna 1892–1896* (Warsaw, 1984), pp. 50, 53; [Stanisław Wojciechowski] *Polska Partya Socjalistyczna w ostatnich pięciu latach* (London, 1900), pp. 69–73; Kulczycki, *Historya*, pp. 238, 263–64; Żychowski, *Polska myśl*, pp. 190–91; Garlicki, *Piłsudski*, p. 42; Suleja, *Polska Partia*, p. 32.

246. On Poles at the Zurich congress: Nettl, *Luxemburg*, p. 73; Żychowski, *Polska myśl*, pp. 197–98; Feliks Tych, "Polskie partie w II Międzynarodówce," in *Historia Drugiej Międzynarodówki*, vol. 2 (Warsaw, 1978), pp. 701–702; Wojciechowski, *Polska Partya*, pp. 70–71; Kulczycki, *Historya*, pp. 258–60.

247. On the early months of the PPS, Kancewicz, *PPS*, pp. 51, 149–52; Kulczycki, *Historya*, pp. 279–80; Wojciechowski, *Polska Partya*, pp. 79–80.

248. On Piłsudski, Wojciechowski, and *Robotnik*, see Feldman, *Dzieje polskiej myśli*, p. 91; Kancewicz, *PPS*, pp. 50–52, 88–89; Wojciechowski, *Polska Partya*, pp. 72–74.

249. Kelles-Krauz in Radom to Ignacy Urbach in Paris, 14 December 1893, *Hoover* (XIX/5).

250. Kazimierz Pietkiewicz, "Niecała No. 12," in *Księga pamiątkowa PPS* (Warsaw, 1923), pp. 39–0.

251. On this first congress, Nettl, *Luxemburg*, p. 75; Żychowski, *Polska myśl*, p. 195; Kulczycki, *Historya*, pp. 276–79.

252. Garlicki, *Piłsudski*, p. 46.

253. Dąbrowski, "Uczniowskie kółka," pp. 41–42, 50; Marjan Malinowski, "Początek i rozwój organizacji P.P.S w Radomiu i okolicy," in *Księga pamiątkowa PPS* (Warsaw, 1923), p. 90; *Materiały do historyi P.P.S. i ruchu rewolucyjnego w zaborze rosyjskim*, vol. 1 (Warsaw, 1907), pp. 292–93; Boniecki, "Radom," p. 83.

254. Malankiewicz to Paris Okhrana, 2 April 1894, *Hoover* (XIX/4B).

255. On 14 June, 1894: Aleksandra Garlicka, *Listy* I, p. 308n8. See also Kelles-Krauz in Vienna to Kelles-Krauzowa in Radom, 26 June 1901, *Listy* II, p. 515.

256. Kazimierz Kelles-Krauz's passport, *Ossolineum* (18/89); Malankiewicz to Paris Okhrana, 2 April and 26 May 1894, *Hoover* (XIX/4B).

CHAPTER 2

1. Janina Kelles-Krauz, "Wokoł biografii i spuścizny Kazimierza Kelles-Krauza," *Z pola walki* 17(3) 1974: 57.

2. The word was out that the Kelles-Krauzes were intending to move by July 1894: Malankiewicz to Paris Okhrana, 24 July 1894, *Hoover* (XIX/4B). They had moved by June 1896: Kelles-Krauz in Paris to Ludwik Gumplowicz in Graz, 22 June 1896, *Listy* I, p. 576.

3. Kelles-Krauz in Paris to CZZSP in London, 28 September 1894, *Listy* I, p. 314.

4. *Michał Luśnia, "*Klasowość naszego programu," Paris 1894. Cited after *Pisma* II, p. 5.

5. [Witold Jodko-Narkiewicz] "Etapy," *Przedświt* 1894 (8–10).

6. Kancewicz, *PPS*, pp. 301–305; Kulczycki, *Historya*, pp. 292–309.

7. On Jędrzejowski and Jodko, see Feliks Tych, "Jędrzejowski Bolesław Antoni," in Tych, *Słownik* II, pp. 718–21; Jan Kancewicz, "Jodko-Narkiewicz Witold Tomasz," ibid., pp. 725–27.

8. Krzywicki, *Wspomnienia*, p. 292.

9. Kancewicz, *PPS*, p. 56.

10. Kancewicz, *PPS*, p. 57.

11. Kelles-Krauz in Paris to CZZSP in London, 7 September 1894, *Listy* I, p. 312.

12. Jerzy Marciniak, "Udział Kazimierza Kelles-Krauza w przygotowaniach socjalistów polskich do międzynarodowego kongresu socjalistycznego w Londynie," *Kwartalnik Historyczny* 1982 (2–3): 301.

13. Kancewicz, *PPS*, p. 53; Feldman, *Dzieje polskiej myśli*, p. 103.

14. Wojciechowski in London to Kelles-Krauz in Paris, 12 September 1894, *Archiwum Lewicy*, 305/II/20, book III, card 24.

15. *Materiały* I, p. 87.

16. Kelles-Krauz in Paris to CZZSP in London, 14 September 1899, *Listy* II, p. 279.

17. Wojciechowski in London to Kelles-Krauz in Paris, 14 October 1894, *Archiwum Lewicy*, 305/II/20, book III, card 192.

18. Kelles-Krauz in Paris to CZZSP in London, 17 October 1894, *Listy* I, p. 317.

19. Kelles-Krauz in Paris to CZZSP in London, 29 November 1894, *Listy* I, p. 326.

20. Limanowski, *Pamiętniki*, p. 425.

21. Sokolnicki, *Czternaście lat*, p. 17.

22. Kelles-Krauz in Paris to CZZSP in London, 18 December 1894, *Listy* I, p. 330.

23. Kelles-Krauz in Paris to CZZSP in London, 19 December 1894, *Listy* I, p. 333.

24. Kelles-Krauz, "Klasowość," pp. 5–6.

25. Kelles-Krauz, "Klasowość," pp. 7–8.

26. Kelles-Krauz, "Klasowość," pp. 9–10.

27. He may also have had before him Luxemburg's response to the Paris program, "Pod bat opinii publicznej," published in the summer of 1894, though he never refers to it.

28. Kelles-Krauz, "Klasowość," p. 13. See "Protokoły 1-ego Zjazdu Socjal- demokracji Królestwa Polskiego, odbytego w Warszawie 10-ego i 11-ego marca 1894 r.," *Sprawa Robotnicza* 1894 (4).

29. Wandycz, *Lands*, p. 176.

30. Kelles-Krauz, "Klasowość," p. 12. Kelles-Krauz relied upon Lassalle's argument that constitutions reflect societies, which he borrowed from Stanisław Grabski. Perl, *Dzieje ruchu*, pp. 376–77.

31. Kelles-Krauz, "Klasowość," p. 14.

32. Kelles-Krauz, "Klasowość," p. 15.

33. According to Robert Stuart (*Marxism at Work* [Cambridge, 1992], p. 26n22), this remark of Marx's ("If that's Marxism, I'm not a Marxist"), quoted by Engels in a letter to Bernstein in 1882, found its way into the French press only in 1900. Kelles-Krauz may have been trying to break a press taboo. In any event, calling on Marx's authority to cast aspersions on Guesde's party was a rather shocking attack. See also Steenson, *After Marx*, pp. 310–11.

34. Kelles-Krauz, "Klasowość," p. 15.

35. Kelles-Krauz, "Klasowość," pp. 15–16.

36. Kelles-Krauz, "Klasowość," pp. 16–17.

37. Julius Braunthal, *History of the International* (London, 1966), p. 287.

38. George Lichtheim, *A Short History of Socialism* (London, 1970), pp. 215–16.

39. James Joll, *The Second International* (London, 1955), pp. 70–73; S. F. Kissin, *War and the Marxists* (London, 1988), pp. 110–11. Kelles-Krauz was not present at the congress, so may not have realized that Nieuwenhuis had proposed the general strike in the context of the debate over how best to prevent a European war. Though Kelles-Krauz, unlike Piłsudski, was not optimistic that war could bring revolution in Poland, he was no pacifist, and did not rule out the possibility.

40. Kelles-Krauz, "Klasowość," pp. 15–17

41. Kelles-Krauz, "Klasowość," p. 18.

42. Kelles-Krauz, "Klasowość," pp. 27–28.

43. Kelles-Krauz, "Klasowość," p. 19. *Robotnik* had begun to do so, but Kelles- Krauz had not yet seen these issues. Kulczycki, *Historya*, p. 240.

44. Kelles-Krauz, "Klasowość," pp. 20–22.

45. Andrzej Ajnenkiel, "Stulecie urodzin Kelles-Krauza," *Nauka Polska* 1973 (1): 141.

46. Luxemberg in Paris to Jogiches in Zurich, 21 March 1895; Róża Luksemburg, *Listy do Leona Jogichesa-Tyszki*, ed. Feliks Tych, vol. 1 (Warsaw, 1968), p. 75. Hereafter *Jogiches* I and *Jogiches* II.

47. Aleksander Kochański, *Listy* I, p. 321n2.

48. "Kazimierz Kelles-Krauz," *Przedświt* 1905 (6–8): 230.

49. Wojciechowski, *Wspomnienia*, pp. 88–89.

50. Garlicki, *Piłsudski*, p. 51.

51. Nissen, *War*, p. 109.

52. For this resolution, see *Archiwum Lewicy*, 305/II/3, section 3, cards 4–5. For a discussion of the congress, see Kancewicz, *PPS*, p. 54.

53. Luxemberg in Paris to Jogiches in Zurich, 21 March 1895, *Jogiches* I, p. 75.

54. Malankiewicz reported her presence on 17 November 1894: Malankiewicz to Paris Okhrana, *Hoover* (XIX/4B).

55. Nettl, *Luxemburg*, p. 79.

56. Nettl, *Luxemburg*, p. 70.

57. Luxemburg in Paris to Jogiches in Zurich, 21 March 1895, *Jogiches* I, p. 75.

58. Luxemburg in Paris to Jogiches in Zurich, 28 March 1895, *Jogiches* I, p. 95.

59. [Rosa Luxemburg] Maciej Rożga, "Niepodległa Polska a sprawa robotnicza," Paris 1895. For discussions of Luxemburg's anti-independence stance: Andrzej Walicki, "Rosa Luxemburg and the National Question," *Slavic and East European Review* 41(4) 1983; Feliks Tych, "Róża Luksemburg," in Barbara Skarga, ed., *Polska myśl filozoficzna i społeczna*, vol. 3 (Warsaw, 1977); Leszek Kołakowski, *Main Currents of Marxism*, vol. 2 (Oxford, 1978), pp. 90–94.

60. Luxemburg, "Niepodległa Polska," pp. 9–11.

61. Luxemburg, "Niepodległa Polska," pp. 13–17.

62. Luxemburg, "Niepodległa Polska," pp. 26–27.

63. Luxemburg, "Niepodległa Polska," p. 44.

64. In fact, the line between Polish socialist leaders who believed in cooperation with Russia did not run between the two parties, but between the center and left of the PPS. As we have seen in the debate within the PPS over a Russian constitution, the majority of PPS leaders in 1894 and 1895 opposed cooperation with Russian organizations, but a majority of the rank and file seemed to be in favor.

65. See [Józef Piłsudski] "U nas i gdzie indziej," *Robotnik* 27 October 1894 (4): 1–3. Here Piłsudski identified socialism with the task of overthrowing the tsar. In [Józef Piłsudski] "Na posterunku," *Robotnik* June 1895 (7): 2–5, he argued that Poland is part of the west culturally, and that eastern political culture is qualitatively inferior. Socialism falls within this realm of culture.

66. For anecdotes illustrating Piłsudski's attitude, see Leon Wasilewski, *Józef Piłsudski, jakim go znałem* (Cracow, 1981), pp. 52–56.

67. According to Marek Waldenberg, this aspect of tactics was her "major concern." "Z problematyki narodu w polskiej myśli socjalistycznej okresu zaborów," in Janusz Goćkowski and Andrzej Walicki, eds., *Idee i koncepcje narodu w polskiej myśli politycznej czasów porozbiorowych* (Warsaw, 1977), p. 252.

68. Luxemburg, "Niepodległa Polska," p. 38.

69. Luxemburg, "Niepodległa Polska," pp. 56–57.

70. Further evidence for this concern is to be found in *Michał Luśnia,* "W kweslii 'równoległości,'" *Przedświt* 1895 (7): 19–22.

71. Kulczycki, *Historya*, p. 326.

72. Around the beginning of 1894 the Jewish socialist John Mill agreed to deliver a letter from Luxemburg to an SDKP member in Warsaw. The addressee, Kazimierz Ratyński, turned out to be the last member of the party in the entire city not yet under arrest or imprisoned. Shortly thereafter, Ratyński was arrested, and in prison joined the PPS. Henryk Piasecki, *Żydowska Organizacja PPS* (Wroclaw, 1978). p. 23.

73. Kelles-Krauz in Paris to CZZSP in London, 3 August 1895, *Listy* I, p. 393.

74. Kelles-Krauz in Paris to CZZSP in London, 19 July 1895, *Listy* I, p. 401.

75. Kelles-Krauz in Paris to CZZSP in London, 21 January 1896, *Listy* I, p. 491.

76. Kelles-Krauz in Paris to CZZSP in London, 17 November 1895, *Listy* I, p. 462. The person in question was Marcin Kasprzak.
77. Kelles-Krauz in Paris to CZZSP in London, 8 September 1895, *Listy* I, p. 427.
78. Kelles-Krauz in Paris to CZZSP in London, 6 April 1895, *Listy* I, p. 339.
79. Kelles-Krauz in Paris to CZZSP in London, 27 June 1895, *Listy* I, p. 386.
80. At one point, they asked London to send out copies of the pamphlet to all Polish socialist publications, including Luxemburg's *Sprawa Robotnicza*. For protocols of the January meetings of the Paris Section, *Archiwum Lewicy*, 305/II/37, subfile 4, card 19. See also Kelles-Krauz in Paris to CZZSP in London, 3 August 1895, *Listy* I, pp. 333–34.
81. Kelles-Krauz in Paris to CZZSP in London, 21 March 1895, *Listy* I, p. 337.
82. Romuald Mielczarski in Antwerp to CZZSP in London, 12 April 1895, *Archiwum Lewicy*, 305/VII/28, subfile 2, position 8, card 3.
83. Jędrzejowski in London to Kelles-Krauz in Paris, August 1895, *Archiwum Lewicy*, 305/II/21, book V, card 489.
84. He spoke out for decentralization as late as October 1895, but by then he seems to be saying that the Centralizacja should make the sections feel that they contribute to the direction of party activity, rather than arguing that such a contribution would be of value. Kelles-Krauz in Paris to CZZSP in London, 28 October 1895, *Listy* I, p. 451.
85. Kelles-Krauz in Paris to CZZSP in London, 17 November 1895, *Listy* I, pp. 460–461; Kelles-Krauz in Paris to CZZSP in London, 26 November 1895, *Listy* I, p. 468; Kelles-Krauz in Paris to CZZSP in London, 20 July 1895, *Listy* I, pp. 404–405.
86. This summary from Kancewicz, *PPS*, pp. 152–53, 183, 306–307; Kulczycki, *Historya*, pp. 327–28; Wojciechowski, *Wspomnienia*, pp. 98–99.
87. Kancewicz, *PPS*, pp. 152–53. Kulczycki gave the police Piłsudski's name.
88. In Kancewicz's judgement, power was in the hands of Piłsudski, Wojciechowski, and London from fall 1895. *PPS*, p. 184.
89. Kancewicz, *PPS*, p. 98; Wojciechowski, *Polska Partya*, p. 13. The PPS was remarkably successful in hiding their printing presses. The Okhrana was completely in the dark, as it was asking its Paris agent for help. Malankiewicz made the sale but incorrect guess that *Robotnik* was printed inside "a rich person's house in Warsaw." Malankiewicz to Paris Okhrana, 25 October 1895, *Hoover* (XIX/4B).
90. Garlicki, *Piłsudski*, p. 59.
91. "Na Emigracyi. W Paryżu," *Przedświt* 1895 (5): 13. This actually appeared somewhat later, as it covered events that took place in May. *Przedświt*, though theoretically a monthly, appeared about nine times a year.
92. *Michał Luśnia*, "Święto Majowe Zagranicą. Francja," *Przedświt* 1895 (5): 17–21. Kelles-Krauz used the pseudonym "Michał Luśnia," and later "Elehard Esse" in his party writings and correspondence. Kelles-Krauz's friend Zygmunt Rostkowski, now suffering from a neural disorder, had used the pseudonym

"Luśnia" in their Aryele days. "Elehard" was one of Kelles-Krauz's middle names. (Another of his middle names was "Radosław," hence his pseudonym in the legal press, "K. Radosławski.") Ironically, the Okhrana had already known him by his true name, though it did not seem to know that Luśnia or Esse was Kelles-Krauz.

93. Michał Luśnia, "Ze świata. Francja," *Przedświt* 1895 (10-11): 19–20.

94. Michał Luśnia, "Ze świata. Francja," *Przedświt* 1896 (4): 15–19.

95. Michał Luśnia, "Ze świata. Francja," *Przedświt* 1895 (6): 10–13.

96. Michał Luśnia, "Ze świata. Francja," *Przedświt* 1895 (8): 15–16.

97. Michał Luśnia, "Ze świata. Francja," *Przedświt* 1895 (12): 19–26.

98. Kelles-Krauz, "Równoległość."

99. *Bulletin Officiel du Parti Socialiste Polonais* June 1895 (1), cover. Hereafter "*Bulletin.*" For a list of the French publications to which the *Bulletin* was sent: Kelles-Krauz in Paris to CZZSP in London, 27 April 1895, *Listy* I, pp. 348–49.

100. Motz in Paris to CZZSP in London, spring 1895, *Archiwum Lewicy*, 305/VII/ 29, subfile 6, card 14.

101. Piłsudski to Kelles-Krauz, *Niepodległość* 15: 451, cited after Jerzy Myślinski, *Polska prasa socjalistyczna w okresie zaborów* (Warsaw, 1982), p. 77.

102. Kelles-Krauz in Paris to CZZSP in London, 8 October 1895, *Listy* I, p. 437.

103. Kelles-Krauz in Paris to CZZSP in London, 22 June 1895, *Listy* I, p. 386.

104. Kelles-Krauz in Paris to CZZSP in London, 22 May 1895, *Listy* I, p. 364.

105. Kelles-Krauz in Paris to CZZSP in London, 27 April 1895, *Listy* I, p. 347.

106. Kelles-Krauz in Paris to CZZSP in London, 6 April 1895, *Listy* I, p. 338.

107. Kelles-Krauz in Paris to CZZSP in London, 12 December 1894, *Listy* I, p. 328; Kancewicz, *PPS*, p. 66.

108. [Kazimierz Kelles-Krauz] "Lettre ouverte du Parti Socialiste Polonais au Ve Congrès Pénitentiaire Internationale," *Bulletin* July 1895 (2): 1–7.

109. Leon Wasilewski, *Zarys dziejów Polskiej Partii Socjalistycznej w związku z historią socjalizmu polskiego w trzech zaborach i na emigracji* (Warsaw, n.d.), p. 53

110. [Kazimierz Kelles-Krauz] "La tsarisme devant le Congrès Pénitentiaire," *Bulletin* September 1895 (3): 1. The resolution apparently took its language from the July article. Kelles-Krauz in Paris to CZZSP in London, 19 July 1895, *Listy* I, 402.

111. Kelles-Krauz in Paris to CZZSP in London, 18 December 1894, *Listy* I, p. 330.

112. Malankiewicz to Paris Okhrana, 30 April 1896, *Hoover* (XIX/4B). "Towarzystwo Robotników Polskich."

113. Kelles-Krauz in Paris to CZZSP in London, 4 January 1896, *Listy* I, p. 481; Kelles-Krauz in Paris to CZZSP in London, 19 July 1895, *Listy* I, p. 402; Kelles-Krauz in Paris to CZZSP in London, 3 July 1895, *Listy* I, p. 393.

114. Four years later, Kelles-Krauz recalled the process of establishing his status as leader of the section: "God as my witness, I never tried to push ahead of [Motz],

only took up each project that presented itself, while he always didn't have the time; and so it happened that the outstanding role in Paris was left to me. He doesn't have anything against me, nor I him, but as a result of this, our relations, though very friendly, are basically not intimate." Kelles-Krauz in Paris to CZZSP in London, 14 September 1899, *Listy* II, p. 279

115. *Bulletin*, 3, September 1895, p. 4.

116. Malankiewicz to Paris Okhrana, 27 April 1895, *Hoover* (XIX/4B).

117. Malankiewicz to Paris Okhrana, 14 April 1896, *Hoover* (XIX/4B).

118. Malankiewicz to Paris Okhrana, 10 May 1896, *Hoover* (XIX/4B).

119. "Szapira" to Russian Embassy in Paris, 27 July 1894, *Hoover* (XIX/4B).

120. Malankiewicz to Paris Okhrana, 28 July 1894, *Hoover* (XIX/4B).

121. Malankiewicz to Paris Okhrana, 31 July 1894, *Hoover* (XIX/4B).

122. Kelles-Krauz in Paris to CZZSP in London, 4 August 1897, *Listy* I, p. 709.

123. Kelles-Krauz in Paris to CZZSP in London, 26 October 1895, *Listy* I, p. 448.

124. Kelles-Krauz in Paris to CZZSP in London, 26 October 1895, *Listy* I, pp. 448–49.

125. Jędrzejowski in London to Kelles-Krauz in Paris, 9 November 1895, *Archiwum Lewicy*, 305/II/21, book VI, cards 356–57.

126. Kelles-Krauz's attendance at this congress provides a good example of the kind of intelligence Malankiewicz could, and could not, provide to the Okhrana. He knew that Kelles-Krauz was leaving for Geneva, but did not know why. Malankiewicz to Paris Okhrana, 27 December 1895, *Hoover* (XIX/4B).

127. Kelles-Krauz in Paris to CZZSP in London, 21 January 1896, *Listy* I, p. 491; "Kazimierz Kelles-Krauz," *Przedświt* 6–8 (1905): 235.

128. Kancewicz, *PPS*, p. 54.

129. For example, Kelles-Krauz in Paris to CZZSP in London, 25 October 1895, *Listy* I, p. 452.

130. Braunthal, *International*, p. 250.

131. This account of the Zurich Congress from Nettl, *Luxemburg*, p. 73; Żychowski, *Polska myśl*, pp. 197–98; Tych, "Polskie partie," pp. 701–702; Wojciechowski, *Wspomnienia*, pp. 70–71; Kulczycki, *Historya*, pp. 258–60.

132. Kelles-Krauz in Paris to CZZSP in London, 17 November 1895, *Listy* I, pp. 462–63.

133. Jędrzejowski in London to Kelles-Krauz in Paris, 9 November 1895, *Archiwum Lewicy*, 305/II/21, book VI, cards 356–57.

134. For Kelles-Krauz's proposal and the final resolution: *Archiwum Lewicy*, 305/ II/ 72, cards 34a, 35.

135. Jędrzejowski in London to Kelles-Krauz in Paris, 9 November 1895, *Archiwum Lewicy*, 305/II/21, book VI, cards 356–57.

136. Lorentowicz, *Spojrzenie*, pp. 232–33.

137. Kancewicz, *PPS*, p. 129.

138. Feliks Tych, "The Polish Question at the International Socialist Congress in London in 1896," *Acta Poloniae Historica* 46 (1982): 100.

139. Jędrzejowski in London to Kelles-Krauz in Paris, 9 November 1895, *Archiwum Lewicy*, 305/II/21, book VI, cards 356–57.

140. Feliks Tych, *Socjalistyczna irredenta* (Cracow, 1982), p. 150.

141. Tych, *Irredenta*, p. 149. The original version of the resolution submitted by Kelles-Krauz laid even more stress on Russia: *Archiwum Lewicy*, 305/VII/50, card 134.

142. Liebknecht added the words "and despots" after the word "capitalists," and the words "and autonomy" after the word "independence." Kelles-Krauz in Paris to CZZSP in London, 17 January 1896, *Listy* I, p. 486; Tych, *Irredenta*, p. 151.

143. Walentyna Najdus, "Działacze zachodnioeuropejskich partii socjalistycznych o narodzie i ojczyźnie," *Kwartalnik Historyczny* 75(4) 1978: 993.

144. For collections of their writings on the Polish question: Karl Marx, *Przyczynki do historii kwestii polskiej* (Warsaw, 1971), and Helena Michnik, ed., *Marks I Engels o Polsce* (Warsaw, 1960).

145. Marx, *Przyczynki*, p. 77; Adam Ciołkosz, "Karl Marx and the Polish Insurrection of 1863," *The Polish Review* 10(4) 1965: 21.

146. Tych, "Polskie partie," p. 98.

147. Walicki, *Polska, Rosja, marksizm*, pp. 44–45.

148. Walicki, *Polska, Rosja, marksizm*, p. 48.

149. Walicki, *Polska, Rosja, marksizm*, p. 35.

150. Walicki, *Polska, Rosja, marksizm*, p. 30.

151. Ciołkosz, "Karl Marx"; Tych, "Polskie partie," p. 97.

152. Michalski, *Socjalizm*, pp. 46–47.

153. Marciniak, "Udział," p. 69.

154. J. L. Talmon, *The Myth of Nation and the Vision of Revolution* (London, 1980), p. 125. See also Tych "Luksemburg," p. 488, and Rosa Luxemburg, "Wstęp" to Rosa Luxemburg, ed., *Kwestia polska a ruch socjalistyczny* (Cracow, 1905), p. iv.

155. The Okhrana knew of the gathering two weeks ahead of time. Malankiewicz correctly predicted that strife between the SDKP and the PPS would bring about the failure of the enterprise. Malankiewicz to Paris Okhrana, 14 January 1896, *Hoover* (XIX/4B).

156. Kelles-Krauz in Paris to CZZSP in London, 8 September 1895, *Listy* I, p. 427.

157. Kelles-Krauz in Paris to CZZSP in London, 2 February 1896, *Listy* I, p. 495.

158. Kelles-Krauz in Paris to CZZSP in London, 2 February 1896, *Listy* I, p. 495.

159. Theodore Zeldin, *France*, vol. 1 (Oxford, 1973), p. 756.

160. Kelles-Krauz in Paris to CZZSP in London, 2 February 1896, *Listy* I, p. 495.

161. Stuart, *Marxism at Work*, pp. 24–25; Zeldin, *France*, p. 745.

162. Kelles-Krauz in Paris to CZZSP in London, 2 February 1896, *Listy* I, pp. 496–497. See also Limanowski, *Pamiętniki*, p. 495.

163. Kelles-Krauz in Paris to CZZSP in London, 2 February 1896, *Listy* I, p. 497.

164. Kelles-Krauz in Paris to CZZSP in London, 2 February 1896, *Listy* I, p. 496.

165. [Kazimierz Kelles-Krauz] "Za granicą. Francja," *Przedświt* 1896 (1-3): 26–28.

166. Tych, "Polish Question," p. 104.

167. Aleksander Kochański, *Listy* I, p. 483n8; Kelles-Krauz in Paris to CZZSP in London, 2 February 1896, *Listy* I, p. 484.

168. Kelles-Krauz in Paris to CZZSP in London, 24 February 1896, *Listy* I, p. 515.

169. Kelles-Krauz in Paris to CZZSP in London, 13 July 1895, *Listy* I, p. 390.

170. Kelles-Krauz in Paris to CZZSP in London, 17 January 1896, *Listy* I, p. 485.

171. Kelles-Krauz in Paris to CZZSP in London, 27 July 1897, *Listy* I, p. 706.

172. Louis Dubreuilh, "Martyrs de Pologne," *Petite République* 29 January 1896: 1. Dubreuilh knew Kelles-Krauz well, and doubtless drew from [Kazimierz Kelles- Krauz] "Le Dixième Anniversaire du Martyre des Quatre Socialistes Polonais," *Bulletin* January 1896(6).

173. Wojnarowska had been a member of Kelles-Krauz's social democrats in 1892 and 1893, but had joined the SDKP immediately upon its founding in summer 1893. She was on good terms with French socialist leaders such as Vaillant, Lafargue, and Guesde, as well as with the Russians Plekhanov and Lavrov.

174. Kelles-Krauz in Paris to CZZSP in London, 15 March 1896, *Listy* I, p. 524.

175. Kelles-Krauz in Paris to CZZSP in London, 15 March 1896, *Listy* I, pp. 523–26.

176. Jędrzejowski in London to Kelles-Krauz in Paris, 20 March 1896, *Archiwum Lewicy*, 305/II/21, book VII, card 385.

177. Golde in Paris to Jędrzejowski in London, March 1896, *Archiwum Lewicy*, 305/II/21, book VII, card 385.

178. Polska Partia Socjalistyczna, "Pamiątka Majowa" (London, 1896), pp. 36–56.

179. R. Luksemburg, "Neue Strömungen in der polnischen sozialistischen Bewegung in Deutschland und Österreich," *Die Neue Zeit* 6 May 1896 (33): 216n.

180. Kelles-Krauz in Paris to CZZSP in London, 15 February 1896, *Listy* I, p. 512.

181. R. Luksemburg, "Neue Strömungen in der polnischen sozialistischen Bewegung in Deutschland und Österreich," *Die Neue Zeit* 29 April-6 May 1896 (32-33): 176–81, 206–216.

182. A misleading argument, as the Polish socialists in Austria, while part of Austrian social democracy, had often made clear that they considered theirs to be a special case; and Polish socialists in Germany were weak and beholden to the SDP. The position of Polish socialism in Germany and Austria will be discussed in chapter 4.

183. Luxemburg, *Kwestia*, pp. 1–17.

184. Najdus, "Działacze," p. 989.

185. Kołakowski, *Main Currents* II, pp. 184–85.

186. Jędrzejowski in London to Labriola in Rome, 28 April 1896, in Antonio Labriola, *Korespondencja* (Warsaw, 1986), pp. 491–94.

187. Labriola in Rome to Jędrzejowski in London, 3 May 1896, *Korespondencja*, pp. 495–97.

188. Labriola in Rome to Jędrzejowski in London, 9 May 1896, *Korespondencja*, pp. 509–510.

189. Labriola in Rome to Jędrzejowski in London, 11 May 1896, *Korespondencja*, pp. 511–12.

190. Labriola in Rome to Jędrzejowski in London, 31 May 1896, *Korespondencja*, pp. 516–17.

191. Antonio Labriola, "L'independenza della Polonia al Congresso di Londra," *Critica Sociale* 16 May 1896 (10): 148–49, cited after Luxemburg, *Kwestia*, pp. 79–80.

192. Luxemburg, *Kwestia*, pp. 80–83.

193. Rosa Luxemburg, "La questione polacca al congresso interaazionale di Londra," *Critica Sociale* 16 July 1896 (14), reprinted in Luxemburg, *Kwestia*, pp. 83–89.

194. Labriola in Rome to Jędrzejowski in London, 19 May 1896, *Korespondencja*, p. 514.

195. Jędrzejowski in London to Kelles-Krauz in Paris, 22 May 1896, *Archiwum Lewicy*, 305/11/22, book VIII, cards 155–56.

196. Kelles-Krauz in Paris to CZZSP in London, 26 May 1896, *Listy* I, pp. 558–59.

197. Aleksander Kochański, *Listy* I, p. 560n3.

198. Labriola in Rome to Jędrzejowski in London, 3 May 1896, *Korespondencja*, pp. 495–97.

199. Labriola in Rome to Jędrzejowski in London, 3 May 1896, *Korespondencja*, pp. 495–97.

200. George Lichtheim, *Marxism in Modern France* (London, 1966), p. 16.

201. Jędrzejowski in London to Labriola in France, 5 May 1896, *Korespondencja*, pp. 497–502; Kelles-Krauz in Paris to CZZSP in London, 15 May 1896, *Listy* I, p. 550.

202. Labriola in Rome to Jędrzejowski in London, 11 May 1896, *Korespondencja*, pp. 511–12.

203. Labriola in Rome to Jędrzejowski in London, 22 May 1896, *Korespondencja*, p. 514.

204. Labriola in Rome to Jędrzejowski in London, 31 May 1896, *Korespondencja*, 516–17.

205. Labriola in Rome to Jędrzejowski in London, 9 May 1896, *Korespondencja*, 509–510.

206. For Ignacy Daszyński's recollection of this friendship and loyalty, his *Pamiętniki*, vol. 1 (Warsaw, 1957), p. 215.

207. Najdus, "Działacze," pp. 989–90.

208. Jędrzejowski in London to Labriola in France, 2 June 1896, *Korespondencja*, pp. 519–23.

209. [Viktor Adler and Ignacy Daszyński] E. Haecker, "Der Sozialismus in Polen," *Die Neue Zeit* 3 June 1896 (37): 324–31, cited after Luxemburg, *Kwestia*, pp. 17–26.

210. Labriola in Rome to Jędrzejowski in London, 22 May 1896, *Korespondencja*, p. 515.

211. Viktor Adler, *Briefwechsel mit August Bebel und Karl Kautsky* (Vienna, 1954), p. 207, cited after Tych, "Polish Question," p. 112, and Nettl, *Luxemburg*, p. 97.

212. Jędrzejowski in London to Kelles-Krauz in Paris, 16 June 1896, *Archiwum Lewicy*, 305/11/22, book VIII, card 211.
213. Kelles-Krauz in Paris to CZZSP in London, 29 June 1896, *Listy* I, p. 580.
214. Luxemburg in Paris to Jogiches in Zurich, July 1896, *Jogiches* I, p. 115.
215. Jędrzejowski in London to Kelles-Krauz in Paris, 16 June 1896, *Archiwum Lewicy*, 305/11/22, book VIII, card 211.
216. Luxemburg in Paris to Jogiches in Zurich, July 1896, *Jogiches* I, p. 117.
217. Luxemburg in Paris to Jogiches in Zurich, 26 July 1896, *Jogiches* I, p. 129.
218. Kelles-Krauz in Paris to CZZSP in London, 19 July 1896, *Listy* I, p. 595.
219. Piłsudski in London to CKR PPS in Poland, 15 July 1896, *Niepodległość* 16 (1937): 500, cited after Tych, "Polish Question."
220. Kelles-Krauz in Paris to CZZSP in London, 15 March 1896, *Listy* I, p. 523.
221. Kelles-Krauz in Paris to CZZSP in London, 15 May L896, *Listy* I, p. 550.
222. Kazimierz Kelles-Krauz, "Czy jesteśmy patriotami w właściwym znaczeniu tego słowa?," *Pisma* I, pp. 31–35. Translation of unpublished French text.
223. Kelles-Krauz, "Jesteśmy patriotami?" p. 35.
224. Jędrzejowski in London to Kelles-Krauz in Paris, 6 July 1896, *Archiwum Lewicy*, 305/11/22, book VIII, cards 310–11.
225. [Kazimierz Kelles-Krauz] "Les motifs de notre programme," *Bulletin* July 1896 (9): 1.
226. Kelles-Krauz, "Les motifs," p. 2.
227. Rosa Luxemburg, "Der Sozialpatriotismus in Polen," *Die Neue Zeit* 41 (1 July 1896): 459–70, cited after Luxemburg, *Kwestia*, pp. 26–36.
228. Steenson, *Kautsky*, p. 96.
229. [Witold Jodko-Narkiewicz] "Zur Taktik der polnischen Sozialdemokratie," *Vorwärts*, 15-17 July 1896: 163–65, cited after Luxemburg, *Kwestia*, pp. 62–69.
230. Georgii Plekhanov, "Zur Taktik der polnischen Sozialdemokratie," *Vorwärts* 23 July 1896; cited after Luxemburg, *Kwestia*, pp. 70–71.
231. As Walentyna Najdus notes, Luxemburg's article had two parts, and the first did not appear because the editors of *Vorwärts* noticed that its arguments were almost identical to Plekhanov's. *SDKPiL a SDPRR* (Wrocław, 1973), p. 43.
232. Kelles-Krauz in Paris to CZZSP in London, 29 June 1896, *Listy* I, p. 581.
233. For an account of the two cultures of the SPD worker, loyal patriotic and socialist, see Guenther Roth, *The Social Democrats of Imperial Germany* (Totowa, 1963), pp. 212–48.
234. Ignaz Auer in Berlin to Karl Kautsky, 23 July 1896, quoted by Tych, "Polish Question," p. 135. Michalski (*Socjalizm*, p. 92) agrees with Tych that the "crushing majority" of SPD members opposed Polish independence at this time. This issue will be encountered again in chapter 4.
235. Lorentowicz, *Spojrzenie*, p. 230.
236. William Harvey Maehl, *August Bebel, Shadow Emperor of the German Workers* (Philadelphia, 1980), pp. 205–206, 342.

237. Maehl, *Bebel,* p. 343.

238. August Bebel to Viktor Adler, 29 September 1898, in Viktor Adler, *Briefwechselmit August Bebel und Karl Kautsky* (Vienna, 1954), p. 252, cited after Nettl, *Luxemburg,* pp. 102–103.

239. Czubiński, *Międzynarodowy,* p. 31.

240. Tych, "Polish Question," p. 104.

241. Luxemburg in Paris to Jogiches in Zurich, 13 July 1896, *Jogiches* I, p. 124.

242. He did polemicize with Luxemburg in *Vorwärts,* but only on 11 November 1896. Nettl, *Luxemburg,* p. 98.

243. Some Polish socialists noticed quite early that Adler was more supportive of their cause than were German leaders, see Stanisław Grabski to Władysław Grabski, 12 June 1893, *Hoover XIX/4.*

244. Lichtheim, *Marxism,* pp. 6–9.

245. Zeldin, *France,* p. 745.

246. Lorentowicz, *Spojrzenie,* p. 228.

247. Bebel and Adler: Joll, *Second International,* p. 118; Plekhanov: Nettl, *Luxemburg,* p. 69.

248. Karl Kautsky, "Finis Poloniae?" *Die Neue Zeit* 1896 (42–43): 484–91, cited after Luxemburg, *Kwestia,* pp. 37–57. For discussion, Marek Waldenberg, *Kwestie narodowe w Europie Środkowo-Wschodniej* (Warsaw, 1992), pp. 214–15; Marciniak, "Udział," pp. 71–73.

249. Even its moderate terms brought Kautsky trouble with members of the Vorstand, notably Ignaz Auer. Hans-Ulrich Wehler, *Sozialdemokratie und Nationalstaat* (Göttingen, 1971), pp. 136–37.

250. *Histoire de la IIe Internationale,* vol. 10 (Geneva, 1980), p. 201.

251. Kelles-Krauz in Paris to CZZSP in London, 28 October 1895, *Listy* I, p. 451; Kelles-Krauz in Paris to CZZSP in London, 11 November 1895, *Listy* I, p. 458; Kelles-Krauz in Paris to CZZSP in London, 21 June 1896, *Listy* I, p. 573.

252. Kelles-Krauz in Paris to CZZSP in London, 26 September 1895, *Listy* I, p. 620.

253. Kelles-Krauz in Paris to CZZSP in London, 24 September 1895, *Listy* I, p. 618.

254. Luxemburg in Paris to Jogiches in Zurich, 17 July 1896, *Jogiches* I, p. 128.

255. *IIe Internationale* 10, p. 211.

256. Żychowski, *Polska myśl,* p. 206.

257. Lansbury was later to be one of the founders of the British Labour Party.

258. Jędrzejowski in London to Labriola in Rome, 8 July 1896, *Korespondencja,* pp. 534–35.

259. *IIe Internationale* 10, p. 114.

260. "Provisional Standing Orders," *IIe Internationale* 10, p. 108.

261. Jędrzejowski in London to Labriola in Rome, 13 August 1896, *Korespondencja,* p. 542; Ignacy Daszyński, "Wspomnienia," *Księga Pamiątkowa PPS* (Warsaw, 1923), pp. 152–53.

262. *IIe Internationale* 10, pp. 222–23.

263. Jędrzejowski in London to Labriola in Rome, 13 August 1896, *Korespondencja*, p. 542.

264. *IIe Internationale* 10, p. 223.

265. Jędrzejowski in London to Labriola in Rome, 13 August 1896, *Korespondencja*, p. 542.

266. *IIe Internationale* 10, p. 221.

267. This is Najdus's interpretation ("Działacze," p. 988), as well as Jędrzejowski's.

268. Jędrzejowski in London to Labriola in Rome, 13 August 1896, *Korespondencja*, pp. 539–541.

269. Jędrzejowski in London to Kelles-Krauz in Paris, 19 September 1896, *Archiwum Lewicy*, 305/11/22, book IX, cards 97–98.

270. Ronaldo Munck claims that Kautsky was the author of the compromise resolution (*The Difficult Dialogue: Marxism and Nationalism* (London, 1986), p. 30), and cites Georges Haupt. Haupt wrote only that the compromise resolution was "apparently" ("vraisemblablement") authored by Kautsky, and gave no evidence in support of his (mistaken) supposition. "Les marxistes face à la question national. L'histoire du problème," in Georges Haupt, et al, *Les Marxistes et la Question Nationale* (Paris, 1974), p. 40.

271. *IIe Internationale* 10, p. 226; Piłsudski in London to CKR PPS in Poland, 4 August 1896, *Niepodległość* 17: 60, cited after Tych, "Polish Question."

272. [Kazimierz Kelles-Krauz] "Pologne, Arménie, et Mlle Rose Luxemburg," *Bulletin* January 1897 (12): 21–22.

273. Jędrzejowski in London to Labriola in Rome, 5 May 1896, *Korespondecja*, pp. 497–502.

274. For his article in the 25 July 1896 edition of *Sachsische Arbeiter-Zeitung*, which he then edited, see Luxemburg, *Kwestia*, pp. 57–61. Stephen Bronner's description of Helphand as "a major force on the international left before he turned to German chauvinism" reveals the difficulties of some observers in perceiving that internationalist rhetoric could serve as a veil for nationalism. *A Revolutionary for our Times: Rosa Luxemburg* (London, 1981), p. 68.

275. Kancewicz, *PPS*, p. 204.

276. Luxemburg in Paris to Jogiches in Zurich, 12 July 1896, *Jogiches* I, p. 115.

277. *IIe Internationale* 10, p. 222.

278. Jędrzejowski in London to Kelles-Krauz in Paris, 1 December 1896, *Archiwum Lewicy*, 305/11, book IX, card 421.

279. Jędrzejowski in London to Kelles-Krauz in Paris, 19September 1896, *Archiwum Lewicy*, 305/11/22, book IX, cards 97–98. See Górski, *Idea*, p. 41.

CHAPTER 3

1. Kelles-Krauz in Paris to CZZSP in London, 13 November 1898, *Listy* II, p. 99; Kelles-Krauz in Vienna to Kelles-Krauzowa in Radom, 27 May 1901, *Listy* II, p. 499.

2. Kelles-Krauz in Paris to Kelles-Krauzowa in Radom, 6 July 1899, *Listy* II, p. 209.

3. Kelles-Krauz in Paris to Witold Jodko-Narkiewicz in Cracow, 7 July 1900, *Listy* II, p. 355.

4. Janina Kelles-Krauz, "Mój ojciec," p. 92.

5. For example, *K. Radosławski*, "Wystawa Paryska. August Rodin," *Prawda* 20(31–32) 1900: 373–74, 385–86.

6. Janina Kelles-Krauz, "Mój ojciec," p. 92; Bieńkowski, "Kelles-Krauz Kazimierz," p. 140. On Poles, Paris, and *fin-de-siècle* art: Franciszek Ziejka, *Paryż młodopolski* (Warsaw, 1993).

7. Kelles-Krauz's attitude toward religion was less obstinate than in younger days. See Andrzej Chwalba, *Sacrum i rewolucja* (Cracow, 1992).

8. Janina Kelles-Krauz, "Mój ojciec," p. 93.

9. These restaurants were the background for many a revealing conversation. On one occasion, Ignacy Daum of the Paris Section learned that the Guesdists had unwittingly dispatched an Okhrana agent as their friendly emissary to Russian socialists in the Russian Empire. Kelles-Krauz in Paris to CZZSP in London, 6 August 1897, *Listy* I, p. 712.

10. Kancewicz, *PPS*, 59; Leon Wasilewski, "Z roboty zagranicznej P.P.S.," in *Księga pamiątkowa PPS* (Warsaw, 1923), p. 172.

11. Anna Żarnowska, "Kazimierz Kelles-Krauz," *Pisma* I, p. x.

12. Kelles-Krauz in Paris to Odo Bujwid in Cracow, September 1900, *Listy* II, p. 393.

13. Kelles-Krauz in Paris to CZZSP in London, 7 February 1898, *Listy* II, p. 17; Kelles-Krauz in Paris to Komitet Zagraniczny PPS in London, 16 February 1900, *Listy* II, p. 328. Hereafter "KZPPS."

14. Bieńkowski, "Kelles-Krauz Kazimierz," p. 140.

15. Żarnowska, "Kelles-Krauz," p. x.

16. Sokolnicki, *Czternaście lat*, p. 18.

17. Koszutski, *Walka młodzieży*, p. 58; Kelles-Krauz in Paris to Kelles-Krauzowa in Radom, 15 August 1899, *Listy* II, p. 248; Kelles-Krauz in Paris to CZZSP in London, 3 March 1895, *Listy* I, p. 335.

18. Kelles-Krauz in Pinchat to Kelles-Krauzowa in Paris, 26 September 1896, *Listy* I, p. 621.

19. Koszutski, *Walka młodzieży*, p. 144; Żarnowska, "Kelles-Krauz," p. x.

20. Nettl, *Luxemburg*, p. 110.

21. Kelles-Krauz in Paris to CZZSP in London, 9 December 1898, *Listy* II, p. 107.

22. Kelles-Krauz in Paris to CZZSP in London, 12 October 1896, *Listy* I, p. 634.

23. This account drawn from: Lorentowicz, *Spojrzenie wstecz*, pp. 195–210; Bożena Krzywobłocka, *Cezaryna Wojnarowska* (Warsaw, 1979), pp. 156–58; [Kazimierz Kelles-Krauz] *Bulletin* January 1896 (6): 1; [Kazimierz Kelles-Krauz] "L'affaire Sawicki," *Bulletin* July 1896 (8): 7; "Sprawa Sawickiego," *Przedświt* 1896 (5): 18; Malankiewicz to Paris Okhrana, 26 June 1894, *Hoover* (XIX/4B); Kelles-Krauz in Paris to CZZSP in London, 5 August 1895, *Listy* I, p. 411.

24. Kelles-Krauz in Paris to CZZSP in London, 27 July 1895, *Listy* I, p. 408.

25. Kelles-Krauz in Paris to CZZSP in London, 13 October 1895, *Listy* I, p. 444.

26. Malankiewicz to Paris Okhrana, 10 May 1896, *Hoover* (XIX/4B).

27. Malankiewicz to Paris Okhrana, 27 September 1896, *Hoover* (XIX/4B).

28. On the shelter's history, Krzywobłocka, *Wojnarowska*, pp. 140–41.

29. Kelles-Krauz in Paris to CZZSP in London, 4 August 1897, *Listy* I, p. 708.

30. Kelles-Krauz in Paris to CZZSP in London, 12 October 1896, *Listy* I, p. 634.

31. Kelles-Krauz in Paris to CZZSP in London, 7 May 1899, *Listy* II, p. 161; Kelles-Krauz in Paris to CZZSP in London, 7 September 1899, *Listy* II, p. 273.

32. Janina Kelles-Krauz, "Mój ojciec," p. 93.

33. Kelles-Krauz in Paris to Gumplowicz in Graz, 18 July 1896, *Listy* I, p. 591.

34. Kelles-Krauz did apply for the Stypendium imienia Śniadeckich: "Korespondencja Sekretarza Generalnego Akademii Umiętności z 1899 roku," *Ossolineum* (19/89).

35. Janina Kelles-Krauz, "Wokoł biografii," p. 57.

36. K. Krauz, "Pięciolecie Instytutu Socjologicznego," *Przegląd Filozoficzny* 4 (1897–1898): 93–113.

37. "Korespondencja Sekretarza Generalnego Akademii Umiętności z 1899 roku," *Ossolineum* (19/89). Kelles-Krauz admitted that the qualifications for membership were not very demanding at first, "Pięciolecie," p. 93.

38. Wacław Olszewicz, "Udział K. Kelles-Krauza w pracach Międzynarodowego Instytutu Socjologii w Paryżu w latach 1893–1901," *Kultura i Społeczeństwo* 9(2) 1965: 175.

39. Janina Kelles-Krauz, "Mój ojciec," p. 92.

40. Casimir de Krauz, "La psychiatrie et la science des idées," *Annales* 1895 (1): 253–303.

41. C. de Krauz, "La loi de la rétrospection revolutionnaire vis à vis de la théorie de l'imitation," *Annales* 1896 (2): 315–38.

42. Alan Swingewood, *A Short History of Sociological Thought* (London, 1993), p. 196.

43. Kelles-Krauz published them as such in "Socjologiczne prawo retrospekcji" (Warsaw, 1898); this appears in *Pisma* II. I will cite according to the French originals.

44. Kelles-Krauz, "Loi," p. 320.

45. Kelles-Krauz, "Idées," p. 283; Kelles-Krauz, "Loi," p. 317.

46. Kelles-Krauz, "Idées," p. 279.

47. Kelles-Krauz, "Loi," p. 320.

48. Kelles-Krauz, "Idées," p. 284; Kelles-Krauz, "Loi," p. 316.

49. Kelles-Krauz, "Loi," p. 323.

50. Kelles-Krauz, "Idées," pp. 280–81, 284.

51. Kelles-Krauz, "Idées," p. 289.

52. Kelles-Krauz, "Idées," pp. 277, 286.

53. Kelles-Krauz, "Idées," p. 292.

54. Edward Abramowski, "Socjologiczne prawo retrospekcji," *Przegląd Filozoficzny* 1898 (2): 80–92, in Edward Abramowski, *Pisma*, vol. 2 (Warsaw, 1928), p. 386.

55. Jerzy Szacki, *Historia myśli socjologicznej*, vol. 2 (Warsaw, 1981), pp. 544–5.

56. Kołakowski, *Main Currents* II, p. 36. See also Steenson, *Kautsky*, pp. 16, 24–25, 31, 52, 63–66.

57. David Morgan, "The 'Orthodox' Marxists," in R. J. Bullen, et al, eds., *Ideas into Politics* (London, 1984), pp. 6–7.

58. Kelles-Krauz, "Idées," p. 290.

59. Kelles-Krauz, "Idées," p. 254.

60. Kelles-Krauz, "Idées," p. 286. Marx did leave behind one passage which supports Kelles-Krauz: "The first reaction against the French revolution and the period of the enlightenment bound up with it was to see everything as medieval and romantic ... The second reaction is to look beyond the middle ages into the primitive age of each nation, and that corresponds to the socialist tendency." Marx to Engels, 25 March 1868, Karl Marx, *Pre-capitalist Economic Formations* (London, 1978), pp. 140–1.

61. H. Stuart Hughes, *Consciousness and Society* (New York, 1958), p. 37.

62. He escapes Swingewood's generalization that Marxists in the 1890s considered Marxism as a natural science. *Sociological*, p. 194.

63. On Kautsky's view of Marxism as a positivist science of determinist laws, see Jukka Gronow, *On the Formation of Marxism*, (Helsinki, 1986), pp. 50–54.

64. Abramowski believed that Kelles-Krauz's theory "opened the field." See Abramowski, "Socjologiczne," p. 400. Though Ludwik Krzywicki was skeptical ("Wstęp" to Kazimierz Kelles-Krauz, *Materializm ekonomiczny* (Cracow, 1908), in *Pisma* II, pp. 4–10), his use of the past was similar to Kelles-Krauz's.

65. Walicki, *Polska, Rosja, marksizm*, p. 175.

66. Michalski, *Socjalizm*, p. 52.

67. Jerzy Jedlicki, "Native Culture and Western Civilization," *Acta Poloniae Historica* 28 (1973): 76; Peter Brock, "The Polish 'Movement to the People,'" *Slavonic and East European Review* 40(1) 1961: 107; Wandycz, *Lands*, pp. 93–94. For Lelewel's influence on the Polish left in immigration, see Kieniewicz, *Historia*, p. 137, and on the Polish left in general, Adam and Lidia Ciołkosz, *Niepodległość i socjalizm 1835–1945* (London, 1982), p. 6.

68. Kieniewicz, *Historia*, p. 90. See also Najdus, *Daszyński*, p. 20.

69. Briefly: Kieniewicz, *Historia*, p. 211. Fully: Walicki, *Romantic Nationalism*.

70. Davies compares Lelewel and Mickiewicz, *Playground* II, p. 39, as does Wandycz, *Lands*, p. 117. Luxemburg was devoted to Mickiewicz her entire life, while Kelles-Krauz (like Piłsudski) preferred Słowacki.

71. Kelles-Krauz in Paris to Camille de Saint-Croix in Paris, 30 December 1898, *Listy* II, pp. 115–16.

72. Kelles-Krauz, "Idées," p. 283. His formulation of the "law" of revolutionary retrospection is as follows: "Each movement which intends to change the principles

of the social system begins by turning toward an epoch of the more or less distant past."

73. It is more interesting to discuss the exceptions, as in Hughes, *Consciousness;* or ignore this dominance altogether, as in Harry Barnes, ed., *An Introduction to the History of Sociology* (Chicago, 1948).

74. K. Krauz, "Rocznik i kongres socyologiczny," *Prawda* 23(35) 1903: 415.

75. Kelles-Krauz in Paris to Stanisław Tarnowski in Cracow, 2 June 1899, *Listy* II, p. 193. The characterization is from Steven Lukes, *Emile Durkheim* (London, 1992), p. 83.

76. Casimir de Krauz, "La théorie organique des sociétés," *Annales* 1898 (4): 260–61.

77. Olszewicz, "Udział," p. 175.

78. At the congress: Casimir de Krauz, "La théorie organique des sociétés," *Annale* 1898 (4): 260–89. To the Paris Society: Casimir de Krauz, "Un Sociologue Polonais: Stanislaw Krusinski," *Annales* 1897 (3): 405–438. The Polish article: Kazimierz Krauz, "Jeszcze o organizmie społecznym," *Prawda* 17(18–19) 1897: 210, 224–25. The letter: Kelles-Krauz in Paris to Tarde in Paris, 15 October 1896, *Listy* I, pp. 634–38.

79. Kelles-Krauz, "Krusiński," pp. 406–407.

80. On Krzywicki's opposition to organicism, Kołakowski, *Main Currents* II, pp. 197–98.

81. Kelles-Krauz, "Théorie organique," pp. 278–79.

82. Kelles-Krauz, "Théorie organique," p. 284.

83. Kelles-Krauz, "Théorie organique," p. 288.

84. Kelles-Krauz, "Théorie organique," pp. 267–76; Kelles-Krauz, "Krusiński," pp. 421–30.

85. Kelles-Krauz, "Théorie organique," p. 280.

86. Kelles-Krauz, "Krusiński," pp. 418, 434.

87. Kelles-Krauz, "Krusiński," pp. 406–407.

88. Ludwik Krzywicki, "Jeszcze o program," *Przegląd Tygodniowy* 1883 (15). I cite after Blejwas, *Realism,* p. 169.

89. Marx and Engels yielded to a similar temptation. Marx's letters to Vera Zasulich reveal his hope that existing Russian communes might serve as a basis for socialism (Karl Marx to Vera Zasulich, 8 March 1881, Marx, *Formations,* pp. 142–53). Raymond Firth argues that Marx's attraction to Morgan's ideas was surprising, given Marx's usually determined empiricism. ("The Sceptical Anthropologist? *Proceedings of the British Academy* 58 (1972): 190.) Joanna Overing suggests that "primitive communism" and "primitive anarchy" are "much more telling of Western evaluations and political desires than of the understandings and practice of peoples to whom they have been applied." ("The anarchy and collectivism of the 'primitive other,'" in C. M. Hann, ed., *Socialism: Ideals, Ideologies, and Local Practice* (London, 1993). This sort of wishful thinking has continued

in anthropology well into this century, in the judgement of Alan Barnard
("Primitive communism and mutual aid: Kropotkin P. A. visits the Bushmen,"
in ibid., pp. 29–31).

90. Lukes, *Durkheim*, p. 46.

91. Lukes, *Durkheim*, p. 47.

92. This view is implicit in the revolutionary retrospection articles, and is spelled out
in Kelles-Krauz in Paris to Tarde in Paris, 15 October 1896, *Listy* I, pp. 635–36.

93. Kelles-Krauz, "Idées," p. 274.

94. Kelles-Krauz in Paris to CZZSP in London, 3 November 1896, *Listy* I, p. 644.

95. For the assessment of the École Libre by another member of the Paris
Section: Sokolnicki, *Czternaście lat*, p. 33.

96. Kelles-Krauz in Paris to CZZSP in London, 3 November 1896, *Listy* I, p. 644.

97. "État de Notes," *Ossolineum* (19/89); Kelles-Krauz in Paris to Tarnowski in
Cracow, 2 June 1899, *Listy* II, p. 192.

98. Exams: Kelles-Krauz in Paris to Jędrzejowski in London, 24 May 1898, *Listy* II,
p. 58. Diploma: "Etat de Notes," *Ossolineum* (19/89).

99. "État de Notes," *Ossolineum* (19/89).

100. Kelles-Krauz, "Loi."

101. Kelles-Krauz in Paris to Tarde in Paris, 15 October 1896, *Listy* I, pp. 634–38.

102. "État de Notes," *Ossolineum* (19/89).

103. Jean Cazeneuve, *Lucien Lévy-Brühl* (Oxford, 1972), pp. ix–xii.

104. His best known work is *Les Fonctions mentales dans les sociétés inférieures*
(Paris, 1910).

105. On this point, see Anthony Giddens, "A matter of truth," *Times Literary
Supplement*, 29 March 1996, p. 10.

106. Lucien Lévy-Brühl, ed., *Lettres inédites de John Stuart Mill à Auguste Comte*
(Paris, 1899); Lucien Lévy-Brühl, *La Philosophie d'Auguste Comte* (Paris, 1900).

107. *Elehard Esse*, "Comtisme et marxisme" *Revue Socialiste* 197 (1901): 589–605.
In Polish as "Pozytywizm i monistyczne pojmowanie dziejów," *Głos* 18–
20(1904): 283–85, 299–301, 314–15, in *Pisma* I as "Comtyzm i marksizm."

108. Kelles-Krauz, "Comtyzm," pp. 46, 54; and Kelles-Krauz, "Materializm," p. 37,
for example.

109. Kelles-Krauz, "Comtyzm," p. 45.

110. Kelles-Krauz, "Comtyzm," pp. 43–44.

111. Kelles-Krauz, "Comtyzm," p. 51.

112. An effort which is strikingly similar to the aims of Leszek Kołakowski's introduction to his history of Marxism. *Main Currents* I, pp. 9–80.

113. "L'age d'or de Vico au Marxisme" was published as "Wiek złoty, stan natury i
rozwój w sprzecznościach," *Przegląd Filozoficzny* 1903 (3– 4): 313–20, 414–26;
1904 (1): 19–33; and in *Pisma* I.

114. Kelles-Krauz, "Wiek złoty," p. 197.

115. Kazimierz Krauz, "Dialektyka społeczna w filozofii Vica," *Przegląd Filozoficzny* 2 (1901): 172–89, in *Pisma* I.

116. Kelles-Krauz, "Vico," 170. On Vico's theory of knowledge: Isaiah Berlin, *Vico and Herder* (London, 1992), pp. 9–15.

117. Martin Jay, "Vico and Western Marxism," in *Fin-de-Siècle Socialism and Other Essays* (London, 1988), pp. 67–81.

118. Kołakowski, *Main Currents* II, p. 31. Sorel discussed Vico in *Devenir Social*.and Labriola and Lafargue understood Vico as a forerunner to Marx. But the influence of Vico on Marx is a historical question (which is discussed in Martin Jay, *Marxism and Totality* [Los Angeles, 1984], pp. 30–37), to be distinguished from Kelles-Krauz's view that Marx might be improved upon by the application of his own interpretation of Vico.

119. Dick May to Kelles-Krauz in Paris, 23 July 1897, *Ossolineum* (19/89); E. Delbet to Kelles-Krauz in Paris, 15 November 1897, *Ossolineum* (18/89).

120. R., "Szkoły nauk społecznych," *Prawda* 20(43) 1900: 513.

121. Program of Collége Libre des Sciences Sociales, 1900–1901, *Ossolineum* (19/89).

122. Kelles-Krauz in Paris to Kautsky in Berlin, 25 February 1901, *Listy* II, p. 451.

123. Kelles-Krauz, "Szkoły"; Program of College Libre des Sciences Sociales. 1900–1901, *Ossolineum* (19/89).

124. Kelles-Krauz in Paris to Kautsky in Berlin, 2 April 1898, *Listy* II, p. 38. The manuscript eventually appeared as "Musik und Oekonomie," *Die Neue Zeit* 1901–1902 (20): 786–92.

125. Kelles-Krauz in Paris to Kelles-Krauzowa in Radom, 3 August 1899, *Listy* II. p. 255; Kelles-Krauz to La Direction de l'Instruction Publique du Canton de Fribourg, 28 January 1898, *Listy* II, p. 9; "Korespondecja Sekretarza Generalnego Akademii Umiętności z 1899 r.," *Ossolineum* (19/89).

126. Janina Kelles-Krauz, "Wokoł biografii," p. 57.

127. Kelles-Krauz in Paris to La Direction de 1'Instruction Publique du Canton de Fribourg, 28 January 1898, *Listy* II, p. 9; La Direction de l'Instruction Publique du Canton de Fribourg to Kelles-Krauz in Paris, 7 February 1898, *Ossolineum* (19/89).

128. Van den Borrey in Brussels to Kelles-Krauz in Paris, 13 February 1900. *Ossolineum* (19/89).

129. Joll, *Second International*, p. 57; K. Radosławski, "Z ruchu społecznego i artysty-cznego Młodej Belgii," *Krytyka* 1(6) 1901: 395.

130. Kelles-Krauz in Gries to Feldman in Cracow, 13 April 1904, *Listy* II, p. 790.

131. Kelles-Krauz in Brussels to Kelles-Krauzowa in Paris, 20 January 1901, *Listy* II, p. 435; Kelles-Krauz in Brussels to Kelles-Krauzowa in Paris, about 29 January 1901, *Listy* II, p. 445.

132. Van den Borrey in Brussels to Kelles-Krauz in Paris, 4 March 1901, *Ossolineum* (18/89); Diploma from Université Nouvelle, *Ossolineum* (18/89).

133. Students in Paris: Kazimierz Krauz, "Ekonomiczne podstawy pierwotnych form rodziny," *Krytyka* 1900: 555–75, reprinted in *Pisma* I, pp. 63–87. Colleagues in Paris: Olszewicz, "Udział," p. 176. Brussels: Kazimierz Krauz, "J. J. Bachofen," *Prawda* 21 (1901): 43–44, in *Pisma* I. In German: "J.J. Bachofen," *Die Neue Zeit* 20(1)1901–1902:517–24.

134. Kelles-Krauz, "Bachofen," pp. 234–35.

135. Kelles-Krauz, "Podstawy," pp. 67–68.

136. Kelles-Krauz, "Podstawy," pp. 74–77.

137. Kelles-Krauz, "Podstawy," pp. 65–67. As Krzywicki noticed, Kelles-Krauz was careful to distinguish between Marx and Engels. ("Wstęp," 10.) Kelles-Krauz criticized the latter several times, though never the former. He was not the only Polish socialist to take this distinction, unusual in the Second International, for granted: Jędrzejowski once told Kelles-Krauz to be careful not to become like Engels, treating every fact as though it demonstrates a law already known. Jędrzejowski in London to Kelles-Krauz in Paris, 10 November 1896, *Archiwum Lewicy*, 305/II/22, book IX, cards 297–98.

138. Kelles-Krauz knew Bebel's popular *Die Frau und der Sozialismus* (Leipzig, 1883); see Kelles-Krauz in Monachium to Kelles-Krauzowa in Radom, 20 December 1891, *Listy* I, p. 105. This was Bebel's only important contribution to socialist theory.

139. Kelles-Krauz, "Bachofen," pp. 239–10.

140. M. Luśnia, "Konstytucja francuska," *Światło* 1(4) 1898: 158–70. But in his reporting of international women's congresses he emphasized the divergence of interests among women of different classes. About laws limiting working hours, he wrote: "So the majority of ladies at the congress, who have never tasted factory work, energetically protested against such laws, and did so in the name of laissez-faire. A woman should be considered adult and free—let her work in such conditions as she likes. As if that 'as she likes' were not a cruel irony." (Kazimierz Krauz, "Kongres kobiecy," *Prawda* 16[17] 1896: 197–98; 16[18] 1896: 209; in manuscript at *Ossolineum*, signatures 28/77, 291/78, 292/78, pp. 1–2). He was disturbed by the forays of women's groups into international politics. He mocked one speaker at an international women's congress in 1896 for saying that "once we were angels of the hearth, now we'll be angels of peace." (Kazimierz Krauz, "Kongres kobiecy," *Prawda* 12[18] 1892: 209; 12[22] 1892: 256–57; in manuscript at *Ossolineum*, signatures 28/77, 291/78, 292/78).

141. Estera Golde was a lifelong friend of his and Maria's. Before Maria moved to Paris, he and the novelist Gabriela Zapolska were close friends. Kelles-Krauz wrote Maria that his and Zapolska's friendship was on the model of gender relations in a future society, in which men and women will not think of each other solely in terms of sex. Kelles-Krauz in Paris to Kelles-Krauzowa in Radom, 19 April 1892, *Listy* I, p. 150. See also Gabriela Zapolska to Stefan Laurysiewicz, 13 May 1892, Zapolska, *Listy*, p. 322; Zapolska to Laurysiewicz, 18 May 1892,

Zapolska, *Listy,* p. 342; Zapolska to Laurysiewicz, 2 October 1892, Zapolska, *Listy,* p. 387.

142. Kelles-Krauz stood for equality between the genders, regarding the notion of specifically feminine ideals as a distraction. Kazimierz Krauz, "Kwestja kobieca w poezjach Konopnickiej," *Krytyka* 1902: 264–69; in manuscript at *Ossolineum,* signatures 28/77, 291/78, 292/78. See also Marian Stępień, *Rodowód* (Kraków, 1983), p. 223.

143. He praised groups which addressed the problems of working mothers. Kelles-Krauz, "Kongres kobiecy 1892," pp. 5–6. He approved of the Guesdists' intention to write on the place of women within capitalist societies. Ł, "Ze świata. Francja. Piętnasty zjazd Partyi Robotniczej Francuskiej," *Przedświt* 9 (1897): 11. See also K. Krauz, "Sprawa kobieca i rodzinna w Włoszech," *Prawda* 22(31) 1902: 367–68; R., "Pomoc społeczna w gospodarstwie kobiecom," *Prawda* 23(14) 1903: 160–61; K. Krauz, "Opieka nad pracującemi dziećmi," *Prawda* 23(21) 1903: 245–16; K. Krauz, "Kapitalizm i macierzyńswto," *Prawda* 25(3) 1905: 29–30; K. Krauz, "Kapitalizm i dziecieństwo," *Prawda* 25(4) 1905: 44–45.

144. K. Kr., "Uspołecznienie życia codziennego," *Prawda* 12(47) 1892: 560.

145. Kazimierz Krauz, "Ekonomistyczne pojmowanie wieków średnich," *Prawda* 16(26–28) 1896: 307, 319–20, 332–33; in manuscript at *Ossolineum,* signatures 28/ 77, 291/78, 292/78.

146. Kelles-Krauz, "Uliczny," pp. 128–35.

147. *K. Radosławski,* "Trzy typy etyczne," *Głos* 6(2) 1891: 16–17.

148. Krzywicki opposed societies based upon familial links to societies organized through the mediation of things. Tadeusz Kowalik, "Filozofia społeczna Ludwika Krzywickiego," in Skarga, *Filozoficzna* II, pp. 410–12.

149. J. Novicov, "Discours," *Annales* 8 (1902): 93.

150. Szacki, *Historia,* pp. 540–11.

151. Tom Bottomore, *Marxist Sociology* (London, 1975), pp. 17–18; Szacki, *Historia,* p. 542. Croce wrote on Marxism between 1895 and 1899, and Durkheim lectured on socialism in 1895–1896 in Bordeaux. Sorel toyed with the idea of a "materialist theory of sociology" in 1895, and his efforts were noted by Kelles-Krauz (who wrote for Sorel's *Devinir Social*). Kelles-Krauz, however, was both sociologist and socialist, and led a rather busy life in each capacity. On Croce and Sorel, see Tom Bottomore, "Marxist Sociology," in Tom Bottomore and Robert Nisbet, eds., *A History of Sociological Analysis* (London, 1979), p. 127; on Durkheim see Lukes, *Durkheim,* pp. 245–54. On Kelles-Krauz and Sorel, see Kazimierz Krauz, "O tak zwanym 'Kryzysie marksizmu,'" *Przegląd Filozoficzny* 3(2) 1900, cited after *Pisma* I, p. 109.

152. Casimir de Kellès-Krauz, "Qu'est-ce que le Materialisme Économique," *Annales* 1902 (8): 49–91, published in Polish as "Czym jest materializm ekonomiczny," *Prawda* 21(37–39) 1901, and in *Pisma* I, after which I will cite. Shorter articles presenting much the same view are Kazimierz Kelles-Krauz, "Filozofia

marksizmu," *Krytyka* 1(2) 1902: 329–39; and K. Krauz, "Teoria poznania zjawisk gospodarczych," *Prawda* 21(27–28) 1901: 330–32, 343–45.

153. Kelles-Krauz, "Materializm," pp. 13–16.

154. Kelles-Krauz, "Materializm," pp. 19–20. See Kołakowski, *Main Currents* II, p. 213.

155. Kelles-Krauz, "Materializm," pp. 23–24.

156. Julian Hochfeld is one of the few to notice this. See his "Kelles-Krauza— marksizm 'otwarty,'" in *Marksizm, Socjologia, Socjalizm* (Warsaw, 1982), pp. 200–201.

157. Kelles-Krauz, "Materializm," p. 17.

158. Kelles-Krauz, "Materializm," pp. 21–22. This view is much like that expressed by Marx in the *Grundrisse,* which Kelles-Krauz could not have known. Włodzimierz Kaczocha, "Problemy kultury w ujęciu Kelles-Krauza," *Miesięcznik Literacki* 1980 (8): 96.

159. Kelles-Krauz, "Materializm," pp. 20–21.

160. Kelles-Krauz, "Materializm," p. 28.

161. Kelles-Krauz, "Materializm," pp. 26–29.

162. Kelles-Krauz, "Materializm," p. 34.

163. Kelles-Krauz, "Materializm," p. 37. Elsewhere Kelles-Krauz criticized Engels for suggesting that there might be an end to the dialectic. Kelles-Krauz, "Kryzys," p. 115.

164. Kelles-Krauz escapes Lewis Coser's verdict that Marxists have "emphatically not" applied their own methods to Marxism itself. "Marxist Thought in the First Quarter of the 20th Century," *American Journal of Sociology* 75(1) 1972: 173.

165. Kołakowski, *Main Currents* II, pp. 247–54.

166. Kelles-Krauz, "Materializm," pp. 36–37. Much has been made of Kelles-Krauz's use of the term *monoekonomizm.* It should be clear that Kelles-Krauz is far from understanding history in terms of a simple transmission of changes in the means of production upward through the superstructure, which is how this term has usually been understood. In fact, Kelles-Krauz has in mind his conception that society is unitary, and that of the terms that we use to describe phenomena within society, "economic" deserves priority because the events which we consider "economic" are of the greatest psychological importance. As he wrote elsewhere, "economic monism is identical to social phenomenonal- ism." Kelles-Krauz, "Kryzys," 137. This was clear enough to his colleagues: see Guillaume de Greef, *Éloges de Élisée Reclus et de de Kelles-Krauz* (Brussels, 1906), p. 10.

167. Kelles-Krauz, "Materializm," pp. 40–41.

168. Kelles-Krauz in Paris to Tarde in Paris, 15 October 1896, *Listy* I, p. 635.

169. Casimir de Kellès-Krauz, "Réplique," *Annales* 1902 (8): 313.

170. G. Tarde, "Quelques mots sur le matérialisme historique," *Annales* 1902 (8): 284–88.

171. René Worms, "Paroles," *Annales* 1902 (8): 265.

172. Alfred Fouillée, "Le matérialisme historique," *Annales* 1902 (8): 279.

173. Nicolas Abrikossof, "Paroles," *Annales* 1902 (8): 133.

174. Ferdinand Tönnies, "Opinion," *Annales* 1902 (8): 135.

175. J. Novikov, "Discours," *Annales* 1902 (8): 93–95.

176. Charles-M. Limousin, "Discours," *Annales* 1902 (8): 188.

177. Kelles-Krauz, "Réplique," p. 312.

178. Hughes, *Consciousness*, p. 42.

179. Dick Geary, "Max Weber, Karl Kautsky and German Social Democracy," in Wolfgang Mommsen and Jürgen Osterhammel, eds., *Max Weber and his Contemporaries* (London, 1989), p. 355.

180. Lukes, *Durkheim*, pp. 248–49.

181. On Weber's objections to Marxism, see Geary, "Weber," p. 355; John Breuilly, "Eduard Bernstein and Max Weber," in Mommsen, *Weber*, p. 347.

182. Kancewicz, *PPS*, p. 61; Wasilewski, "Z roboty," pp. 168–70.

183. Wasilewski, *Piłsudski*, pp. 10–14.

184. Piłsudski to CZZSP in London, 11 January 1898, *Niepodległość* 1938 (18): 354–57.

185. Wasilewski, *Piłsudski*, p. 16.

186. Kelles-Krauz in Paris to CZZSP in London, 8 November 1898, *Listy* II, p. 291.

187. Kelles-Krauz in Paris to CZZSP in London, 21 February 1898, *Listy* II, p. 23.

188. On relations between the *Przedświt* and *Światło* groups, Wasilewski, *Piłsudski*, p. 18; Kelles-Krauz in Paris to Jędrzejowski in London, 6 February 1898, *Listy* II, pp. 10–12; Kelles-Krauz in Paris to CZZSP in London, 12 February 1898, *Listy* II, p. 20.

189. Wasilewski, *Piłsudski*, p. 21.

190. Kelles-Krauz in Paris to Jędrzejowski in London, 20 October 1898, *Listy* II, p. 93.

191. Kelles-Krauz in Paris to CZZSP in London, 9 December 1898, *Listy* II, p. 105.

192. Piłsudski to CZZSP in London, 17 December 1898, *Niepodległość* 1978 (11): 21.

193. *Materiały* II, pp. 50–71, 75–78.

194. For the motion of 12 November 1899: *Materiały* II, pp. 80–82.

195. On 24 November 1898. "Okólniki za rok 1899," *Archiwum Lewicy*, 305/II/3, card 10.

196. Kelles-Krauz in Paris to CZZSP in London, 8 November 1898, *Listy* II, pp. 290–96.

197. Wojciechowski, *Wspomnienia*, p. 137.

198. Sokolnicki, *Czternaście lat*, p. 27.

199. Foreign Committee: Jędrzejowski in London to Kelles-Krauz in Paris, 15 January 1900, *Archiwum Lewicy*, 305/11/24, book XV, cards 50-51; Kelles-Krauz in Paris to Jędrzejowski in London, 28 January 1900, *Listy* II, 314. Paris Section: Kelles-Krauz in Paris to KZPPS in London, 26 February 1900, *Listy* II, p. 328. "Komitet Zagraniczny."

200. Jan Tomicki, *Polska Partia Socjalistyczna* (Warsaw, 1983), pp. 62–63.

201. Kulczycki, *Historya*, pp. 347–50; Wojciechowski, *Wspomnienia*, p. 113.

202. *Elehard Esse,* "Socialistes polonais et russes," *L'Humanité Nouvelle* 1899 (April): 434–50; published as a pamphlet, Paris 1899; I cite after the translation "Polscy i rosyjscy socjaliści," *Pisma* II, pp. 110–11. A Russian version was published in *Vestnik Russkoi Revoliutsii* in 1902.

203. Kelles-Krauz, "Socjaliści," pp. 116–17.

204. Kelles-Krauz, "Socjaliści," p. 120, especially note 1.

205. Kelles-Krauz, "Socjaliści," pp. 116, 119.

206. Kelles-Krauz, "Socjaliści," pp. 120–22.

207. Piłsudski to CZZSP in London, 22–23 October 1898, *Niepodległość* 1978 (11): 9–10.

208. Wasilewski, *Piłsudski,* pp. 21–25.

209. Kelles-Krauz in Paris to CZZSP in London, 22 April 1899, *Listy* II, p. 151.

210. Kelles-Krauz in Paris to KZPPS in London, 14 December 1900, *Listy* II, pp. 419–20; Jędrzejowski in London to Kelles-Krauz in Paris, 17 December 1900, *Archiwum Lewicy,* 305/11/24, book XVII, cards 464–65.

211. Kelles-Krauz in Paris to KZPPS in London, 14 March 1900, *Listy* II, pp. 462–63.

212. Kelles-Krauz in Paris to KZPPS in London, 3 December 1902, *Listy* II, p. 662.

213. For example, in "Pologne, Armenie, et Mlle Rose Luxemburg," *Bulletin* 12 (January 1897), he called her "the editor of *Sprawa Robotnicza,* which does not exist, the organ of the SDKP, which also does not exist."

214. Jędrzejowski in London to Kelles-Krauz in Paris, 19 September 1896, *Archiwum Lewicy,* 305/II/22, book IX, cards 97–98.

215. [Kazimierz Kelles-Krauz] "L'Alliance Franco-Russe. Lettre ouverte de Parti Socialiste Polonais aux Socialistes Francais," *Bulletin* 17 (January 1897): 4–7.

216. Kelles-Krauz, "Alliance," p. 7.

217. Kelles-Krauz, "Alliance," pp. 11–12.

218. "L' Alliance Franco-Russe," *Bulletin* 18 (March 1897): 1–4.

219. Kelles-Krauz in Paris to CZZSP in London, 5 July 1897, *Listy* II, p. 697.

220. *Elehard Esse,* "Le 'Compromis' Polono-Russe," *Bulletin* 19 (November 1897): 1–9.

221. Wereszycki, *Historia polityczna,* p. 131.

222. Kelles-Krauz, "Compromis," p. 6.

223. Kelles-Krauz, "Compromis," p. 7.

224. Kelles-Krauz, "Compromis," p. 9.

225. On the acquisition of the memo, Garlicki, *Piłudski,* p. 65; Wojciechowski, *Wspomnienia,* p. 127.

226. Joll, *Second International,* pp. 13, 79; George Lichtheim, *Marxism* (London, 1980), p. 280.

227. Kelles-Krauz in Paris to CZZSP in London, 9 December 1898, *Listy* II, p. 106; Kelles-Krauz in Paris to CZZSP in London, 6 January 1899, *Listy* II, p. 122.

228. Wiesław Bieńkowski, *Listy* II, p. 116, notes 6 and 7.

229. *Bulletin* 23 (February 1899).

230. Kelles-Krauz in Paris to Camille de Saint-Croix in Paris, 30 December 1898. *Listy* II, pp. 113–15.
231. [Kazimierz Kelles-Krauz] "Pour la Crète—Contre la Pologne," *Bulletin* 13 (March 1897): 6.
232. Kelles-Krauz in Paris to CZZSP in London, 6 October 1897, *Listy* II, p. 729.
233. *Elehard Esse*, "La politique internationale du proletariat et la question d'Orient," *Devenir Social* 1898 (7–8): 565–89. I will cite after *Elehard Esse*, "Międzynarodowa polityka proletariatu (w kwestii wschodniej)," *Przedświt* 1897 (10): 4–12, reprinted in *Pisma* I.
234. Kelles-Krauz, "Międzynarodowy," p. 36.
235. Kelles-Krauz, "Międzynarodowy," p. 41.
236. Kelles-Krauz, "Międzynarodowy," pp. 45–47.
237. Kelles-Krauz, "Międzynarodowy," pp. 48–49.
238. Kelles-Krauz, "Międzynarodowy," p. 53.
239. [Kazimierz Kelles-Krauz] "Contre la paix du tsar," *Bulletin* 26 (May 1899).
240. Kelles-Krauz, "Międzynarodowy," pp. 52, 54.
241. "I'm curious whether she did it for the Idea, or for fame?" Kelles-Krauz in Paris to CZZSP in London, 13 April 1898, *Listy* II, p. 45.
242. Kelles-Krauz in Antony to KZPPS in London, 9 September 1900, *Listy* II, p. 396.
243. Kelles-Krauz in Paris to KZPPS in London, 26 March 1900, *Listy* II, p. 340.
244. Sokolnicki, *Czternaście lat*, p. 16.
245. Kelles-Krauz in Antony to KZPPS in London, 22 August 1900, *Listy* II, p. 383.
246. Leon Wasilewski in London to Kelles-Krauz in Paris, 15 August 1899, *Archiwum Lewicy*, 305/11/23, book 14, card 124. *Michał Luśnia*, "Niepodległość Polski w programie socjalistycznym" (Paris, 1900); *Michał Luśnia*, "Ostatnie nieporozumienie," *Przedświt* 1900 (7): 7–17; both in *Pisma* II.
247. Kelles-Krauz, "Niepodległość," p. 127.
248. Kelles-Krauz, "Nieporozumienie," p. 173.
249. Kelles-Krauz, "Niepodległość," p. 128.
250. Kelles-Krauz, "Nieporozumienie," pp. 171–72.
251. Kelles-Krauz, "Niepodległość," pp. 132–33.
252. Kelles-Krauz, "Niepodległość," pp. 138, 149.
253. Kelles-Krauz, "Niepodległość," pp. 135–41.
254. Kelles-Krauz, "Nieporozumienie," p. 181.
255. Kelles-Krauz, "Nieporozumienie," pp. 176–77.
256. Kelles-Krauz, "Nieporozumienie," p. 185.
257. Kelles-Krauz, "Niepodległość," p. 131.
258. Kelles-Krauz, "Niepodległość," pp. 146–41.
259. Here Kelles-Krauz is following John Stuart Mill, echoing the position Mill took in his famous debate with Acton. Kelles-Krauz read English with the greatest of difficulty, and it is unclear whether this is a question of direct influence. But see John Stuart Mill, *Considerations on Representative Government* (London, 1861).

Acton's 1862 essay on "Nationality" is reprinted in his *History of Freedom and Other Essays* (London, 1907), pp. 270–301.

260. Kelles-Krauz, "Niepodległość," pp. 134–35.

261. Kelles-Krauz, "Niepodległość," p. 145.

262. Kelles-Krauz, "Nieporozumienie," p. 180.

263. Kelles-Krauz, "Niepodległość," pp. 141–42. For discussion, Walicki, "Luxemburg," p. 576.

264. Kelles-Krauz, "Nieporozumienie," p. 173.

265. Julian Marchlewski, "Le socialisme en Pologne et en Lithuanie," *La Petite République* 5 May 1900, cited after Żychowski, *Polska myśl*, p. 213.

266. Kelles-Krauz, "Nieporozumienie," pp. 170–71.

267. "Socjaldemokracja Królestwa Polskiego i Litwy." Nettl, *Luxemburg*, p. 96; Walicki, "Luxemburg," p. 575.

268. Robert Blobaum, "The SDKPiL and the Polish Question (Revisited)," in John Morrison, ed., *Eastern Europe and the West* (London, 1992), p. 209; Nettl, *Luxemburg*, p. 105.

269. Michalski, "Socjalizm," pp. 96–99.

270. Blobaum, "SDKPiL," p. 209; Żychowski, *Polska myśl*, pp. 211–12.

271. [Rosa Luxemburg] RL, "Der Sozialismus in Russische-Polen," *Vorwärts* 24 August 1900: 3, cited after Wiesław Bieńkowski, *Listy* II, p. 399n7.

272. [Kazimierz Kelles-Krauz] "Mlle Rose Luxemburg," *Bulletin* 23 (February 1899): 19.

273. Kelles-Krauz in Paris to KZPPS in London, 16 February 1900, *Listy* II, p. 331.

274. Kelles-Krauz in Antony to KZPPS in London, 13 September 1900, *Listy* II, p. 401.

275. Kelles-Krauz in Antony to KZPPS in London, 22 August 1900, *Listy* II. pp. 381,383.

276. Kelles-Krauz in Antony to KZPPS in London, 9 September 1900, *Listy* II, p. 394.

277. Kelles-Krauz in Brussels to CZZSP in London, 28 May 1899, *Listy* II, p. 185.

278. Kelles-Krauz in Paris to CZZSP in London, 7 May 1899, *Listy* II, p. 161.

279. There was a Guesdist called Krauss, so Kelles-Krauz asked London to allow a letter stating that this Krauss had agreed to represent the SDKP in Brussels to fall into the Okhrana's hands. Kelles-Krauz in Brussels to CZZSP in London, 28 May 1899, *Listy 11, pp.* 188–89.

280. Michel Winock, "Introduction," *Histoire de la lle Internationale* 13 (Geneva, 1980), p. 13.

281. Kelles-Krauz in Paris to KZPPS in London, 20 September 1900, *Listy* II, p. 406; Kelles-Krauz in Paris to KZPPS in London, 21 September 1900, *Listy* II, p. 407.

282. Kelles-Krauz in Paris to KZPPS in London, 21 September 1900, *Listy* II. p. 407; Jędrzejowski in London to Kelles-Krauz in Paris, 22 September 1900, *Archiwum Lewicy,* 305/11/24, book XVII, cards 122–23.

283. *Materiały* II, 181–85; *IIe Internationale* 13, pp. 64–65; Wasilewski, *Zarys 1925, p.* 87; Żychowski, *Polska myśl, p.* 215; Tych, "Polskie partie," p. 714.

284. Limanowski, *Pamiętniki*, pp. 532–33.

285. The PPS recorded it as 45 minutes, *Materiały* II, p. 185.

286. *IIe Internationale* 13, pp. 65, 202–204.

287. *IIe Internationale* 13, pp. 66, 205.

288. Tych, "Luksemburg," p. 435.

289. Nettl, *Luxemburg*, pp. 260–61.

290. Kelles-Krauz in Antony to KZPPS in London, 9 September 1900, *Listy* II, p. 395.

291. Limanowski, *Pamiętniki*, pp. 532–33.

292. Tych, "Luxemburg," p. 437.

293. Tych, "Polskie partie," p. 714; *IIe Internationale* 13, pp. 339–3.

294. *IIe Internationale* 13, p. 345.

295. As in *Elehard Esse*, "La politique internationale du proletariat et la question d'Orient," *Devenir Social* 1898 (7–8): 565–89. This article prompted Jogiches to tell Luxemburg to "bloody the Baron's nose" by writing against him anonymously, which she declined to do. Luxemburg to Jogiches, 8 January 1899, *Jogiches* I, p. 345.

296. Kelles-Krauz in Brussels to CZZSP in London, 28 May 1899, *Listy* II, pp. 184–85.

297. Kelles-Krauz published his resolution in the *Bulletin* 27 (April–June 1899).

298. Limanowski, *Pamiętniki*, pp. 571–72. See also Andrzej Głowacki, *Międzynarodowy ruch socjalistyczny wobec odbudowy Polski*, (Szczeciń 1974), p. 25; Kieniewicz, *Historia*, 276. There were exceptions, of course, such as Maria Szeliga, founder of the "Alliance Universelle des Femmes" and a leader of the "Ligue des femmes pour le désarmement international," whom Kelles-Krauz took to task after she thanked the tsar "for taking the question of peace into his powerful hands." See Kelles-Krauz in Paris to CZZSP in London, 20 March 1899, *Listy* II, p. 14. On Szeliga: Maria Szeliga to Kazimierz Kelles-Krauz, 16 October 1897, *Ossolineum* (19/89); Krzywobłocka, *Wojnarowska*, p. 135.

299. [Kazimierz Kelles-Krauz] "Contre la paix du tsar," *Bulletin* 26 (May 1899): 3–4.

300. *Bulletin* 27 (April–July 1899).

301. Kissin, *War*, pp. 136–38.

302. Karl Kautsky, *Sozialisten und Krieg* (Prague, 1937), p. 443, cited in Kissin, *War*, p. 166. On the SPD and foreign policy: Steenson, *German*, pp. 65–78.

303. Gary Steenson argues that this lack of practice combined with the fear of Russia left German socialists "with little choice but to back the government." (Steenson, *German*, p. 77.)

304. Kissin, *War*, pp. 185–88.

305. Kelles-Krauz in London to Kelles-Krauzowa in Paris, 4 October 1900, *Listy* II, p. 407.

306. Braunthal, *International*, pp. 255–58; Joll, *Second International*, p. 96.

307. *M. Luśnia,* "Socjalista ministrem," *Przedświt* 1899 (8): 2–8; Kelles-Krauz in
Paris to CZZSP in London, 22 June 1899, *Listy* II, p. 204.

308. Kelles-Krauz in Paris to CZZSP in London, 22 June 1899, *Listy* II, 204. See
also Kelles-Krauz in Paris to CZZSP in London, 17 August 1900, *Listy* II,
p. 251.

309. Kelles-Krauz in Paris to CZZSP in London, 14 August 1899, *Listy* II, p. 241; K.
Radosławski, "Z życia Francji. Ankieta w sprawie pracy nocnej," *Prawda* 20(37)
1900: 442–43; K. Radosławski, "Czyny Milleranda," *Prawda* 22(14), 1902: 172–
73; *Elehard Esse,* "Po dymisyi Milleranda," *Przedświt* 1902 (9): 338–5.

310. Joll, *Second International,* pp. 83–84.

311. *Elehard Esse,* "Socyaliści Francuscy wobec sprawy Dreyfusa," *Przedświt* 1898
(8): 15.

312. Kelles-Krauz in Paris to Kelles-Krauzowa in Radom, 22 July 1899, *Listy* II. p. 221.

313. Kelles-Krauz in Paris to Kelles-Krauzowa in Radom, 9 September 1899, *Listy* II,
p. 275.

314. Kelles-Krauz, "Niepodległość," p. 126.

315. Kelles-Krauz in Paris to Camille de Saint-Croix in Paris, 30 December 1898,
Listy II, p. 115.

CHAPTER 4

1. Janina Kelles-Krauz, "Mój ojciec," p. 94; Kelles-Krauz in Vienna to KZPPS in
London, 16 April 1901, *Listy* II, p. 473.

2. Kelles-Krauz in Vienna to Ludwik Gumplowicz in Graz, 6 July 1902, *Listy* II,
pp. 624–625.

3. Kelles-Krauz in Vienna to KZPPS in London, 9 May 1901, *Listy* II, p. 484;
Bieńkowski, *Kelles-Krauz,* reproduces the Meldungsbuch.

4. His Brussels doctorate did not suffice in Austria. By "Austria" I will mean the
Austrian portion of Austria-Hungary.

5. Kelles-Krauz in Vienna to Wasilewski in London, 27 April 1902, *Listy* II, p. 612.

6. Kelles-Krauz in Vienna to KZPPS in London, 16 April 1901, *Listy* II, p. 474.

7. Kelles-Krauz in Bratislava (Pressburg) to Kelles-Krauzowa in Radom, 14 July
1901, *Listy* II, p. 529.

8. Kelles-Krauz in Paris to Kautsky in Berlin, 25 February 1901, *Listy* II, p. 457.

9. The Polish books he finished will be discussed below. One he did not is *Francja,*
advertized in *Ogniwo* 2(27) 1904: 648. His two books on Marxist sociology for
French publishers were never finished.

10. Kelles-Krauz in Vienna to Kelles-Krauzowa in Radom, 24 June 1901, *Listy* II,
p. 512; Van den Borrey in Brussels to Kelles-Krauz in Vienna, 25 June 1903,
Ossolineum (18/89).

11. Kelles-Krauz in Brussels to Kelles-Krauzowa in Vienna, 6 November 1902, *Listy*
II, pp. 647–48, and the following letters from Brussels for details.

12. Kelles-Krauz in Paris to Kelles-Krauzowa in Vienna, 3 November 1902, *Listy* II, p. 645.

13. Maria Kelles-Krauzowa, "Wspomnienie o Kazimierzu Kelles-Krauzie," *Ossolineum*, signature II 13518, pp. 119–20. This is not his wife, but the wife of his brother Stanisław.

14. K.R., "Uniwersytet ludowy w Wiedniu," *Prawda* 22(13) 1902: 150; Janina Kelles-Krauz, "Wokoł biografii," p. 61.

15. Janina Kelles-Krauz "Wokoł biografii," p. 57.

16. Kelles-Krauz in Brussels to Kelles-Krauzowa in Vienna, 29 November 1902, *Listy* II, p. 658; Kelles-Krauz in Gries to Maria Kelles-Krauz in Vienna, 9 March 1904, *Listy* II, p. 729.

17. Kelles-Krauz in Vienna to Jędrzejowski in London, 2 February 1903, *Listy* II, p. 677.

18. Kelles-Krauz in Vienna to Wasilewski in Cracow, 29 July 1903, *Listy* II, p. 689.

19. Kelles-Krauz in Gries to Motz in Paris, 26 March 1904, *Listy* II, p. 751.

20. Kelles-Krauz in Gries to Kelles-Krauzowa in Vienna, 25 March 1904, *Listy* II, p. 749.

21. Kelles-Krauz in Gries to Kelles-Krauzowa in Vienna, 10 April 1904, *Listy* II, p. 786.

22. Kelles-Krauz in Kosiv to Aleksander Malinowski in London, 10 July 1904, *Listy* II, p. 815.

23. Kelles-Krauz in Gries to Kelles-Krauzowa in Vienna, 31 March 1904, *Listy* II, p. 763; Kelles-Krauz in Gries to Kelles-Krauzowa in Vienna, 11 March 1904, *Listy* II, p. 731.

24. Kelles-Krauz in Gries to Kelles-Krauzowa in Vienna, 29 February 1904, *Listy* II, p. 718; Kelles-Krauz in Gries to Kelles-Krauzowa in Vienna, 30 March 1904, *Listy* II, p. 761.

25. Kelles-Krauz in Vienna to KZPPS in London, 1 December 1903, *Listy* II, p. 707.

26. Kelles-Krauz in Gries to Kelles-Krauzowa in Vienna, 15 March 1904, *Listy* II, p. 736.

27. Kelles-Krauz in Vienna to Kelles-Krauzowa in Radom, 18 May 1901, *Listy* II, pp. 487–88.

28. Janina Kelles-Krauz "Wokoł biografii," p. 58.

29. Janina Kelles-Krauz "Mój ójciec," pp. 91, 94; Janina Kelles-Krauz, "Wokół biografii," p. 61; Maria Kelles-Krauzowa, "Wspomnienie o Kazimierzu Kelles-Krauzie," *Ossolineum*, signature II 13518, p. 119.

30. See *K. Radosławski*, "Alkoholizm i walka z nim," *Prawda* 21(18–22) 1901.

31. Kelles-Krauz in Paris to Golde in Cracow, 7 January 1901, *Listy* II, p. 432; Kelles-Krauz in Vienna to Golde in Cracow, 12 November 1903, *Listy* II, p. 703; Kelles-Krauz in Vienna to Golde in Katowice, 13 November 1904, *Listy* II, p. 832.

32. Janina Kelles-Krauz, "Mój ojciec," p. 94; Limanowski, *Pamiętniki*, p. 643; Kelles-Krauz in Kraków to Jędrzejowski in London, 27 July 1901, *Listy* II, pp. 535–36;

Piłsudski to KZPPS, 25 July 1901, Jędrzejowicz, "Listy," p. 28; Piłsudski to KZPPS, 2 August 1901, Jędrzejowicz, "Listy," p. 29; Kelles-Krauz in Nürnberg to Kelles-Krauzowa in Vienna, 30 October 1901, *Listy* II, p. 641; Kelles-Krauz in Vienna to Piłsudski in Cracow, 6 October 1903, *Listy* II, pp. 700–701.

33. Wehler, *Nationalstaat*, pp. 130–31; Wereszycki, *Historia polityczna*, p. 200; Jerzy Holzer, *PPS: Szkic dziejów* (Warsaw, 1977), p. 159. PPSzp in Polish stands for "Polska Partia Socjalistyczna zaboru pruskiego."

34. Wehler, *Nationalstaat*, pp. 124–25; Wasilewski, *Zarys 1925*, pp. 46, 70.

35. Franciszek Hawranek, *Polska i niemiecka socjaldemokracja na Górnym Śląsku* (Opole, 1977), p. 96; Wehler, *Nationalstaat*, p. 124; Wereszycki, *Historia polityczna*, p. 201.

36. Tych, "Polski ruch," p. 333.

37. Hawranek, *Górny Śląsk*, p. 64; Michalski, *Socjalizm*, p. 79.

38. Wehler, *Nationalstaat*, pp. 136–37; Holzer, *PPS*, p. 76.

39. Hawranek estimates that 70 to 90 percent of workers in Upper Silesia were Polish (*Górny Śląsk*, p. 85). Yet many of these Polish-speaking workers had ambiguous national identities.

40. Wehler, *Nationalstaat*, pp. 140–47.

41. Wehler, *Nationalstaat*, pp. 132–33.

42. Głowacki, *Międzynarodowy*, p. 23.

43. See the responses of leading German socialists to a survey on the Polish question by *Krytyka* in 1901. Knowing that they were writing for a Polish audience, some still advocated Germanization. Editors of *Krytyka, Sprawa polska w opinii Europy* (Cracow, 1901), p. 47. Also Hawranek, *Górny Śląsk*, p. 81; Michalski, *Socjalizm*, p. 82.

44. Hawranek, *Górny Śląsk*, p. 69.

45. Daszyński, *Pamiętniki*, p. 220; Głowacki, *Międzynarodowy*, p. 23.

46. Lewis Namier, *1848: The Revolution of the Intellectuals* (Oxford, 1992), pp. 49–50, 53, 86–87. Namier's verdict (p. 53) on the SPD and Poland is as follows: "In short, the difference between the apostles of German Social-Democracy, the exponents of German liberalism, and the Prussian Junkers, concerned merely the point in time when they reached the acme of Realpolitik, the degree of sincerity with which they admitted it in public, and the means they had of translating their views into practice."

47. Daszyński, *Pamiętniki*, p. 219.

48. Peter Nettl, "The German Social Democratic Party as a Political Model," *Past and Present* 30 (April 1965): 65–95; Joll, *Second International*, p. 118; Michalski, *Socjalizm*, p. 78.

49. Marek Waldenberg, *Wzlot i upadek Karola Kautsky'ego*, vol. 1 (Cracow, 1972), pp. 578–85; Hawranek, *Górny Śląsk*, p. 205.

50. Hawranek, *Górny Śląsk*, pp. 82–83.

51. Hans-Ulrich Wehler, *The German Empire 1871–1918* (Oxford, 1993), p. 82.

52. Gary Steenson, *Not One Man! Not One Penny!* (Pittsburgh, 1981), p. 77.

53. Hawranek, *Górny Śląsk*, pp. 165–68.

54. Hawranek, *Górny Śląsk*, p. 170; Nettl, *Luxemburg*, p. 175; Wehler, *Nationalstaat*, pp. 151–52.

55. Hawranek, *Górny Śląsk*, pp.175–78, 190.

56. Wehler, *Nationalstaat*, p. 153.

57. Luxemburg in Berlin to Jogiches, January 1900, *Jogiches* II, pp. 10–11; Luxemburg in Berlin to Jogiches, 11 March 1902, *Jogiches* II, p. 238; Bronner, *Luxemburg*, p. 49; Wehler, *Nationalstaat*, p. 151.

58. Hawranek, *Górny Śląsk*, pp. 172–73; *Materiały* II, p. 180; Głowacki, *Międzynarodowy*, pp. 42–43.

59. Nettl, *Luxemburg*, p. 133.

60. Wehler, *Nationalstaat*, p. 151; Wasilewski, *Zarys 1925*, pp. 171–72; Wereszycki, *Historia polityczna*, p. 181; Hawranek, *Górny Śląsk*, pp. 71–72.

61. [Kazimierz Kelles-Krauz] "La Question polonaise au Congrès de Hambourg,"' *Bulletin* 19 (November 1897): 9–10.

62. Wasilewski, "Z roboty," p. 179; Hawranek, *Górny Śląsk*, p. 191.

63. Kelles-Krauz in Vienna to Jodko-Narkiewicz in Lviv (Lwów), 6 May 1901, *Listy* II, p. 481; M. *Luśnia*, "Kwestia samorządu," *Przedświt* 1901 (8): 287–90.

64. Wasilewski, *Zarys 1925*, p. 163.

65. Kelles-Krauz in Bratislava (Pressburg) to Kelles-Krauzowa in Radom, 14 July 1901, *Listy* II, p. 528.

66. Kelles-Krauz in Vienna to KZPPS in London, 4 July 1901, *Listy* II, pp. 522–523.

67. Hawranek, *Górny Śląsk*, pp. 201–202; Najdus, "Działacze," pp. 101–102.

68. Viktor Adler, "Der Lübecker Parteitag," *Arbeiter Zeitung* 269 (1901): 1–2; "Goście wiedenscy w Berlinie," *Naprzód* 273 (1901): 3.

69. Kelles-Krauz in Vienna to Golde in Katowice and KZPPS in London, 8 October 1901, *Listy* II, pp. 550–557.

70. Kelles-Krauz in Vienna to KZPPS in London, 11 November 1901, *Listy* II, pp. 572–84; Najdus, *Daszyński*, p. 201.

71. Kelles-Krauz in Vienna to KZPPS in London, 8 October 1902, *Listy* II, p. 636.

72. Wehler, *Nationalstaat*, pp. 160–61; Hawranek, *Górny Śląsk*, pp. 229–30; [Władysław Gumplowicz] "Historya niedoszłej zgody," *Przedświt* 1903 (5): 169–80.

73. Kelles-Krauz in Brussels to Czesław Kossobudzki in Berlin, 17 December 1902, *Listy* II, p. 672.

74. Wehler, *Nationalstaat*, pp. 164–65; Hawranek, *Górny Śląsk*, pp. 234–35; Gumplowicz, "Historya," p. 174.

75. Kelles-Krauz in Vienna to Wasilewski in Cracow, 29 July 1903, *Listy* II, p. 688.

76. "Offener Brief der Polnischen Sozialistischen Partei (PPS) Deutschlands an die Deutsche Sozialdemokratie" (Berlin, 1903).

77. "Nasze sprawy w Dreźnie," *Przedświt* 1903 (10): 409–28; Hawranek, *Górny Śląsk*, pp. 242–43; Wasilewski, *Zarys 1925*, p. 131. For Luxemburg's view: Luxemburg

in Dresden to Jogiches, 15 September 1903, *Jogiches* II, pp. 284–85; Luxemburg in Dresden to Jogiches, 16 September 1903, *Jogiches* II, p. 287; Luxemburg in Dresden to Jogiches, 16 September 1903, *Jogiches* II, p. 288.

78. Stanley Pierson, *Marxist Intellectuals and the Working Class Mentality in Germany* (London, 1993), pp. 162–69, gives a detailed account which leaves out the Polish question.

79. Kelles-Krauz in Plankau to Kautsky in Berlin, 11 September 1903, *Listy* II, pp. 690–91.

80. Kelles-Krauz in Vienna to Kautsky in Berlin, 2 November 1903, *Listy* II, p. 702.

81. M. Luśnia, "Porachunek z rewizjonistami," *Przedświt* 1903 (10–12), (in *Pisma* II); Kelles-Krauz in Vienna to Piłsudski in Cracow, 6 October 1994, *Listy* II, p. 701.

82. M. Luśnia, "Unbewaffnete Revolution?" *Die Neue Zeit* 22(1) 1903–1904. He had begun this line of criticism in M. Luśnia, "Widoki rewolucji," *Przedświt* 1902 (8–9): 286–92, 325–33 (in *Pisma* II). Also Massimo Salvadori, *Karl Kautsky and the Socialist Revolution* (London, 1979), pp. 79–80.

83. Karl Kautsky, "Allerhand Revolutionäres," *Die Neue Zeit* 22(1) 1903–1904: 588–98, 620–27, 652–57, 685–95, 732–40. For discussion, Salvadori, *Kautsky*, pp. 89–90; Waldenberg, *Kautsky*, pp. 357–62.

84. Georgii Plekhanov to Karl Kautsky, 28 September 1904, cited after Waldenberg, *Kautsky*, p. 362.

85. Nettl, "Political Model," p. 67.

86. For a chart of the SPD's electoral progress from 1871 to 1912, Joseph Rovan, *Histoire de la Social-Démocratie Allemande* (Paris, 1978), p. 115.

87. Wehler, *German Empire*, p. 83.

88. Vernon Lidtke, *The Alternative Culture* (Oxford, 1985); W. L. Guttsman, *The German Social Democratic Party* (London, 1981), pp. 167–219.

89. Joll, *Second International*, p. 67.

90. Morgan, "Orthodox," pp. 9–11; Kołakowski, *Main Currents* II, pp. 43–50; Salvadori, *Kautsky*, p. 90.

91. Karl Kautsky, "Wie weit ist das kommunistische Manifest veraltet," *Leipziger Volkszeitung*, 25 January 1904, cited after Salvadori, *Kautsky*, p. 87.

92. Karl Kautsky, "Ein sozialdemokratischer Katechismus," *Die Neue Zeit* 7(1) 1893: 368.

93. M. Luśnia, "Po uchwaleniu taryfy celnej," *Przedświt* 1903 (2).

94. Kelles-Krauz in Gries to Feldman in Cracow, 2 April 1904, *Listy* II, p. 772.

95. [Rosa Luxemburg] M.R., "Jeszcze raz Karl Kautsky o kwestii polskiej," *Przegląd Socjalistyczny* 2(2) 1904: 76.

96. She thought Kautsky relied excessively on the "safe domestic fold of old principles" and failed "to address the burning need—to increase the revolutionary aspect of the movement." Luxemburg to Henriette Roland-Hoist, 17 December 1904, cited after Pierson, *Mentality*, p. 190.

97. Luxemburg, *Kwestia*.

98. Kelles-Krauz in Gries to Wasilewski in Cracow, 18 April 1904, *Listy* II, p. 803.

99. Wasilewski to Kelles-Krauz, 14 April 1904, *Niepodległość* 16 (1937): 255.

100. For one account: Marian Bębenek, "Kazimierz Kelles-Krauz wobec rewizjonizmu," 1975.

101. Kelles-Krauz, "Widoki," pp. 228–45; Michał Luśnia, "Rewizja programu agrarnego," *Przedświt* 1904 (9–10) (in *Pisma* II).

102. Elehard Esse, "Zjazd wiedeński i rewizja partyi austryackiej," *Przedświt* 1902 (1); Pierson, *Mentality*, p. 122.

103. Kołakowski, *Main Currents* II, pp. 102–105.

104. K. Krauz, "Nauka, ideał, i czyn," *Prawda* 21(45–6) 1901: 547, 561. Kautsky was also weak in pure philosophy. Kołakowski, *Main Currents* II, p. 35.

105. Kazimierz Krauz, *Portrety zmarłych socjologów* (Warsaw, 1906), cited after *Pisma* I, pp. 375–76.

106. K. Krauz, "Darwinizm w socyologii," *Prawda* 23(43–14) 1903. See also K. Krauz, "Kilka uwag o psychologii w socjologii," *Ogniwo* 2(43) 1904.

107. Kelles-Krauz, "Psychologia," p. 1011.

108. Kelles-Krauz, *Portrety*, pp. 414–15.

109. Kelles-Krauz, *Portrety*, pp. 375–77.

110. Kelles-Krauz, "Nauka," p. 561.

111. K. Krauz, "Sprawa kobieca i rodzinna w Włoszech," *Prawda* 22(31) 1902: 367–68.

112. Kelles-Kraus, "Widoki," pp. 308–310.

113. Kołakowski, *Main Currents* II, p. 213.

114. K. Krauz, "Z powodu kongresu drezdenskiego," *Prawda* 23(42) 1903: 498–99.

115. Though Kelles-Krauz's chief preocuppation was Polish independence, he opposed all colonialism. K. Krauz, "Rocznik i kongres socyologiczny," *Prawda* 23(35) 1903: 415; K. Krauz, "Kapitalizm i ludzkość," *Prawda* 25(5) 1905: 53–54.

116. Kelles-Krauz, *Portrety*, p. 377.

117. The census of 1910 counted 4.9 million Poles in Austria. Waldenberg, *Kwestie narodowe*, p. 28.

118. In effect, the votes of, for example, workers counted for far less than the votes of landowners. On the aims and effects of extending the franchise, see R. A. Kann, *The Multinational Empire* (New York, 1950); and A. J. P. Taylor, *The Habsburg Monarchy, 1809–1918* (London, 1948).

119. K. Radosławski, "Listy z Wiednia," *Prawda* 23(16) 1903: 182–84.

120. Wistrich, *Socialism*, pp. 300–301.

121. Najdus, "Działacze," pp. 995–96.

122. Najdus, *Galicja*, p. 240; Wistrich, *Socialism*, pp. 302–303; Steenson, *After Marx*, p. 178.

123. Najdus, *Galicja*, p. 241.

124. For example: K. R., "Listy z Wiednia," *Prawda* 21(50) 1901: 602–603; K. Radosławski, "Listy z Wiednia. Ugoda z Węgrami i parlament przedlitawski," *Prawda* 22(45) 1902: 530–31; zz., "Koło polskie i wojsko austryackie," *Prawda*

23(9) 1903: 98–99; K. Radosławski, "Listy z Wiednia," *Prawda* 23(16) 1903: 182–84;

125. [Karl Renner] Rudolf Springer, *Der Kampf der Österreichischen Nationen um den Staat* (Vienna, 1902).

126. M. Luśnia, "Program narodowościowy Socjalnej Demokracji Austriackiej a program PPS," *Przedświt* 7–8 (1903), cited after *Pisma* II, p. 282.

127. Kelles-Krauz, "Program," p. 288.

128. Renner would be chancellor (1918–1920) in interwar Austria, and then president (1945–1950) of the Second Austrian Republic. Along with most of the Austro-German political class, he supported union with Germany in 1918. He also supported Anschluss in 1938.

129. K. Radosławski, "Nowa teoria narodowości i państwa w Austryi," *Prawda* 23(7) 1903:74.

130. zz., "List z Wiednia," *Prawda* 23(41) 1903: 483.

131. Talmon, *Nation*, p. 150; Steenson, *After Marx*, p. 173. The curia system was abolished in 1907.

132. On this point, see Talmon, *Nation*, p. 138. According to Taylor, the socialists were also like conservatives in believing that the masses were free of nationalism. *Habsburg Monarchy*, p. 165.

133. Kelles-Krauz, "Nowa teoria," p. 74.

134. zz., "List z Wiednia," *Prawda* 23(41) 1903: 483.

135. Steenson, *After Marx*, p. 213.

136. Kelles-Krauz, "Program," p. 292.

137. Kelles-Krauz, "Program," p. 291. This belief became a certainty in the course of the next two years: see *Michał Luśnia*, "Niepodległość Polski a materialistyczne pojmowanie dziejów," *Krytyka* 7(4–5) 1905, cited after *Pisma* II, pp. 390–91.

138. Kelles-Krauz, "Program," pp. 292–93.

139. Personal communication, 28 July 1993, Warsaw.

140. Jonathan Frankel, *Prophecy and Politics* (Cambridge, 1981), pp. 198–99.

141. Michał Śliwa, "Kwestia żydowska w polskiej myśli socjalistycznej," in Feliks Kiryk, ed., *Żydzi w Małopolsce* (Przemyśl, 1991), p. 276.

142. Robert Blobaum, *Feliks Dzierżyński and the SDKPiL* (Boulder, 1984), p. 34.

143. These are the proportions according to the 1897 Russian census. The city had 140,200 residents in 1897.

144. Daniel Beauvois, "Polish-Jewish relations in the territories annexed by Russia in the first half of the nineteenth century," in Chimen Abramsky, et al, eds., *The Jews in Poland* (Oxford, 1988), p. 88.

145. Harry J. Tobias, *The Jewish Bund in Russia* (Stanford, 1972), pp. xv, 12–13, 53.

146. Moshe Mishkinsky, "Polish Socialism and the Jewish Question," *Polin* 1990 (5).

147. He helped Jewish socialists find means of publishing in Yiddish. Tobias, *Bund*, pp. 46, 52–53.

148. Wereszycki, *Historia polityczna*, p. 87; Blobaum, *Dzierzyński*, p. 11; Corrsin. "Language," p. 69; Kieniewicz, *Historia*, p. 351.

149. Corrsin, "Language," p. 85; Piasecki, *Organizacja*, p. 14.

150. Jerzy Holzer, "Relations between Polish and Jewish left wing groups in interwar Poland," in Abramsky, *Jews in Poland*, pp. 140–41; Joseph Lichten, "Notes on the assimilation and acculturation of Jews in Poland, 1863–1943," ibid., p. 108; Stefan Kieniewicz, "Polish society and the Jewish problem in the nineteenth century," ibid, pp. 74–75.

151. The PPS was not exceptional in this respect. Few SDKP leaders could read Yiddish. Some early leaders of the Bund could not have written an article in Yiddish, for that matter. Tobias, *Bund*, p. 11.

152. For this story, see Wojciechowski, *Wspomnienia*, pp. 112–13; Piasecki, *Organizacja*, pp. 23–33; *Materiały* I, pp. 219–21; and Kancewicz, *PPS*, p. 204. For Mill's recollections (in Yiddish), see John Mill, *Pionem un boyer: memuarn* (New York, 1946–1949).

153. Piasecki, *Organizacja*, p. 34; Tomicki, *PPS*, p. 34.

154. Frankel, *Prophecy*, p. 220; Piasecki, *Organizacja*, pp. 34, 69; Feldman, *Dzieje polskiej myśli*, p. 90, Wojciechowski, *Polska Partya*, pp. 31–32; Wojciechowski, *Wspomnienia*, p. 113; Holzer, "Relations," p. 141; Tobias, *Bund*, pp. 72, 103.

155. Piasecki, *Organizacja*, 45; Holzer, "Relations," p. 140; Śliwa, "Żydowska," p. 276.

156. Frankel, "Prophecy," p. 142.

157. Frankel, "Prophecy," p. 218.

158. Śliwa, "Żydowska," p. 277.

159. Tobias, *Bund*, p. 67.

160. Wojciechowski remembered the slight, *Wspomnienia*, pp. 110–11.

161. Nettl, *Luxemburg*, p. 254.

162. Kelles-Krauz in Paris to CZSSP in London, 6 September 1899, *Listy* II, p. 270; Kelles-Krauz in Paris to CZSSP in London, 14 September 1899, *Listy* II, p. 278; Kelles-Krauz in Paris to CZSSP in London, 26 February 1900, *Listy* II, pp. 328–29; Kelles-Krauz in Paris to CZSSP in London, 27 February 1900, *Listy* II, p. 334; Kelles-Krauz in Paris to KZPPS in London, 3 January 1901, *Listy* II, p. 426.

163. Kelles-Krauz in Paris to Kelles-Krauzowa in Radom, 29 July 1899, *Listy* II, pp. 229–30.

164. Steven Beller, "Class, Culture and the Jews of Vienna, 1900," in Ivar Oxaal, et al, eds., *Jews, Antisemitism, and Culture in Vienna* (London, 1987), pp. 43, 46, 57–58.

165. Wistrich, *Socialism*, pp. 180–84.

166. P. G. J. Pulzer, *The Rise of Political Anti-Semitism in Germany and Austria* (New York, 1964), pp. 166–69, 199; Beller, "Culture," p. 44.

167. Carl Schorske, *Fin-de-Siècle Vienna* (Cambridge, 1987), p. 6.

168. Michael Pollak, "Cultural Innovation and Social Identity in Fin-de-Siècle Vienna," in Oxaal, *Vienna*, p. 63.

169. Pollak, "Innovation," p. 63.

170. I use this term advisedly. Ignacy Daszyński was exempt from the generalizations to follow. From as early as 1891, he considered the Jews a nationality deserving of the appropriate rights and protections. On his unusual stand, see Najdus, *Daszyński*, pp. 83, 153 and Frankel, *Prophecy*, p. 177. As early as 1881 a program of Galician socialists included a mention of the Jews as a nationality. Roman Wapiński, *Polska i małe ojczyzny polaków* (Wrocław, 1994), p. 182.

171. On Kautsky, the SPD, and orthodoxy: Wistrich, *Socialism*, pp. 16–18, 138–39, 143–44, 146, 153; Waldenberg, *Kautsky*, p. 581. On the Austro-Germans: Pulzer, *Anti-Semitism*, p. 267; Wistrich, *Socialism*, pp. 251, 306–307; Robert Wistrich, "Social Democracy, Antisemitism and the Jews of Vienna," in Oxaal, *Vienna*, p. 117.

172. Pulzer, *Anti-Semitism*, p. 168; Wistrich, *Socialism*, pp. 168–69, 248–49, 269.

173. Pollak, "Innovation," pp. 66–67.

174. Wistrich, *Socialism*, pp. 208–209.

175. Marsha Rozenblit, "The Jews of Germany and Austria," in Robert Wistrich, ed., *Austrians and Jews in the Twentieth Century* (London, 1992), p. 9.

176. Pulzer, *Anti-Semitism*, p. 138; Rozenblit, "The Jews," p. 8.

177. Walter Weitzmann, "The Politics of the Viennese Jewish Community, 1890–1914," in Oxaal, *Vienna*, p. 140.

178. Kazimierz Krauz, "Z powodu kongresu syonistów," *Prawda* 22(14) 1902: 162.

179. Kelles-Krauz, "Syoniści," p. 162.

180. Kelles-Krauz, "Syoniści," p. 175.

181. Kelles-Krauz in Vienna to KZPPS in London, 11 June 1902, *Listy* II, p. 617; Kelles-Krauz in Plankau to Jędrzejowski in London, 13 September 1903, *Listy* II, p. 699. A sign of his interest in mutual Polish-Jewish portrayal is K. Radosławski, "Judyta i Rachela," *Prawda* 22(4) 1902: 44–45.

182. Henryk Piasecki, *Sekcja żydowska PPSD i żydowska partia socjalno- demokratyczna* (Wrocław, 1982), p. 53.

183. Alicja Pacholczykowa, "Cederbaum (wcześniej Zetterbaum) Maksymilian," in Tych, *Słownik* I, p. 291.

184. Max Zetterbaum, "Zur materialistischen Geschichtsauffassung," *Die Neue Zeit* 21 (1902–1903): 399–407, 498–506, 524–31.

185. Kelles-Krauz in Vienna to Kelles-Krauzowa in Radom, 25 May 1901, *Listy* II, p. 494.

186. Kelles-Krauz in Vienna to KZPPS in London, 6 December 1901, *Listy* II, p. 591.

187. Jędrzejowski in London to Kelles-Krauz in Vienna, *Archiwum Lewicy*, 305/11/25, book XIX, cards 633–34.

188. Kelles-Krauz in Vienna to KZPPS in London, 12 February 1902, *Listy* II, pp. 601–602.

189. Piłsudski to Kelles-Krauz in Vienna, 17 February 1902, *Niepodległość* 13 (1980): 8–10.
190. Frankel, *Prophecy*, pp. 164, 171; Ezra Mendelson, *Class Struggle in the Pale* (Cambridge, 1970), p. 136; Tobias, *Bund*, pp. 163–64. John Mill, influenced by his experiences in Warsaw, and convinced that the PPS was not entirely wrong to consider the national question part of the socialist agenda, had been pressing for some such change. See Tobias, *Bund*, p. 107.
191. Tobias, *Bund*, p. 161.
192. Cited after Śliwa, "Żydowska," p. 277. On the Bund's reaction: Tobias, *Bund*, pp. 286–87. On PPS-Bund relations in 1903: Piasecki, *Organizacja*, pp. 72, 76–78, 85, 90; Żychowski, *Polska myśl*, pp. 255–56.
193. Frankel, *Prophecy*, p. 200.
194. Luxemburg's position was odd, as she demanded autonomy for her own organization. Tobias, *Bund*, pp. 291–93.
195. Frankel, *Prophecy*, pp. 175, 227–28; Tobias, *Bund*, pp. 177–205.
196. Keiles-Krauz in Vienna to Jędrzejowski in London, 4 May 1903, *Listy* II, p. 682.
197. Kelles-Krauz in Vienna to Wasilewski in London, 15 March 1902, *Listy* II, p. 611.
198. Kelles-Krauz insisted on preserving this conclusion, despite opposition from London. Kelles-Krauz in Plankau to Wasilewski in Cracow, 12 July 1903, *Listy* II, p. 687.
199. Kelles-Krauz, "Program," pp. 294–96.
200. *Michał Luśnia*, "W kwestii narodowości żydowskiej," *Krytyka* 6(1–2) 1904, in *Pisma* II, pp. 318–41. Feldman offered to publish the article as a pamphlet, but Kelles-Krauz replied that its "heretical content" would prevent the PPS from distributing it in Russian Poland. Kelles-Krauz in Vienna to Feldman in Cracow, 13 January 1904, *Listy* II, p. 710. On Feldman, see Dąbrowski, "Feldman," and Ezra Mendelson, "Jewish Assimilation in Lvov," *Slavic Review* 28(4) 1969.
201. Kelles-Kraus, "Kwestia," p. 337.
202. Kelles-Kraus, "Kwestia," pp. 323–24. Stanisław Barański had argued in 1889 that nationality is a question of consciousness, and that by this criterion the Jews should be considered a nationality. Moshe Mishkinsky, "A Turning Point in the History of Polish Socialism and its Attitude Toward the Jewish Question," *Polin* 1986(1): 120–21.
203. Kelles-Kraus, "Kwestia," pp. 324, 326.
204. Kelles-Kraus, "Kwestia," pp. 324–27.
205. Kelles-Kraus, "Kwestia," pp. 326–27.
206. Kelles-Kraus, "Kwestia," pp. 330–35.
207. Kelles-Kraus, "Kwestia", pp. 338–40.
208. Śliwa, "Żydowska," p. 274.
209. Piasecki, *Organizacja*, pp. 101–104.
210. Wapiński, *Ojczyzny*, pp. 173–74.

211. Michael Sobelman, "Polish Socialism and Jewish Nationality," *Soviet Jewish Affairs* 20(1) 1990: 48, 54.
212. zz., "List z Wiednia," *Prawda* 24(45) 1904: 530–31.
213. Dmowski's *Myśli nowoczesnego Polaka* was published in 1903, Zygmunt Balicki's *Egoizm narodowy wobec etyki* in 1901.
214. Dąbrowski, "Feldman," p. 74.
215. Garlicki, *Piłsudski*, pp. 77–78.
216. Garlicki, *Piłsudski*, p. 79; Anna Żarnowska, *Geneza rozłamu w Polskiej Partii Socjalistycznej* (Warsaw, 1965), p. 88. The arrest also precipitated a secession from the party, in which a small number of members led by Ludwik Kulczycki quit to form the PPS-Proletariat.
217. Żarnowska, *Rozłam*, p. 92.
218. Żarnowska, *Rozłam*, pp. 89–91; Garlicki, *Piłsudski*, pp. 20, 72, 79.
219. Holzer, *PPS*, p. 33.
220. Ignacy Pawłowski, *Geneza i działalność Organizacji Spiskowo-Bojowej PPS* (Wrocław, 1976), pp. 28–29.
221. Kelles-Krauz in Gries to Motz in Paris, 26 March 1904, *Listy* II, p. 752.
222. Kelles-Krauz in Gries to Kelles-Krauzowa in Vienna, 2 March 1904, *Listy* II, p. 731.
223. This is not to say that Kelles-Krauz went uncriticized. Władysław Studnicki and Stanislaw Grabski, who passed through the PPS as they moved to the right, accused him of dogmatism. K. Kr., "O prawdę," *Prawda* 22(11–12) 1902: 131, 142–3.
224. Kelles-Krauz in Vienna to KZPPS in London, 12 February 1902, *Listy* II, p. 600.
225. Kelles-Krauz in Vienna to KZPPS in London, 12 February 1902, *Listy* II, p. 600.
226. He made cooperation with a Russian party contingent upon its acceptance of the PPS program. He was frustrated by the fact that he could find few Russian socialists who agreed that the independence of Poland was desirable. Kelles-Krauz in Vienna to *Vestnik Russkoi Revoliutsii*, 10 March 1902, *Listy* II, pp. 604–605.
227. *Michał Luśnia*, "Niepodległość Polski a materialistyczne pojmowanie dziejów," *Krytyka* 7(4–5) 1905, in *Pisma* II, pp. 370–94.
228. Although he addressed a few ironic remarks in the direction of the party's right wing: "Pojmowanie," pp. 372–73.
229. Michalski, *Socjalizm*, pp. 98–99; Blobaum, "SDKPiL," p. 211.
230. Kelles-Krauz, "Pojmowanie," p. 371.
231. *Michał Luśnia*, "Rozmowy towarzyszy o socjalizmie i patriotyzmie, konstytucy i niepodległości" (London, 1904). This pamphlet also repeats Kelles-Krauz's arguments against a Russian constitution.
232. Kelles-Krauz, "Pojmowanie," pp. 374–76.
233. Kelles-Krauz was right about this: the former Congress Kingdom no longer held a special place within Russian industry, and Russian industrialists were

asking for protection against "foreign" competition from Warsaw and Łódź. Ihnatowicz, "Przemyśl," pp. 87–89.

234. Kelles-Krauz had developed these argumemts earlier on the example of Finland: El. Es., "Rynki rosyjskie a Finlandya," *Przedświt* 1901 (6): 226–29. The division of Polish lands did lead to some notable economic disadvantages for the former Congress Kingdom: coal had to be imported from the Donets' basin rather than Silesia, oil from Baku rather than Galicia. Wandycz, *Lands*, p. 205.

235. Luxemburg was of course correct that at least some of the bourgeoisie opposed independence for fear of losing markets. Ihnatowicz, "Przemyśl," p. 92.

236. Kelles-Krauz, "Pojmowanie," pp. 376–82.

237. Kelles-Krauz, "Pojmowanie," pp. 384–85.

238. [Kazimierz Kelles-Krauz] "Dlaczego dążymy do niepodległości," *Robotnik* 14 December 1903 (53): 5.

239. Kelles-Krauz, "Dlaczego," p. 6.

240. Kelles-Krauz, "Pojmowanie," pp. 386–87.

241. Kelles-Krauz, "Dlaczego" p. 5.

242. Kelles-Krauz, "Pojmowanie," pp. 392–93.

243. K. Radosławski, "Krytyka zasady narodowości" *Prawda* 23(42) 1903: 496–97.

244. Kelles-Krauz in Vienna to KZPPS in London, 11 November 1901, *Listy* II, p. 574.

245. Kelles-Krauz in Vienna to KZPPS in London, 23 June 1902, *Listy* II, p. 619.

246. Kelles-Krauz, "Rocznik," p. 415.

247. K. Radosławski, "Listy z Wiednia," *Prawda* 21(24) 1901: 290–92; K. Radosławski, "Listy z Wiednia. Z polytiki socjalnej," *Prawda* 21(29) 1901: 351–53; K. Krauz, "Obowiązkowe towarzystwa rolnicze," *Prawda* 22(5-6) 1902: 58,70–71; K. Radosławski, "Czyny Milleranda," *Prawda* 22(14) 1902: 172–73; K.Rad., "Robotnicy rolni w Belgii," *Prawda* 22(27) 1902: 322–23; Rad., "Stan ruchu współdzielczego w Anglii," *Prawda* 22(36) 1902: 430–31; K. Krauz, "Opieka nademigrantami," *Prawda* 23(21) 1903: 258–59; K. Radosławski, "Międzynarodowa ochrona pracy," *Prawda* 23(44) 1903: 522–23; K. R., "Prawa człowieka i prawodawstwo fabryczne w Ameryce," *Prawda* 24(4) 1904: 42–43; K. Krauz, "Międzynarodowa ochrona pracy," *Prawda* 24(43) 1904: 509–510; K. Krauz, "Izby pracy," *Prawda* 24(44) 1904: 522–23; K. Krauz, "Postępy prawodawstwa pracy," *Prawda* 24(46,50) 1904: 549–50, 598–99; K. Krauz, "Sprawa pomocników handlowych," *Prawda* 25(8) 1905: 87–88; K. Krauz, "Liga kupujących," *Prawda* 25(9) 1905: 101–103; K. Krauz, "Reforma górnicza w Prusach," *Ogniwo* 3(23-24) 1905: 522–23, 547–48; Kazimierz Krauz, "Ochrona prawna robotników rolnych," in *Myśl* (Warsaw, 1904), pp. 152–61.

248. Kazimierz Krauz, "Demokracja w nowoczesnym ustroju państwowym," *Głos* 1905 (issues 1, 3, 4, 8, 11, 12, 13, 14, 17, 18, and 21), cited after *Pisma* II, pp. 397–93,464–470 and *passim*. At a more popular level: Kazimierz Krauz, "Jak się narody rządzą" (Warsaw, 1906).

249. Kelles-Krauz, "Demokracja," p. 396. His preference for a strong parliament was probably a reaction to the weakness of the German and Austrian legislatures.

250. Kelles-Krauz, "Demokracja," p. 402.

251. Kelles-Krauz, "Demokracja," pp. 403, 415.

252. K. Krauz, "Z dziedziny nauk państwowych. Esmein i uzasadnienie demokracy i." *Prawda* 25(7) 1905: 79.

253. Kelles-Krauz, *Portrety,* p. 391.

254. Kelles-Krauz, "Narody," p. 14.

255. Kelles-Krauz in Vienna to KZPPS in London, 12 February 1902, *Listy* II, p. 600.

256. Kazimierz Krauz, "Rzut oka na rozwój socjologii w XIX wieku," in Stanisław Grabski and Kazimierz Krauz, *Rzut oka na rozwój ekonomii i socjologii w XIX wieku* (Warsaw, 1901); in *Pisma* I, pp. 282–313. For a German version, see Kazimierz Kelles-Krauz, *Die Sociologie im 19. Jahrhundert* (Berlin, 1902).

257. [Kazimierz Kelles-Krauz] "Ruch społeczny w starożytności," *Głos* 1903 (21,22, 24, 26), and in *Pisma* I, pp. 138–68.

258. Kazimierz Krauz, *Portrety zmarłych socjologów* (Warsaw, 1906), in *Pisma* I, pp. 315–415.

259. Kelles-Krauz, *Portrety,* p. 319.

260. Kelles-Krauz, *Portrety,* p. 322.

261. Kelles-Krauz, *Portrety,* p. 364.

262. Kelles-Krauz, "Z ruchu"; Stępień, *Rodowód,* p. 218.

263. Schorske, *Vienna,* p. 8; Wojciech Cesarski, "L. Krzywicki i K. Kelles-Krauz o alienacji estetycznej," *Studia Estetyczne* 5 (1968): 232.

264. He wrote a few other articles attempting to explain art in sociological terms, most after his arrival in Vienna: K. Krauz, "Muzyka i ekonomia," *Prawda* 21(1–2) 1901: 8, 20–21; K. Krauz, "Powstawanie stylów z gospodarstwa społecznego," *Prawda* 22(21–22) 1902: 246–47, 259–60; K. Krauz, "Przemyśl i sztuka," *Prawda* 23(14) 1903: 163–64.

265. Kazimierz Krauz, "Kilka głównych zasad rozwoju sztuki," in *Poradnik dla samoukόw,* vol. 2 (Warsaw, 1905), cited after *Pisma* I, pp. 420, 425; Kelles-Krauz, "Muzyka," p. 8.

266. Kelles-Krauz, "Sztuka," p. 436.

267. Kelles-Krauz, "Sztuka," pp. 438–39.

268. Kelles-Krauz, "Sztuka," pp. 429, 460.

269. Kelles-Krauz, "Sztuka," p. 424.

270. Kelles-Krauz, "Sztuka," pp. 442, 460.

271. Kelles-Krauz, "Sztuka," pp. 447, 462, 464.

272. Kelles-Krauz, "Sztuka," p. 460.

273. Kelles-Krauz, "Sztuka," p. 453.

274. Kelles-Krauz, "Muzyka," p. 8.

275. Kelles-Krauz, "Sztuka," pp. 470–72.

276. Kelles-Krauz, "Sztuka," pp. 474, 476.

277. Kelles-Krauz, "Muzyka," p. 8.

278. Kelles-Krauz, "Powstawanie," p. 246; Kelles-Krauz, "Muzyka," pp. 483, 510–13, 517.

279. Kelles-Krauz,"Sztuka," p. 528.

280. Kelles-Krauz, *Portrety,* p. 364.

281. Kazimierz Krauz, "Współzawodnictwo i współdziałanie," *Głos* 1901: 768.

282. Kelles-Krauz, "Sztuka," p. 536.

283. Kelles-Krauz, "Sztuka," pp. 532, 534, 536.

284. Kelles-Krauz, "Sztuka," pp. 537, 541.

285. Kelles-Krauz, "Sztuka," p. 545.

286. Kelles-Krauz, "Sztuka," p. 547.

287. Like his fellow Polish Marxists Krzywicki and Marchlewski, Kelles-Krauz stood out in the Second International by not demanding that progressive artists adhere to realism. Andrzej Lipiński, "Myśl socjologicza Kazimierza Kelles-Krauza," *Biuletyn Kwartalny Radomskiego Towarzystwa Naukowego* 22(2) 1988:35; Cesarski, "Alienacja," p. 230.

288. Kelles-Krauz, "Sztuka," pp. 539, 548–49.

289. Kelles-Krauz in Vienna to Feldman in Cracow, 24 November 1903, *Listy* II, p. 704.

290. Jerzy Myśliński, "Uniwersytet Wakacyjny w Zakopanem," *Przegląd Historyczno-Oświatowy* 6(1) 1963: 9.

291. Kazimierz Krauz, "Wolny polski Uniwersytet wakacyjny," *Krytyka* 1 (6) 1904: 455–64; K., "Otwarcie wyższych kursów wakacyjnych w Zakopanem," *Gazeta Polska* 212 (1904), read in *Ossolineum* (18/89).

292. Kelles-Krauz in Gries to Feldman in Cracow, 13 April 1904, *Listy* II, p. 791; Myśliński, "Uniwersytet," pp. 10–11; P. Margor, "Pierwszy rok uniwersytetu zakopiańskiego," *Krytyka* 2(10) 1904: 237.

293. Limanowski, *Pamiętniki,* p. 583.

294. Myśliński, "Uniwersytet," p. 19.

295. Dąbrowski, "Feldman," p. 102.

296. Kelles-Krauz in Vienna to Feldman in Cracow, 24 November 1903, *Listy* II, p. 704.

297. Myśliński, "Uniwersytet," pp. 11–12.

298. Limanowski, *Pamiętniki,* p. 573; Myśliński, "Uniwersytet," p. 11.

299. Kelles-Krauz in Gries to Feldman in Cracow, 11 April 1904, *Listy* II, p. 791; Kelles-Krauz in Gries to Kelles-Krauzowa in Vienna, 11 April 1904, *Listy* II, p. 787.

300. Janina Kelles-Krauz, "Mój ojciec," p. 94.

301. Margor, "Pierwszy rok," pp. 233–35; Andrzej Mawkgrafski to Police Department in Petersburg, 2 September 1904, *Archiwum Główne Akt Dawnych, Kancelaria Pomocnika General-Gubernatora Warszawskiego do spraw policyjnich,* p. 87.

302. Myśliński, "Uniwersytet," p. 8.

303. Margor, "Pierwszy rok," p. 239.

304. Andrzej Mawkgrafski to Police Department in Petersburg, 2 September 1904, *Archiwum Główne Akt Dawnych, Kancelaria Pomocnika General-Gubernatora Warszawskiego do spraw policyjnich*, p. 87.

305. Students: Leon Wasilewski, "Towarzystwo Wyższych Kursów Wakacyjnych," *Prawda* 24(27) 1904: 438; Margor, "Pierwszy rok," p. 232. Attenders: Dąbrowski, "Feldman," p. 102.

306. Mawkgrafski to Police Department in Petersburg, 2 September 1904, *Archiwum Główne Akt Dawnych, Kancelaria Pomocnika General-Gubernatora Warszawskiego do spraw policyjnich*, p. 87.

307. Mawkgrafski to Police Department in Petersburg, 2 September 1904, *Archiwum Główne Akt Dawnych, Kancelaria Pomocnika General-Gubernatora Warszawskiego do spraw policyjnich*, p. 87.

308. Kelles-Krauz in Paris to Kelles-Krauzowa in Vienna, 5 October 1904, *Listy* II, p. 827.

309. Wojciechowski, *Wspomnienia*, pp. 163–64; Garlicki, *Piłsudski*, p. 87.

310. Garlicki, *Piłsudski*, p. 88.

311. Kelles-Krauz in Gries to Wasilewski in Cracow, 18 April 1904, *Listy* II, p. 802; Keiles-Krauz in Kosiv to Aleksander Malinowski in London, 10 July 1904, *Listy* II, pp. 815–16.

312. Sokolnicki, *Czternaście lat*, pp. 134–35; Żarnowska, *Rozłam*, pp. 138–40. This interpretation of Kelles-Krauz's intentions is based on M. Luśnia, "Przedwczesny realizm," *Przedświt* 9 (1904): 376–81.

313. Żarnowska, *Rozłam*, p. 142. For Kelles-Krauz's view, see *Interim*, "Z całej Polski," *Krytyka* 1(1) 1905: 75–79.

314. Żarnowska, *Rozłam*, pp. 108–111, 148–53; Pawłowski, *Geneza*, pp. 105–108.

315. Pawłowski, *Geneza*, pp. 38–39,42–43; Wojciechowski, *Wspomnienia*, p. 162; Suleja, *Polska Partia*, p. 70.

316. Kelles-Krauz in Vienna to KZPPS in London, 1 December 1904, *Listy* II, p. 834.

317. Kelles-Krauz in Vienna to KZPPS in London, 28 December 1904, *Listy* II, p. 841.

318. Janina Kelles-Krauz, "Mój ojciec," p. 95.

319. Steenson, *Kautsky*, p. 137. It was published as *Michael Lusnia*, "Die Lage in Polen und Litauen," *Sozialistische Monatshefte* 9(1) 1905: 234–41.

320. Kelles-Krauz in Vienna to Jędrzejowski in Cracow, 16 February 1905, *Listy* II, p. 849.

321. *Interim*, "Z całej Polski," *Krytyka* 1(2) 1905: 161–67.

322. *Interim*, "Z całej Polski" *Krytyka* 1(3) 1905: 250–55.

323. PPS membership reached some 55,000, SDKPiL membership reached some 30,000.

324. Garlicki, *Piłsudski*, pp. 89, 93, 100; Żarnowska, *Rozłam*, pp. 131–32; Pawłowski, *Geneza*, p. 49.

325. Żarnowska, *Rozłam*, pp. 178–84; Pawłowski, *Geneza*, pp. 55–56; Wasilewski, *Zarys 1925*, p. 163.

326. Kelles-Krauz in Vienna to Jodko-Narkiewicz in Cracow, 16 March 1905, *Listy* II, p. 852; Kelles-Krauz in Vienna to Piłsudski in Cracow, 18 March 1905, *Listy* II, pp. 856–57.

327. Garlicki, *Piłsudski*, p. 95.

328. Kelles-Krauz in Vienna to Piłsudski in Cracow, 18 March 1905, *Listy* II, pp. 856–57.

329. Interim, "Z całej Polski," *Krytyka* 1(5) May 1905: 420.

330. Janina Kelles-Krauz, "Mój ojciec," p. 95. For an outline of his projected book on historical materialism, see *Ossolineum* (18/89).

331. Żarnowska, *Rozłam*, pp. 198–202.

332. Three of whom, Wojciechowski bitterly recalled, were of Jewish descent. *Wspomnienia*, p. 170.

333. Narrative accounts: Żarnowska, *Rozłam*, pp. 215–23, 226–29; Garlicki, *Piłsudski*, pp. 99–101.

334. Stanisław Kalabiński and Feliks Tych, *Czwarte powstanie czy pierwsza rewolucja* (Warsaw, 1969), pp. 170–72.

CONCLUSION

1. Bukowiński, "Kazimierz Krauz," p. 293.

2. "Kazimierz Kellés-Krauz," *Przedświt* 6–8 (1905): 235.

3. Limanowski, *Pamiętniki*, pp. 601–602.

4. Garlicki, *Piłsudski*, p. 224; Górski, *Idea*, p. 49.

5. Eric Hobsbawm, "Introduction: Inventing Traditions," in Eric Hobsbawn and Terence Ranger, eds., *The Invention of Tradition* (Cambridge, 1993), p. 13.

6. Stephen Turner and Regis Factor, *Max Weber and the dispute over reason and value* (London, 1984), pp. 57–61.

7. I have in mind the young Lukács; or in his own later words, "the author of *History and Class Consciousness*."

8. In general, Kelles-Krauz's preference for culture over economics is characteristic of Western Marxism. Walter Benjamin and the scholars of the Institute of Social Research in Frankurt also turned their attention to art. Like Kelles-Krauz, the members of the Frankfurt School wrote about the family and tradition under capitalism. Kelles-Krauz's arguments about repressed needs anticipated Marcuse's use of the term.

9. It would be mistaken to think that Kelles-Krauz was a patriotic Marxist simply because he was Polish. Most Polish Marxists of the time took a much more hesitant, or even hostile, stance toward national independence. Interestingly, Kelles-Krauz found allies among European Marxists who were, as he was, historicist and influenced by Vico and Hegel: Labriola, Sorel, and Herr.

Notes to pages 190–195

10. This is not to say that Kelles-Krauz disregarded the differences among nations. He was alert to the fact that different kinds of national histories posed different intellectual and political problems for nationalists—for example, that nations with a state tradition will try to restore former state boundaries, while nations without a state tradition will rely on ethnographic claims. But he concentrated on the essential aspirations which nationalisms have in common.

11. Kelles-Krauz's place in the Marxist tradition on this question is treated very well in Marian Bębenek, *Teoria narodu i kwestia narodowa u Kazimierza Kelles-Krauza* (Cracow, 1987).

12. K. Radosławski, "Liczmany nauki i polityki," *Krytyka* 4(3) 1902: 165–71; Kelles-Krauz, "Darwinizm," pp. 525–26.

13. Tim Snyder, "Czy obywatele nie potrzebują ojczyzny?" *Społeczeństwo otwarte* 7-8 (1994): 21–23.

14. Jerzy Szacki, "Koncepcja narodu w socjologii i historii," in *Dylematy historiografii idei* (Warsaw, 1991), pp. 353–55.

15. Walicki, "Luxemburg," p. 582.

16. Eric Hobsbawn and Terence Ranger, eds., *The Invention of Tradition* (Cambridge, 1993); Ernest Gellner, *Nations and Nationalism* (Oxford, 1983); Benedict Anderson, *Imagined Communities* (London, 1983).

17. Julian Barnes, *Flaubert's Parrot* (London, 1985), p. 38.

Bibliography

MANUSCRIPT SOURCES

*Archives of the Paris Okhrana, Hoover Institution,
Stanford, United States.*

Summary of honor court proceedings of Jan Lorentowicz, Index Number XIX, folder 2.

Letters seized from Stanisław and Władysław Grabski, Index Number XIX, folder 5.

Reports of E. H. Brunet to Paris Okhrana, Index Number XIX, folder 2A.

Reports of Bronisław Malankiewicz to Paris Okhrana, Index Number XIX, folder 4B.

*Archiwum Lewicy (Oddział VII), Archiwum Akt Nowych,
Warsaw, Poland.*

Letters from PPS leaders to Kazimierz Kelles-Krauz, Index Number 305.

Archiwum Główne Akt Dawnych, Warsaw, Poland.

Rewizja Inflant (tak zwana Metryka Litewska), signature IV B.28, p. 288.

Sumariusz Metryki Litewskiej, signature IV, p. 163. Metryka Koronna, signature ks. 131, p. 66.

Kancelaria Pomocnika Generał-Gubernatora Warszawskiego do spraw policyjnich, file 87.

Biblioteka Polska, Paris, France.

Papers of Kazimierz Kelles-Krauz's acquaintances in Paris.

Dział Rękopisów, Biblioteka Zakładu Narodowego im.
Ossolińskich "Ossolineum" Wrocław, Poland.

Papers of Kazimierz Kelles-Krauz, unsorted materials, folders 18/89 and 18/ 90.
Copies of articles by Kazimierz Kelles-Krauz, signatures 28/77, 291/78, 292/ 78.
Maria Kelles-Krauzowa, "Wspomnienie o Kazimierzu Kelles-Krauzie," signature
II 13518.

PRINTED SOURCES[*]
1. Primary Sources

a. **Correspondence**

Kazimierz Kelles-Krauz, *Listy,* 2 vols., eds. Feliks Tych et al. Warsaw, 1984. *Listy* I and
Listy II
Antonio Labriola, *Korespondencja,* Warsaw, 1986.
Labriola, *Korespondencja*
Róża Luksemburg, *Listy do Leona Jogichesa-Tyszki,* 2 vols., ed. Feliks Tych. Warsaw,
1968.
Jogiches I and *Jogiches* II
Józef Piłsudski, "Listy Józefa Piłsudskiego," ed. Władysław Pobóg-Malinowski and
Leon Wasilewski, *Niepodległość* 1937 (15).
Józef Piłsudski, "Listy Józefa Piłsudskiego," ed. Władysław Pobóg-Malinowski and
Leon Wasilewski, *Niepodległość* 1938 (18).
Józef Piłsudski, "Listy Józefa Piłsudskiego," *Niepodległość* 1939 (20).
"Listy Józefa Piłsudskiego z okresu PPS," ed. Wacław Jędrzejewicz, *Niepodległość*
1978 (11).
Jędrzejewicz, "Listy"
"Listy Józefa Piłsudskiego z okresu PPS," ed. Wacław Jędrzejewicz, *Niepodległość*
1980 (13).
Leon Wasilewski, "Listy Leona Wasilewskiego," ed. Stanisław Giza, *Niepodległość* 1937 (16).
Gabriela Zapolska, *Listy,* vol. 1. Warsaw, 1980, Zapolska, *Listy*

b. **Collections of Documents**

Materiały do historyi P.P.S. i ruchu rewolucyjnego w zaborze rosyjskim od r. 1893-1904,
vols. 1 and 2. Warsaw, 1907 and 1911. *Materiały I* and *Materiały II*
Histoire de la IIe Internationale, vol. 10, Congrès Internationale Socialiste des Travailleurs
et des Chambres Syndicales Ouvrières, Londres 26 Juillet–2 Août 1896. Geneva, 1980.

---

[*] In the endnotes following each chapter, I have given the full citation the first time a source
is used, and a short title reference thereafter. The form of the short title reference is given
here just beneath the full citation.

IIe Internationale 10

Histoire de la IIe Internationale, vol. 13, Congrès Socialiste Internationale, Paris, 23-27 Septembre 1900. Geneva, 1980.

IIe Internationale 13

c. Memoirs and Diaries

Ignacy Daszyński, *Pamiętniki,* vol. 1. Warsaw, 1957.

Daszyński, *Pamiętniki*

Ignacy Daszyński, "Wspomnienia. Przyczynek do dziejów PPS," *Księga Pamiątkowa PPS,* pp. 150–58. Warsaw, 1923.

Stanisław Grabski, *Pamiętniki,* vol. 1. Warsaw, 1989.

Grabski, *Pamiętniki*

Ludwik Krzywicki, *Wspomnienia,* vol. 2. Warsaw, 1958.

Krzywicki, *Wspomnienia*

Bolesław Limanowski, *Pamiętniki,* vol. 2 (1870–1907). Warsaw, 1958.

Limanowski, *Pamiętniki*

Jan Lorentowicz, *Spojrzenie wstecz.* Warsaw, 1935.

Lorentowicz, *Spojrzenie*

Kazimierz Pietkiewicz, "Niecała No. 12," in *Księga pamiątkowa PPS,* pp. 39–43. Warsaw, 1923.

Stanisław Radwan, "Wspomnienia z życia koleżeńskiego w latach 1889–1905," in *Jednodniówka Zjazdu Koleżeńskiego Radomiaków w dniu 6,7, i 8 maja 1923 r. w Radomiu.* Warsaw, 1924

Michał Sokolnicki, *Czternaście lat.* Warsaw, 1936.

Sokolnicki, *Czternaście lat*

sp., "Wspomnienia z dwóch lat (1892–1893)," *Z Pola Walki,* pp. 28–34. London, 1904.

sp., "Wspomnienia"

Leon Wasilewski, "Z roboty zagranicznej P.P.S.," in *Księga pamiątkowa PPS,* pp. 164–83. Warsaw, 1923.

Wasilewski, "Z roboty"

Stanisław Wojciechowski, *Moje wspomnienia,* vol. 1. Lviv [Lwów] and War-saw, 1938.

Wojciechowski, *Wspomnienia*

Stefan Żeromski, *Dzienniki.* Warsaw, 1965.

d. Collected Publications by Kelles-Krauz

Kazimierz Kelles-Krauz, *Pisma wybrane,* 2 vols. Warsaw, 1962.

Pisma I and *Pisma* II

Kazimierz Krauz, "J. J. Bachofen," *Prawda* 21(43) 6 October 1901; 21(44) 13 October 1901. [In *Pisma* II, pp. 226–40.]

[Kazmierz Kelles-Krauz] Elehard Esse, "Comtisme et marxisme," *Revue Socialiste* 197 (1901): 589–605. Published in Polish as "Pozytywizm i monistyczne pojmowanie dziejów," *Głos* 1904 (18): 283–85; 1904 (19): 299–301; 1904 (20): 314–15. [In *Pisma* II as "Comtizm i marksizm," pp. 42–62.]

Kazimierz Kelles-Krauz, "Czy jesteśmy patriotami we właściwym znaczeniu tego słowa?" [In *Pisma* II, pp. 31–35.]

Kelles-Krauz, "Jesteśmy patriotami?"

Kazimierz Krauz, "Czym jest materializm ekonomiczny," *Prawda* 21(37) 1 September 1901: 450–51; 21(38) 8 September: 462–63; 21(39) 15 September: 375–76. [In *Pisma* I, pp. 11–41.]

Kelles-Krauz, "Materializm"

Kazimierz Krauz, "Demokracja w nowoczesnym ustroju państwowym," *Głos* 1905 (1): 1–2; 1905 (3): 41–43; 1905 (4): 59–61; 1905 (8): 105–108; 1905 (11): 154–56; 1905(12): 171–72; 1905(13): 187–89; 1905(14): 203–205; 1905 (17): 252–53; 1905 (18): 267–68; 1905 (21): 314–16. [In *Pisma* II, pp. 397–463.]

Kelles-Krauz, "Demokracja"

Kazimierz Krauz, "Dialektyka społeczna w filozofii Vica," *Przegląd Filozoficzny* 1901 (2): 172–89. [In *Pisma* I, pp. 169–87.]

Kelles-Krauz, "Vico"

Kazimierz Krauz, "Ekonomiczne podstawy pierwotnych form rodziny," *Krytyka* 1900: 555–75. [In *Pisma* I, pp. 63–87.]

Kazimierz Krauz, "Kilka głównych zasad rozwoju sztuki," in *Poradnik dla samouków* 2 (Warsaw, 1905): 887–1013. [In *Pisma* I, pp. 420–529.]

Kelles-Krauz, "Sztuka"

[Kazimierz Kelles-Krauz] Elehard Esse, "Międzynarodowa polityka proletariatu (w kwestii wschodniej)," *Przedświt* 1897 (10): 4–12. [In *Pisma* II, pp. 36–60.]

[Kazimierz Kelles-Krauz] Michał Luśnia, "Niepodległość Polski a materialistyczne pojmowanie dziejów," *Krytyka* 7(4) April 1905: 277–85; 7(5) May 1905: 400–412. [In *Pisma* II, pp. 370–94.]

Kelles-Krauz, "Pojmowanie"

[Kazimierz Kelles-Krauz] Michał Luśnia, "Niepodległość Polski w programie socjalistycznym," Paris, 1900. [In *Pisma* II, pp. 125–68.]

Kelles-Krauz, "Niepodległość"

Kazimierz Krauz, "O tak zwanym 'Kryzysie marksizmu,'" *Przegląd Filozoficzny* 1900 (3)2: 87–94; 1900 (3)3: 80–99. [In *Pisma* II as "Kryzys marksizmu," pp. 108–137.]

Kelles-Krauz, "Kryzys"

[Kazimierz Kelles-Krauz] Michał Luśnia, "Ostatnie nieporozumienie," *Przedświt* 1900 (7): 7–17. [In *Pisma* II, pp. 168–85.]

Kelles-Krauz, "Nieporozumienie"

[Kazimierz Kelles-Krauz] M. Luśnia, "Porachunek z rewizjonistami," *Przedświt* 1903 (10): 435–40; 1903 (11–12): 471–78. [In *Pisma* II, pp. 297–317.]

Kazimierz Krauz, *Portrety zmarłych socjologów.* Warsaw, 1906. [In *Pisma* I, pp. 315–15.]

Kelles-Krauz, *Portrety*

[Kazimierz Kelles-Krauz] M. Luśnia, "Program narodowościowy Socjalnej Demokracji Austriackiej a program PPS," *Przedświt* 1903 (7): 276–83; 1903 (8): 333–41. [In *Pisma* II, pp. 275–96.]
Kelles-Krauz, "Program"

[Kazimierz Kelles-Krauz] Michał Luśnia, "Rewizja programu agrarnego," *Przedświt* 1904 (9): 360–70; 1904 (10): 413–41. [In *Pisma* II, pp. 342–69.]

[Kazimierz Kelles-Krauz], "Ruch społeczny w starożytności," *Głos* 1903 (21): 336–37; 1903 (22): 350–51; 1903 (24): 381–84; 1903 (26): 416–18. [In *Pisma* I, pp. 138–68.]

Kazimierz Krauz, "Rzut oka na rozwój socjologii w XIX wieku," in Stanisław Grabski and Kazimierz Krauz, *Rzut oka na rozwój ekonomii i socjologii w XIX wieku.* Warsaw, 1901. [In *Pisma* I, pp. 282–313.]
Kelles-Krauz, "Rzut oka"

[Kazimierz Kelles-Krauz] Michał Luśnia, "Sartor sarritus albo czy się Ostoja ostoi?," *Przedświt* 1898 (11): 11–17. [In *Pisma* II, pp. 61–101.]

[Kazimierz Kelles-Krauz] Elehard Esse, "Socialistes polonais et russes," *L'Humanité Nouvelle* April 1899: 434–50; and as a pamphlet, Paris 1899. [In translation in *Pisma* II as "Polscy i rosyjscy socjaliści," pp. 104–126.]
Kelles-Krauz, "Socjaliści"

[Kazimierz Kelles-Krauz] M. Luśnia, "Widoki rewolucji," *Przedświt* 1902 (8): 286–92; 1902 (9): 325–33. [In *Pisma* II, pp. 227–51.]
Kelles-Krauz, "Widoki"

[Kazimierz Kelles-Krauz] Michał Luśnia, "W kwestii narodowości żydowskiej," *Krytyka* 6(1) 1904: 52–61; 6(2) 1904: 120–30. [In *Pisma* II, pp. 318–41.]
Kelles-Kraus, "Kwestia"

Kazimierz Krauz, "Wiek złoty, stan natury i rozwój w sprzecznościach," *Przegląd Filozoficzny* 1903 (3): 313–20; 1903 (4): 414–26; 1904 (1): 19–33. [In *Pisma* I, pp. 188–225.]
Kelles-Krauz, "Wiek złoty"

e. Uncollected Publications by Kelles-Krauz

Bulletin: Bulletin Officiel du Parti Socialiste Polonais
Annales: Annales de l'Institut International de Sociologie

[Kazimierz Kelles-Krauz] "L'affaire Sawicki," *Bulletin Officiel du Parti Socialiste Polonais* 8 (July 1896): 7.

[Kazimierz Kelles-Krauz] K. Radosławski, "Alkoholizm i walka z nim," *Prawda* 21(18) 21 April 1901: 220–21; 21(19) 28 April: 232–33; 21(20) 5 May: 246–47; 21(21) 12 May: 257–58; 21(22) 19 May: 269–71.

[Kazimierz Kelles-Krauz] "L'Alliance Franco-Russe. Lettre ouverte du Parti Socialiste Polonais aux Socialistes Frančais," *Bulletin Officiel du Parti Socialiste Polonais* 12 (January 1897): 1–17.
Kelles-Krauz, "Alliance"

[Kazimierz Kelles-Krauz] "L'Alliance Franco-Russe," *Bulletin Officiel du Parti Socialiste Polonais* 13 (March 1897): 1–4.

Kazimierz Krauz, "Antysemitizm we Francji," *Prawda* 13(14) 8 April 1893: 158–59; 13(15) 15 April 1893: 170–71; 13(16) 22 April 1893: 183–84.

[Kazimierz Kelles-Krauz] Michał Luśnia, "Aryele," in "Majówka," supplement to *Naprzód* 14(97) 1 May 1905: 5–6.

K. Krauz, "Badanie z historii rodziny," *Prawda* 23(17) 25 April 1903: 199–200.

[Kazimierz Kelles-Krauz] K. Radosławski, "Bajarz dla herbowych próżniaków," *Prawda* 24(3) 16 January 1904: 32–33.

[Kazimierz Kelles-Krauz] Michał Luśnia, "Carmaux," *Przedświt* 1895 (12): 19–26.

K. Krauz, "Coignard i Bergeret, czyli metamorfoza skeptyka," *Prawda* 22(33) 16 August 1902: 392–93; 22(34) 23 August 1902: 406–407.

[Kazimierz Kelles-Krauz] Elehard Esse, "Le 'Compromis' Polono-Russe," *Bulletin Officiel du Parti Socialiste Polonais* 19 (November 1897): 1–9.

Kelles-Krauz, "Compromis"

[Kazimierz Kelles-Krauz] "Au Congrès de Londres," *Bulletin Officiel du Parti Socialiste Polonais* 10 (September 1896): 1–2.

[Kazimierz Kelles-Krauz] "Contre la paix du tsar," *Bulletin Officiel du Parti Socialiste Polonais* 26 (May 1899).

[Kazimierz Kelles-Krauz] K. Radosławski, "Cuda zamorskie," *Prawda* 22(35) 30 August 1902: 411–13.

[Kazimierz Kelles-Krauz] K. Radosławski, "Czyny Milleranda," *Prawda* 22(14) 5 April 1902: 172–73.

K. Krauz, "Darwinizm w socyologii," *Prawda* 23(43) 24 October 1903: 512—13; 23(44) 31 October 1903: 525–26.

Kelles-Krauz, "Darwinizm"

[Kazimierz Kelles-Krauz] "Le Dixième Anniversaire du Martyre des Quatre Socialistes Polonais," *Bulletin Officiel du Parti Socialiste Polonais* 6 (January 1896): 1–3.

[Kazimierz Kelles-Krauz] "Dlaczego dążymy do niepodległości," *Robotnik* 53 (14 December 1903): 5–8.

Kelles-Krauz, "Dlaczego"

[Kazimierz Kelles-Krauz] E. E., "Dwa kierunki w socyalizmie włoskim," *Przedświt* 1903 (1): 9–15.

K. Krauz, "Dwaj etnologowie, Adolf Bastian i Eliasz Reclus," *Prawda* 25(12) 19 March 1905: 440–41.

[Kazimierz Kelles-Krauz] K. Radosławski, "Dziennik służącej. Octave Mirbeau. Le Journal d'une femme de chambre," *Prawda* 21(49) 24 November 1901: 595–96.

Kazimierz Krauz, "Ekonomistyczne pojmowanie wieków średnich," *Prawda* 16(26) 1896: 307; 16(27) 1896: 319–20; 16(28) 1896: 332–33. [Read in manuscript at Ossolineum, signatures 28/77, 291/78, 292/78.]

Kazimierz Kelles-Krauz, "Filozofia marksizmu," *Krytyka* 1(2) February 1902: 329–39.

[Kazimierz Kelles-Krauz] M. Luśnia, "Francuskie partie polityczne," *Światło* 1(3) 1898: 118–26. [Read in manuscript at Ossolineum, signatures 28/77, 291/78,292/78.]

Kazimierz Krauz, "Historia Polski na podstawie ekonomicznej," *Prawda* 22(8) 22 February 1902: 91–92; 22(9) 1 March 1902: 102–104; 22(10) 8 March 1902: 114–15; 22(11) 15 March 1902: 128–29.

Kazimierz Krauz, "Indywidualizm w dziennikarstwie," *Prawda* 13(45) 1893: 535–36. [Read in manuscript at Ossolineum, signatures 28/77, 291/78, 292/78.]

K. Krauz, "Instytut Socjologiczny w Brukseli," *Prawda* 23(5) 31 January 1903: 56; 23(6) 7 February 1903: 68.

K. Krauz, "Izby pracy," *Prawda* 23(44) 29 October 1904: 522–23.

Kazimierz Krauz, "Jak się narody rządzą." Warsaw, 1906.

Kelles-Krauz, "Narody"

Kazimierz Krauz, "Jeszcze o organizmie społecznym," *Prawda* 17(18) 19 April 1897: 210; 17(19) 26 April: 224–25.

[Kazimierz Kelles-Krauz] K. Radosławski, "Judyta i Rachela," *Prawda* 22(4) 25 January 1902: 44–45.

K. Krauz, "Kapitalizm i dziecieństwo," *Prawda* 25(4) 28 January 1905:44–45.

K. Krauz, "Kapitalizm i ludzkość," *Prawda* 25(5) 11 February 1905: 53–54.

K. Krauz, "Kapitalizm i macierzyńswto," *Prawda* 25(3) 21 January 1905: 29–30.

K. Krauz, "Kilka uwag o psychologii w socjologii (Z ostatniego kongresu socjologicznego)," *Ogniwo* 2(43) 22 October 1904: 1011–1012. Kelles-Krauz, "Psychologia"

[Kazimierz Kelles-Krauz] zz., "Koło polskie i wojsko austryackie," *Prawda* 23(9) 28 February 1903: 98–99.

Kazimierz Krauz, "Kongres kobiecy," *Prawda* 12(18): 22 (1892). [Read in manuscript at Ossolineum, signatures 28/77, 291/78, 292/78.] Kelles-Krauz, "Kongres kobiecy 1892"

Kazimierz Krauz, "Kongres kobiecy," *Prawda* 17 (1896): 197–98; 18 (1896): 209. [Read in manuscript at Ossolineum, signatures 28/77, 291/78, 292/ 78.]

Kelles-Krauz, "Kongres kobiecy 1896"

K. Krauz, "Konrad czy Hamlet," *Prawda* 23(11) 14 March 1903: 127–28; 23(12) 21 March 1903: 141–42; 23(13) 28 March 1903: 52.

[Kazimierz Kelles-Krauz] M. Luśnia, "Konstytucja francuska," *Światło* 1(4) 1898: 158–70.

[Kazimierz Kelles-Krauz] K. Radosławski, "Krytyka zasady narodowości," *Prawda* 23(42) 17 October 1903: 496–97.

[Kazimierz Kelles-Krauz] Michał Luśnia, "Kryzys Trade-Unionizmu," *Przedświt* 1902 (11-12): 423–30.

[Kazimierz Kelles-Krauz] r., "Kuno i War," *Przedświt* 1896 (1–3): 17.

[Kazimierz Kelles-Krauz] M. Luśnia, "Kwestia samorządu," *Przedświt* 1901 (8): 287–90.

Kazimierz Krauz, "Kwestja kobieca w poezjach Konopnickiej," *Krytyka* 1902: 264–69. [Read in manuscript at Ossolineum, signatures 28/77, 291/78, 292/78.]

[Kazimierz Kelles-Krauz] M. Luśnia, "Kwestya agrarna w parliamencie francuskim," *Przedświt* 1898 (3): 5–9.

[Kazimierz Kelles-Krauz] Michael Luśnia, "Die Lage in Polen und Litauen," *Sozialistische Monatshefte* 9(1) 1905: 234–41.

[Kazimierz Kelles-Krauz], "Lettre ouverte du Parti Socialiste Polonais au Ve Congrès Pénitentiaire Internationale," *Bulletin Officiel du Parti Socialiste Polonais* 2 (July 1895): 1–7.

[Kazimierz Kelles-Krauz] K. Radosławski, "Liczmany nauki i polityki," *Krytyka* 4(3) March 1902: 165–71.

K. Krauz, "Liga kupujących," *Prawda* 25(9) 11 March 1905: 101–103.

[Kazimierz Kelles-Krauz] zz., "List z Wiednia," *Prawda* 23(41) 27 September 1903: 482–84.

[Kazimierz Kelles-Krauz] zz., "List z Wiednia," *Prawda* 23(46) 14 November 1903: 542–43.

[Kazimierz Kelles-Krauz] zz., "List z Wiednia," *Prawda* 24(45) 23 October 1904: 530–31.

[Kazimierz Kelles-Krauz] zz., "List z Wiednia," *Prawda* 24(49) 3 December 1904: 581–82.

[Kazimierz Kelles-Krauz] zz., "List z Wiednia," *Prawda* 25(6) 18 February 1905: 64–66.

[Kazimierz Kelles-Krauz] K. Radosławski, "Listy z Wiednia," *Prawda* 21(24) 2 June 1901: 290–92.

[Kazimierz Kelles-Krauz] K. Radosławski, "Listy z Wiednia," *Prawda* 21(24) 15 June 1901: 290–92.

[Kazimierz Kelles-Krauz] K. R., "Listy z Wiednia," *Prawda* 21(50) 1 December 1901: 602–603.

[Kazimierz Kelles-Krauz] K. R., "Listy z Wiednia," *Prawda* 21(50) 14 December 1901: 602–603.

[Kazimierz Kelles-Krauz] K. R., "Listy z Wiednia," *Prawda* 22(17) 26 April 1902: 195–97.

[Kazimierz Kelles-Krauz] K. Radosławski, "Listy z Wiednia," *Prawda* 23(16) 18 April 1903: 182–84.

[Kazimierz Kelles-Krauz] zz., "Listy z Wiednia," *Prawda* 23(19) 9 May 1903: 218–20.

[Kazimierz Kelles-Krauz] zz., "Listy z Wiednia. Sprawa Erhardta," *Prawda* 23(4) 24 January 1903: 42–43.

[Kazimierz Kelles-Krauz] K. Radosławski, "Listy z Wiednia. Ugoda z Węgrami i parlament przedlitawski," *Prawda* 22(45) 8 November 1902: 530–31.

[Kazimierz Kelles-Krauz] K. Radosławski, "Listy z Wiednia. Z polytiki socjalnej," *Prawda* 21(29) 7 July 1901: 351–53.

[Kazimierz Kelles-Krauz] K. Radosławski, "Listy z Wiednia. Z polytiki socjalnej," *Prawda* 21(29) 20 July 1901: 351–53.

[Kazimierz Kelles-Krauz] K. Radosławski, "Literatura francuska. Dramat tytonów. Danton. Trois actes de Romain Rolland," *Prawda* 21(44) 20 October 1901: 535–37.

[Kazimierz Kelles-Krauz] K. Radosławski, "Literatura francuska. Idealizm Zoli," *Prawda* 21(35) 18 August 1901: 427–29.

C. de Krauz, "La loi de la rétrospection revolutionnaire vis-à-vis de la théorie de l'imitation," *Annales de l'Institut International de Sociologie* 2 (1896): 315–38.

Bibliography   281

Kelles-Krauz, "Loi"

[Kazimierz Kelles-Krauz] K. Radosławski, "Lucyan Muhlfeld," *Prawda* 23(18) 2 May 1903:214–15.

[Kazimierz Kelles-Krauz] "Mlle Rose Luxemburg," *Bulletin Officiel du Parti Socialiste Polonais* 23 (February 1899): 19–20.

K. Krauz, "Metoda ankiet monograficznych," *Prawda* 22(28) 12 July 1902: 330–32; 22(29) 19 July 1902: 343–45.

[Kazimierz Kelles-Krauz] K. Radosławski, "Międzynarodowa ochrona pracy," *Prawda* 23(43) 22 October 1904: 509–510; 23(44) 31 October 1903: 522–23.

Kazimierz Krauz, "Mieszkanie za darmo," *Prawda* 13(31) 5 August 1893: 367–68; 13(32) 12 August 1893: 378–79.

[Kazimierz Kelles-Krauz] "Les motifs de notre programme," *Bulletin Officiel du Parti Socialiste Polonais* 9 (July 1896): 1–5.

Kelles-Krauz, "Les motifs"

[Kazimierz Kelles-Krauz] Elehard Esse, "Le mouvement socialiste à l'étranger. Pologne," *Devenir Social* 1898 (5): 445–63.

[Kazimierz Kelles-Krauz] Elehard Esse, "Le mouvement socialiste à l'étranger. Pologne," *Devenir Social* 1898 (11): 817–38.

K. Krauz, "Muzyka i ekonomia," *Prawda* 21(1) 4 January 1901: 8; 21(2) 11 January 1901:20–21.

Kelles-Krauz, "Muzyka"

[Kazimierz Kelles-Krauz] 1., "Na Emigracyi. W Paryżu," *Przedświt* 1895 (5): 13.

[Kazimierz Kelles-Krauz] M. Luśnia, "Nasza broń klasowa," *Światło* 1(1) 1898: 15–20.

K. Krauz, "Nauka, ideał i czyn," *Prawda* 21(45) 27 October 1901: 547; 21(46) 2 November 1901: 561.

Kelles-Krauz, "Nauka"

[Kazimierz Kelles-Krauz] K. Radosławski, "Nowa teoria narodowości i państwa w Austryi," *Prawda* 23(7) 14 February 1903: 74; 23(8) 21 February 1903: 86–87; 23(9) 28 February 1903: 99–101; 23(11) 14 March 1903: 122–24.

Kelles-Krauz, "Nowa teoria"

[Kazimierz Kelles-Krauz] K. Radosławski, "Nowe Dziewiętnaścioro Przykazań, czyli Koniec demokracyi chrześciańskiej," *Krytyka* 1(4) April 1904: 273–79.

[Kazimierz Kelles-Krauz] K. Kr., "O prawdę. In Verba magistri?," *Prawda* 22(11) 15 March 1902: 131; 22(12) 22 March 1902: 142–43.

K. Krauz, "Obowiązkowe towarzystwa rolnicze," *Prawda* 22(5) 1 February 1902: 58; 22(6) 8 February 1902: 70–71.

Kazimierz Krauz, "Ochrona prawna robotników rolnych," in *Myśl*, Warsaw 1904: 152–61.

[Kazimierz Kelles-Krauz] "Offener Brief der Polnischen Sozialistischen Partei (PPS) Deutschlands an die Deutsche Sozialdemokratie," Berlin 1903.

K. Krauz, "Opieka nad emigrantami," *Prawda* 23(21) 30 May 1903: 258–59.

K. Krauz, "Opieka nad pracującemi dziećmi," *Prawda* 23(20) 23 May 1903: 245–46.

K. Krauz, "Oświata w dziełach Zoli," *Prawda* 23(10) 22 February 1903: 116–18.

[Kazimierz Kelles-Krauz] K., "Otwarcie wyższych kursów wakacyjnych w Zakopanem," *Gazeta Polska* 212 (1904).

[Kazimierz Kelles-Krauz] Michał Luśnia, "Państwo konspiracyjne i Skarb Narodowy," *Przedświt* 1895 (10-11): 9–10.

K. Krauz, "Pięciolecie Instytutu Socjologicznego," *Przegląd Filozoficzny* 4 (1897-1898): 93–113.

Kelles-Krauz, "Pięciolecie"

[Kazimierz Kelles-Krauz] Elehard Esse, "Po dymisyi Milleranda," *Przedświt* 1902 (9): 338–45.

[Kazimierz Kelles-Krauz] M. Luśnia, "Po uchwaleniu taryfy celnej," *Przedświt* 1903 (2): 44–52.

[Kazimierz Kelles-Krauz] Elehard Esse, "La politique internationale du proletariat et la question d'Orient," *Devenir Social* 1898 (7-8): 565–89.

[Kazimierz Kelles-Krauz] "Pologne, Arménie, et Mlle Rose Luxemburg," *Bulletin Officiel du Parti Socialiste Polonais* 12: 21–22 (January 1897).

[Kazimierz Kelles-Krauz] Michał Luśnia, "Pomnik Mickiewicza," *Przedświt* 1897 (4): 4–5.

[Kazimierz Kelles-Krauz] R., "Pomoc społeczna w gospodarstwie kobiecem," *Prawda* 23(14) 4 April 1903: 160–61.

K. Krauz, "Postępy prawodawstwa pracy," *Prawda* 24(46) 30 October 1904: 549–50; 24(50) 10 December 1904: 598–99.

[Kazimierz Kelles-Krauz] K. Radosławski, "Postępy społeczne w Włoszech," *Prawda* 23(15) 11 April 1903: 173–75.

[Kazimierz Kelles-Krauz] K. Radosławski, "Poszukiwania. Odpowiedź Orońska," *Wisła* 25(4) July-August 1901: 489–501; 25(5) September-October 1901: 619–33 Kelles-Krauz, "Poszukiwania"

[Kazimierz Kelles-Krauz] "Pour la Crète—Contre la Pologne," *Bulletin Officiel du Parti Socialiste Polonais* 13 (March 1897): 6.

K. Krauz, "Powstawanie stylów z gospodarstwa społecznego," *Prawda* 22(21) 24 May 1902: 246–47; 22(22) 31 May 1902: 259–60.

Kelles-Krauz, "Powstawanie"

[Kazimierz Kelles-Krauz] K. R., "Prawa człowieka i prawodawstwo fabryczne w Ameryce," *Prawda* 24(4) 23 February 1904: 42–43.

[Kazimierz Kelles-Krauz] C. Halak, "Próba agitacyi na wsi przed laty dziesięciu," *Przedświt* 1902 (1): 21–24.

Kelles-Krauz, "Próba"

[Kazimierz Kelles-Krauz] K. Radosławski, "Proletariat uliczny i jego poezja miłosna," *Krytyka* 5(2) 1896: 61–71; 5(3): 128–35

Kelles-Krauz, "Uliczny"

[Kazimierz Kelles-Krauz] M. Luśnia, "Przedwczesny 'realizm,'" *Przedświt* 1904 (9): 376–81.

K. Krauz, "Przemysł i sztuka," *Prawda* 23(14) 4 April 1903: 163–64. Kelles-Krauz, "Przemysł"

[Kazimierz Kelles-Krauz] K. Kr., "Przemysł rosyjski w oświetleniu urzędowem," *Prawda* 22(46) 15 November 1902: 549–50; 22(47) 22 November 1902: 562–63; 22(48) 29 November 1902: 574–75.

K. Krauz, "Przeszłość w terazniejszość," *Prawda* 21(26) 16 June 1901: 319— 20.

Casimir de Krauz, "La psychiatrie et la science des idées," *Annales de l'Institut International de Sociologie* 1 (1895): 253–303.

Kelles-Krauz, "Idées"

Casimir de Kellès-Krauz, "Qu'est-ce que le materialisme économique," *Annales de l'Institut International de Sociologie* 8 (1902): 49–91.

Casimir de Kellès-Krauz, "Quelques observations sur la psychologie dans la sociologie," *Annales de l'Institut International de Sociologie* 10 (1904): 281–87.

[Kazimierz Kelles-Krauz] "La question polonaise au Congrès de Hambourg," *Bulletin Officiel du Parti Socialiste Polonais* 19 (November 1897): 9–12.

[Kazimierz Kelles-Krauz] Michał Luśnia, "Rachunek," *Przedświt* 10–11 (1896): 11–15.

K. Krauz, "Radykalizm w Francji," *Ekonomista* 14 (6 July 1900): 113–15; 15 (13 July 1900): 122–24; 16 (20 July 1900): 131; 17 (27 July 1900): 138–39.

K. Krauz, "Reforma górnicza w Prusach," *Ogniwo* 3(23) 10 June 1905: 522–23; 3(24) 17 June 1905: 547–48.

Casimir de Kellès-Krauz, "Réplique," *Annales de l'Institut International de Sociologie* 8 (1902): 307–327.

(Kazimierz Kelles-Krauz] K. Rad., "Robotnicy rolni w Belgii," *Prawda* 22(27) 5 July 1902: 322–23.

K. Krauz, "Robotnik Dramaturg," *Prawda* 22(49) 23 November 1902: 585.

K. Krauz, "Rocznik i kongres socyologiczny," *Prawda* 23(35) 29 August 1903:415–16.

Kelles-Krauz, "Rocznik"

[Kazimierz Kelles-Krauz] Michał Luśnia, "Rok 1848 w Francji," *Przedświt* 1898 (8): 4–8.

[Kazimierz Kelles-Krauz] Michał Luśnia, "Rozmowy towarzyszy o socyalizmie i patriotyzmie, konstytucyi i niepodległości." London 1904.

Kelles-Krauz, "Rozmowy"

K. Krauz, "Ruchy chłopskie na Węgrzech," *Prawda* 25(14) 15 April 1905: 161–62; 25(15) 22 April 1905: 174–75.

[Kazimierz Kelles-Krauz] El. Es., "Rynki rosyjskie a Finlandya," *Przedświt* 1901 (6): 226–29.

Kazimierz Kelles-Krauz, *Die Soziologie im 19. Jahrhundert*. Berlin, 1902.

Casimir de Krauz, "Un Sociologue Polonais. Stanislaw Krusinski," *Annales de l'Institut International de Sociologie* 3 (1897): 405–138. Kelles-Krauz, "Krusinski"

[Kazimierz Kelles-Krauz] M. Luśnia, "Socjalista ministrem," *Przedświt* 1899 (8): 2–8.

[Kazimierz Kelles-Krauz] Elehard Esse, "Socyaliści francuscy wobec sprawy Dreyfusa," *Przedświt* 1898 (8): 14–17.

K. Krauz, "Sprawa kobieca i rodzinna w Włoszech," *Prawda* 22(31) 2 August 1902: 367–68.

K. Krauz, "Sprawa pomocników handlowych," *Prawda* 25(8) 4 March 1905: 87–88.

[Kazimierz Kelles-Krauz] Rad., "Stan ruchu współdzielczego w Anglii," *Prawda* 22(36) 6 September 1902: 430–31.

[Kazimierz Kelles-Krauz] Michał Luśnia, "Święto Majowe Zagranicą. Francja," *Przedświt* 1895 (5): 17–21.

[Kazimierz Kelles-Krauz] M. L., "XVI Kongres Partyi Robotniczej Francuskiej," *Przedświt* 1898 (10): 3–6.

[Kazimierz Kelles-Krauz] R., "Szkoły nauk społecznych," *Prawda* 20(43) 14 October 1900: 513.

Kelles-Krauz, "Szkoły"

[Kazimierz Kelles-Krauz] zz., "Szowinizm i demokracya," *Prawda* 24(5) 30 January 1904:50–51.

[Kazimierz Kelles-Krauz] zz., "Szowinizm i kultura," *Prawda* 24(1) 2 January 1904: 5.

K. Krauz, "Teoria poznania zjawisk gospodarczych," *Prawda* 21(27) 6 July 1901: 330–32; 21(28) 13 July: 343–45.

[Kazimierz Kelles-Krauz] K. Radosławski, "Testament papieża," *Prawda* 22(16) 19 April 1902: 186–87.

Casimir de Krauz, "La théorie organique des sociétés," *Annales de l'Institut International de Sociologie* 4 (1898): 260–89.

Kelles-Krauz, "Théorie organique"

K. Krauz, "Towarzystwo, moda i prawo," *Prawda* 23(3) 17 January 1903: 31–32; 23(4) 24 January 1903: 44–15.

Kazimierz Kelles-Krauz, Wilhelm Feldman, and Odo Bujwid, "Towarzystwo wyższych kursów wakacyjnych," *Krytyka* 1(5) May 1904: 418–19.

[Kazimierz Kelles-Krauz] K. Radosławski, "Trylogia Pawła Adams," *Prawda* 23(23) 6 June 1903: 274; 23(24) 13 June 1903: 286–87.

[Kazimierz Kelles-Krauz] K. Radosławski, "Trzy typy etyczne: honor, cnota, pożytek," *Głos* 6(2) 10 January 1891: 16–17.

[Kazimierz Kelles-Krauz] "Le tsarisme devant le Congrès pénitentiaire," *Bulletin Officiel du Parti Socialiste Polonais* 3 (September 1895): 1–4.

[Kazimierz Kelles-Krauz] M. Luśnia, "Unbewaffnete Revolution?" *Die Neue Zeit* 22(1) 1903–1904: 559–67.

[Kazimierz Kelles-Krauz] K. R., "Uniwersytet ludowy w Wiedniu," *Prawda* 22(13) 28 March 1902: 150.

[Kazimierz Kelles-Krauz] K. Kr, "Uspołecznienia życia codziennego," *Prawda* 12(47) 19 November 1892: 560.

Kazimierz Kelles-Krauz E. Esse, "W Bremie," *Przedświt* 1904 (10-12): 443–50.

[Kazimierz Kelles-Krauz] Michał Luśnia, "W kwestii 'równoległości,'" *Przedświt* 1895 (7): 19–22.

Kelles-Krauz, "Równoległość"

Kazimierz Krauz, "Wolny polski Uniwersytet wakacyjny," *Krytyka* 1(6) June 1904: 455–64

[Kazimierz Kelles-Krauz] K. Radosławski, "Wróg studentek," *Prawda* 15(23) 8 June 1895: 15(24) 15 June 1895: 283–84.

Kazimierz Krauz, "Współzawodnictwo i współdziałanie," *Głos* 1901 (36, 37, 38, 39, 43, 44, 45, 47, 49).

Kazimierz Kelles-Krauz] M. Luśnia, "Wybory w Francji," *Przedświt* 1898 (6): 11–14.

[Kazimierz Kelles-Krauz] K. Radosławski, "Wyodrębnienie Galicyi," *Prawda* 21(50) 8 December 1901: 614–15; 21(51) 15 December 1901: 626–27.

Kazimierz Kelles-Krauz] K. Radosławski, "Wystawa Paryska. August Rodin," *Prawda* 20(31) 22 July 1900: 373–74; 20(32) 29 July 1900: 385–86.

[Kazimierz Kelles-Krauz] K. Radosławski, "Wystawa paryska. Character ogólny," *Prawda* 20(27) 24 June 1900: 321–23.

Kazimierz Kelles-Krauz] K. Radosławski, "Wystawa paryska. Ekonomia społeczna," *Prawda* 20(35) 19 August 1900: 418–19.

[Kazimierz Kelles-Krauz] K. Radosławski, "Wystawa paryska. Szkoła wystawy," *Prawda* 20(28) 1 July 1900: 332–33.

[Kazimierz Kelles-Krauz] Interim, "Z całej Polski," *Krytyka* 1(1) January 1905: 75–79.

[Kazimierz Kelles-Krauz] Interim, "Z całej Polski," *Krytyka* 1(2) February 1905: 161–67.

[Kazimierz Kelles-Krauz] Interim, "Z całej Polski," *Krytyka* 1(3) March 1905: 250–55.

[Kazimierz Kelles-Krauz] Interim, "Z całej Polski," *Krytyka* 1(5) May 1905: 420–23.

K. Krauz, "Z dziedziny nauk państwowych. Esmein i uzasadnienie demokracyi," *Prawda* 25(7) 25 February 1905: 77–79.

K. Krauz, "Z dziedziny nauk społecznych. Pollock i umowa społeczna," *Prawda* 34(39) 24 September 1904: 463–64.

K. Krauz, "Z powodu kongresu drezdeńskiego," *Prawda* 23(42) 17 October 1903: 498–99.

Kazimierz Krauz, "Z powodu kongresu syonistów," *Prawda* 22(14) 5 April 1902: 161–62; 22(15) 12 April 1902: 174–75.

Kelles-Krauz, "Syoniści"

[Kazimierz Kelles-Krauz] K. Radosławski, "Z ruchu społecznego i artystycznego Młodej Belgii," *Krytyka* 1(5-6) May-June 1901: 308–312, 395–401.

Kelles-Krauz, "Z ruchu"

Kazimierz Krauz, "Z wystawy paryskiej," *Prawda* 20(45) 28 October 1900: 536–37; 20(46) 4 November 1900: 550–51; 20(47) 11 November 1900: 562–63; 20(49) 25 November 1900: 584–85.

[Kazimierz Kelles-Krauz] K. Radosławski, "Z życia Francji," *Prawda* 20(13) 18 March 1900: 148–50.

[Kazimierz Kelles-Krauz] K. Radosławski, "Z życia Francji," *Prawda* 20(15) 31 March 1900: 167–74.

[Kazimierz Kelles-Krauz] K. Radosławski, "Z życia Francji," *Prawda* 20(16) 8 April 1900: 188–89.

[Kazimierz Kelles-Krauz] K. Radoslawski, "Z życia Francji. Ankieta w sprawie pracy nocnej," *Prawda* 20(37) 1900: 442–43.

[Kazimierz Kelles-Krauz] K. Radoslawski, "Z życia Francji. Masoneryia," *Prawda* 20(22) 20 May 1900: 260–61.

[Kazimierz Kelles-Krauz] K. Radoslawski, "Z życia Francji. Projekt prawa o trybunałach rozjemczych," *Prawda* 20(50) 2 December 1900: 596–97.

[Kazimierz Kelles-Krauz] K. Radoslawski, "Z życia Francji. Retrospekcja przewrotowa na gorącym uczynku," *Prawda* 20(39) 16 September 1900: 462–64; 20(40) 23 September 1900: 476–77.

[Kazimierz Kelles-Krauz] K. Radoslawski, "Z życia Francji. Zarodki organizacyi produkcyi," *Prawda* 20(24) 3 June 1900: 284–86.

[Kazimierz Kelles-Krauz] "Za granicą. Francja," *Przedświt* 1896 (1–3): 26–28.

K. Krauz, "Zarysy Francyi Współczesnej," *Prawda* 23(1) 3 January 1903: 3–4; 23(2) 10 January 1903: 14–16.

[Kazimierz Kelles-Krauz] Michał Luśnia, "Ze świata. Francja," *Przedświt* 1895 (10–11): 19–20.

[Kazimierz Kelles-Krauz] Michał Luśnia, "Ze świata. Francja," *Przedświt* 1896 (4): 15–19.

[Kazimierz Kelles-Krauz] Michał Luśnia, "Ze świata. Francja," *Przedświt* 1896 (6): 10–12.

[Kazimierz Kelles-Krauz] Michał Luśnia, "Ze świata. Francja," *Przedświt* 1896 (8): 15–16.

[Kazimierz Kelles-Krauz] Ł., "Ze świata. Francja. Piętnasty zjazd Partyi Robotniczej Francuskiej," *Przedświt* 1897 (9): 9–11.

[Kazimierz Kelles-Krauz] Elehard Esse, "Zjazd wiedeński i rewizja partyi austryackiej," *Przedświt* 1902 (1): 11–18.

f. Publications by Other Authors

Edward Abramowski, "Kazimierz Krauz. Socjologiczne prawo retrospekcji. Odbitka z 'Ateneum.' Warszawa, 1898 r.," *Przegląd Filozoficzny* 2 (1898) 80–92. [Cited after Edward Abramowski, *Pisma,* vol. 2, pp. 386–00. Warsaw, 1928.]

[Edward Abramowski] Z. R. Walczewski, "Społeczeństwo rodowe." Kraków. 1890. [Cited from Edward Abramowski, *Pisma,* vol. 4, pp. 1–37. Warsaw. 1928.]

Nicolas Abrikossof, "Paroles," *Annales de l'Institut International de Sociologie* 8 (1902): 133–34.

Lord Acton, *History of Freedom and Other Essays.* London, 1907.

Viktor Adler, "Der Lübecker Parteitag," *Arbeiter Zeitung* 269 (1 October 1901): 1–2.

August Bebel, *Kobieta i socyalizm.* Cracow, 1907.

Edward Bellamy, *Looking Backward, 2000–1887.* New York, 1986. [Originally published 1888.]

Bellamy, *Looking Backward*

Edward Bellamy, "Postscript: The Rate of the World's Progress," in *Looking Backward 2000–1887.* New York, 1986.

"Bellamy," *Przedświt* 1898 (7): 17.

Antoni Brzeszkiniewicz et al., "Odezwa delegacyi polskiej," *Przedświt* 1896 (7): 1–3.

Władysław Bukowiński, "Kazimierz Krauz. Wspomnienie pozgonne," *Prawda* 25(25) 1 July 1905: 293.

Bukowiński, "Kazimierz Krauz"

Adolphe Coste, "Paroles," *Annales de l'Institut International de Sociologie* 8 (1902): 129–32.

Émile Durkheim, *Le Socialisme*. Paris, 1928.

Friedrich Engels, *The Origin of the Family, Private Property, and the State*, in Karl Marx and Friedrich Engels, *Selected Works in One Volume*. London, 1991.

Alfred Fouillée, "Le matérialisme historique," *Annales de l'Institut International de Sociologie* 8 (1902): 278–82.

[Stanisław Gierszyński] Oficer piechoty, "Wojsko i rewolucja," *Przedświt* 1902 (7): 243–51.

"Goście wiedeńscy w Berlinie," *Naprzód* 273 (5 October 1901): 3.

Guillaume de Greef, *Éloges de Élisée Reclus et de Kellès-Krauz*. Brussels, 1906.

de Greef, *Éloges*

[Władysław Gumplowicz] "Historya niedoszłej zgody," *Przedświt* 1903 (5): 169–80.

Gumplowicz, "Historya"

[Witold Jodko-Narkiewicz] A. W., "Kwestya niepodległości w programach socyalistów polskich." Lviv [Lwów], 1901.

Frederyk Katchner, *Katechism Historyi Filozofii*, trans. Kazimierz Kelles-Krauz. Warsaw, 1902.

Karl Kautsky, "Allerhand Revolutionäres," *Die Neue Zeit* 22 (1903–1904): 588–98, 620–27, 652–57, 685–95, 732–40.

Karl Kautsky, "Ein sozialdemokratischer Katechismus," *Die Neue Zeit* 7(1) 1893.

"Kazimierz Kelles-Krauz," *Przedświt* 1905 (6–8): 227–35.

"Kazimierz Krauz. Wspomnienie," *Ogniwo* 3(26) 1 July 1905: 585–87.

[Ludwik Krzywicki] J. F. Wolski, *Początki cywilizacji. Na zasadzie i jako uzupełnienie badań Lewisa H. Morgana*. Paris, 1885.

Ł, "Bunt Łódzki w r. 1892," *Z Pola Walki*, pp. 25–28. London, 1904. "Lettre de Russie," *Le Soleil* 17 May 1891.

Lucien Lévy-Brühl, ed., *Lettres inédites de John Stuart Mill à Auguste Comte*. Paris, 1899.

Lucien Lévy-Brühl, *La Philosophie d'Auguste Comte*. Paris, 1900.

Charles-M. Limousin, "Discours," *Annales de l'Institut International de Sociologie* 8 (1902): 187–90.

[Rosa Luxemburg] M. R., "Jeszcze raz Karl Kautsky o kwestii polskiej," *Przegląd Socjalistyczny* 2(2) 1904: 76.

Róża Luksemburg, ed., *Kwestia polska a ruch socjalistyczny*. Cracow, 1905. Luxemburg, *Kwestia*

R. Luksemburg, "Neue Strömungen in der polnischen sozialistischen Bewegung in Deutschland und Österreich," *Die Neue Zeit* 32–33, 1896, pp. 176–81, 206–216.

[Rosa Luxemburg] Maciej Rózga, "Niepodległa Polska a sprawa robotnicza," Paris 1895.

Luxemburg, "Niepodległa Polska."

Karl Marx, *Pre-capitalist Economic Formations*. London, 1978.

Marx, *Formations*

Karl Marx, *Przyczynki do historii kwestii polskiej. Rękopisy z lat 1863–1864*. Warsaw, 1971.

Marx, *Przyczynki*

John Stuart Mill, *Considerations on Representative Government*. London, 1862.

Lewis Henry Morgan, *Ancient Society*. Tucson, 1985. [Originally published 1877.]

"Nasz program," *Przegląd Robotniczy* 1 (September 1900).

"Nasze sprawy w Dreźnie," *Przedświt* 1903 (10): 409–428.

"Notatki naukowe. Annales de l'Institut Internationale de Sociologie," *Prawda* 22(24) 14 June 1902: 282–83.

J. Novicov, "Discours," *Annales de l'Institut International de Sociologie* 8 (1902): 93–95.

Theodor Hermann Pantenius, *Die von Keiles. Ein Roman aus Livlands Vergangenheit*. Bielefeld and Leipzig, 1885.

[Józef Piłsudski] "Na posterunku," *Robotnik* June 1895 (7): 2–5. [Józef Piłsudski, ed.] *Tajne dokumenty rządu rosyjskiego*. London, 1898.

[Józef Piłsudski] "U nas i gdzie indziej," *Robotnik* 27 October 1894 (4): 1–3.

"Pogrzeb tow. Kazimierza Krauza," *Naprzód* July 1905 (2): 3.

Polska Partia Socjalistyczna, "Pamiątka Majowa." London, 1896.

PPS, "Pamiątka"

"Protokoły 1-ego Zjazdu Socjaldemokracji Królestwa Polskiego, odbytego w Warszawie 10-ego i 11-ego marca 1894 r.," *Sprawa Robotnicza* April 1894.

[Karl Renner] Rudolf Springer, *Kampf der Österreichischen Nationen um den Staat*. Vienna, 1902.

"Rentrée en Scène. Le Mouvement Social en Russie," *Le Matin* 11 March 1892.

"Les Socialistes polonais," *La Bataille* 17 May 1891.

"Les Socialistes polonais," *La Libre Parole* 27 September 1894.

Sprawa polska w opinii Europy. Cracow, 1901.

"Sprawa Sawickiego," *Przedświt* 1896 (5): 18.

G. Tarde, "Quelques mots sur le matérialisme historique," *Annales de l'Institut International de Sociologie* 8 (1902): 283–89.

Ferdinand Tönnies, "Opinion," *Annales de l'Institut International de Sociologie* 8(1902): 135.

"Tydzień polityczny," *Prawda* 23(40) 3 October 1903: 469–70.

Lester F. Ward, "Paroles," *Annales de l'Institut International de Sociologie* 8 (1902): 185–86.

Leon Wasilewski, "Towarzystwo Wyższych Kursów Wakacyjnych," *Prawda* 24(27) 10 September 1904: 437–38.

Widoki Radomia. Warsaw, 1899.

Stanislaw Wojciechowski, ed., *Polska Partya Socjalistyczna w ostatnich pięciu latach*. London, 1900.

Wojciechowski, *Polska Partya*

René Worms, "Paroles," *Annales de l'Institut International de Sociologie* 8 (1902): 265–70.

Max Zetterbaum, "Zur materialistischen Geschichtsauffassung," *Die Neue Zeit* 21 (1902–1903): 399–407, 498–506, 524–31.

"Zjazd międzynarodowy," *Przedświt* 1896 (7): 5–7.

2. Secondary Sources

Chimen Abramsky, Maciej Jachimczyk, and Antony Polonsky, eds., *The Jews in Poland*. Oxford, 1988.

Abramsky, *Jews in Poland*

Andrzej Ajnenkiel, "Stulecie urodzin Kelles-Krauza. Kwestia narodowa w myśli teoretycznej Kazimierza Kelles-Krauza na sesji PTN, Radom 26 V 1972 r." *Nauka Polska* 1973 (1): 139–45.

Alain-Fournier, *Le Grand Meaulnes*. Paris, 1983. [Originally published in 1913.]

Benedict Anderson, *Imagined Communities. Reflections on the Origin and Spread of Nationalism*. London, 1983.

Perry Anderson, *Considerations on Western Marxism*. London, 1989.

Perry Anderson, *Lineages of the Absolutist State*. London, 1974.

Rosemary Ashton, *Little Germany. Exile and Asylum in Victorian England*. Oxford, 1986.

Ashton, *Little Germany*

Shlomo Avineri, "Marxism and Nationalism," in Jehuda Reinharz and George L. Mosse, eds., *The Impact of Western Nationalisms*, pp. 283–304. London, 1992.

Bronisław Baczko, "Prawo retrospekcji przewrotowej Kelles-Krauza," *Myśl Współczesna* 1949 (8-9).

Alan Barnard, "Primitive Communism and Mutual Aid. Kropotkin P. A. Visits the Bushmen," in C. M. Hann, ed., *Socialism. Ideals, Ideologies, and Local Practice*, pp. 27–42. London, 1993.

Julian Barnes, *Flaubert's Parrot*. London, 1985.

Leon Baumgarten, ed., *Krakowski komisarz policji na służbie carskiego wywiadu*. Cracow, 1967.

Baumgarten, *Komisarz*

Daniel Beauvois, "Polish-Jewish Relations in the Territories Annexed by Russia in the First Half of the Nineteenth Century," in Chimen Abramsky, Maciej Jachimczyk, and Antony Polonsky, eds., *The Jews in Poland*, pp. 78–90. Oxford, 1988.

Marian Bębenek, "Kazimierz Kelles-Krauz wobec rewizjonizmu," *Zeszyty Naukowe Uniwersytetu Jagiellonskiego. Prace z Nauk Politycznych* 1975 (8): 7–51.

Marian Bębenek, *Teoria narodu i kwestia narodowa u Kazimierza-Kelle s Krauza*. Cracow, 1987.

David Bell, Douglas Johnson, and Peter Morris, eds., *A Biographical Dictionary of French Political Leaders since 1870*. Cambridge, 1990.

Steven Beller, "Class, Culture, and the Jews of Vienna, 1900," in Ivar Oxaal, Michael Pollak, and Gerhard Botz, eds., *Jews, Antisemitism, and Culture in Vienna*, pp. 93–58. London, 1987.

Beller, "Culture"

Julian Benda, *The Treason of the Intellectuals*. London, 1969.

Isaiah Berlin, *Karl Marx*. Oxford, 1978.

Isaiah Berlin, *Vico and Herder*. London, 1992.

Wiesław Bieńkowski, "Kazimierz Kelles-Krauz jako historyk," *Studia Historyczne* 41 (1) 1973: 65–79.

Wiesław Bieńkowski, *Kazimierz Kelles-Krauz. Życie i dzieło.* Wrocław, 1969.

Bieńkowski, *Kelles-Krauz*

Wiesław Bieńkowski, "Kelles-Krauz Kazimierz Radosław Elehard," in Feliks Tych et al., eds., *Słownik biograficzny działaczy polskiego ruchu robotniczego,* vol. 3 (K), pp. 138–41. Warsaw, 1992.

Bieńkowski, "Kelles-Krauz Kazimierz"

Wiesław Bieńkowski, "Kelles-Krauz Stanisław Maciej," in Feliks Tych et al., eds., *Słownik biograficzny działaczy polskiego ruchu robotniczego,* vol. 3 (K), pp. 141–43. Warsaw, 1992.

Wiesław Bieńkowski, "Kelles-Krauzowa Maria Katarzyna z d. Goldsteyn," in Feliks Tych et al., eds., *Słownik biograficzny działaczy polskiego ruchu robotniczego,* vol. 3 (K), pp. 143–44. Warsaw, 1992.

Stanislaus A. Blejwas, *Realism in Polish Politics. Warsaw Positivism and National Survival in Nineteenth Century Poland.* New Haven, 1984.

Blejwas, *Realism*

Lucjan Blit, *The Origins of Polish Socialism.* Cambridge, 1971.

Robert Blobaum, *Feliks Dzierżyński and the SDKPiL. A Study of the Origins of Polish Communism.* Boulder, 1984.

Blobaum, *Dzierżyński*

Robert Blobaum, "The Revolution of 1905–1907 and the Crisis of Polish Catholicism," *Slavic Review* 47(4) Winter 1988: 667–86.

Robert Blobaum, "The SDKPiL and the Polish Question (Revisited)," in John Morrison, ed., *Eastern Europe and the West,* pp. 207–18. London, 1992

Blobaum, "SDKPiL"

Maurice Bloch, *Marxism and Anthropology.* Oxford, 1991.

Jerome Blum, *The End of the Old Order in Rural Europe.* Princeton, 1978.

Blum, *Old Order*

Adam Boniecki, *Herbarz Polski,* vol. 12. Warsaw, 1908.

Jan Boniecki, "Radom w okresie 1865–1918. Stosunki polityczno-społeczne," in Stefan Witkowski et al., eds., *Radom. Dzieje miasta w XIX i XX w.* Warsaw, 1985.

Boniecki, "Radom"

Jerzy W. Borejsza, "Rewolucjonista polski. Szkic do portretu," in *Piękny wiek XIX,* pp. 423–82. Warsaw, 1984.

Tom Bottomore, "Marxism and Sociology," in Tom Bottomore and Robert Nisbet, eds., *A History of Sociological Analysis,* pp. 118–48. London, 1979.

Tom Bottomore, *Marxist Sociology.* London, 1975.

Julius Braunthal, *History of the International.* London, 1966.

Braunthal, *The International*

John Breuilly, "Eduard Bernstein and Max Weber," in Wolfgang Mommsen and Jürgen Osterhammel, eds., *Max Weber and his Contemporaries,* pp. 345–54. London, 1989.

Peter Brock, "The Polish Identity," in W. J. Stankiewicz, ed., *The Tradition of Polish Ideals*, pp. 23–51. London, 1981.

Peter Brock, "The Polish 'Movement to the People'. An Early Chapter in the History of East-European Populism," *Slavonic and East European Review* 40(1) December 1961: 99–122.

Stephen Bronner, *A Revolutionary for our Times. Rosa Luxemburg*. London, 1981.

Bronner, *Luxemburg*

Jean Cazeneuve, *Lucien Lévy- Brühl*. Oxford, 1972.

Wojciech Cesarski, "L. Krzywieki i K. Kelles-Krauz o alienacji estetycznej," *Studia Estetyczne* 1968 (5): 229–46.

Cesarski, "Alienacja"

Andrzej Chwalba, *Sacrum i rewolucja. Socjaliści polscy wobec praktyk I symboli religijgnych*. Cracow, 1992.

Chwalba, *Sacrum*

Stanisław Ciesielski, *Niepodległość i socjalizm*. Warsaw, 1986.

Stanisław Ciesielski, "Przedmowa" to Kazimierz Kelles-Krauz, *Naród i historia. Wybor pism*, pp. 5–31. Warsaw, 1989.

Adam Ciołkosz, "Karl Marx and the Polish Insurrection of 1863," *The Polish Review* 10(4) 1965: 8–51.

Ciołkosz, "Karl Marx"

Adam Ciołkosz, *Ludzie P.P.S.* London, 1967.

Adam and Lidia Ciołkosz, *Niepodległość i socjalizm, 1835–1945*. London, 1982.

Stephen D. Corrsin, "Language Use in Cultural and Political Change in Pre-1914 Warsaw. Poles, Jews, and Russification," *Slavonic and East European Review* 68(1) January 1990: 69–90.

Corrsin, "Language Use"

Lewis A. Coser, "Marxist Thought in the First Quarter of the 20th Century," *American Journal of Sociology* 77(1) July 1972: 173–201.

Bohdan Cywiński, *Rodowody niepokornych*. Paris, 1985.

Cywiński, *Rodowody*

Antoni Czubiński, "Ruch socjalistyczny w Europie wobec odbudowy państwa polskiego," *Kwartalnik Historyczny* 75(3) 1978: 621–41.

[Józef Dąbrowski] J. Grabiec, *Czerwona Warszawa przed ćwierć wiekiem*. Poznań, 1925.

Józef Dąbrowski, "Uczniowskie kółka tajne w Radomiu w latach 1889-1904," in *Jednodniówka Zjazdu Koleżeńskiego Radomiaków w dniu 6,7, i 8 maja 1923 r. w Radomiu*. Warsaw, 1924.

Dąbrowski, "Uczniowskie kółka"

[Józef Dąbrowski] J. Grabiec, "Wilhelm Feldman jako publicysta i działacz społeczny," in *Pamięci Wilhelma Feldmana*, pp. 61–104. Cracow, 1922.

Dąbrowski, "Feldman"

Norman Davies, *God's Playground. A History of Poland*, vols. 1 and 2. New York, 1982.

Davies, *Playground* I and *Playground* II

Horace B. Davis, *Nationalism and Socialism. Marxist and Labor Theories of Nationalism to 1917.* New York, 1967.

Włodzimiera Drewniewska, "Sylwetki malarzy radomskich," in Jerzy Jędrzejewicz, ed., *Radom. Szkice z dziejów miasta,* pp. 210–24. Warsaw, 1961.

Seweryn Dziamski, *Zarys polskiej filozoficznej myśli marksistowskiej, 1878–1939.* Warsaw, 1973.

Grzegorz Ekiert, "Kazimierz Kelles-Krauz. From Marxism to Sociology," in Piotr Sztompka, ed., *Masters of Polish Sociology,* pp. 67–81. Wrocław, 1984.

Wilhelm Feldman, *Dzieje polskiej myśli politycznej w okresie porozbiorowym,* vol. 3. Warsaw, 1920.

Feldman, *Dzieje polskiej myśli*

Stanisław Filipowicz, "Wstęp" to Kazimierz Kelles-Krauz, *Historia i rewolucja,* pp. v–lv. Warsaw, 1983.

Raymond Firth, "The Sceptical Anthropologist? Social Anthropology and Marxist Views on Society," *Proceedings of the British Academy* 58 (1972): 177–214.

Jonathan Frankel, *Prophecy and Politics. Socialism, Nationalism, and the Russian Jews, 1862–1917.* Cambridge, 1981.

Frankel, *Prophecy*

Aleksandra Garlicka, "Kazimierz Krauz. Dziennikarz Polski," *Kwartalnik Historii Prasy Polskiej* 26(2): 41–50.

Andrzej Garlicki, *Józef Piłsudski, 1867-1935.* Warsaw, 1988.

Garlicki, *Piłsudski*

Marek Gawlik, "Początki przemysłu garbarskiego w Radomiu," in Jerzy Jędrzejewicz, ed., *Radom. Szkice z dziejów miasta,* pp. 128–36. Warsaw, 1961.

Peter Gay, *The Dilemma of Democratic Socialism. Eduard Bernstein's Challenge to Marx.* New York, 1962.

Dick Geary, "Max Weber, Karl Kautsky, and German Social Democracy," in Wolfgang Mommsen and Jürgen Osterhammel, eds., *Max Weber and His Contemporaries,* pp. 355–66. London, 1989.

Geary, "Weber"

Alexander Gella, "The Life and Death of the Old Polish Intelligentsia," *Slavic Review* 30(1) March 1971: 1–27.

Gella, "Life and Death"

Ernest Gellner, "Foreword" to C. M. Hann, ed., *Socialism. Ideals, Ideologies, and Local Practice.* London, 1993.

Ernest Gellner, *Nations and Nationalism.* Oxford, 1983.

Ernest Gellner, "La trahison de la trahison des clercs," in Ian MacLean et al., eds., *The Political Responsibility of Intellectuals.* pp. 17–28. Cambridge, 1990.

Anthony Giddens, "A Matter of Truth," *Times Literary Supplement,* 29 March 1996: 10.

Andrzej Głowacki, "Działalność Kazimierza Kelles-Krauza w między-narodowym ruchu socjalistycznym na rzecz sprawy polskiej," *Biuletyn Kwartalny Radomskiego Towarzystwa Naukowego,* 22(2) 1988: 39–43.

Andrzej Głowacki, *Międzynarodowy ruch socjalistyczny wobec odbudowy Polski, 1889-1918.* Szczecin, 1974.

Głowacki, *Międzynarodowy*

Teofil Głowacki, "Kazimierz Kelles-Krauz. Człowiek i dzieło," *Przegląd Socjalistyczny* 3(7-9): 15–20.

Piotr Górski, *Socjalistyczno-niepodległościowa idea narodu polskiego, 1908-1914.* Cracow, 1994.

Górski, *Idea*

Jukka Gronow, *On the Formation of Marxism. Karl Kautsky 's Theory of Capitalism, the Marxism of the Second International, and Karl Marx's Critique of Political Economy.* Helsinki, 1986.

Konstanty Grzybowski, *Historia państwa i prawa Polski,* vol. 4. Warsaw, 1982.

W. L. Guttsman, *The German Social Democratic Party, 1875–1933.* London, 1981.

C. M. Hann, "Introduction. Social Anthropology and Socialism," in C. M. Hann, ed., *Socialism. Ideals, Ideologies, and Local Practice,* pp. 1–26. London, 1993.

C. M. Hann, ed., *Socialism. Ideals, Ideologies, and Local Practice.* London, 1993.

Hann, *Socialism*

Chris Harman, "The Return of the National Question," *International Socialism* 56 (Autumn 1992): 3–62.

Georges Haupt, "From Marx to Marxism," in *Aspects of International Socialism, 1871–1914,* pp. 1–22. Cambridge, 1986.

Georges Haupt, "Les marxistes face à la question nationale. L'histoire du probleme," in Georges Haupt, Michael Lowy, Claudie Weil, *Les marxistes et la question natio-nale, 1848–1914,* pp. 10–61. Paris, 1974.

Franciszek Hawranek, *Polska i niemiecka socjaldemokracja na Górnym Śląsku w latach 1890–1914.* Opole, 1977.

Hawranek, *Górny Śląsk*

Stanisław Herbst, *Wojna inflancka, 1600–1602.* Warsaw, 1937.

Charles C. Herod, *The Nation in the History of Marxian Thought. The Concept of Nations with History and Nations Without History.* The Hague, 1976.

Alexander Hertz, "The Case of an Eastern European Intelligentsia," *Journal of Central European Affairs* 11(1) January–April 1951: 10–26.

Hertz, "Intelligentsia"

Adam Heymowski, "Les armoiries étrangères augmentées en Pologne." Liège, 1977.

Adam Heymowski, *Herbarz Inflant Polskich z roku 1778.* Buenos Aires, 1964.

John-Paul Himka, *Socialism in Galicia. The Emergence of Polish Social Democracy and Ukrainian Radicalism.* Cambridge, 1983.

Himka, *Socialism in Galicia*

Eric Hobsbawm, "Introduction" to Karl Marx, *Pre-capitalist Economic Formations,* pp. 9–66. London, 1978.

Eric Hobsbawm, "Introduction: Inventing Traditions," in Eric Hobsbawn and Terence Ranger, eds., *The Invention of Tradition,* pp. 1–14. Cambridge, 1993.

Eric Hobsbawn and Terence Ranger, eds., *The Invention of Tradition*. Cambridge, 1993.

Eric Hobsbawm, *Nations and Nationalism since 1780*. Cambridge, 1991.

Julian Hochfeld, "Kelles-Krauza—marksizm 'otwarty,'" in *Marksizm, Socjologia, Socjalizm. Wybór Pism*, pp. 190–202. Warsaw, 1982.

H. Hołda-Róziewicz, "Kazimierz Kelles-Krauz," in Barbara Skarga, ed., *Polska myśl filozoficzna i społeczna*, vol. 3. Warsaw, 1977.

Jerzy Holzer, *PPS. Szkic dziejów*. Warsaw, 1977.

Holzer, *PPS*

Jerzy Holzer, "Relations between Polish and Jewish Left-wing Groups in Interwar Poland," in Chimen Abramsky, Maciej Jachimczyk, and Antony Polonsky, eds., *The Jews in Poland*, pp. 140–46. Oxford, 1988.

Holzer, "Relations"

Adam Hrebenda, "Miejsce Bolesława Limanowskiego w polskim ruchu robotnyczym," in Stanisław Michalkiewicz and Zbigniew Żechowski, eds., *Nestor polskiego socjalizmu czy tylko demokrata? Studia o Bolesławie Limanowskim*, pp. 45–62. Katowice, 1987.

Toby E. Huff, *Max Weber and the Methodology of the Social Sciences*. London, 1984.

H. Stuart Hughes, *Consciousness and Society*, New York, 1958. Hughes, *Consciousness*

Ireneusz Ihnatowicz, "Przemysł, handel, finanse," in Stefan Kieniewicz, ed., *Polska XIX wieku. Państwo—społeczeństwo—kultura*, pp. 56–94. War-saw, 1982.

Ihnatowicz, "Przemysł"

Ireneusz Ihnatowicz, "Uniwersytet Warszawski w latach 1869–1899," in Stefan Kieniewicz, ed., *Historia Uniwersytetu Warszawskiego*, pp. 440–56. War-saw, 1981.

Ihnatowicz, "Uniwersytet"

Martin Jay, *Marxism and Totality*. Los Angeles, 1984.

Martin Jay, "Vico and Western Marxism," in *Fin-de-Siècle Socialism and Other Essays*, pp. 67–81. London, 1988.

Jerzy Jedlicki, "Holy Ideals and Prosaic Life," in Stanislaw Gomulka and Antony Polonsky, eds., *Polish Paradoxes*. London, 1990.

Jerzy Jedlicki, "Inteligencja," in Józef Bachórz and Alina Kowalczykowa, eds., *Słownik literatury polskiej XIX wieku*, pp. 373–77. Wrocław, 1991.

Jedlicki, "Inteligencja"

Jerzy Jedlicki, *Jakiej cywilizacji Polacy potrzebują*. Warsaw, 1988.

Jedlicki, *Jakiej cywilizacji*

Jerzy Jedlicki, "Kwestia nadprodukcji inteligencji w Królestwie Polskim po powstaniu styczniowym," in Ryszarda Czepulis-Rastenis, ed., *Inteligencja polska pod zaborami*, pp. 218–59. Warsaw, 1978.

Jedlicki, "Nadprodukcja"

Jerzy Jedlicki, "Native Culture and Western Civilization," *Acta Poloniae Historica* 28 (1973): 63–85.

Jerzy Jedlicki, *Nieudana próba kapitalistycznej industrializacji*. Warsaw, 1964.

Jerzy Jedlicki, "Szlachta," in Józef Bachórz and Alina Kowalczykowa, eds., *Słownik literatury polskiej XIX wieku*, pp. 919–23. Wrocław, 1991.

Jedlicki, "Szlachta"

Jednodniówka Zjazdu Koleżeńskiego Radomiaków w dniu 6,7, i 8 maja 1923 r. w Radomiu. Warsaw, 1924.

Jednodniówka

Jerzy Jędrzejewicz, ed., *Radom. Szkice z dziejów miasta.* Warsaw, 1961.

Jędrzejewicz, *Radom*

Wacław Jędrzejewicz, *Pilsudski. A Life for Poland.* London, 1982.

Stanisław Jedynak, "Etyka Kazimierza Kelles-Krauza," *Biuletyn Kwartalny Radomskiego Towarzystwa Naukowego,* 22(2) 1988: 24–25.

Witold Jodko-Narkiewicz, *Zarys dziejów P.P.S.* Warsaw, 1917.

Richard Johnson, "Zagranichnaia Agentura. The Tsarist Political Police in Europe," in George L. Mosse, ed., *Police Forces in History.* London, 1975, pp. 17–38.

Johnson, "Agentura"

James Joll, *The Second International.* London, 1955.

Joll, *Second International*

James Joll, *Intellectuals in Politics.* London, 1960. Tony Judt, *Marxism and the French Left.* Oxford, 1986.

Włodzimierz Kaczocha, "Problemy kultury w ujęciu Kelles-Krauza," *Miesięcznik Literacki* 1980 (8) August: 94–100.

Elżbieta Kaczyńska and Dariusz Drewniak, *Ochrana.* Warsaw, 1992.

Kaczyńska, *Ochrana*

Stanisław Kalabiński and Feliks Tych, *Czwarte powstanie czy pierwsza rewolucja. Lata 1905-1907 na ziemach polskich.* Warsaw, 1969.

Andrzej Kamiński, "Neo-Serfdom in Poland and Lithuania," *Slavic Review* 34(2) June 1975: 253–68.

Jan Kancewicz, "Golde-Strożecka Estera," in Feliks Tych et al., eds., *Słownik biograficzny działaczy polskiego ruchu robotniczego,* vol. 2 (E-J), pp. 286–87. Warsaw, 1987.

Kancewicz, "Golde"

Jan Kancewicz, "Jodko-Narkiewicz Witold Tomasz," in Feliks Tych et al., eds., *Słownik biograficzny działaczy polskiego ruchu robotniczego,* vol. 2 (E-J), pp. 725–27. Warsaw, 1987.

Jan Kancewicz, *Polska Partia Socjalistyczna, 1892-1896.* Warsaw, 1984.

Kancewicz, *PPS*

R. A. Kann, *The Multinational Empire.* New York, 1950.

Antoni Karbowiak, *Młodzież polska akademicka za granicą, 1795–1910.* Cracow, 1910.

Janina Kasprzakowa, "Wokoł biografii i spuścizny Kelles-Krauza," *Z Pola Walki* 17(3) 1974: 49–56.

Walter Kaufmann, *Nietzsche. Philosopher, Psychologist, Antichrist.* Princeton, 1974.

Janina Kelles-Krauz, "Mój ojciec—Kazimierz Kelles-Krauz," *Miesięcznik Literacki* 1972 (9) September: 88–95.

Janina Kelles-Krauz, "Mój ojciec"

Janina Kelles-Krauz, "Wokoł biografii i spuścizny Kelles-Krauza," *Z Pola Walki* 17(3) 1974: 56–68.

Janina Kelles-Krauz "Wokół biografii"

Michał Kelles-Krauz, "Kazimierz Kelles-Krauz na tle historii rodziny," *Biuletyn Kwartalny Radomskiego Towarzystwa Naukowego* 22(2) 1988: 49–50.

Michał Kelles-Krauz, "Historia rodziny"

Stefan Kieniewicz, *Historia Polski, 1795–1918*. Warsaw, 1970.

Kieniewicz, *Historia*

Stefan Kieniewicz, "Polish society and the Jewish problem in the Nineteenth Century," in Ghimen Abramsky, Maciej Jachimczyk, and Antony Polonsky, eds., *The Jews in Poland*, pp. 70–77. Oxford, 1988.

Stefan Kieniewicz, *Powstanie styczniowe*. Warsaw, 1972.

S. F. Kissin, *War and the Marxists*. London, 1988.

Kissin, *War*

Leszek Kołakowski, *The Alienation of Reason. A History of Positivist Thought*. Garden City, 1968.

Leszek Kołakowski, *Main Currents in Marxism*, vol. 1, *The Origins*, and vol. 2, *The Golden Age*. Oxford, 1978.

Kołakowski, *Main Currents I, Main Currents II*

Leszek Kołakowski, *Główne nurty marksizmu*, vol. 3. Paris, 1978.

Stanisław Koszutski, *Walka młodzieży polskiej o wielkie ideały*. Warsaw, 1928.

Koszutski, *Walka młodzieży*

Tadeusz Kowalik, "Filozofia społeczna Ludwika Krzywickiego," in Barbara Skarga, ed., *Polska myśl filozoficzna i społeczna*, vol. 2. Warsaw, 1975.

Ludwik Krzywicki, "Krauz Kazimierz Keiles," *Wielka Encyklopedia Powszechna Ilustrowana*, vol. 39–40, p. 813. Warsaw, 1907.

Ludwik Krzywicki, "Wstęp" to Kazimierz Kelles-Krauz, *Materializm ekonomiczny*. Cracow, 1908. [Cited after *Pisma I*, pp. 4–10.]

Krzywicki, "Wstęp"

Bożena Krzywobłocka, *Cezaryna Wojnarowska*. Warsaw, 1979.

Krzywobłocka, *Wojnarowska*

[Ludwik Kulczycki] Mieczysław Mazowiecki, *Historya polskiego ruchu socjalistycznego w zaborze rosyjskim*. Cracow, 1903.

Kulczycki, *Historya*

Adam Kuper, *The Invention of Primitive Society*. London, 1991.

Joanna Kurczewska, *Naród w socjologii i ideologii polskiej*. Warsaw, 1979.

R. F. Leslie, ed., *The History of Poland since 1863*. Cambridge, 1980.

Richard D. Lewis, "Marxist Historiography and the History Profession in Poland, 1944–1955," in John Morison, ed., *Eastern Europe and the West*, pp. 219–28. New York, 1992.

Joseph Lichten, "Notes on the Assimilation and Acculturation of Jews in Poland, 1863–1943," in Chimen Abramsky, Maciej Jachimczyk, and Antony Polonsky, eds., *The Jews in Poland*, pp. 106–124. Oxford, 1988.

George Lichtheim, *Marxism. A Historical and Critical Study*. London, 1980.

Lichtheim, *Study*

George Lichtheim, *Marxism in Modern France*. London, 1966.

Lichtheim, *Marxism*

George Lichtheim, "Oriental Despotism," in *The Concept of Ideology and Other Essays*, pp. 62–93. New York, 1967.

George Lichtheim, *A Short History of Socialism*. London, 1970.

Lichtheim, *Socialism*

Vernon L. Lidtke, *The Alternative Culture. Socialist Labor in Imperial Germany*. Oxford, 1985.

Andrzej Lipiński, "Myśl socjologiczna Kazimierza Kelles-Krauza," *Biuletyn Kwartalny Radomskiego Towarzystwa Naukowego* 22(2) 1988: 27–37.

Zofia Lissa, "Kazimierz Kelles-Krauz. Początki marksistowskiej myśli muzycznej w Polsce," *Muzyka* 11(2) 1966: 8–35.

Jan Luboński, "Historja gimnazjum radomskiego od 1685 do 1897 r.," in *Jednodniówka Zjazdu Koleżeńskiego Radomiaków w dniu 6,7, i 8 maja 1923 r. w Radomiu*. Warsaw, 1924.

Luboński, "Historja gimnazjum radomskiego"

Jan Luboński, *Monografia historyczna miasta Radomia*, Radom 1907.

Luboński, *Monografia historyczna*

Steven Lukes, *Emile Durkheim. His Life and Work. A Historical and Critical Study*. London, 1992.

Lukes, *Durkheim*

Steven Lukes, *Marxism and Morality*. Oxford, 1987.

William Harvey Maehl, *August Bebel, Shadow Emperor of the German Workers*. Philadelphia, 1980.

Maehl, *Bebel*

Maria Maj, "Kolegium Pijarów," in Jerzy Jędrzejewicz, ed., *Radom. Szkice z dziejów miasta*, pp. 152–61. Warsaw, 1961.

Marjan Malinowski, "Początek i rozwój organizacji P.P.S. w Radomiu i okolicy," in *Księga pamiątkowa PPS*, pp. 90–95. Warsaw, 1923.

Malinowski, "Początek i rozwój organizacji P.P.S."

Gustaw Manteuffel, *Inflanty polskie*. Poznań, 1879.

Gustaw Manteuffel, *O starodawnej szlachcie krzytacko-rycerskiej na kresach inflanckich*. Lviv [Lwów], 1912.

Ryszard Manteuffel-Szoege, *Inflanty, Inflanty*. Warsaw, 1991.

Jerzy Marciniak, "Udział Kazimierza Kelles-Krauza w przygotowaniach socjalistów polskich do międzynarodowego kongresu socjalistycznego w Londynie 1896," *Kwartalnik Historyczny* 1982 (2–3): 301–311.

P. Margor, "Pierwszy rok uniwersytetu zakopiańskiego," *Krytyka* 2(10) 1904: 232–44.

Margor, "Pierwszy rok"

Stanisław Markiewicz, "Spuścizna bogata i cenna," *Nowe Drogi* 1972 (3) March: 124–32.

Ezra Mendelsohn, *Class Struggle in the Pale*. Cambridge, 1970.

Ezra Mendelsohn, "Jewish Assimilation in L'viv. The Case of Wilhelm Feldman,"
    Slavic Review 28(4) 1969: 577–96.
Ryszard Michalski, Socjalizm a niepodległość w polskiej myśli socjalistycznej, 1878–1918.
    Toruń, 1988.
Michalski, Socjalizm
Zbigniew Mikołejko, "Kazimierz Kelles-Krauz. Religia w strukturze materializmu
    ekonomicznego," Studia Religioznawcze 24 (1988): 151–76.
Susanne Miller and Heinrich Potthoff, A History of German Social Democracy.
    New York, 1986.
Miller and Potthof, History
Moshe Mishkinsky, "A Turning Point in the History of Polish Socialism and its
    Attitude Toward the Jewish Question," Polin 1 (1986): 111–29.
Moshe Mishkinsky, "Polish Socialism and the Jewish Question on the Eve of the
    Establishment of the Polish Socialist Party (PPS) and Social Democracy of the
    Kingdom of Poland (SDKP)," Polin 5 (1990): 250–71.
Wojciech Modzelewski, Naród i postęp. Problematyka narodowa w ideologii i myśli
    społecznej pozytywistów warszawskich. Warsaw, 1977.
Modzelewski, Naród i postęp
Alina Molska, "Wstęp" to Alina Molska, ed., Pierwsze pokolenie marksistów polskich,
    pp. v-xci. Warsaw, 1962.
Wolfgang Mommsen and Jürgen Osterhammel, eds., Max Weber and His Contemporaries.
    London, 1989.
Mommsen, Weber
Barrington Moore, Social Origins of Dictatorship and Democracy. London, 1967.
David W. Morgan, "The 'Orthodox' Marxists. The First Generation of a Tradition," in
    R. J. Bullen, H. Pogge von Strandman, and A. B. Polonsky, eds., Ideas into Politics.
    Aspects of European History, 1880–1950, pp. 4–14. London, 1984.
Morgan, "Orthodox"
Ronaldo Munck, The Difficult Dialogue. Marxism and Nationalism. London, 1986.
Munck, Dialogue
Robert Musil, Les désarrois de l'élève Törless. Paris, 1960. [Originally published in 1906.]
Jerzy Myślinski, Polska prasa socjalistyczna w okresie zaborów. Warsaw, 1982.
Myślinski, Polska prasa
Jerzy Myślinski, "Uniwersytet Wakacyjny w Zakopanem w r. 1904. Towarzystwo
    Wyższych Kursów Wakacyjnych," Przegląd Historyczno-Oświatowy 6(1) 1963: 7–19.
Myślinski, "Uniwersytet"
Norman Naimark, The History of the "Proletariat. " The Emergence of Marxism in the
    Kingdom of Poland, 1870–1887. New York, 1979.
Naimark, Proletariat
Walentyna Najdus, "Działacze zachodnioeuropejskich partii socjalistycznych o
    narodzie i ojczyźnie," Kwartalnik Historyczny 75(4) 1978: 995–1013.
Najdus, "Działacze"

Waletyna Najdus, *Ignacy Daszyński, 1866–1936*. Warsaw, 1988.

Najdus, *Daszyński*

Walentyna Najdus, *Polska Partia Socjalno-Demokratyczna Galicji i Śląska, 1890–1919*. Warsaw, 1983.

Najdus, *Galicja*

Walentyna Najdus, *SDKPiL a SDPRR, 1893–1907*. Wrocław, 1973.

Lewis Namier, *1848. The Revolution of the Intellectuals*. Oxford, 1992. Namier, *1848*

Peter Nettl, "The German Social-Democratic Party as a Political Model," *Past and Present* 30 (April 1965): 65–95.

Nettl, "Political Model"

Peter Nettl, *Rosa Luxemburg*, vol. 1. London, 1966.

Nettl, *Luxemburg*

Ephraim Nimni, *Marxism and Nationalism. Theoretical Origins of a Political Crisis*. London, 1991.

Jan Offenberg, *Stan umysłów wśród młodzieży akademickiej w latach 1885–1890*. Warsaw, 1929.

Offenberg, *Stan umysłów*

Wacław Olszewicz, "Udział K. Kelles-Krauza w pracach Międzynarodowego Instytutu Socjologii w Paryżu w latach 1893–1901," *Kultura i Społeczeństwo* 9(2) 1965: 174–76.

Olszewicz, "Udział"

Juliusz Ostrowski, *Księga herbowa rodów polskich*. Warsaw, 1899.

Joanna Overing, "The Anarchy and Collectivism of the 'Primitive Other.' Marx and Sahlins in the Amazon," in C. M. Hann, ed., *Socialism. Ideals, Ideologies, and Local Practice*. London, 1993.

Ivar Oxaal, Michael Pollak and Gerhard Botz, eds., *Jews, Antisemitism, and Culture in Vienna*. London, 1987

Oxaal, *Vienna*

Ivar Oxaal, "The Jews of Young Hitler's Vienna," in Ivar Oxaal, Michael Pollak, and Gerhard Botz, eds., *Jews, Antisemitism, and Culture in Vienna*, pp. 11–38. London, 1987.

Alicja Pacholczykowa, "Cederbaum (wcześniej Zetterbaum) Maksymilian," in Feliks Tych et al., eds., *Słownik biograficzny działaczy polskiego ruchu robotniczego*, vol. 1 (A-D), pp. 291–92. Warsaw, 1978.

Ignacy Pawłowski, *Geneza i działalność Organizacji Spiskowo-Bojowej PPS, 1904–1905*. Wrocław, 1976.

Pawłowski, *Geneza*

Jan Pazdur, *Dzieje Kielc, 1864–1939*. Wrocław, 1973.

[Feliks Perl] Res, *Dzieje ruchu socjalistycznego w zaborze rosyjskim*, vol. 1. Warsaw, 1910.

Perl, *Dzieje ruchu*

Henryk Piasecki, *Sekcja żydowska PPSD i żydowska partia socjalno-demokratyczna, 1892–1919/20*. Wrocław, 1982.

Henryk Piasecki, *Żydowska Organizacja PPS, 1893–1907*. Wrocław, 1978.
Piasecki, *Organizacja*
Stanley Pierson, *Marxist Intellectuals and the Working Class Mentality in Germany*. London, 1993.
Pierson, *Mentality*
Józef Piłsudski, *Pisma*, Marcin Król and Wojciech Karpiński, eds. Warsaw, 1985.
John Plamenatz, *German Marxism and Russian Communism*. London, 1954.
Michael Pollak, "Cultural Innovation and Social Identity in *Fin-de-Siècle* Vienna," in Ivar Oxaal, Michael Pollak, and Gerhard Botz, eds., *Jews, Antisemitism, and Culture in Vienna*, pp. 59–74. London, 1987.
Pollak, "Innovation"
P. G. J. Pulzer, *The Rise of Political Anti-Semitism in Germany and Austria*. New York, 1964.
Pulzer, *Anti-Semitism*
Roman Rosdolsky, *Engels and the "Nonhistoric " Peoples. The National Question in the Revolution of 1848*, trans. and ed. John-Paul Himka. Glasgow, 1986.
Guenther Roth, *The Social Democrats of Imperial Germany*, Totowa NJ, 1963.
Joseph Rovan, *Histoire de la Social-Démocratie Allemande*. Paris, 1978.
Marsha L. Rozenblit, "The Jews of Germany and Austria. A Comparative Perspective," in Robert S. Wistrich, ed., *Austrians and Jews in the Twentieth Century*, pp. 1–18. London, 1992.
Rozenblit, "The Jews"
Norman Rush, "What Was Socialism … And Why We Will All Miss It So Much," *The Nation* 24 January 1994: 90–94.
Leonas Sabaliunas, *Lithuanian Social Democracy in Perspective, 1893-1914*. Durham, 1990.
Massimo Salvadori, *Karl Kautsky and the Socialist Revolution*. London, 1979.
Salvadori, *Kautsky*
Adam Schaff, "Kazimierz Kelles-Krauz," *Nowe Drogi* 1949 (1): 1–12.
Carl E. Schorske, *Fin-de-Siècle Vienna. Politics and Culture*. Cambridge, 1987.
Schorske, *Vienna*
Hugh Seton-Watson, *Nations and States. An Inquiry into the Origins of Nations and the Politics of Nationalism*. London, 1977.
Seton-Watson, *Nations and States*
Tadeusz Sierocki, "Abramowski Edward Józef," in Feliks Tych et al., eds., *Słownik biograficzny działaczy polskiego ruchu robotniczego*, vol. 1 (A-D), pp. 40–43. Warsaw, 1978.
Thomas W. Simons, Jr., *Eastern Europe in the Postwar World*. New York, 1991.
Thomas W. Simons, Jr., "The Peasant Revolt of 1846 in Galicia. Recent Polish Historiography," *Slavic Review* 30(4) December 1971: 795–817.
Barbara Skarga, ed., *Polska myśl filozoficzna i społeczna*, vols. 2 and 3. Warsaw, 1975, 1977.

Skarga, *Filozoficzna* II, *Filozoficzna* III

Božidar Slapšak, "Archaeology and Contemporary Myths of the Past," *Journal of European Archaeology* 1(2) 1993: 191–95.

Michał Śliwa, "Kwestia żydowska w polskiej myśli socjalistycznej," in Feliks Kiryk, ed., *Żydzi w Małopolsce*, pp. 273–88. Przemyśl, 1991.

Śliwa, "Żydowska"

Tim Snyder, "Czy obywatele nie potrzebują ojczyzny?" *Społeczeństwo Otwarte* 1994(7-8): 21–23.

Michael Sobelman, "Polish Socialism and Jewish Nationality. The Views of Kazimierz Kelles-Krauz," *Soviet Jewish Affairs* 20(1) Spring 1990: 47–55.

Sobelman, "Jewish"

Edmund Staszyński, *Polityka oświatowa caratu w Królestwie Polskim.* Warsaw, 1968.

Staszyński, *Polityka oświatowa*

Gary P. Steenson, *After Marx, Before Lenin. Marxism and Socialist Working-Class Parties in Europe, 1884–1914.* Pittsburgh, 1991

Steenson, *After Marx*

Gary P. Steenson, *Karl Kautsky, 1854–1938. Marxism in the Classical Years.* Pittsburgh, 1978.

Steenson, *Kautsky*

Gary P. Steenson, *"Not One Man! Not One Penny!" German Social Democracy, 1863–1914.* Pittsburgh, 1981.

Steenson, *German*

Marian Stępień, *Rodowód.* Cracow, 1983.

Stępień, *Rodowód*

Robert Stuart, *Marxism at Work. Ideology, Class, and French Socialism during the Third Republic.* Cambridge, 1992.

Stuart, *Marxism at Work*

Włodzimierz Suleja, *Polska Partia Socjalistyczna. Zarys dziejów.* Warsaw, 1988.

Suleja, *Polska Partia*

Alan Swingewood, *A Short History of Sociological Thought.* London, 1993.

Swingewood, *Sociological*

Jerzy Szacki, "Dylematy historii idei," in *Dylematy historiografii idei*, pp. 11–19. Warsaw, 1991.

Jerzy Szacki, *Historia myśli socjologicznej*, vol. 2. Warsaw, 1981. Szacki, *Historia*

Jerzy Szacki, "Gdzież są ci nasi inteligenci?" in *Dylematy historiografii idei*, pp. 364–72. Warsaw, 1991.

Jerzy Szacki, "Intellectuals between Politics and Culture," in Ian MacLean et al., eds., *The Political Responsibility of Intellectuals*, pp. 229–46. Cambridge, 1990.

Jerzy Szacki, "Koncepcja narodu w socjologii i historii," in *Dylematy historiografii idei*, pp. 351–63. Warsaw, 1991.

Jerzy Szacki, "Refleksje nad historią socjologii," in *Dylematy historiografii idei*, pp. 20–37. Warsaw, 1991.

Jerzy Szacki, "Socjologia i historia," in *Dylematy historiografii idei*, pp. 342–50. Warsaw, 1991.

Jerzy Szacki, "Tradycja," in *Dylematy historiografii idei*, pp. 238–55. Warsaw, 1991.

Jerzy Szacki, "Tezy o inteligencji polskiej," in *Dylematy historiografii idei*, pp. 372–80. Warsaw, 1991.

Jerzy Szacki, "Wokół polskiej 'zdrady klerków,'" in *Dylematy historiografii idei*, pp. 402–418. Warsaw, 1991.

J. L. Talmon, *The Myth of Nation and the Vision of Revolution. The Origins of Ideological Polarisation in the Twentieth Century.* London, 1980.

Talmon, *Nation*

A. J. P. Taylor, *The Habsburg Monarchy, 1809-1918.* London, 1948.

Testis, "Pamiętniki dyrektora gimnazjum radomskiego," in *Zwierciadło Polskie*, pp. 68–81. Warsaw, 1915.

Testis, "Pamiętniki dyrektora"

Cecilia Tichi, "Introduction" to Edward Bellamy, *Looking Backward, 2000–1887*, pp. v–xi. New York, 1986.

Harry J. Tobias, *The Jewish Bund in Russia.* Stanford, 1972.

Tobias, *Bund*

Jan Tomicki, "Dębski Aleksander," in Feliks Tych et al., eds., *Słownik biograficzny działaczy polskiego ruchu robotniczego*, vol. 1 (A-D), pp. 572–73. Warsaw, 1978.

Jan Tomicki, *Polska Partia Socjalistyczna, 1892–1948.* Warsaw, 1983.

Tomicki, *PPS*

Elisabeth Tooker, "Foreward" to Lewis Henry Morgan, *Ancient Society*, pp. vi–xvi. Tucson 1985.

Jerzy Topolski, "Polish Historians and Marxism after World War II," *Studies in Soviet Thought* 43(2) March 1992: 169–83.

Stephen Turner and Regis Factor, *Max Weber and the Dispute over Reason and Value. A Study in Philosophy, Ethics, and Politics.* London, 1984.

Feliks Tych, "Grabski Stanisław," in Feliks Tych, ed., *Słownik biograficzny polskiego ruchu robotniczego*, vol. 2 (E-J), p. 349. Warsaw, 1987.

Feliks Tych, "Jędrzejowski Bolesław Antoni," in Feliks Tych et al., eds., *Słownik biograficzny działaczy polskiego ruchu robotniczego*, vol. 2 (E-J), pp. 718–21. Warsaw, 1987.

Feliks Tych, "The Polish Question at the International Socialist Congress in London in 1896. A Contribution to the History of the Second International," *Acta Poloniae Historica* 46 (1982): 97–140.

Tych, "Polish Question"

Feliks Tych, "Polski ruch robotniczy," in Stefan Kieniewicz, ed., *Polska XIX wieku. Państwo-społeczeństwo—kultura*, pp. 312–54. Warsaw, 1982. Tych,

Tych, "Polski ruch"

Feliks Tych, "Polskie partie w II Międzynarodówce," in *Historia Drugiej Międzynarodówki*, vol. 2. Warsaw, 1978.

Tych, "Polski partie"

Feliks Tych, "Przypomnieć Kelles-Krauza," *Polityka* 25(1318) 7 August 1982: 12–13.

Feliks Tych, "Róża Luksemburg," in Barbara Skarga, ed., *Polska myśl filozoficzna i społeczna*, vol. 3. Warsaw, 1977.

Tych, "Luksemburg"

Feliks Tych et al., eds., *Słownik biograficzny działaczy polskiego ruchu robotniczego*, vols. 1–3. Warsaw, 1978, 1987, 1992.

Tych, *Słownik* I, *Słownik* II, *Słownik* III

Feliks Tych, "Słowo wstępne" to Róża Luksemburg, *Listy do Leona Jogichesa-Tyszki*, vol. I, pp. v-xlvii. Warsaw, 1968.

Feliks Tych, *Socjalistyczna irredenta*. Cracow, 1982.

Tych, *Irredenta*

Feliks Tych, "Wstęp," to Kazimierz Kelles-Krauz, *Listy*, vol. I, pp. 5–27. Wrocław, 1984.

Feliks Tych, *Związek Robotników Polskich. Anatomia wczesnej organizacji robotniczej*. Warsaw, 1974.

Seweryn Uruski, *Rodzina. Herbarz szlachty polskiej*, vol. 13. Warsaw, 1911.

Uruski, *Rodzina*

Elizabeth Kridl Valkenier, "The Rise and Decline of Official Marxist Historiography in Poland, 1945–1987," *Slavic Review* 44(4) 1985: 661–80.

Elizabeth Kridl Valkenier, "Stalinizing Polish Historiography. What Soviet Archives Disclose," *East European Politics and Societies*, 7(1) 1993: 109–134.

Marek Waldenberg, *Kwestie narodowe w Europie Środkowo-Wschodniej*. Warsaw, 1992.

Waldenberg, *Kwestie narodowe*

Marek Waldenberg, *Wzlot i upadek Karola Kautsky'ego*, vol. 1. Cracow, 1972.

Waldenberg, *Kautsky*

Marek Waldenberg, "Z problematyki narodu w polskiej myśli socjalistycznej okresu zaborów," in Janusz Goćkowski and Andrzej Walicki, eds., *Idee i koncepcje narodu w polskiej myśli politycznej czasów porozbiorowych*, pp. 246–66. Warsaw, 1977.

Andrzej Walicki, *Philosophy and Romantic Nationalism. The Case of Poland*. Oxford, 1982.

Walicki, *Romantic Nationalism*

Andrzej Walicki, *Poland Between East and West. The Controversies over Self-Definition and Modernization in Partitioned Poland*. Cambridge, Massachusetts, 1994.

Andrzej Walicki, *Polska, Rosja, marksizm. Studia z dziejów marksizmu i jego recepcji*. Warsaw, 1983.

Walicki, *Polska, Rosja, marksizm*

Andrzej Walicki, "Rosa Luxemburg and the National Question," *Slavonic and East European Review* 66(4) October 1983: 565–82.

Walicki, "Luxemburg"

Andrzej Walicki, *Stanislaw Brzozowski and the Beginnings of "Western Marxism."* Oxford, 1989.

Walicki, *Brzozowski*

Andrzej Walicki, "Three Traditions in Polish Patriotism," in Stanisław Gomulka and Antony Polonsky, eds., *Polish Paradoxes*. London, 1990.

Andrzej Walicki, ed., *Zarys dziejów filozofii polskiej, 1815–1918*. Warsaw, 1983.

Piotr Wandycz, *The Lands of Partitioned Poland, 1795–1918*. Seattle, 1974.

Wandycz, *Lands*

Roman Wapiński, *Polska i małe ojczyzny Polaków*. Wrocław, 1994.

Wapiński, *Ojczyzny*

Mrs. Humphry Ward, *Robert Elsmere*. Lincoln, 1967. [Originally published in 1888.]

Leon Wasilewski, *Józef Piłsudski. Jakim go znałem*. Cracow, 1981.

Wasilewski, *Piłsudski*

Leon Wasilewski, "Międzynarodówka robotnicza wobec hasła niepodległości Polski," *Niepodległość* 1930 (2): 32–42.

Leon Wasilewski, *Zarys dziejów Polskiej Partji Socjalistycznej*. Warsaw, 1925.

Wasilewski, *Zarys 1925*

Zygmunt Wdowiszewski, "Tytuły polskie nadawane cudzoziemcom," *Materiały do biografii, genealogii, i heraldyki polskiej* 1966 (3): 9–26.

Zygmunt Wdowiszewski, "Regesty nobilitacji w Polsce (1404–1794)," *Materiały do biografii, genealogii, i heraldyki polskiej* 1977 (9).

Hans-Ulrich Wehler, *The German Empire, 1871–1918*. Oxford, 1993.

Wehler, *German Empire*

Hans-Ulrich Wehler, *Sozialdemokratie und Nationalstaat*. Göttingen, 1971.

Wehler, *Nationalstaat*

Walter R. Weitzmann, "The Politics of the Viennese Jewish Community, 1890–1914," in Ivar Oxaal, Michael Pollak, and Gerhard Botz, eds., *Jews, Antisemitism, and Culture in Vienna*, pp. 121–51. London, 1987.

Henryk Wereszycki, *Historia polityczna Polski, 1864–1918*. Wroclaw, 1990.

Wereszycki, *Historia polityczna*

Jerzy J. Wiatr, *Marksistowska teoria rozwoju społecznego*. Warsaw, 1973.

Jerzy J. Wiatr, *Naród i państwo. Socjologiczne problemy kwestii narodowej*. Warsaw, 1969.

Maria Wierzbicka, "Próba charakterystyki poglądów Kazimierza Kelles-Krauza na dzieje Polski," *Z Pola Walki* 1969 (3): 3–15.

Robert S. Wistrich, "The Kreisky Phenomenon. A Reassessment," in Robert S. Wistrich, ed., *Austrians and Jews in the Twentieth Century*, pp. 234–246. London, 1992.

Robert S. Wistrich, "Social Democracy, Antisemitism and the Jews of Vienna," in Ivar Oxaal, Michael Pollak, and Gerhard Botz, eds., *Jews, Antisemitism, and Culture in Vienna*. London, 1987.

Robert S. Wistrich, *Socialism and the Jews. The Dilemmas of Assimilation in Germany and Austria-Hungary*. London, 1982.

Wistrich, *Socialism*

Stefan Witkowski, "Struktura współczesnego przemysłu radomskiego," in Jerzy Jędrzejewicz, ed., *Radom. Szkice z dziejów miasta*, pp. 137–44. Warsaw, 1961.

Jan Woleński, "Philosophy inside Communism. The Case of Poland," *Studies in Soviet Thought* 43(2) March 1992: 93–100.

Marta Zahorska, "Spór o inteligencję w polskiej myśli społecznej do I wojny światowej," in Ryszarda Czepulis-Rastenis, ed., *Inteligencja polska pod zaborami*, pp. 180–216. Warsaw, 1978.

Zahorska, "Spór"

Zasłużeni ludzie Radomia. Radom, 1967.

Adam Zamoyski, *The Polish Way. A Thousand-Year History of the Poles and Their Culture.* London, 1987.

Anna Żarnowska, *Geneza rozłamu w Polskiej Partii Socjalistycznej, 1904-1906.* Warsaw, 1965.

Żarnowska, *Rozłam*

Anna Żarnowska, "Kazimierz Kelles-Krauz (1872–1905)," introduction to *Pisma* I, pp. vii–xxiii. Warsaw, 1962.

Żarnowska, "Kelles-Krauz"

Anna Żarnowska, "Religion and Politics. Polish Workers c. 1900," *Social History* 16(3) 1991: 299–316.

Theodore Zeldin, *France,* vol. 1. Oxford, 1973.

Zeldin, *France*

Stefan Żeromski, *Syzyfowe prace.* Warsaw, 1973. [Originally published in 1897.]

Franciszek Ziejka, *Paryż młodopolski.* Warsaw, 1993.

Marian Żychowski, *Polska myśl socjalistyczna XIX i XX wieku.* Warsaw, 1976.

Żychowski, *Polska myśl*

Index